Harvard Studies in Business History • 51

Published with the support of the
Harvard Business School

EDITED BY

Walter A. Friedman
Lecturer
Director, Business History Initiative

AND

Geoffrey Jones
Isidor Straus Professor of Business History Faculty Chair,
    Business History Initiative

Harvard Business School

SUSIE J. PAK

GENTLEMEN BANKERS

THE WORLD OF J. P. MORGAN

HARVARD UNIVERSITY PRESS   Cambridge, Massachusetts, and London, England
2013

Library of Congress Cataloging-in-Publication Data

Pak, Susie.
Gentlemen bankers : the world of J. P. Morgan / Susie Pak.—1 Edition.
    pages cm
  Includes bibliographical references and index.
  ISBN 978-0-674-07303-6
  1. J.P. Morgan & Co.—History. 2. Banks and banking—United States—
History. 3. Bankers—United States—Biography. 4. Morgan, J. Pierpont
(John Pierpont), 1837–1913. I. Title.
  HG2471.P35 2013
  332.1'230973—dc23   2012051088

For Greg & Wyatt

Contents

gentlemen bankers

IN DECEMBER 1912, J. Pierpont Morgan (1837–1913) was called before the U.S. House of Representatives to testify on his alleged role in the monopolization of financial capital in the United States. The Money Trust Investigation, also known as the Pujo Hearings, studied the origins of the Panic of 1907, which had seriously demoralized faith in the banking industry. Because Morgan, America's most powerful private banker, was largely credited with bringing an end to the panic, the Pujo Committee was anxious for him to explain the source of his influence and power. Given that Morgan rarely made public statements of any kind, his appearance at the hearings was a singular event in his history and that of his bank, not in the least because he surprised everyone by denying he had control over anyone or anything. He testified, "I do not feel that I have vast power. . . . I am not seeking it, either."

Morgan's critics were convinced that he was being evasive, but he was actually sharing important insight into his world. He did not deny that he had an elevated standing in the financial community and he readily acknowledged that he had many long-standing relationships to other well-connected individuals and financial institutions. But Morgan argued that if he had any influence at all, it stemmed only from the trust given to him by others. Stating that trust was "the fundamental basis of business" and believing that trust was not something one could control much less monopolize, Morgan rejected the idea that he had any direct control over anyone, even members of his own firm.

Morgan continued to surprise the committee by declaring that trust had nothing to do with money. Though he confirmed that his bank held more than $81 million in corporate deposits (in excess of the firm's own capital), he downplayed the importance of his financial resources stating, ". . . I do not compete for deposits. I do not care whether they ever come, but they do come." Arguing that an individual's access to credit had little to do with money, he told the committee he knew "lots of men . . . who can borrow any amount, whose credit is unquestioned" without the money to back them. The reason for this, Morgan said, was that trust was based, "before money or anything else," on a person's character. In what is a well-known statement, Morgan testified, ". . . A man I do not trust could not get money from me on all the bonds in Christendom." Implicitly, he meant that his character (and the character of his partners) was the basis of his firm's capital and reputation.[1]

Twenty years later, when his son, J. P. Morgan Jr., or Jack Morgan (1867–1943), testified as the bank's senior partner at the U.S. Senate investigation into the securities business (also called the Pecora Hearings), Morgan reiterated his father's beliefs that confidence and character were the foundation of their business.[2] He said, "As to the theory that [the private banker] may become too powerful, it must be remembered that any power which he has comes, not from the possession of large means, but from the confidence of the people in his character and credit . . . not financial credit, but that which comes from the respect and esteem of the community."[3]

While it is tempting to be cynical, and their critics certainly were, Pierpont and Jack Morgan's sentiments were not just for show. They may have been self-serving, but they were not insincere. Until they were forced to testify in front of Congress, no one outside the Morgan firm had confirmation of how much the bank or its partners were worth. Private bankers, who were members of unlimited liability partnerships like the Morgans, were personally liable for their profits and losses, but they were not required to make information about their capital and liabilities public.[4] Given this context of opacity and risk, the Morgans assumed that their individual character served as the primary indicator of their trustworthiness and credit.

Of course, the Morgans' definition of character did conceal much, but not because they were being evasive or disingenuous. They never explicitly articulated what kind of character created trust because they simply took it for granted. For this reason, they did not dwell on any conflicts or inconsistencies between their actions and their beliefs. They believed their reputation and status to be sufficient proof of their character and of the trust given to them by "the people." At the same time, the Morgans understood that their character was not just a reflection of their individual attributes. Even though they thought of their values as timeless and universal, they appreciated that their reputation was an expression of their standing in a larger "community."[5]

This awareness is very significant because it meant the Morgans also understood that they did not independently determine the content of good character. The Morgans did not decide on their own that certain rights and privileges were natural and valued. They came to this understanding within the context of a community, a society, and a history. Their emphasis on trust was itself an example of how deeply they were embedded in the institutions and society of their time.[6] It is not that money did not matter, as the Morgans' testimonies seemed to claim, but that it mattered because other historical conditions were present, which gave it meaning and made it possible. As Marx once noted, "Men make history, but not in circumstances of their own choosing."[7]

The idea that the world of finance is part of a larger society may appear simple and self-evident. But despite the fact that the Morgans talked repeatedly about trust, reputation, and community, and even though they testified to the personal nature of private banking, studies of their economic power have not traditionally included an analysis of their social environment. A vast amount of effort has gone into the study of the Morgans' business, which have tremendously added to our understanding of their economic networks and practices. In general, however, studies of the Morgans and private banking have focused almost exclusively on their business ties in an economic context. While this partly reflects tendency of academic fields to focus on discrete questions in concise time periods, it is also apparent in disciplines that take the long view, such as history.[8]

In many ways, these choices simply followed the Morgans' lead. From the Morgans' perspective, the separation of the study of their business and their personal lives was perfectly natural. Ironically, even though the Morgans assumed that a private banker's life outside the business world reflected his character, they also operated as though the two spheres were entirely separate. Given the Morgans' emphasis on character and trust, this artificial separation between their social and economic networks seemed very out of place. What made it even more peculiar was the fact that it was neither universal nor arbitrary. As we shall see, it was most apparent in their interactions with German Jewish bankers, especially Kuhn, Loeb & Co., a private American bank that was their strongest competitor and an important collaborator.

The deliberate yet assumed nature of the separation between the business and domestic spheres of private bankers was the first indication that it must have been extremely significant. In other words, it was so important, so normal, that it was taken for granted. Unfortunately, that means it has also been easy to overlook. Historical actors can only leave evidence of things that were there. They do not leave evidence, for example, of things that were absent or that they deliberately excluded. Nor are they always aware of their own inconsistencies and contradictions. Thus, when we organize our studies in ways that deliberately or inadvertently adopt the parameters of our subjects, we can take their prejudices for granted. We can also obscure the fact that their choices have a history, as do the limitations in which they are made. For this reason, we cannot rely on the Morgans to directly explain how they organized their network because they took much of it for granted even while they were actively involved in creating it.

This book takes a broad view of the Morgans' relationships, combining and drawing on the studies of the Morgans' social and business relations that have come before it.[9] It is not a biography of the Morgans but a history of their network, meaning it studies their relationships and how they were organized. It imagines the Morgans' network as a series of layers radiating from the core and moving progressively outward, studying the ways in which they were tied to each other and to other elite bankers like themselves. Most importantly, it also examines their ties to persons and groups whom they considered to be far removed and different from their world.

The purpose of this book is not simply to create a more comprehensive map of the Morgans' relations. Its goal is to study which relationships were important to the Morgans, to understand the conditions that made them meaningful, and to identify the work that made them possible. When we look broadly at the Morgans' relations, what do they tell us about how the Morgans were able to establish and maintain trust? Why and when did they separate their economic and social networks? Did this structure engender trust or undermine it?[10] Trust is and was central to the functioning of financial markets, but what was the basis for that trust and how did it change under different conditions with respect to different actors? Focusing on the history of the bank during the period in which the New York house was an unlimited liability private partnership, the book asks: What does the structure of the firm's relations tell us about the world in which elite private bankers lived and worked? Ultimately, what do their relations tell us about the source of the Morgans' influence?

The book begins with Pierpont and Jack Morgan, who were by custom and legal agreement the most senior members of the firm. Between 1895–1940, when J. P. Morgan & Co. was a private unlimited liability partnership,[11] they invited sixty-five men to join them as partners in the House of Morgan (thirty-nine in the American houses and twenty-six in the European houses).[12] Who were the men the Morgans entrusted to be their partners? Did they come from similar socio-economic backgrounds as the seniors? Were they men of the same race, religion, class, ethnicity, age, and nationality? Did they share a similar ancestry? Did they marry? Were they married to women of similar background? How did they raise their children? Did they live close together? Did they frequent the same social organizations? Did they have different interests, skill sets, and education? Did they share equal responsibilities and benefits as Morgan partners? What was the rate of attrition and why did partners leave? Did the makeup of the firm change over time and did the identity of the firm also change? In other words, how did the Morgans create cohesion as a firm and did this change over time?

In addition to studying intrafirm ties, the book looks at the Morgans' relationships outside the firm, focusing on their peers and collaborators. The Morgans did not do business with just anyone. They were very aware that when they did business with another firm, they associated their name and their reputation with the leading members of that firm. Their choices were an important statement of their identity and how they saw themselves in relationship to others.[13] Who did the Morgans do business with? Where did they do business and under what conditions? Who did they avoid doing business with and why? Did they do business with firms that were similar to them or was their economic community more diverse? Did their most important collaborators change over time? Were their intrafirm ties similar to that of other firms? Were social ties important with all or some of their peers? In other words, how did they create cohesion and trust across firm boundaries?

Though many of these questions may appear to be basic and have been studied to varying degrees in other texts, this book studies these questions within the larger context of the Morgans' relationships, which includes a complete record of their syndicate participants between 1895 and 1934 and an extensive database of their affiliations to social, cultural, and educational organizations in that time.[14] From these simple questions and a considerable amount of quantitative and qualitative data, the book creates a picture that contradicts some of our most entrenched views of the Morgans and the world of elite American finance in which they were leading members. Situating the Morgans in a wider historical and social context, the book reveals a world distinctive not for its homogeneity, as their world is often assumed and portrayed to be, it illuminates a world that had a wide diversity of participants, whose interests were deeply interconnected and not entirely complementary.[15] In other words, the Morgans were not powerful because they were exactly the same or had exactly the same interests as everyone with whom they worked or interacted. Nor were they connected equally to everyone in the same way, to the same degree, or in the same context. As we shall see, recognizing the significance of this diversity is the key to understanding their influence and power.

Here I should note that though the House of Morgan has a much older pedigree than the New York firm of J. P. Morgan & Co., and though the financial community in New York has a history that long predates the late nineteenth century, these histories are not repeated in this book for several reasons.[16] If the book maps and analyzes the complex relations of a community of elite bankers from the perspective of its leading bank, it is also a study of the United States at a particular moment in its history, the Progressive and interwar periods. As the emphasis on history might suggest, the questions and issues the book studies are unique to that time, one characterized by the consolidation of the American economy, the diversification of American society, and the growth of American state power at home and abroad.[17] These conditions were central to how the Morgans' network was organized in this period, and as we shall see, they were largely responsible for the circumstances that led to the end of private banking at the Morgans by 1940.[18]

The Pujo investigation was but one example of the tremendous challenges that the Morgans faced during the Progressive and interwar periods, a time when they were the object of passionate Congressional critique and popular scorn. The story of their network demonstrates both their flexibility and resources, specifically their relational capital, in dealing with external challenges. Even during these trying times, the Morgans maintained active cooperative relationships with multiple agencies in the American government and with important non-governmental and non-economic institutions in American society.[19] These conflicted ties were another sign that their network was much more complex than it appeared. They pointed to the ways in which the Morgans' network crossed national and international boundaries. They signaled the external influences that would shape their efforts to create and maintain trust with their collaborators, associates, and clients, including the American state. Most importantly, they were a sign of how embedded the Morgans were in larger institutional networks not entirely of their own making.

The Morgans' cooperative ties with the American government were particularly evident in the realm of international finance, where their business and experience extended into areas that affected American foreign policy interests. Their partnership in the international arena involved other elite American bankers, including their competitors, whose interests were also tied to the American nation-state. Again, these multiple relations were an example of the diversity and strength of the Morgan's network, but they also demonstrated how they operated under conditions where conflict, both actual and potential, was always present. Nowhere is this complex structure more apparent than in the Morgans' relationship with Kuhn, Loeb & Co.[20]

Established in New York in 1867, Kuhn, Loeb & Co.'s senior partner was Jacob H. Schiff (1847–1920), a German Jewish immigrant who was the son-in-law of one of the founders, Solomon Loeb. During his lifetime, Schiff was a major figure in American private banking and his reputation was second to only that of Pierpont Morgan.[21] Kuhn, Loeb & Co.'s name has since been lost to history, but before the Second World War, it was one of the most powerful firms in investment banking, far outranking other banks with similar nineteenth century pedigree, such as Goldman, Sachs (f. 1869). As we shall see, the Morgans' relationship with Kuhn, Loeb is essential to understanding how their network was organized and most importantly, how it was tied to the society at large.

Like the Morgans, Kuhn, Loeb had extensive ties to international bankers and banking houses.[22] While their strongest ties were with German bankers, Kuhn, Loeb also distinguished themselves from the Morgans in the area of East Asian finance. Having successfully financed the Japanese war against Russia in 1904–1905, the firm garnered considerable prestige as Japan's leading foreign bankers. The Morgans were able to hold their ground, however, when it came to China. In 1909, at the behest of the American government, they became the leading American bank of an international group of bankers called the International Banking Consortium to China (IBC) in order to secure America's share in financing what was known as the Hukuang railway. Though the Morgans were never very enthusiastic about lending money to China, the prestige associated with leadership in the IBC was important to them as a statement of their status as America's premier international bankers. Like Kuhn, Loeb, they understood how a bank's reputation was enhanced by its proximity to a sovereign power.[23]

Kuhn, Loeb & Co. was also one of the original banks in the Hukuang railway agreement. Though not the leading bank, it took an active role in the IBC in order to protect its own "position and prestige" and to prevent it from becoming a Morgan affair.[24] Relations within the IBC were generally cooperative, however, because the Morgans and Kuhn, Loeb had many ideological similarities regarding modern finance and business-government relations. They were largely united, for example, in their views regarding the expansion of American (and Japanese) empire in East Asia.[25] Most importantly, their relationship in the IBC was indicative of a larger trend toward cooperation within the financial community, particularly at the elite level even among competing banks.[26] Kuhn, Loeb and J. P. Morgan & Co. also had partners who sat on the boards of the other two banks in the Hukuang agreement, First National Bank of New York and National City Bank.[27] All three banks ranked among the Morgans' top collaborators in syndicate participations between 1895 and 1934.

On the face of it, these relationships seem to confirm the impression that New York's elite bankers formed a "community of interest," whose purpose was to monopolize credit and dominate financial networks. Economic self-interest was assumed to be the basis for trust and collaboration. The economic data do not, however, tell the full story of the Morgans' network, particularly with regard to Kuhn, Loeb. When we look more carefully, we also find that the Morgans' relations with Kuhn, Loeb were characterized by a constant tension. Most importantly, this tension was expressed in such personal language and social terms that it could not be entirely explained by international politics or economic competition. This book, which emerged from an earlier study of private banking and American foreign policy, began as an investigation into the origin and meaning of this conflict.

Surprisingly, despite the fact that Kuhn, Loeb was an important participant in the Morgan syndicates, very little is known about the actual aggregate structure and details of their economic collaboration. Because of the traditional separation between social and economic spheres of activity, very little is known about the nature of the social relations between the two banks except that the partners were not close.[28] Because Morgan partners were all native-born Americans of Christian background and Kuhn, Loeb partners were largely German-born immigrants of Jewish background, this social distance was thought to reflect primarily personal and individual choices or ethno-national and religious differences. It was largely taken for granted as the norm in the financial community, where Anglo-American banks and German Jewish banks were organized around separate spheres of influence.[29] Most importantly, because the separation did not appear to affect their economic collaboration, it was assumed that it did not matter. Again, the basis for trust and cooperation was assumed to be the pursuit of economic profit or money.

When we look at the way the Morgans and their associates lived their lives, from where they lived to whom they married to where they educated their children, everything says that those assumptions do not accurately represent their history or relationships. When we look at how they chose their partners and their collaborators, how they went about building trust and relationships, and how they talked about what was important to them, we are reminded of Pierpont and Jack Morgan's claims that money was not the most important consideration to their determination of trust and character. For all these reasons, the conflict with Kuhn, Loeb could not be explained solely as the outcome of economic competition, nor could their cooperation, particularly given the distance that characterized their social relations.

The key to understanding the Morgans' network is recognizing that private banking was at its core a personal business. A private banking partnership was not a simply a job. It was an identity that required constant vigilance, a process, or a mode of becoming, that was fragile because of its dependence on relationships to others. If private banking was a way of life,

a banker's social ties were as much a statement of his identity and reputation
as his economic associations. Given that private bankers relied upon non-
economic ties to create trust, what role did their social relations play in the
structure of their economic networks? How were those ties important to the
functioning of financial markets? What did it mean when they did not
exist, as was the case with Kuhn, Loeb & Co.?

If economic motive was not enough of a basis for the creation of trust, as
the Morgans themselves claimed, it could not be insignificant that elite
bankers in the late nineteenth and early twentieth centuries lived in largely
separate communities identified by their race, religion, and national origin.
While they may have seen this separation as natural, they also expended a
great amount of time and energy to maintain those boundaries. In other
words, the social distance that the Morgans had with Kuhn, Loeb was not
an accident or a coincidence. It was a sign of the embeddedness of the financial community in the larger society, whose meaning must be studied.

When we map the Morgans' network, it becomes clear that they were
not immune to the larger issues that plagued their society. Social and economic interaction across religious and racial lines within their network was
structured in ways that were quite complex. While they were most apparent
in their ties to Jewish bankers, they also extended far beyond those relationships to other collaborators whom the Morgans also considered separate
and different from themselves. As we shall see, the Morgans' relationship
with Kuhn, Loeb was important precisely because it signaled not only the
presence of other relations and actors in the world of finance, such as Japanese bankers; it was also significant because it pointed to the role played by
persons traditionally considered far removed from the source of their power,
such as women. In other words, different groups were not only present in
the Morgans' network, the structure of their exclusion or inclusion was very
much interrelated, a fact that has been completely ignored in the study of
the values and practices of *gentlemen* banking.

The larger question, of course, is how this changes our understanding of
their economic power. If, as the book claims, trust is essential to the functioning of financial markets, and if social relations are central to the ways in
which financial markets function, what do the Morgans' relationships tell
us about the conditions under which alliances were formed in the world of
elite private bankers before the Second World War? When the Morgans'
relationships are studied broadly and when they are not parsed into preex-

isting categories, it becomes clear that their network was not homogeneous. If the Morgans' network was not homogeneous or collusive, and if their influence was not based on their monetary capital, as they claimed, what was the source of their power? Ironically, their network's diversity offers one theory for why it was so difficult for the bank's critics to prove that the Morgans' power was based on collusion and control.[30] The reality was that the Morgans did not need direct control and did not need to work in an entirely collusive environment in order pursue their interests.[31] As we shall see, their network may have been diverse but it was not equal.

When the Morgans talked about their influence being based on the confidence of others, this book understands this to mean that their influence stemmed from their specific position within a national and international network that enabled and supported their interests and relationships. Though that is not what the Morgans meant when they talked about character, that is essentially what it entailed. In other words, the story of their influence is as much about their historical context as it is about the history of the bank and its partners. That is the story their relationships tell and that is the history to which we now turn.

CHAPTER ONE

Gentlemen Banking Before 1914

WHEN PIERPONT MORGAN was born in 1837, the United States was barely sixty years old, a union of states uneasily bound together across ideological, economic, and geographic divisions. Morgan was in his late fifties when he reorganized his father and mentors' firms into what became the House of Morgan. By that time, the United States had become a nation by fire, an industrializing country with communications, transportation, and technological advances far beyond what had been available before the Mexican-American and Civil Wars. The Morgans' position within the financial community was dependent upon this growth in American national infrastructure. Their rise to the apex of American finance was aided by certain historical and structural factors that encouraged economic consolidation, such as the relative position of the United States to Europe and the limited government regulation of private banking.

The firm's ties that developed under these conditions, including the relationships and traditions of gentlemen bankers, became the focus of progressive critics and government investigators at the Pujo Hearings. If the Morgans' relationships have traditionally been perceived as a collusive and homogeneous network, this perception of gentlemen banking relationships and power, including its private nature, hid the extent to which their interests were enabled by fundamental inequalities. These encompassed the divisions that deeply troubled American republican society in the post-Civil War, including those considered to be far removed from the concerns of elite businessmen and capitalists.

GENTLEMEN BANKERS BEFORE 1914

Pierpont Morgan was born in Hartford, Connecticut in 1837. His mother, Juliet, was the daughter of a Unitarian minister and a descendant of James Pierpont, one of the founders of Yale University. Morgan's father, Junius, was the grandson of a Unitarian minister and a descendant of Joseph Morgan, one of the founders of the Aetna Insurance Company. By the early 1840s, the Morgan family had already accumulated a substantial fortune. Pierpont was the first of Juliet and Junius's five children and the only surviving son. The year before Junius joined George Peabody as his partner in London, Pierpont graduated from public school in Boston. He was sent to Germany to study at the University of Gottingen after which he began his apprenticeship in New York in 1857.[1]

After George Peabody retired, Junius founded the firm of J. S. Morgan & Co. (JSM & Co.) in London (1864). In 1871, Junius merged the Morgan interests with those of Anthony Drexel (1826–1893), a Philadelphia merchant banker, whose father, Francis, was the founder of the Drexel bank. Together, they formed Drexel, Morgan & Co. (DM & Co.) with Pierpont as its head. DM & Co. served as JSM & Co.'s American arm. While Drexel himself had two sons, they were unwilling or unable to take up his position. After Junius died in 1890 and Drexel died in 1893, Pierpont Morgan founded J. P. Morgan & Co. based in New York, which became the leading branch of a newly organized house.

In total, there were four firms in the House of Morgan. The Philadelphia firm was renamed Drexel & Co. (D & Co.).[2] JSM & Co. remained the British branch of the House of Morgan until 1909 when it was renamed Morgan, Grenfell & Co. (MG & Co.).[3] The Paris branch, which had been founded in 1868 under the Drexel interests, was called Morgan, Harjes & Co. (MH & Co.). It was renamed Morgan et Cie. after the death of Herman

Harjes (1875–1926), who was the son of its founder, John Harjes.[4] Only J. P. Morgan & Co. and Drexel & Co. partners were bound by the same partnership agreement. The American branches were partners as firms in the European houses. The Paris and London branches had their own agreements though some partners overlapped.[5] Under Pierpont's leadership, the banks worked together and were identified as one collective—an international house whose expertise was in the American market.

As merchant or gentlemen bankers, the Morgans' roots lay in the business of international trade. The fact that the Morgans had multiple branches on both sides of the Atlantic was critical to their success because the different houses provided each other with access to information on the ground at a time when reliable information was expensive and rare.[6] Merchant or gentlemen banking traditionally had a high barrier to entry because it was extremely personal, a structure designed to limit risk in a historical context that offered little formal protections or structures to enforce contracts across national boundaries and vast distances.[7] Using the bank's "name and credit" through instruments such as the "bills of exchange" and "commercial letter of credit," merchant bankers like the Morgans were able to provide a multitude of financial services from supplying credits for international trade to foreign exchange to loans to governments to underwriting, while also navigating multiple currencies, laws, customs, and languages.[8] The Morgans' relations in international trade were a central part of the family bank's business in investment banking.

The fortune of the House of Morgan was also closely tied to American industrial and national development. At a time when the United States was a debtor nation in need of capital, they became an important intermediary between European investors and America's first big business, the railroads. From their connections in merchant banking and international trade, they built a financial network for railroads and industries in the United States. If their prominence in the United States stemmed largely from their position as a bridge between the United States and Europe, the significance of their position was heightened by the differences between the two spaces that were being bridged, particularly before the First World War.

Unlike England, which had a central bank since the seventeenth century, the United States (though much younger in years) did not develop a central bank until 1913.[9] This was only one of the considerable structural advantages the European markets had over the American market, which tended to favor private international bankers.[10] In the decentralized environment of the "new world," private banks had considerable influence in the field of foreign finance because of the ways in which the legal structure gave them advantages over their competitors. After the passage of the National Banking Act in 1863, nationally chartered commercial banks faced more state regulation than private banks and were prevented from opening branches abroad. Blocked from moving into international finance on their own, they formed working relationships with private banks, in some cases through interlocking directorships, ties between firms formed by the common membership of an individual director.[11]

These ties allowed commercial banks like National City Bank (f. 1812) and First National Bank of New York (f. 1863), which were founded as banks to further government and national development, to take advantage of the experience and connections of private banks like J. P. Morgan & Co., which then took advantage of the deposits and reach of its collaborators.[12] The relationships were solidified through formal economic ties and, as we shall see, personal ties between partners and directors.[13] As long as competition and access to capital were limited, and until corporations had the ability to raise substantial funds through surplus profits, private banks had the potential for enormous influence, relative to even their considerable reputations and connections. Through a legal and economic structure that allowed them to access reserves of other banks, commercial banks, who were made in effect national depositories, became the collaborators of elite private banks, not their competitors.[14]

Whether or not Pierpont Morgan was conscious of the structural and historical factors that worked in his favor, he disliked competition, believing it to be wasteful and inefficient. That much was evident in the Morgans' active embrace of a cooperative structure known as the syndicate. While the history of syndicates dates back centuries, syndicates were first utilized in the United States in the early nineteenth century. The first underwriting syndicate appeared after the Civil War. Syndicates became more frequent by the late nineteenth century as circumstances changed such that one party could not assume all the risk and provide all the capital necessary in the economic expansion of the United States starting with the railroads, the pioneers of American big business.[15]

The general process of creating a syndicate began when a client, such as a railroad, needed to raise a large amount of capital (usually several million dollars) for improvements, acquisitions, or refunding of debt and approached the Morgans to underwrite a bond offering. (Between 1894 and 1934, approximately 50 percent of all Morgan undertakings involved railroads. Other clients included industrials [19 percent], state or national governments [13 percent], or utilities [9 percent].) (See Table 1.) The Morgans would then approach other banks with an offer to share in the underwriting. Very close associates and friends, such as First National and National City, might be allotted participations on the same terms as the Morgans. They were called the managing group.

Table 1   J. P. Morgan & Co.'s Syndicate Books Summary Characteristics, 1894–1934

Description	Total No.	% of Deals
Total # of Separate Deals (according to the syndicate book title listings)	1,660	Preliminary total
Total # of Deals (includes all the deals noted within the content of the syndicate books)	1,827	Actual total
Total # of Deals Originated by J. P. Morgan & Co. Only	1,240	68%
# of Deals Given by Others	587	32%
# of Syndicates*	843	N/A
# of Purchases*	271	N/A
# of Selling*	477	N/A
# of Loans*	54	N/A
# of Miscellaneous (Includes Reorganizations/No Action Taken/Transfers)*	106	N/A
Clients: Railroads	919	50%**
Clients: Foreign	277	15%**
Clients: Governments	232	13%**
Clients: Shipping	17	1%**
Clients: Utility & Communications	158	9%**
Clients: Industry & Manufacturing	349	19%**
Clients: Individuals	11	.6%**
Clients: Other/Miscellaneous	87	5%**

   * Note that one deal listed in a syndicate book could have many different stages that included syndicates, purchases, and sales.
   ** % of actual total. Note that this refers to the percentage of deals that had a client of that type. For example, a client could be coded both as "foreign" and as "government."
   Source: J. P. Morgan & Co. Syndicate Books, ARC 108–ARC 119, Pierpont Morgan Library (PML)

Other banks would be invited to participate as members of the purchasing group with the amount of the participation set by the Morgans usually on terms slightly less advantageous than the managing group. The final group was called the distributing group and like the other groups could be made up of individuals, banks, trust companies, or other types of syndicate participants. The distributing group was usually the largest group and the least prestigious. Their responsibility was to sell the offering to the public and other institutions. The Morgans were usually allotted a fee for their services, usually either one-half of 1 percent or 1 percent of the entire amount, but they also made profit on the difference between the terms of the managing, purchasing, and distribution groups. At each stage, the Morgans kept a certain portion of the syndicate for themselves, but the majority of the underwriting was done by the participants with few exceptions. (See Table 2.)

Participation in a syndicate had many benefits; the most obvious one was to profit at less risk than one might have on one's own; the less obvious but more important benefit was to expand and strengthen one's network.[16] Syndicates were also informal in that they did not involve contracts and were meant to avoid lengthy and expensive legal conflicts. In other words, they were monitored by a community and not by a state legal structure, which did not either exist or did not function efficiently to enforce contracts between parties. Syndicates could also be used as a way to control the

Table 2   J. P. Morgan & Co.'s Syndicates Participants by Type, 1894–1934*

Type of Syndicate Participant	# of Participants of Type	Total # of Participations	Total Amount**	# of Participations with Amount Unknown
Commercial banks***	280	2,212	$3,662,000,000	44
Private firms	670	3,698	$3,426,000,000	154
Security companies	16	569	$2,093,000,000	21
Trust companies	197	1,237	$1,117,000,000	40
Individuals	1,168	2,398	$827,000,000	159
TOTAL	2,331	10,114	$11,125,000,000	418

*Does not include insurance companies, savings banks, and others (e.g., trusts and estates, universities, and churches)
**Rounded to the nearest million
***Does not include foreign banks (of which there were 39)
Source: J. P. Morgan & Co. Syndicate Books, ARC 108–ARC 119, Pierpont Morgan Library (PML)

competition by including those who could seriously challenge or disadvantage or attack the price of the issue.[17] Syndicates thus encouraged the formation of a cooperative community across competing economic groups. They were indicative of the general trend toward economic consolidation and cooperation at the turn of the century.[18]

The House of Morgan's American syndicate data, which included substantial international issues, show the extent to which the Morgan bank did not work alone. Between 1894 and 1914, J. P. Morgan & Co. managed 352 syndicates for a total of approximately $4.3 billion. This was unlike actions related to purchases, for example, which J. P. Morgan & Co. usually acted on its own or for a client.[19] The syndicate books show 1,530 different syndicate participants with a total of 5,424 distinct participations during that time. The listed profit (for 71 percent of the syndicates) was over $40 million.[20] The firm took for itself only about 32 percent of all the syndicates it sponsored (about $1.38 billion). The portion of the total given to firms outside the House of Morgan was approximately $3.55 billion.[21] The top ten participants, in terms of the amount allotted, included: commercial banks (three), private firms (six), and one individual, John D. Rockefeller Sr. The top ten syndicate participants alone accounted for $1.94 billion or 55 percent of the total participations allotted to others, not including the House of Morgan branches. (See Table 3.)

Table 3 J. P. Morgan & Co.'s Top Ten Syndicate Participants, 1894–1914

Name	Amount*	# of Cases Amount Unknown
First National Bank of New York	$544,000,000	7
National City Bank	$495,000,000	4
Kidder, Peabody & Co.	$239,000,000	2
Kuhn, Loeb & Co.	$210,000,000	2
Lee, Higginson & Co.	$119,000,000	
Harvey Fisk & Sons	$92,000,000	1
Baring Bros. & Co.	$86,000,000	
Baring Magoun & Co.	$56,000,000	1
Deutsche Bank	$51,000,000	
John D. Rockefeller Sr.	$50,000,000	1
TOTAL:	$1,942,000,000	18

*Rounded to the nearest million

Source: J. P. Morgan & Co. Syndicate Books, ARC 108–ARC 119, Pierpont Morgan Library (PML)

During this time, J. P. Morgan & Co. participated in 660 different deals involving other firms (including syndicates, joint accounts, and other activities) out of a total of 898 (or 74 percent) deals listed in its syndicate books (such as stock purchases and sales). Out of those 660 deals, 308 were syndicate participations given to J. P. Morgan & Co. by other banks or firms or 47 percent of the 74 percent (34 percent of all the firm's deals listed in its syndicate books for that period). The total amount of syndicates initiated by others was more than $3.5 billion, and the amount of the participations given to J. P. Morgan & Co. alone was close to $300 million.[22] Syndicate participations given to the bank and offered by the bank were clearly an important part of its business.[23] More importantly, as we shall see, they also provide a map of the firm's economic network.

Multiple considerations went into the kind, method, size, and structure of a syndicate. As syndicates became larger, the process was also divided into the origination and purchase of a flotation and the selling and distribution of the issue. All of these decisions were made by the leading bank, who alone determined how and with whom risk and profit would be shared. The leading bank thus also determined the distribution of prestige or symbolic capital. Participation enhanced one's reputation and gave others an indication of one's resources and standing within the financial community.[24] Over time, the state would try to depersonalize investment banking in an attempt to make it more transparent, more accessible, more socially responsive, more stable and standardized, and, theoretically, more democratic. These actions would be vehemently resisted by the banking community, who saw the syndicate structure as an inherently more efficient management of risk and more considerate of the needs of both investor and client.

As the Morgans' syndicates suggest, the structure of banking syndicates was cooperative but hierarchical. Starting in the nineteenth century, syndicates took on the structure of a pyramid, with few firms at the apex. This structure developed historically because members of the financial community as a whole looked for leaders to allocate risk and manage prices in an environment of limited information and few safety nets. In practice this meant that even people not within the apex firms supported the pyramid structure; in other words, the syndicate system was able to maintain discipline in the investment banking industry overall. A firm's position in the pyramid was directly related to future business, current income, and prestige, and it spoke volumes about its relationship to the managing bank and to other banks in the syndicate.[25] For this reason, the amount of participation could also cause "dissatisfaction" or "jealousy."[26]

At the apex level, however, bankers like the Morgans did not compete over price. And though they competed over relationships with clients, which were "based on past performance, current reputation, and faithful adherence to the industry's 'informal code of conduct,'"[27] once a bank had an established relationship with a client, it was understood that the relationship would be respected and no action would take place without prior discussion with the precedent bank.[28] Like the syndicate, this informal code of conduct or the "gentlemen banker's code" guided the cooperation and monitored competition among banks.[29] As Jack Morgan would later explain, "The private banker is a member of a profession which has been practiced since the Middle Ages. In the process of time there has grown up a code of professional ethics and customs, on the observance of which depend his reputation, his fortune, and his usefulness to the community in which he works."[30]

The gentlemen's code was indicative of the wider community to which the Morgans were tied, one that was governed by rules not defined directly by the state. Though it implied that a banker felt a personal even "moral responsibility" regarding the quality of the bonds he issued, the extent to which this was true could only be judged by his reputation, whose meaning and definition extended beyond the financial world.[31] Because the Morgans were private, no one outside the firm had direct access to information about their organization and capital, their relationships or their syndicates. The lack of transparency became a major issue during and after the Panic of 1907. By that time, Pierpont Morgan's reputation was such that he would be directly called upon to use his enormous social, economic, and symbolic capital to vouch for and thus save multiple banking institutions from bankruptcy. His leadership during the Panic of 1907 marked the apex of his career, but it also exposed the weaknesses of an entire financial structure and the consequences of a system built on secrecy and largely accountable only to itself.

THE PANIC OF 1907

The Panic of 1907 began with an entrepreneur named F. Augustus Heinze (1869–1914). Born in Brooklyn, Heinze was the son of German and Irish parents and a graduate of Columbia University's Mining School. By the age of thirty, he had become major figure in the mining of copper in Butte, Montana. The year before the panic, when he was thirty-six, Heinze sold his copper interests for $12 million and moved back to New York, where he became the president of the Mercantile National Bank.[32] In October 1907, Heinze tried to corner the stock of the United Copper Company, and his failure to do so toppled his broker, Gross & Kleeberg, his brother's firm, Otto C. Heinze & Co., and threatened the dissolution of the Mercantile National Bank.

Heinze's close relationship with Charles T. Barney, the president of the Knickerbocker Trust Company, led to a run on the Trust. The Knicker-bocker cleared its checks through the National Bank of Commerce, a member of the New York Clearing House. The National Bank met Knicker-bocker's depositors' demands for two days before losing confidence in the Trust. Without the National Bank's support or outside assistance, the Knickerbocker failed on October 22, 1907.[33] Barney, who was the son of a banker, a graduate of Williams College, and brother-in-law to the former Secretary of the Navy, William C. Whitney, shot himself on November 14. Friends said it was because "he couldn't stand the loss of prestige."[34]

Knickerbocker's failure created a domino effect as depositors lost confi-dence and credit disappeared.[35] The panic spread and led to the failure of several banks and trust companies, the near suspension of the New York Stock Exchange, and the specter of the bankruptcy of the City of New York. During the crisis, the financial community turned to Morgan, which was itself a statement of his reputation and the hierarchical and intercon-nected structure of the community. In March of that year when the stock exchange was beginning to show signs of turmoil, financial leaders like Jacob Schiff, William Rockefeller, Edward Harriman, and Henry Clay Frick converged on the Morgan offices to discuss possible strategies for calming the markets.[36] By October, consultations with Morgan began in earnest.

The day before the Knickerbocker Trust closed, the officers of the Trust went to J. P. Morgan & Co.'s offices and asked to speak with Morgan directly. While they were there, word reached the Morgans that the Bank of Com-merce "had sent out a notice" stating that they would stop clearing for the Trust. That night, officers of the Trust had a meeting at Morgan's library with Morgan and two of his partners, Charles Steele and George W. Perkins. Perkins recalled, "At this meeting it became evident that the Knickerbocker situation was pretty desperate and, unless taken promptly in hand, would certainly cause a run on that company which might spread to others." The group then moved to Sherry's, a well-known restaurant patronized by New York society, located on the corner of 44th Street and 5th Avenue, where the Morgan partners had dinner in a private dining room. The Trust officers met in another room at Sherry's and they spent several hours in conference. About one in the morning, the Trust officers decided they would open the doors of the Trust "to see whether help could be extended to them by other financial institutions—in this way giving such other institutions time to investigate the Trust Company's assets and general condition."[37]

The next day, Benjamin Strong, then a member of Bankers Trust, was asked by Henry Davison to make an examination of the Knickerbocker's assets while a line of depositors waited outside of the Trust Co.'s main office.[38] Pierpont Morgan, George F. Baker of First National, James Stillman of National City, and James T. Woodward of Hanover National were waiting inside to find the results of his investigation. According to Strong, it was not determined that the Trust was insolvent. Strong said he simply was not given enough time "to give any assurances upon which any pledge of assistance could be based." Strong recalled, "In another 24 hours it might have been possible to do so."[39]

In Perkins's account, it was believed that the examination had been completed. He wrote, ". . . the bankers downtown felt that the Trust Company was not solvent . . . and that its assets were of a nature that would make liquidation slow and tedious in any event." Moreover, because the trust companies were not able to act collectively, Perkins said, "It did not seem, advisable, therefore to render it any help."[40] Strong was at the Trust when it closed. He told Thomas Lamont years later, "The consternation on the faces of the people on that line, many of them men whom I knew, I shall never forget."[41]

After the Knickerbocker suspended, Perkins wrote, "We all realized then that we were 'in for it'; that there would undoubtedly be runs on other Trust Companies and that the situation had become exceedingly grave." That is exactly what happened. Day and night for several weeks, Morgan, his partners Davison, Steele, and Perkins, and his associates were on call to answer to the frantic visits of bankers, make decisions about the solvency of institutions, and find capital and solutions for those whose failure would further demoralize confidence. Meetings were held at Morgan's office and his private library on Madison Avenue and 36th Street, which had just been completed the year before.

Pierpont Morgan believed that the trust companies were not able to organize because they lacked the personal ties necessary for collective action. At one point, he told Benjamin Strong, "When [the presidents of the trust companies] came into the [Morgan] office they had to be introduced to each other, and I don't think much can be expected from them."[42] The premium Morgan placed on close ties proved to be the deciding factor in the outcome of the panic. When the dust settled, Morgan, along with George F. Baker (1840–1931) of First National Bank, James Stillman (1850–1918) of National City Bank, and a "rescue party" that included Hanover National Bank and Bankers Trust Company, were attributed with stopping the panic and organizing the financial community and the capital needed to keep the major institutions afloat.[43]

George F. Baker, in particular, was a key figure during the panic. One of Morgan's closest friends and collaborators, Baker was a major figure in the banking community with networks that rivaled Morgan's.[44] Born in western New York, the seventh generation of a New England family, Baker's entry into banking began like Morgan with a family connection and an apprenticeship.[45] Unlike Morgan, Baker's family was not wealthy, but his father's eventual career in public service created ties to leading public officials, including William Seward, Lincoln's Secretary of State, which served useful when Baker embarked on a career at the age of sixteen.

After attending public school in New York and Massachusetts, Baker began working as a clerk in the New York Banking Department. There he met John Thompson, who became one of the founders of the First National Bank of New York in 1863. Baker began at First National as a teller and moved up eventually to becoming one of the board directors. In 1877, he became president of the bank, which expanded enormously under his tenure.[46] Morgan had great respect for Baker and their mutual affection set the stage for a long-term relationship, which was a model of the strength and informal nature of personal relations in the banking community. As Jack Morgan once stated, "[Baker and Pierpont Morgan] understood each other perfectly, worked in harmony, and there was never any need of written contracts between them."[47]

Unlike Baker, James Stillman was not close friends with Morgan, but he had other important ties that made him a formidable ally. Stillman was born in Texas and raised in New York City. His father was a cotton broker. He was educated at private schools and began working at the age of sixteen in his father's brokerage house, Smith, Woodward & Stillman, where he became a partner at the age of twenty-two. Stillman joined National City Bank of New York's board in 1884 and succeeded the president, Moses Taylor, who died in 1891. Like Baker and Morgan, Stillman "had an extraordinary talent for forming alliances with the rich and powerful of his day. This talent [was] the foundation of his success in investment banking." Stillman was closely tied to William Rockefeller, president of Standard Oil Company; two of his daughters married into the Rockefeller family. Their connection added to National City's reputation as the bank of Standard Oil and its status as the nation's biggest bank.[48]

The panic marked a turning point in the depth and strength of the relationships, if not between Morgan, Baker, and Stillman, certainly in the relationships of the three banks, J. P. Morgan & Co., First National Bank, and National City Bank.[49] In the period after the panic, the two banks became so important to the Morgan syndicates that they simply were referred to as "The Banks." Their "usual" portion of the underwriting on original terms (the same terms as Morgan received) was one-quarter each (J. P. Morgan & Co. took the other half). Between 1894 and 1934, First National, National City, and National City Co., National City's securities affiliate, dominated the top ten syndicate participants by total amount, participations, and number of unique clients (i.e., highest diversity of clients). (See Table 4.) Their ties were critical to the Morgans' ability to place large issues with banks and financial institutions, one reason why they were considered to be an apex house. Their relationships also enabled the Morgans to finance large projects and undertake daunting tasks, such as underwriting bond issues for New York City.[50]

Though Baker and Stillman's support was central to the effort to inject confidence into the banking community and though they were also well-known figures, attention centered on the figure of Pierpont Morgan. Being a private banker, Morgan was not limited by the same rules as Baker or Stillman, whose banks received their charters from the state. Not having to answer to anyone, Morgan seemed to be guided only by his own force of will. He was heralded as the "Jupiter" or the "Colossus of Wall Street." The *New York Times* called him, "A Bank in Human Form."[51]

If the panic marked the moment in time "Morgan's leadership of

Table 4   J. P. Morgan & Co.'s Top Ten Syndicate Participants, 1894–1934

Name	1894–1934 Total*	# of Cases Amount Unknown	Total # of Participations	Total # of Unique Clients
First National Bank (NY)	$2,171,000,000	12	709	189
National City Co.	$1,658,000,000	8	391	110
National City Bank	$889,000,000	6	346	114
Kidder, Peabody & Co.	$753,000,000	5	164	71
Kuhn, Loeb & Co.	$592,000,000	2	164	67
Guaranty Trust Co.	$389,000,000	5	137	68
Lee, Higginson & Co.	$353,000,000	3	149	64
Guaranty Co.	$320,000,000	3	94	37
Harris, Forbes & Co.	$303,000,000	2	113	47
Bankers Trust Co.	$298,000,000	7	167	72
TOTAL	$7,726,000,000	53	Average: 243.4	Average: 83.9

* Rounded to the nearest million
Source: J. P. Morgan & Co. Syndicate Books, ARC 108–ARC 119, Pierpont Morgan Library (PML)

American finance reached its peak," it was also the point that the tide began to gain momentum against him. Morgan was accused of having started the crisis himself to financially enrich himself and his firm.[52] He was also criticized for having arbitrarily decided who would fail and succeed irrespective of the damage to the depositors or the economy at large. Less hostile critics argued that the financial system could not give one man that much power, even if he worked for the greater good, as Morgan sincerely believed he had.

Morgan's role in the Panic of 1907 added to his legendary status, but it also fueled the political movement for financial reform. Unlike Andrew Carnegie, who wrote the "Gospel of Wealth," a treatise on how the ends justify the means, or John D. Rockefeller, whose blatant support of Social Darwinian theories led him to state that God had made him rich, Pierpont Morgan did not publicize his opinions about the source of his wealth and power. He also did little to counter negative public perceptions. His cold and distant persona, his intense sense of privacy and personal conviction, and his devotion to client confidentiality were interpreted, quite accurately, as a rejection of the idea that he had to explain his actions to anyone. All contributed to the impression that he was aloof from the national crisis caused by the very institutions he had helped to create.

By the first decade of the twentieth century, the popular perception of Morgan as the leader of an economic conspiracy that threatened the order and ideals of American society began to gain a political voice. Against what they saw as an impenetrable wall of indifference between themselves and the financial and industrial elite, political reformers turned to the American government to speak for their interests. What they found was growing support in Congress, the White House, and the Supreme Court for the idea that the government had the obligation and power to protect American democracy from the evils of big business. In January 1912, the House of Representatives passed a resolution authorizing an investigation into the existence of a money trust stating in part:

> Whereas it has been charged, and there is reason to believe that the management of the finances of many of the great industrial and railroad corporations of the country engaged in interstate commerce is rapidly concentrating in the hands of a few groups of financiers in the city of New York. . . . Whereas it has been further charged and is generally believed that these same groups of financiers have so entrenched themselves in their control of the aforesaid financial and other institutions and otherwise in the direction of the finances of the country that they are thereby enabled to use the funds and property of the great national banks and other moneyed corporations in the leading money centers to control the security and commodity markets to regulate the interest rates for money; to create, avert, and compose panics; to dominate the New York Stock Exchange and various clearing-house associations throughout the country. . . . Therefore be it Resolved, That the Members now or hereafter constituting the Committee on Banking and Currency . . . is authorized and directed . . . to fully investigate and inquire into each and all of the above-recited matter. . . . [53]

Named after Arséne Pujo (1861–1939), a Louisiana congressman who sat as chairman of the committee, the Pujo Investigation focused on cooperative relationships within the financial community.[54] Its goal was to prove the existence of a monopoly on credit, which Woodrow Wilson had declared in 1911, was "the great monopoly in this country."[55] During the hearings, J. P. Morgan & Co.'s inner workings were brought out into the public sphere in a spectacular and unfavorable light. The man who was chosen for this task was Samuel Untermyer, a New York lawyer whom the Morgan partners learned to hate so much they referred to him as the "beast."[56]

PHOTO I House of Representatives Special Subcommittee of Banking and Currency to Investigate "Money Trusts" also known as the "Pujo Committee" [McMorran of MI, Hayes of CA, Neeley of KS, Guernsey of ME, Pujo of LA (Chairman), Daughtery of MO, Byrnes of SC, a clerk, Heald of DE, a clerk, Samuel Untermyer, lead counsel], 1912, (Library of Congress, Prints & Photographs Division, [reproduction number LC-H261–1924])

THE MONEY TRUST INVESTIGATION

Samuel Untermyer (1858–1940) was born in Virginia, the son of Jewish immigrants from Germany. His father, who fought for the Confederate Army, died shortly after the Civil War. Raised in New York City and a graduate of the City College of New York and Columbia University Law School, Untermyer started a law partnership with his brother, Isaac, and his half-brother, Randolph Guggenheimer, in 1879.[57] The law firm, Guggenheimer & Untermyer (later Guggenheimer, Untermyer & Marshall) remained largely a family affair. Untermyer's other brother, Maurice, joined in 1890.[58] A former Columbia classmate, Louis Marshall, who married his cousin, Florence Lowenstein, joined the firm in 1895.[59] Another partner, T. L. Herrmann, was married to Untermyer's niece.[60] Untermyer's son, Alvin, joined the firm in 1906.[61]

Like many others, Untermyer was deeply influenced by the Progressive reform movements of the late nineteenth and early twentieth century. A successful lawyer and businessman in his own right, he handled many important cases in his career,[62] but he achieved his greatest fame as counsel for the Pujo Investigation, the year after he presented a talk titled, "Is there a Money Trust?" at the Financial Forum.[63] In his talk, Untermyer granted that under the existing law, "There is no definite union or aggregation of the money powers in the financial world," but he continued:

> If, however, we mean by this loose elastic term 'Trust' as applied to the con-centration of the 'Money Power' that there is a close and well-defined 'com-munity of interest' and understanding among the men who dominate the financial destinies of our country and who wield fabulous power over the fortunes of others through their control of corporate funds belonging to other people, our investigators will find a situation confronting us far more serious than is popularly supposed to exist.[64]

Politically, Untermyer was a progressive Democrat, influential within the party though he never held public office. He was a Democratic National Convention delegate from 1904 until 1916, and later stumped for Wilson in 1912 and 1916.[65] Though he was also a strong critic of Theodore Roosevelt's distinction between "good" and "bad" trusts, Untermyer's ideas on state responsibility were more in line with that of Roosevelt's New Nationalism than Wilson's New Freedom. He believed in the power of an activist gov-ernment. In 1904, he told the Commercial Travelers' League that the presi-dent and attorney general had to "teach respect and fear for the law" to "the small body of reckless and foolhardy rich and powerful men who are vic-timizing the people and imperiling the industrial future of our country."[66] Untermyer advocated the "government ownership of public utilities," but he was also a strong defender of the capitalist order. He felt his role was to be a voice for the minority stockholder and the consumer, who paid the differ-ence between the "real" price and the selling price and were the primary victims of the trusts and large corporations.[67]

Untermyer was wealthy, reportedly a millionaire before the age of thirty, but he was not a member of the social or financial elite. He had only indirect ties to members of the elite investment banking community, politically and socially, and he had no fear of losing any current or future relationship with the men he was asked to confront on the stand. Despite Untermyer's ties with Louis Marshall, who was brother-in-law to Jewish scholar Judas Magnes and a close associate of Kuhn, Loeb & Co.'s Jacob Schiff, he was also not of the German Jewish "Our Crowd," the Jewish social and economic elite in New York.[68] These qualities, as well as his grasp of economic practices and his extensive legal experience, made him an exceptional choice for the lead counsel of the Pujo Investigation.

During the hearings, Untermyer questioned the leaders of every major bank in New York, the New York Clearing House Association, and the New York Stock Exchange, among others. He had a great ability to break down complicated transactions and make them understandable to a general audience. He was, by all accounts, a formidable prosecutor.[69] He was relentless in his goal to obtain "the facts," as he called it, and he refused to let witnesses get by with "I don't know" and "I don't recall." When witnesses were evasive, and they were quite often, Untermyer would say pointedly, "Will you not answer my question?" He told one witness, "I should prefer not to put any questions to you that you would prefer not to answer, but I have a duty to perform and so have you."[70] Other times he would ask if the witness was actually serious or say rhetorically, "We will not try to fence will we?" He was quick to point out if he thought a witness was making what he called "speeches" and had absolutely no hesitation in asking extremely direct questions in the most unapologetic manner. One of his favorite phrases was, "Let us see about that."[71]

The Morgan partners hated Untermyer with an undying passion. This was particularly true for the younger and newer partners, who were very protective of their "senior." They believed Untermyer to be ambitious and impertinent, a combination that describes possibly the lowest qualities they could fault in a person. Because they saw the Pujo Investigation as a direct attack on the firm, the partners responded by trying to dig up dirt on both him and Chairman Pujo.[72] The Morgans also hired William Spurgeon, the managing editor of the *Washington Evening Post* as a sort of publicity counsel. Morgan partner Thomas W. Lamont wanted Untermyer smeared as an "irresponsible muck-raker."[73] Fundamentally, they regarded outsiders of his kind to be envious and resentful.[74]

To the extent that the term "envy" implies the desire to have something

PHOTO 2 Samuel Untermyer, undated
(Library of Congress, Prints & Photographs
Division, [reproduction number LC-DIG-
ggbain-31626])

that one does not possess which is possessed by another, envy would not be
an accurate reflection of Untermyer's relationship to the Morgan bank.
Also, though the Morgan partners would have disagreed, Untermyer was
not out to malign their character or intentions.[75] During the investigation,
his focus on the Morgan firm was clear, and he did not hesitate to ask the
most difficult questions, but his goal was not to personalize the hearings.
On numerous occasions, Untermyer repeatedly stated that he was not interested in the details of personal business or affairs, which as we shall see, was
an important distinction. At one point, he said, ". . . We are not impugning
these gentlemen or their motives, and we have no intention of doing so."[76]
He told Pierpont Morgan directly that he had "no desire to intrude upon
your private business."[77]

Untermyer's feelings on Morgan were complex. The fact that Morgan
only testified to that which he could verify personally as an individual made
it difficult for Untermyer to prove that Morgan was part of a larger trust.
Untermyer also encountered Morgan on the stand as an individual, for
whom he had a measure of respect. After the investigation, Untermyer said,
"Whatever may be one's view of the perils to our financial and economic

system of the concentration of the control of credit, the fact remains, and is generally recognized, that Mr. Morgan was animated by high purpose and that he never knowingly abused his almost incredible power."[78] Regardless of what he felt about Morgan as a person, Untermyer felt little obligation to respect the rules and boundaries of the gentlemen banking profession. His distance from Morgan's world was reflected in the fact that the Pujo Hearings were an investigation, meaning that the committee first had to gather information, which as outsiders, they did not have.

Empowered by the state, Untermyer and the prosecution questioned and gathered information for approximately eight months between May 1912 and January 1913, an effort that was repeatedly questioned and tested.[79] William Rockefeller, for example, refused to even testify and evaded the subpoena to appear in Washington. The Pujo Committee was forced to station men for more than half a year at his various residences but was not able to serve him.[80] Morgan was much less evasive, but he and his partners, as well as his friends like George Baker, disputed the committee's claim that it had a right to information that they considered to be private and confidential. It was only after Congress passed a law empowering the committee that the hearings resumed after a six-month recess between June and December 1912. Even then the committee was not given all the information that was requested.[81]

The Pujo Committee commissioned a statistician named Lawrence W. Scudder to catalogue formal economic ties between the nation's leading private banks, national banks, trust companies, insurance companies, industrials, and railroads. The morning of Pierpont Morgan's appearance at the hearings, Scudder presented a massive chart that documented the overlapping directorships or interlocking directorates of the top banking houses and major financial institutions.[82] With aggregate capital resources in the tens of billions of dollars, the resulting network was so impressive and Morgan's position so indisputably central that it seemed unnecessary to look any further for the source of his power.[83] Nevertheless, the committee was anxious for Morgan to explain his influence for himself.

For his part, once he took the stand, Morgan was unfailingly polite and frank when it came to giving testimony. Fundamentally, he acted like someone in charge, and he was not afraid to name names or be held accountable unlike many of the other witnesses. He told Untermyer, "Anything that you would like to ask I will try to answer."[84] Several times, he stated that he

PHOTO 3 Louisa Morgan Satterlee, Pierpont Morgan, and Jack Morgan, Washington, DC, 1912 (Library of Congress, Prints & Photographs Division, [reproduction number LC-DIG-hec-01824])

would accept final responsibility for any action taken by his partners and his firm and would swear by anything his partners had done.[85] Though he could not remember every detail or transaction, he did not act as though he was deliberately evasive and thus, he was not treated as a hostile witness. It is difficult to say if Untermyer reciprocated Morgan's attitude because Morgan was who he was or because Morgan behaved in a manner unlike other witnesses. Though his partners may have disagreed, their exchange was not exceptionally negative relative to that of other witnesses of similar stature.[86]

When they got to the issue of control, however, Morgan and Untermyer seemed to be speaking entirely different languages. Fundamentally, they could not agree on what the question was. Untermyer would ask a question and Morgan would make a statement about something that seemed entirely different. The reason was that if Untermyer's goal was to show that the practices Morgan and his friends regarded as good and necessary put all others at a disadvantage and caused a national economic catastrophe, this was a conclusion that Morgan could not accept or even consider. The idea that he personally, knowingly or unknowingly, destabilized the national economy for monetary gain challenged his traditions, his way of life, and his sense of honor and conviction. It was so incomprehensible, he would say things that Untermyer simply could not believe or understand, such as, "I do not care anything about the money." He also told Untermyer that he had no power, which seemed to fly in the face of common sense and reality.[87]

Pierpont Morgan was not alone in trying to convince Untermyer of the higher moral code of bankers. About a month later, George F. Baker testified at the hearings and made many of the same points stating, "There would not be much business done if it was not done on confidence."[88] Baker had a more contentious meeting with Untermyer. His friend Edward Tuck later wrote to him, "What an outrage that our best men should be summoned to appear under the authority of the U.S. Government almost in the attitude of criminals before a committee of cheap politicians and business ignoramuses to be cross-questioned by an unprincipled and pettifogging Jew."[89]

Baker's testimony was made more antagonistic by his counsel Fisher A. Baker, who was also his uncle.[90] Fisher kept interrupting the proceedings trying to clarify comments Baker had made. He exasperated Untermyer and was warned several times by Chairman Pujo.[91] At one point when Baker could not remember the details of a bond issue in 1905, Fisher protested by saying, "You must remember, Mr. Untermyer, that he is 73 years old. . . ." After order was restored, Untermyer said, "It is not at all surprising, Mr. Baker, that you should not remember everything." To which Baker replied, "I am not like you, Mr. Untermyer."[92] After Baker testified, Jack Morgan cabled his father, "G. F. Baker had rather hard time [in] Washington but did magnificently. The beast was both rude and insulting to him."[93]

The attack on the traditions and beliefs of gentlemen bankers helped to create feelings of solidarity among the competing firms as each senior partner went through the experience of testifying in front of Congress, including German Jewish bankers, who received no leniency from Untermyer.[94] The Morgan partners were impressed with Jacob Schiff's testimony on the stand and the way in which he affirmed the proper values and practices of gentlemen banking to which both houses were committed.[95]

PHOTO 4 George F. Baker (with cane) and George F. Baker Jr. (holding his arm), Washington DC, January 1913, (Library of Congress, Prints & Photographs Division, [reproduction number LC-DIG-ggbain-12883])

Like Baker, Schiff had a contentious interaction with Untermyer. Several times Untermyer asked Schiff, "Will you not answer my question?" To which Schiff would reply, "I will answer it in my own way." Untermyer questioned Schiff at length about his relations with J. P. Morgan & Co. and their understanding not to interfere in each other's business. Schiff said, "I would describe it in this way, that it is not good form to create unreasonable interference or competition. A large banking house or small banking house . . . should respect itself. After the negotiation has once been begun, it should not endeavor to get it away from somebody else."[96]

Like the Morgans, Schiff used terms like "honor" and "moral responsibility" to describe the practices of "gentlemen" bankers. Though he did not completely agree with the Morgans with regard to voting trusts or holding companies (he did not like them), offering participations to individuals in syndicates (Kuhn, Loeb did rarely), or holding corporation deposits (Kuhn, Loeb did not do so), Schiff's emphasis on individual freedom and character was entirely consistent with the Morgans. "We do not make brains," he said. "Brains are created by a higher Power." Schiff told Untermyer, "I would not limit, in any instance, individual freedom in anything, because I believe the law of nature governs that better than any law of man."[97] Jack Morgan cabled his father, "Jacob H. Schiff on stand yesterday; made admirable witness. Managed make one point quite clear, namely that he was in favour of largest possible liberty to the individual and felt that banking business could be stifled by too much law."[98]

THE DEATH OF PIERPONT MORGAN

During and after the investigation, Morgan and his partners were greatly disturbed by the way in which the Pujo Committee's findings were presented to the public.[99] They did not deny that they were members of an exclusive fraternity, but they did not believe that their economic ties constituted proof of a monopoly on money or credit. They were not, however, blind to the writing on the wall.

On March 13, 1913, Jack Morgan wrote James Stillman that the firm would be reducing its stock holding interests, stating, "The Untermyer enquiry and the press generally have indicated a feeling on the part of the public that J. P. Morgan & Company ought not to have large stock-holding interests in our financial institutions. . . . We all feel that it behooves us to pay more or less attention to public feeling of that kind. . . ."[100] This shift in the firm's attitude signaled the fact that the partners knew times were changing though they could not have known how quickly events would come to pass.

Tired and worn out by the hearings, Pierpont Morgan went abroad in January 1913 with his daughter Louisa. Before he left for his trip, he met with George Baker, whom he told he had to "consider the possibility that [he] might not return." On March 31, 1913, about three months after he testified at the Pujo Hearings, Morgan died in his sleep in Rome at the age of seventy-five. The diagnosis was that he had had "a general nervous and physical breakdown." Within his inner circle, the consensus was that the strain and injustice of the Pujo prosecution had been too much for him.[101] "The king is dead," Frank A. Vanderlip of National City wrote James Stillman. "All New York is at half-mast. There are no cries of, 'Long life [sic] the king,' for the general verdict seems to be that there will be no other

king; that Mr. Morgan, typical of the time in which he lived, can have no
successor, for we are facing other days."[102]

Reeling from their loss, the Morgan partners also had to contend with
the fallout from the hearings, which continued to rain down upon them in
the form of political and economic reforms. In February 1913, the Sixteenth
Amendment had been ratified after having been passed by Congress in
1909, allowing the government to levy an income tax.[103] In December 1913,
Woodrow Wilson, by then president, signed the Federal Reserve Act, which
led to the creation of a national banking reserve system of twelve privately
controlled banks with a central board of governors, which became the
depository for commercial banks. Taking stock of the new environment,
Jack Morgan announced on January 1, 1914, that he and four other senior
partners would step down from dozens of their board memberships, a move
that anticipated the government's passage of the Clayton Antitrust Act
(1914), which determined interlocking directorates to be illegal if they could
be proven to reduce competition.[104]

From the point of view of the Morgans' critics, the new legislation and the
banking community's responses were an important victory, the successful
culmination to a long, arduous political process.[105] After wringing concessions out of the banking community, one had to ask, however, if the state and
Progressive reformers were successful in achieving a more competitive playing
field. While there was certainly more regulation, the changes did not make
the banking community any less hierarchical, any less consolidated, or any
less secret. They also did not make the banking community any more open,
any less distant. Though government reforms may have limited their direct
influence, they did not fundamentally change the structure, the methods, or
many of the relationships within the financial community.[106] What factors
and conditions made this possible? Though the Morgan partners had to
acknowledge national interests to an extent they never had previously, they
found ways to adapt. They were not against making compromises, particularly if they could do so on their own terms.[107]

When Jack Morgan made the decision to drop off the boards of numerous
companies, he did not hide the fact that the firm was responding to public
sentiment even though he disagreed with the substance of the criticisms. He
said, "Although the fact may not be generally understood, we have always
undertaken directorships with extreme reluctance, and only in response to
an implied obligation that we keep in close touch with these properties
whose securities we have recommended and sold to the public." Like Mor-

gan's London partners, Morgan did not believe that the resignations would have an effect on the securities of those companies, if done in a proper manner. He went on to say, "We believe, however, that without being directors we can still keep in sufficiently close touch with the progress of these properties, and yet relieve ourselves of unnecessary responsibilities."[108]

Morgan made the same argument when he wrote privately to James Stillman about the firm's stock-holding interests. When he wrote, "We all feel that it behooves us to pay more or less attention to public feeling of that kind," he went on to say, "particularly as our relations to our friends do not depend on our stock-holding interests."[109] Frank Vanderlip wrote Stillman that Morgan was giving up stock-holdings because he and his partners believed they were of "little advantage" and because "relations were personal and would continue" without them.[110] Later, Morgan told Vanderlip again that he was "absolutely confident that the present relationships are built on personalities rather than on stock ownership, and that they will continue unaltered."[111] These sentiments about the importance of personal ties were explicitly reaffirmed by Benjamin Strong Jr., the president of Bankers Trust. About two weeks after Morgan's announcement in January 1914, Strong wrote George F. Baker Jr. of First National Bank, "Legislation won't bother us if we are surrounded by such good friends as you and I both have down town; and it's the best asset we have." Ten months later, Strong was appointed the governor of the Federal Reserve Bank of New York.[112]

If Morgan and his partners were willing to sacrifice formal economic ties and commitments, such as interlocking directorships or stock holdings, it was because they privately and publicly acknowledged the loss of those ties would not alter the ways they did business.[113] By agreeing to a certain degree of intervention in their formal economic ties then, they safeguarded the most important aspect of their work, the freedom of association and the existence of a separate and private sphere in the world of business.[114] These concessions were possible because their critics also shared their values with regard to the right of private association. The significance of this common ground cannot be overstated. Deriving from a mutual embeddedness in American society, it would also enable the Morgans, as we shall see, to leave private banking and become a public corporation by mid-century.

It is important to note that the structure in question was similar to but distinct from the traditional conceptualization of a private and a public sphere where the private sphere is understood as a space where labor is unpaid and relations are informally organized, and the public is its opposite, a space of paid labor and political activity and the free market. This categorization did not apply to the Morgans or to any of their banking associates in the early twentieth century, who universally believed their relationships and those of their banks to be entirely private.[115]

What is traditionally called a private sphere more closely resembles what the Morgans defined a "domestic sphere." In the private world of the home, tradition was epitomized by the relationships of the bourgeois family, husband and wife, master and servant, parent and child. The private world of business was ruled by tradition as exemplified by the gentlemen banker's code, the informal code of conduct that mediated competitive relationships within the banking community. In both the economic and social spheres of the private world, the language of tradition was moralistic and religious, which advanced the view that their relations were held to a different and higher standard.

For the next generation of Morgan partners, who would carry on after Pierpont Morgan's death, the fact that the state focused only on the Morgans' formal economic ties within a public sphere had enormous implications for the potential for economic reform. It meant there were certain kinds of relationships upon which the state would not infringe, in particular, those related to private association for both firms and individuals in business and in society. In this regard, the Morgans found critical support in the most unlikely allies, including Louis D. Brandeis, whose writings did much to extend the impact of the Money Trust Investigation well into the twentieth century.

THE PROGRESSIVE CRITIQUE

Louis D. Brandeis (1856–1941) was the son of German Jewish immigrants, who immigrated to the United States in 1848. He was born in Louisville, Kentucky where his father ran a grain business. In 1875, he entered Harvard Law School where he excelled and later became a lecturer. In July 1879, he and his classmate Samuel D. Warren opened the law office of Warren & Brandeis in Boston. The son of a well-educated, cultured, and intellectual family, Brandeis was deeply influenced by the reform culture in New England, and he became involved in many reform efforts from transportation, to insurance, to child labor.[116] Like Untermyer, Brandeis was a millionaire in his own right, but he was not a member of the same social circles as the Morgan partners. He was also a Democrat. Over time he became a close confidant of Woodrow Wilson, who appointed him to the Supreme Court in 1916.

Brandeis had experience battling Morgan trusts having tackled the New Haven Railroad in 1907 and U.S. Steel in 1911. His experience with these large combinations led him to question the veracity of the argument that the Morgans were conservative bankers, who ran their properties for the benefit of others.[117] Several years before the Pujo Investigation, Brandeis wrote a critique of gentlemen banking arguing that interlocking director- ates gave bankers the opportunity to take advantage of both their clients and investors.[118] Like Untermyer, he believed that greater economic trans- parency was a benefit to the public welfare and a necessity for democracy. In 1913, he began a series of articles on the Money Trust in *Harper's Weekly* titled "Breaking the Money Trust," which were widely read. The articles were published the following year as a book titled, *Other People's Money and How the Bankers Use It.*[119]

In 1913 after the first articles were published, Morgan partner Thomas W. Lamont asked his old Harvard classmate, Norman Hapgood (1868–1937), the owner of *Harper's Weekly,* to set up a meeting with Brandeis.[120] A protégé of Morgan senior partner Henry P. Davison, Lamont started at Bankers Trust and moved to First National Bank when Davison became a Morgan partner. He followed Davison to J. P. Morgan & Co. in 1911.[121] A native- born son of a Methodist minister of Scotch-Irish extraction, Lamont was raised in the Hudson Valley of New York and educated at Philips Exeter Academy and Harvard University. Having written for the *Harvard Crimson,* Lamont began his career in journalism and never lost his interest in the power of mass communication. (Lamont owned the *New York Evening Post* from 1918 to 1922 and the *Saturday Review of Literature* from 1924 to 1948). As a former journalist, Lamont had a deep understanding of the importance of public image, which necessitated interacting with the media outlets that had become increasingly more influential since the turn of the century.[122]

The Pujo Hearings were a particularly important moment for Lamont, who had just recently joined the firm. During this time, he began to cement his status as the "ambassador" or "the principle image maker and ideologist of the House of Morgan."[123] Unlike his senior partners, Pierpont and Jack Morgan, Lamont was personable and outgoing, a man comfortable in the spotlight. Deeply identified with the Morgan bank, its history, and prestige,

Lamont would become the Morgan bank's bridge to the outside world, its public face and most ardent defender in the post-Pujo era. He would eventually rise through the ranks to become the firm's senior member after Jack Morgan's death in 1943 and retain that status until his own death in 1948. Ambitious and enormously self-confident, Lamont's goal in meeting with Brandeis, a man more than ten years his senior and recognized to be of vast intellect, was no less than to try and convince Brandeis that he had been mistaken all along.[124]

Lamont and Brandeis met in December 1913 at the University Club, a private men's club in New York where a majority of the American Morgan partners were members.[125] During their conversation, both repeated many of the arguments they had already made in other settings. Lamont persistently referred to the Money Trust as the "so-called Money Trust," emphasizing his belief that the Money Trust was fictitious. Lamont insisted that the Morgan firm had no power and did not make a lot of money. He claimed that directorships on company boards were responsibilities, unsolicited and undesired, necessary for good business. He defended Morgan as extremely patriotic, stating that his first concern had not been for profit for the firm but for how it would "affect the general situation." Lamont also implied that if Morgan had power, it was only because others gave it to him based on their assessment of his character. Like Morgan, Lamont did not see the banking fraternity as dangerous to the public. He believed that their relationships, such as their presence on the boards of companies, led to greater fiscal conservatism and was a source of value for their investors, one they also claimed would benefit the greater good.[126]

Not surprisingly, Brandeis disagreed with most of Lamont's positions. His main issue had to do with the question of trust. Like Untermyer, he had seen enough financial malfeasance that he did not trust men to do the right thing, especially the Morgans. He also questioned the Morgans' logic that economic crises were caused by men of bad character and their implication that their character protected the common good. By their logic, the Morgans implied that only persons of bad character went bankrupt, a theory that Untermyer, for example, had gone to great lengths to dispute during the Pujo Hearings by demonstrating the solvency of banks that had been destroyed. For Brandeis, Untermyer, and others outside of this elite group, the Morgans' ties, combined with an environment of limited government regulation of private banks, industrial consolidation, and secrecy, were the root of economic instability.

Despite their differences, Brandeis and Lamont did agree on one critical point. During their talk, Brandeis told Lamont, "I am a believer in individual property and in the rights of the individual." He stated that the Money Trust was dangerous because "it hampers the freedom of the individual." He said, "The only way that we are going to work out our problems in this country is to have the individual free, not free to do unlicensed things, but free to work and to trade without the fear of some gigantic power threatening to engulf him every moment, whether that power be a monopoly in oil or in credit."[127] Brandeis's arguments reflected his belief in the ability of capitalism to be beneficial, if regulated properly, and the ability of the social system to lead to freedom and presumably equality if the conditions were right for the protection of property. As such, his critique of the Morgan bank, like that of Untermyer, while extremely unpleasant for Lamont and the firm, was not fundamentally contradictory to capital.[128]

With the exception of some populist and socialist thinkers, most Progressive-era reformers did not think to challenge individualism and the right to private property.[129] Though Marx would have disagreed, they believed that capitalism could be beneficial if reformed properly and managed by experts. Even the argument of *Other People's Money* was essentially one that was based on the right to private property. Its main contention was over the rightful owner.[130] Just as Untermyer had argued in 1911 at the Financial Forum, Brandeis was not challenging the right of the wealthy to use their money as they saw fit. His argument was that investment bankers gambled with "corporate funds belonging to other people," or "other people's money."[131] He believed that the profits that bankers earned did not rightfully belong to them because they were made by using the funds of ordinary citizens, who had no say in how their money was invested. For this reason, he focused on the lack of transparency and on ties, such as interlocking directorates, through which bankers were alleged to have gained access to "other people's money" in the form of the funds and deposits of insurance companies, trust companies, and commercial banks.[132]

Lamont and Brandeis's conversation shows they shared a fundamental commitment to the right of privacy. In practice this meant that despite Brandeis's appreciation for the ways in which the Morgans' position in the financial community rested upon their relationships, and despite his emphasis on transparency, he never considered the possibility of legislating what were considered to be personal associations, which he considered to be central to the rights of the individual. For Brandeis, the state's justification for its interference into the affairs of private business was precisely to defend the rights of the individual to exist separate from it. Thus, when the Morgans agreed to step off of interlocking directorates or reduce stock-holding interests, they agreed to expand the boundaries of the firm's business under public scrutiny, but they also reaffirmed its limitations. In their efforts, whether they realized it or not, Brandeis was an important ally.

This is not to say that Brandeis or Untermyer's disagreements with investment bankers were fictitious. They were real adversaries for Morgan and his bank, with whom they had mostly negative contact and from whom they remained largely separate, each side brooding in the conviction of their righteousness. But if we try to understand the differences in their relative positions within American society and appreciate their ideological commonalities, a much more socially complex reality emerges, one that has been overshadowed by the controversy of the Money Trust. The key is appreciating the extent to which both private bankers and progressive critics were embedded in their society and their time. By studying the situation more broadly, we can see other questions and interests related to the division between public and private property that would have the greatest long-term consequences for any economic reform, the shape it would take and whose interests it would support.

RACIAL INEQUALITY AND THE RIGHT TO PRIVACY

Brandeis actually wrote the standard on the right to privacy, which he tied directly to the right to property. In an essay in the *Harvard Law Review* (1890), Brandeis stated, "The right of property in its widest sense, including all possession, including all rights and privileges, and hence embracing the right to an inviolate personality, affords alone that broad basis upon which the protection which the individual demands can be rested." Thus, he included in the right to property, "every form of possession—intangible, as well as tangible" including "the right to enjoy life, the right to be let alone."[133] After Brandeis ascended to the bench in 1916 and until he retired in 1939, he continued to defend the right to privacy as one of the most important rights in the civilized world (*Olmstead v. United States* 1928).[134]

Brandeis's support for the right to privacy was so fundamental that despite his reputation for supporting causes of social justice, he accepted the precedent set by the Supreme Court's 1896 decision, *Plessy v. Ferguson*.[135] Best known for establishing the separate but equal doctrine that served as the foundation for Jim Crow, *Plessy v. Ferguson* was also a landmark case on the right to property and the right to privacy. It stated that while the Fourteenth Amendment prevented states from discriminating against its citizens, the amendment's jurisdiction did not extend to the actions of private individuals.[136]

The court's decision was intimately tied to its understanding of racial inequality. It assumed that inequality was based on assessment of individuals, who were defined and judged differently because of supposedly natural and immutable characteristics. All individuals were not privy to the same rights because all individuals were not considered inherently equal. In other words, the law would not legislate against private discrimination because social customs and traditions, including those that determined whiteness to be a form of property, were beyond the scope of the law. Justice Henry Brown argued:

> Legislation is powerless to eradicate racial instincts or to abolish distinctions based upon physical differences, and the attempt to do so can only result in accentuating the difficulties of the present situation. If the civil and political rights of both races be equal, one cannot be inferior to the other civilly or politically. If one race be inferior to the other socially, the Constitution of the United States cannot put them on the same plane.[137]

Contrary to the court's view that property was based on individual abilities, the *Plessy* case demonstrates the larger historical conflicts at stake in the private versus public debate. It serves as a reminder that private property was about relationships, not just privileges or possessions. It was also implicitly a structure of exclusion, one that was not "natural" as many Progressives also believed, but was so deeply embedded in American society that a civil war had been fought over its definition.[138]

The *Plessy* decision may seem far afield from the world of banking given the almost complete absence of African Americans in the field of investment banking before the late twentieth century, but this is not the case.[139] If it was an example of the historical stakes inherent in the debate over the right to property, it was also a sign of the social and political conditions that structured economic relations at that time, which were as important to private investment bankers as the state of American national development. In practice, the *Plessy* decision had important consequences and not just for the segregated South or for African Americans.

Because the Morgan partners on both sides of the Atlantic were white, Protestant men, it has been assumed that gender and race were not significant to them or to their work. Nothing could be further from the truth. For the Morgan bank and partners, the *Plessy* case meant that as long as the scope of the Fourteenth Amendment did not apply to the actions of private individuals, and as long as the right to property, privacy, and association retained a broad spectrum of support from a cross-section of diverse parties, so too would their ability to pursue private, as opposed to public, relationships through which they communicated and accessed resources and information.

In other words, the social hierarchies deeply embedded in the customs, traditions, and the legal institutions of the country also served to further the development of interclass and intraclass alliances around the protection of private behavior from state intervention, one whose implications would be apparent not only in domestic affairs but also international politics. And precisely because certain ties, in particular those based on perceived differences, were so critical to the ways in which economic networks of private bankers were organized and made meaningful, they were taken for granted. This was so much so the case that the ways in which state power supported this structure were also made virtually invisible.

Unfortunately, historians have made natural the idea that the history of investment banking can be written separate from the history of race relations that was so central to the structure of American society at that time. In doing so, they have affirmed the popular perception that the financial world operated by its own rules separate from the rules of its society. Businessmen may not have originated social and economic hierarchies, but they were affected by them, also deeply committed to them, and enabled by them. That race and gender hierarchies were important to the world of gentlemen bankers and their relations within the financial sphere is the subject to which we now turn.

## CHAPTER TWO

The Social World of Private Bankers

TO SAY THAT African Americans were absent from the world of investment banking is not to say that race was unimportant to gentlemen bankers or even that they had no relationships of importance with persons of African American descent. In their lifetimes, Pierpont Morgan and his son, Jack, did have one significant relationship with a person of African American descent. It was not, however, within the world of finance and had one important reservation. That person was Belle da Costa Greene, their private librarian.

Greene (1879–1950) was born in Washington, DC, and raised in New York City. Her father, Richard Theodore Greener, was the first African American man to graduate with an undergraduate degree from Harvard University (Class of 1870). A graduate of the University of South Carolina's Law School and an associate of Booker T. Washington, Greener was one of the rare African Americans in the foreign service. During Theodore Roosevelt's presidency, he served as U.S. Commercial Agent in Vladivostok and consul in Bombay, India. He later became the dean of Howard University's law school.[1] As her name suggests, despite her father's relative social capital, Belle Greene apparently had no contact with him. She lived with her mother, who "was listed variously in New York city directories as Greener, Greene, and V.V. (Van Vliet)."[2]

Greene's relationship to the Morgans has been of great contemporary interest because after her death it was revealed that during the entire time she was known to the Morgan family, she passed as a white woman. Whether or not the Morgans knew of her family's racial background is a matter of speculation, but her correspondence with Morgan indicates that she identified herself as being white or of the same race as him.[3] Given that she did "pass" and given the structure of "passing," it is difficult to argue that it would not have mattered.[4] The fact is that she did pass as a white woman and Morgan never acknowledged her to be anything but white.

Greene claimed that her complexion was from her maternal Portuguese grandmother, Genevieve da Costa Van Vliet, though her grandmother's real name was Hermione C. Peters.[5] She was introduced to Morgan by his nephew Junius while working as a librarian at Princeton University. She worked for Pierpont Morgan from December 1905 until his death in March 1913 and for Jack Morgan until 1924, when he formally donated the Morgan library and it became a public institution. She remained the head of the Morgan library and retired in 1948. In 1949, the year before she died, *Time* magazine did a story on Greene that remarked upon her mysterious and private ways. It stated that she been born abroad, "Portugal, some friends guessed."[6]

By all accounts and judging from their correspondence, Greene and Pierpont had a close relationship. Though she clearly deferred to Pierpont, calling him "Big Chief," she became an important figure in the art world because of her proximity to the Morgans and of the trust she was given to negotiate purchases for their famed art collection.[7] She was very attached to Morgan, the man to whom she wrote in what would be her last letter before his death, "I do hope that you will never know the distress, I may well say torture that we suffered here upon learning that you were ill. It was almost unbearable . . ." (Underline in the original).[8] After Morgan died, she wrote, "My heart and life are broken."[9]

Little has been studied in regard to the significance of Morgan's relationship with Greene in his work in the field of finance. Greene was also a woman and thus ensconced in Morgan's domestic world on Madison Avenue

PHOTO 5 Belle Greene, October 1, 1929 (Library of Congress, Prints & Photographs Division, [reproduction number LC-USZ62–93225])

not on Wall Street. At the time, women were not allowed on the Morgan bank's trading floor and only invited to the bank on New Year's Day when the bank was closed.[10] Greene's race also distinguished her from other women even in Morgan's private circles. The fact that she had to pass as a white woman to enter into the inner sanctum of the Morgans' world, domestic or public, is itself a significant statement about the hierarchies of their world.

The very invisibility of African Americans reminds us that the society in which the Morgans lived was an unequal one in terms of race and gender. But unfortunately, the exclusion of African Americans from the social and economic spheres of gentlemen bankers has also allowed historians to write as if race did not matter. As we shall see, the Morgans' nonbanking interests, particularly those related to their social relations or social capital, were structurally important to the internal organization of the firm and to their relations outside the firm.[11] By mapping the relationship between their social and economic networks in their time, we will see how central these hierarchies were to the structure and organization of private banking.

THE MORGAN MEN BEFORE THE FIRST WORLD WAR

Like most merchant banks in the late nineteenth and early twentieth century, the House of Morgan was structured as a private unlimited liability partnership. Operating in an environment where missing information was a given, legal institutions were largely absent, and international relations were complex, merchant banks built their networks on their reputation and through their relationships.[12] Because reputations, like trust, took a long time to build, private investment banking traditionally had a high barrier to entry.[13] And like trust, reputations could be lost quickly and at any time. The loss of reputation could mean both the end of a firm and catastrophic personal ruin.[14] Finding partners who could be entrusted with the name and reputation of a firm was thus critical to the survival and prosperity of a merchant bank.[15]

Before the First World War, the House of Morgan chose its partners from kinship networks like most merchant banks.[16] Family was the traditional place from which to draw capital, entrepreneurial skill, and human resources because it had a built-in basis for trust.[17] Given that the partnership was a long-term commitment of a partner's individual capital, kinship ties among partners also ensured the firm's capital was kept in the family and in the firm. For families based in business, kinship ties within the firm could also strengthen ties within the family. The closeness of social relations between kin also made it possible to monitor one's partners.[18] Business organizations identified with kinship groups also had the advantage of being able to project strength, unity, and continuity in a way that was reaffirmed by the most fundamental organizational unit in society.[19]

Families are complex and their organization is dependent upon external structures, legal, social, and cultural. In other words, they are not simply biological; they are social institutions. In general, however, attention to the internal organization of merchant banks has focused on their networks as kin groups with an emphasis on biological ties. Historically, at least since the nineteenth century in the United States and Europe, the family has been understood and accepted as the normative and dominant social unit.[20] With regard to the Morgans, the focus on the family structure has unfortunately served to overshadow other organizational elements that became more important as the century progressed and the bank became less defined by kin.

Between 1895 and 1900, there were twenty-four partners in the House of Morgan: J. P. Morgan & Co., J. S. Morgan & Co., Morgan, Harjes & Co., and Drexel & Co. Twelve, or 50 percent, had kinship ties within the firm. Morgan family members among the English partners included Walter Hayes Burns, Pierpont's brother-in-law.[21] In Paris, the Harjes family was part of the founding members of a firm that was inherited from Drexel.[22] In the American houses, J. P. Morgan & Co., the New York house, and Drexel & Co., the Philadelphia house, there were fourteen partners, seven who were bound by kinship ties. Besides Pierpont and Jack Morgan and Pierpont's son-in-law William Pierson Hamilton (a descendant of Alexander Hamilton), there were George S. Bowdoin (also a descendant of Alexander Hamilton), Bowdoin's son Temple, and two partners who were related to the Drexel family: Anthony Drexel's son-in-law James W. Paul Jr. and J. Hood Wright's stepson Edward M. Robinson, whose father John M. Robinson had also been a member of the Drexel firm (Wright married Robinson's widow).[23] (See Tables 5, 6, and 7.)

During the early period, a majority of American partners also shared a common social background. Most were the descendants of early settlers. Their wives also came from old American stock, and their fathers had also been merchants, bankers, or lawyers. Partners like Arthur E. Newbold, Robert Bacon, Charles H. Coster, and Charles Steele were not tied to others by kinship, but they were similar to the other senior partners in background.[24] Arthur Newbold's father was a merchant banker in Philadelphia. Newbold's wife, Harriet Dixon, was the granddaughter of George Mifflin Dallas, U.S. vice president under President James Polk and former U.S. ambassador to Great Britain under President Franklin Pierce.[25] Charles Coster's grandfather, who was Dutch, immigrated in the late eighteenth century. His family was involved in merchant trade between New York and the East and West Indies and his maternal grandfather, Nathaniel Prime, was also a New York banker. Robert Bacon's "ancestors were among the first settlers of Massachusetts."[26] His father, William B. Bacon, was also a merchant banker, "a prominent merchant in the China trade, [and an] agent for the London banking firm of Baring Brothers."[27] Charles Steele's ancestor, Henry Steele, immigrated to the American colonies from England in 1730. Steele's father, Isaac Nevett Steele, was also a lawyer and diplomat from Maryland, who served as the charge d'affaires to Venezuela, 1849–1853. Steele's mother, Rosa Landonia, was the daughter of John Nelson, the Attorney General of the United States.[28] (See Table 8.)

Table 5 The House of Morgan American Partners, 1895–1919
(Refers to the date of entry into the partnership)

Name	Main Affiliation	Date of Birth	Date of Death	Date Became Partner in Newly Formed J. P. Morgan & Co./Drexel & Co.*	Date Left Firm if Before Death
J. P. Morgan Sr.	Senior Partner	1837	1913	1895	
J. P. Morgan Jr.	Senior Partner	1867	1943	1895	
Robert Bacon	JPM & Co.	1860	1919	1895	1902
George S. Bowdoin	JPM & Co.	1833	1914	1895	1899
Temple Bowdoin	JPM & Co.	1863	1914	1895	
Charles H. Coster	JPM & Co.	1852	1900	1895	
Arthur E. Newbold	Drexel & Co.	1859	1920	1895	
James W. Paul Jr.	Drexel & Co.	1851	1908	1895	
Edward M. Robinson	Drexel & Co.	1868	1910	1895	
Edward T. Stotesbury	Drexel & Co.	1849	1938	1895	
George C. Thomas	Drexel & Co.	1839	1909	1895	1905
W. Pierson Hamilton	JPM & Co.	1869	1950	1900	1922
Charles Steele	JPM & Co.	1857	1939	1900	
Edward F. Whitney	JPM & Co.	1857	1928	1900	1911
George W. Perkins	JPM & Co.	1862	1920	1901	1910
Henry P. Davison	JPM & Co.	1867	1922	1909	
Thomas W. Lamont	JPM & Co.	1870	1948	1911	
William H. Porter	JPM & Co.	1861	1926	1911	
Horatio G. Lloyd	Drexel & Co.	1867	1937	1912	
Dwight W. Morrow	JPM & Co.	1873	1931	1914	1927
Edward R. Stettinius	JPM & Co.	1865	1925	1916	
Thomas Cochran	JPM & Co.	1871	1936	1917	

* Traditionally a partner's entry to a firm happened on the last day of the year. For example, 12/31/1899 is thus listed as 1900. Also refers to the date entered JPM & Co. (as opposed to only Drexel & Co.).

Source: "Articles of Partnership, 1894–1908" and "Articles of copartnership, J. P. Morgan & Co., 1916–1939," Morgan Firm Papers, ARC 1195, Boxes 1 and 5, PML. For sources of biographical information on individual partners, see endnotes.

Table 6 The House of Morgan British Partners, 1895–1940*

Name	Main Affiliation*	Date of Birth	Date of Death	Date Became Partner**	Date Left the Firm if Before Death	Family Tie to Another Partner (When Joined Firm)	Private (US)/Public (UK) Preparatory School or University if Known
J. P. Morgan Sr.	Senior Partner	1837	1913	1890		Yes	St. Paul's, Harvard University
J. P. Morgan Jr.	Senior Partner	1867	1943	1898		Yes	
Robert Gordon	JSM & Co.	1829	1918	1885	1900		The Academy (Dunfries, Scotland)
Frederick William Lawrence	JSM & Co.	N/A	N/A	1885	1900		
Walter H. Burns	JSM & Co.	1838	1897	1890		Yes	Harvard University
Clinton E. Dawkins	JSM & Co.	1859	1905	1900			Cheltenham, Balliol College, Oxford
Walter Spencer Morgan Burns	JSM & Co./MG & Co.	1872	1929	1898	1909	Yes	Eton, Trinity College, Cambridge
Edward Charles Grenfell	JSM & Co./MG & Co.	1870	1941	1904			Harrow, Trinity College, Cambridge
Vivian Hugh Smith	JSM & Co./MG & Co.	1867	1956	1905		Yes	Eton, Cambridge
Charles Frederick Whigham	MG & Co.	1872	1938	1912/1918***			
Michael George Herbert	MG & Co.	1893	1932	1924			

Table 6 (continued)

Name	Main Affiliation*	Date of Birth	Date of Death	Date Became Partner**	Date Left the Firm if Before Death	Family Tie to Another Partner (When Joined Firm)	Private (US)/Public (UK) Preparatory School or University if Known
Thomas Sivewright Catto	MG & Co.	1879	1959	1928	1941		
Randal Hugh Vivian Smith	MG & Co.	1898	1968	1930	1967	Yes	Eton, Sandhurst
Francis James Rennell Rodd	MG & Co.	1895	1978	1933	1967	Yes	Eton, Balliol College, Oxford
William Edward, 2nd Viscount Harcourt	MG & Co., Ltd.	1908	1973	1939	1967	Yes	Eton, Oxford
Wilfred William Hill Hill-Wood	MG & Co., Ltd.	1901	1980	1939	1967		Eton, Trinity College, Cambridge

* The House of Morgan's European branches have a much older pedigree than J. P. Morgan & Co. Only firms and partners of firms between 1895 and 1940 were included in the table with the exception of a copartnership agreement made between J. P. Morgan and John Harjes in 1893 after the death of Anthony Drexel. (According to the 1893 partnership agreement, J. P. Morgan was "acting in the name of Drexel & Co., Drexel, Morgan & Co.") The British firms are as follows: J. S. Morgan & Co. (1864–1909), Morgan, Grenfell & Co. (1909–1934), Morgan, Grenfell & Co. Ltd. (1934–1988). Though MG Ltd. was legally separate from the other Morgan houses, the relationships continued as before, so they are included.

** Traditionally a partner's entry to a firm happened on the last day of the year. For example, 12/31/1894 is thus listed as 1895. In the case of Morgan, Grenfell & Co., Ltd., this could also mean the date became a director.

*** Charles F. Whigham made general partner in 1918. He became a salaried partner in 1912. (Kathleen Burk, *Morgan, Grenfell 1838–1988: The Biography of a Merchant Bank* (New York: Oxford University Press, 1989): 65).

Source: Records of the Morgan firms, ARC 1195; Box 5, Folder: Articles of copartnership, 1893, Folder: Articles of copartnership, 1907–9, Folder: Articles of copartnership, 1927–1928; Box 6, Folder: Articles of copartnership, 1931, Folder: Articles of copartnership, 1932–33, Folder: Articles of copartnership, 1934, Folder: Articles of copartnership, 1937, Folder: Articles of copartnership, 1941; Box 3, Folder: Articles of Co-partnership: J. S. Morgan & Co., 1882–1884; Folder: Articles of Co-partnership: J. S. Morgan & Co., 1885–1889, Folder: Articles of Co-partnership: J. S. Morgan & Co., 1898–1899, PML. For sources of biographical information on individual partners, see endnotes and esp. Kathleen Burk, *Morgan, Grenfell 1838–1988* and Vincent P. Carosso, *The Morgans: Private International Bankers, 1854–1913* (Cambridge, MA: Harvard University Press, 1987).

Table 7 The House of Morgan French Partners, 1895–1940*

Name	Main Affiliation*	Date of Birth	Date of Death	Date Became Partner**	Date Left the Firm if Before Death	Family Tie to Another Partner (When Joined Firm)	University if Known (Received BA or Higher Degree)
J. P. Morgan Sr.	Senior Partner	1837	1913	1871		Yes	
J. P. Morgan Jr.	Senior Partner	1867	1943	1898		Yes	Harvard University
John Henry Harjes	DH & Co./ MH & Co.	1830	1914	1893	1908	Yes	
John Henry Harjes Jr.	DH & Co./ MH & Co.	N/A	N/A	1893	1908***	Yes	
Hermann Peter Herold	DH & Co./ MH & Co.	N/A	N/A	1893	1909****		
Oscar Othon Siegel	DH & Co./ MH & Co.	N/A	1917	1893	1906		
Henry Herman Harjes	MH & Co./ M et Cie.	1875	1926	1898		Yes	
John Ridgely Carter	MH & Co./ M et Cie.	1862	1944	1914	1940		Trinity College (CT), Maryland University Law
Nelson Dean Jay	MH & Co./ M et Cie.	1883	1972	1920	1955		Knox College
Bernard Shirley Carter	MH & Co./ M et Cie.	1893	1961	1924		Yes	Harvard University, Harvard Law
Benjamin Joy	M et Cie.	1882	1968	1928	1934		Harvard University

Table 7 (continued)

Name	Main Affiliation*	Date of Birth	Date of Death	Date Became Partner**	Date Left the Firm if Before Death	Family Tie to Another Partner (When Joined Firm)	University if Known (Received BA or Higher Degree)
Maurice Charles Alphonse Paul Pesson-Didion	M et Cie.	c. 1883	N/A	1931	N/A		
Alan Vasey Arragon	M et Cie.	1893	1974	1933	N/A		Northwestern University
Harry Ashton Watkins	M et Cie.	1905	1976	1934	1941		Williams College

* Only firms and partners of firms between 1895 and 1940 were included in the table with the exception of a copartnership agreement made between J. P. Morgan and John Harjes in 1893 after the death of Anthony Drexel. (According to the 1893 partnership agreement, J. P. Morgan was "acting in the name of Drexel & Co., Drexel, Morgan & Co.") The firms are as follows: Morgan, Harjes & Co. (1895–1926), Morgan et Cie. (1926–1945). [Preceded by Drexel, Harjes & Co., 1868–1895 with ties to Drexel, Morgan & Co., 1871–1894. Morgan et Cie. became Morgan et. Cie., Ltd. 1945–1975.]

** Traditionally a partner's entry to a firm happened on the last day of the year. For example, 12/31/1894 is thus listed as 1895.

*** John H. Harjes Jr. is listed in the partnership agreements until 1908, but the exact date he left is unknown.

**** Hermann Peter Herold is listed in the partnership agreements until 1909, but the exact date he left is unknown.

Source: Records of the Morgan firms, ARC 1195: Box 5, Folder: Articles of copartnership, 1893, Folder: Articles of copartnership, 1907–9, Folder: Articles of copartnership, 1927–1928; Box 6, Folder: Articles of copartnership, 1931, Folder: Articles of copartnership, 1932–33, Folder: Articles of copartnership, 1934, Folder: Articles of copartnership, 1937, Folder: Articles of copartnership, 1941; Box 3, Folder: Articles of Co-partnership: J. S. Morgan & Co., 1882–1884; Folder: Articles of Co-partnership: J. S. Morgan & Co., 1885–1889, Folder: Articles of Co-partnership: J. S. Morgan & Co., 1898–1899, PML. For sources of biographical information on individual partners, see Chapters 2 and 5 endnotes and esp. Vincent P. Carosso, *The Morgans: Private International Bankers, 1854–1913* (Cambridge, MA: Harvard University Press, 1987).

During the course of the twentieth century, the Morgan firm's demographic characteristics began a subtle shift away from those that had given the founding partners a social basis for cohesion. It became less and less a family-based firm and, while the bank remained solidly Christian, less socially homogeneous. This was a pattern evident in all the branches of the House of Morgan. Between 1910 and 1915, for example, there were seventeen partners in the House of Morgan, twelve in J. P. Morgan & Co. and Drexel & Co. Of these twelve men only four had family ties to another partner or to a retired partner of the firm.[29] Moreover, in the American branches, starting at the turn of the century and until the end of the First World War, it was more common to see partners enter the firm whose biographical narratives read more like the model of the self-made man of "country birth," a native-born son from a previously well-to-do family or a family of limited means from non-English or non-Dutch background, and whose wives may not have been from elite old stock backgrounds but were also native born.[30]

This "populist" trend was best personified by Thomas W. Lamont, whose autobiography, *My Boyhood in a Parsonage* (1946), emphasized his humble, pious, and solidly American origins.[31] Like most of the new partners, who were born after the Civil War and came of age during the Gilded Age, Lamont was native born. And like many families of prominent men of his calling, Lamont's family had a background in the church.[32] Though his family was not wealthy, Lamont's family did not come from a working class or immigrant background. Like his older brother, Hammond, Lamont was able to attend Philips Exeter preparatory school and then Harvard University, Jack Morgan's alma mater. Lamont's ties to Exeter and Harvard were, by his own admission, his first step to becoming a Morgan partner, though shared school ties did not become a significant point of commonality among Morgan partners until after 1920.[33]

Like Lamont, newer partners before the First World War—George Perkins, Henry P. Davison, Horatio G. Lloyd, William H. Porter, Dwight W. Morrow, Edward R. Stettinius, and Thomas Cochran—had nonbanking family backgrounds.[34] Perkins's father was an insurance agent and the former head of a reformatory.[35] Both Lloyd and Porter's fathers were farmers.[36] Morrow's father was a math teacher and later the president of a college.[37] Stettinius's father was a wholesale grocer.[38] Davison's father was a farming implements salesman.[39] Unlike their senior partner and his son, the newer

Table 8 The House of Morgan American Partners, 1895–1919: Biographical Data
(Refers to the date of entry into the partnership)

Name	Family Tie to Another Partner (When Joined Firm)*	Occupation of Father if Known	Religion if Known	Attended American University (Received BA or Higher Degree)	Occupation of Wife's Father if Known**
J. P. Morgan Sr.	Yes	Merchant banker	Episcopalian		Merchant/Lawyer
J. P. Morgan Jr.	Yes	Merchant banker	Episcopalian		Merchant
Robert Bacon		Merchant & Shipper	Episcopalian	Yes	Importer
George S. Bowdoin	Yes	Lawyer	Episcopalian	Yes	Shipping merchant & Collector of the port
Temple Bowdoin	Yes	Banker	Episcopalian	Yes	Merchant
Charles H. Coster		Merchant	Episcopalian		Auctioneer
Arthur E. Newbold		Banker	Episcopalian	Yes	Farmer
James W. Paul Jr.	Yes	Lawyer	N/A		Merchant banker
Edward M. Robinson	Yes	Banker	N/A		Merchant
Edward T. Stotesbury		Sugar refiner	Episcopalian		N/A/Lawyer
George C. Thomas		Merchant	Episcopalian		Ironmaster
W. Pierson Hamilton	Yes	Businessman & Steel wheel manufacturer	Episcopalian	Yes	Banker/Farmer
Charles Steele		Lawyer & Diplomat Shipmaster & Merchant	Episcopalian	Yes	Broker
Edward F. Whitney			N/A	Yes	

Name		Religion		
George W. Perkins	Insurance agent	Presbyterian		Lawyer & Insurance agent
Henry P. Davison	Farming implements salesman & Inventor	Episcopalian		Wholesale grocer
Thomas W. Lamont	Minister	Presbyterian	Yes	Men's collar and shirt manufacturer
William H. Porter	Farmer	Presbyterian		Clerk
Horatio G. Lloyd	Farmer	Episcopalian	Yes	Military general & Lawyer
Dwight W. Morrow	President of college & Professor	Presbyterian	Yes	Railroad executive
Edward R. Stettinius	Wholesale grocer	Episcopalian	Yes	Tobacconist
Thomas Cochran	Lawyer & Dealer in Real Estate	Presbyterian		Farmer

*If a partner was related to another partner at the time of the reorganization in 1895, this was counted as a family tie.

** Separation of different occupations with a slash refers to multiple marriages.

Source: For sources of biographical information on individual partners, see endnotes, especially Chapter 2 and for the earlier period, Vincent P. Carosso, *The Morgans: Private International Bankers, 1854–1913* (Cambridge, MA: Harvard University Press, 1987) and Vincent P. Carosso, "The Morgan Houses: The Seniors, Their Partners, and Their Aides," *American Industrialization, Economic Expansion, and the Law*, ed. Joseph R. Frese, S. J and Jacob Judd (Tarrytown, NY: Sleepy Hollow Press, 1981): 1–36.

American partners had little prior exposure to Europe. Their entrée into the firm was based in large part on their association with firms connected to the Morgan firm like New York Life (Perkins), First National Bank (Davison and Lamont), Chemical National Bank (Porter), General Electric Co. via the law firm Reed, Simpson, Thacher & Bartlett (Morrow), Diamond Match Co., (Stettinius), and Liberty National Bank (Davison and Cochran).

Several key partners came to the attention of the firm through certain deals or events that required interfirm cooperation like the Panic of 1907 (Lamont), the First World War (Stettinius), and, after the war, the reconstruction of Germany (Gilbert). This is one commonality they shared with partners who entered before or in 1900, who were not family members and came from firms with whom the Morgans had ties: Robert Bacon (Lee, Higginson & Co., E. Rollins Morse & Bros.), Charles Coster (Fabbri & Chauncey), and E. F. Whitney (Jacob Rogers & Co.). These examples and the fact that new partners generally contributed very little initial capital to the Morgans lent credence to the perception that the Morgans were more meritocratic than their competitors.[40]

It is important to recognize that the Morgan firm chose its partners and associates from a particular background. In other words, the identity of the firm was a goal, not a given. If the Morgan identity was the result of concerted efforts and decisions, their cohesion was not the consequence of natural, inherent, or immutable characteristics. Even their religious affiliation, which was such an important sign of one's rank and class in American society, was subject to change. Christian identity was not, in other words, monolithic. The vast majority of the Morgan partners were Episcopalian, like their senior, which was also consistent with elites in other cities during this time.[41] But they were not entirely so, and they were not necessarily born into the Episcopalian faith.[42] Lamont was raised Methodist as his father was a Methodist minister, but he became a member of a Presbyterian church.[43] Edward Stettinius was raised Catholic, but he converted to Episcopalianism, the religion of his wife. Later in his life, he was not able to reconcile his beliefs and resigned his position as vestryman in St. James Episcopal Church. (When he died, however, he was buried in the cemetery of an Episcopal church in Long Island).[44]

As their individual histories suggest, each partner was part of the world outside the firm, with his own interests and past. His behavior and values were reflective of his "habitus," which, while international in scope, was local in practice.[45] For all of the Morgan men, becoming a partner, the Holy Grail of banking partnerships, became an important part of their identity. It was a sign they had arrived at a greater position in the world than the one to which they had been born.[46] For the same reason, they, like most of the future partners of the House of Morgan, would implicitly have to confront the issues of authenticity and belonging in ways that were not asked of the founding partners. Even though diversification allowed the firm to access resources and talent beyond the family, it created other challenges with regard to social cohesion.

With the exception of E. F. Whitney, who was a bachelor, each partner was also the head of a family unit.[47] Because of the personalized structure of the firm, a partner's behavior in the outside world and that of his family reflected upon the character of the firm, the degree of his identification with the firm, his respect for the senior partner, and his taste, conservatism, and judgment. Whatever his background, a Morgan partner had to find a way to become part of the group, to take on the mantle of the Morgan partnership. In these matters, they looked for direction to their senior and men of his class and social standing. Their choices reinforced their tie to the firm as an institution, to the other partners, and to the identity of the firm, which they adopted as their own.

THE DOMESTIC SPHERE

The first indication that the division between social and economic worlds does not conform to the reality of investment banking is the fact that being a successful private banker involved more than one's abilities. It also involved the projection of an identity that others could respect, an essentially conservative image that signified the stability, decency, and confidence that was central to the reputation of the bank.

The early Morgan partners' morals and values were similar to those of upper-class Victorian England, which influenced the social world in which they lived. Within that society, the family was the central unit, one that was reinforced and recognized by law and custom, and one that defined separate and unequal spheres for men and women based on cultural and historical understandings of gender, law, and religious doctrine. The domestic sphere was supposedly a private one, but it was reinforced by public and social customs and structures. Within this world of bourgeois relations, a man's domestic life, like his marital status, was a statement of his "standing in the community and state."[48] This was the case for the entire period in which the firm was a private partnership.

In many ways, in the period before the Second World War, the Morgan partnership was structurally similar to the institution of marriage. Partners shared the risks and benefits of the firm's business, contributed to its social and economic capital, and were bound by legal ties and kinship. Relationships with partners involved the sharing of information, resources, and responsibilities. In 1927, Thomas W. Lamont wrote Jack Carter, one of the Paris Morgan partners, that the New York partners were spending a great amount of time and thought on who would replace Herman Harjes, the senior partner in Paris, who died in a riding accident the year before. "When it comes to your choosing a partner," Lamont wrote, "it is just as difficult and just as important as choosing a wife."[49]

Like a marriage, a partnership was assumed to be a close, long-term relationship. As reflected in the rate of attrition, the strength of a Morgan partnership was substantial. Historically, major changes in the Morgan firm's partnership were involuntary, instigated by the death of a partner. Of the twenty-seven partners in J. P. Morgan & Co. and Drexel & Co. who left the firm between 1895 and 1940, fifteen partners died while still a partner. Another twelve left while still alive, but included Henry S. Morgan, William Ewing, and Harold Stanley, who left in 1935 to form Morgan Stanley & Co. after the passage of the Glass-Steagall Act.[50] Not including H. S. Morgan, Ewing, and Stanley, approximately 63 percent of the partners who left between 1895 and 1940 did so only because they died. Of the remaining 37 percent (nine partners), two left citing poor health: Robert Bacon in 1902 and George C. Thomas in 1904.[51] Two partners left for prestigious opportunities outside the field of banking. Dwight Morrow left in 1927 to become ambassador to Mexico under President Calvin Coolidge, who was a close friend and had been a classmate at Amherst College. (He later served as a senator for New Jersey).[52] Thomas S. Gates left in 1930 to become the president of the University of Pennsylvania.[53]

Three partners left for destinations unknown. George Bowdoin, one of the original members of J. P. Morgan & Co., left in 1900. Edward F. Whitney left in 1910 stating that he "desired to retire from active business."[54] Thomas Newhall, who left in 1936, died in 1947 of a self-afflicted gunshot wound, in what was reported as an accidental shooting.[55] At least in the case of Bowdoin, who was the great-great-grandson of Alexander Hamilton, and, according to Jack Morgan, "a life-long friend of Father (Pierpont Morgan) and a very great gentleman," it is certain that he did not leave because of a rift with Pierpont Morgan. (Bowdoin's son, Temple, was also a Morgan partner at that time).[56]

The same is probably not true for William Hamilton, Pierpont Morgan's son-in-law and another Alexander Hamilton descendant, who left in 1922. In 1924 Hamilton remarried in California, and it was only then that it became public that he and Juliet Morgan, Morgan's daughter, had divorced. Though publicly the firm said that Hamilton was leaving the firm to look after his "private investments," Jack Morgan's cryptic letters to his mother speak otherwise.[57] In 1923, the year after Hamilton left the firm and the year before Hamilton remarried, Morgan wrote to his mother stating that "Billy" had gone crazy. He said, "If I did not honestly believe him insane there is nothing I could not be willing to do to annoy him. . . ."[58]

George W. Perkins, who became a partner in 1900 and left in 1910, also did not leave the firm on good terms. The fact that Perkins was a bit of a rogue and had a healthy sense of ego is readily apparent in his testimony at the Pujo Hearings. He was one of the few witnesses, if not the only witness, who refused Untermyer's request to stop talking.[59] Perkins had come from New York Life, and when he first arrived at the Morgans, he refused to give up his formal connections with the insurance company against Morgan's objections. Perkins also had a female secretary, which diverged from Morgan's practice of excluding women from the bank.[60] These incidents demonstrate Perkins's desire to conduct business his way, which eventually led to conflicts with Morgan. According to Lamont, Perkins was asked to leave because Morgan felt he had not handled some deals in a satisfactory manner. In any case, Perkins left the House of Morgan under a shadow, but he was one of the few to do so.[61]

Morgan's London house of J. S. Morgan & Co. (Morgan, Grenfell & Co.) followed a similar pattern. Of seven partners/directors, who left between 1895 and 1940 (not including Pierpont Morgan), four (Robert Gordon, Frederick William Lawrence, Oscar Othon Siegel, and Walter Spencer Morgan Burns) retired before they died. If we include Pierpont Morgan, Edward Charles Grenfell, who died in 1941, Thomas S. Catto, who left in 1941, and Jack Morgan, who died in 1943, the percentage decreases to 36 percent. Of the four houses, Morgan, Harjes & Co. (Morgan et Cie.) was the relative exception.[62] Of twelve men who were partners between 1895 and 1940 (not including Pierpont or Jack Morgan), seven left during that period, approximately six before they died. (The percentage also increases if we include Harry Watkins, who left in 1941. Two are unknown.)

Morgan, Harjes & Co., was the least prestigious of the four houses in terms of its relative stature in its respective country as well as its standing in the House of Morgan (with the close second of Drexel & Co., which was, however, highly regarded in Philadelphia circles). But given the fact that most of the partners were American, it is more likely that a partner's desire to return to the United States played an important factor.[63] With this exception, when we look at the Morgan bank as a whole between 1895 and 1940, the majority of the American and British partners did not leave " 'til death do us part." In other words, the bonds between partners were considerable. The Morgan partnership was not exactly like a marriage in the late nineteenth and early twentieth centuries, of course, in that it was homosocial. The exclusion of women did not imply, however, that they were not important. Rather, the social organization of the partners was closely tied to their relationships with women but in complicated ways.

Because individual needs, desires, and choices could bring one's own commitments into question, an important characteristic of a successful banker was his sense of discretion. History is full of stories of people who do not always do what they should do or want to do. Many upstanding Victorians in England were known to have lived un-Victorian lifestyles, and their American compatriots were no exception.[64] Pierpont Morgan, for example, was estranged from his wife, Fanny Tracy Morgan (1842–1924), for many years.[65] Around the 1890s, he began to have affairs with other women. His affairs with Mrs. Edith Randolph, whom Fanny referred to in her diary as "Mrs. R.," and Mrs. Adelaide Douglas were hinted at in the society pages and were known to those in close proximity to him.[66] Though he was not "furtive," he was more open in his behavior when in Europe, or away from home (and his wife), and "he surrounded himself with people he trusted not to talk."[67]

Morgan held his staff and his partners to the same standard.[68] Discretion, not monogamy, was the key to a banker's image, though even the most discreet of affairs could have unfortunate and public consequences. In 1915, partner Henry P. Davison (1867–1922) was engaged in an extramarital affair with Mrs. Adele Boocock. The Boococks and Davisons had been neighbors, and Adele was a good friend of Davison's wife, Kate. Adele's husband, Howard, was the treasurer of the Astor Trust Co. and a Yale graduate (A.B. 1900). After Howard found out about the affair, he came home early from work, dressed for dinner, and read the newspaper in his library. Then he went into the drawing room, shot and killed his wife while she was playing the piano, and committed suicide. He did not leave a suicide note. The *New York Times* reported that the couple's relatives said the Boococks were "perfectly happy" or "ideally happy" and that no reason could be found for his actions. Because Davison's involvement remained entirely hidden, the firm itself was not affected by his actions, though the personal consequences were certainly great.[69]

The importance of discretion highlights the fact that a private banker's reputation depended on how he was seen by others.[70] The appearance of Morgan's commitment to the institution of marriage is an example of how he saw his relationships outside the firm and his behavior in the world outside of business as being tied to his identity and reputation as a merchant banker, one that had to represent stability, reliability, and conservative values. Though Morgan was not bound by "bourgeois convention" and though "in his attitudes and behavior he had more in common with the British aristocracy—and with his father—than with the social arbiters of the American drawing room," he did abide by certain New York society rules. Divorce, for example, was out of the question.[71]

The fact that a banker's image was tied to that of his family life shows that his status affected many others outside the firm. Even though Morgan and his wife did not get along, he also never considered divorce because of his appreciation for what it would do to Fanny, and how it would affect her sense of self and her social standing—how others viewed and treated her. His compromise was to respect her position as his wife but to spend as much time apart from her as possible. Fanny, while not happy with the arrangements, accepted the state of things.[72] She compensated for the lack of love in her marriage with her relationship to her children, particularly her only son, Jack, with whom she was very close.[73]

As an individual, Fanny did not have many alternatives.[74] Because she was a woman, her position in life and her status was intimately united with that of her father, her husband, and her son. Jack acknowledged her situation, writing to her in 1889, "There are certainly some drawbacks to belonging to a busy man no matter how fine he may be as I believe you have sometimes found out."[75] Had Fanny tried to divorce Morgan, it would have meant the reorganization of her identity and her entire world—emotionally, culturally, physically, socially, and financially. Even though her position depended in large part on the ways in which her political, cultural, social status was determined by her gender, she would have suffered the consequences largely on her own or as a private individual. Given that she lacked political rights and economic self-sufficiency, and knowing what divorce would mean to her children, personally and socially, she, like the majority of the women in the partners' families, took Morgan's interests as her own.

To be sure, not every family member was entirely cooperative. Families are complex, and conflict is not uncommon. Pierpont Morgan had a complicated relationship with Anne, his youngest child. Even though she became Pierpont's traveling companion after the marriage of her sister, Louisa, Anne was also deeply involved in public activities that did not sit well with her father. She never married and she actively developed her own interests and passions, such as women's worker reform and labor movements.[76] Lamont's son, Corliss, had similar sentiments about the working class but went further by becoming a socialist and a supporter of communist Russia.[77]

Like other families, elite families were not monolithic, but they were able to accommodate what appeared to be largely the quirks and opinions of individuals as long as conflict within the family remained private. Particularly if those individuals continued to be dependent upon the financial and social capital of their fathers, heads of families had substantial leverage because of the ways in which the social and economic status of the individual family member was dependent upon the status of the family in general, for both men and women. This was the case with Anne Morgan, who received annual income from her father and who was much in demand in women's and civic clubs precisely because she was the daughter of Pierpont Morgan.[78]

Though elite white women like Fanny Morgan were themselves circumscribed by patriarchy, they could gain positions of influence for themselves and they closely policed the relations of the family.[79] They were equally committed to protecting their houses "from bad lots," a term Jack Morgan used when writing to his mother in 1898.[80] Both the men and women of the house had strong ideas about what kind of people they could interact with, where to live, and so on. In general, they did not create these ideas on their

PHOTO 6 J. Pierpont Morgan and his wife, Frances Tracy Morgan, with their first grandson, Junius Spencer Morgan, and Mr. & Mrs. Henry Sturgis Grew, parents of Jessie Morgan (J. P. Morgan Jr.'s wife), 1892 in Cragston, NY (The Pierpont Morgan Library, New York)

own. They followed preexisting hierarchies with regard to class, social, and economic status, as did the other families of the social and economic elite. Thus, families were private, but they were also members of a larger community. For the Morgan partners, this community was the Anglo-American social elite centered in New York City.

NEW YORK SOCIETY

That the other partners followed Pierpont Morgan's lead in questions of image and taste was also reflected in their places of residence, which were in step with New York's elite in the late nineteenth and early twentieth centuries. Around the time of the Civil War, New York's elite social classes lived in the areas around Fifth Avenue, Washington Square, Union Square, and Gramercy Park. Having "moved northward from City Hall" or north of Houston Street, they continued the steady march uptown.[81] Toward the end of the nineteenth century, though some elites stayed in traditional areas like Gramercy Park, "a bastion of correct society" since the Mexican War, many congregated between the Thirties and mid-Fifties between Fifth Avenue and Park Avenue, where the Vanderbilts had settled in the 1880s. By the 1920s, they moved up into the Sixties and Seventies along the east side of Central Park.[82] As the city grew and as the technology of transportation expanded, the upper classes continued to move northward to neighborhoods that were designed to exclude the poor (and by the midcentury, out of the city).[83] During this time, a family's neighborhood became a sign of its social status.[84]

In the 1850s, when Pierpont Morgan was still a young man, he travelled by omnibus (a "horse-drawn wagon"), which he noted in his personal account ledger. The first omnibus appeared in New York City in the 1829, followed by the first horse railway (a horse-drawn wagon that ran on iron rails) that opened in 1832 and ran between Prince and Fourteenth Street along the Bowery.[85] By 1856, tracks for the horsecars ran up to Sixtieth Street along Second and Third Avenues. In 1860, thirty-six million passengers rode the horse railways in New York.[86] As a result of the transportation developments, "The northern boundary of the zone of concentrated settlement moved from Houston Street to Forty-Second Street." In the 1860s, the elevated rail lines were introduced to the city. By 1869, they ran from Dey Street to Thirteenth Street along Greenwich Street and Ninth Avenue. And by the 1880s, elevated trains ran up Second, Third, Sixth, and Ninth Avenues to the Harlem River.[87]

By the time J. P. Morgan & Co. was formally organized in 1895, the city had developed a transportation system of omnibuses, horsecarts, and elevated trains allowing for greater geographic expansion on the island and across the water. Judge J. H. Reed, who was Andrew Carnegie's chief counsel, recalled riding the "L" or the elevated train with Morgan to Carnegie's house in 1901 in order to obtain from Carnegie a formal letter that Carnegie agreed to sell his steel interests to Morgan. Elbert H. Gary also recounted a time when he traveled with Morgan on public transport after an important meeting negotiating with John W. Gates over the price for his interests that would also become a part of U.S. Steel.[88] Later in his life, Morgan no longer used public transport. He traveled by his yacht, the Corsair, and he rented a private cab (single-horse drawn carriage) from New York Cab Co. in the late nineteenth century. By the turn of the century, Morgan also had an automobile, and after the Panic of 1907, he had a car specially built for him and had a private chauffer. His world and that of other elites still depended, however, on the growth and development of transportation and city infrastructure.[89]

By 1904, New York City's first subway, the Interborough Rapid Transit (IRT) subway, was completed, accelerating that trend.[90] Kuhn, Loeb & Co.'s senior partner Jacob Schiff often walked from his home on the Upper East Side to his office in downtown Manhattan, but he was among the first chosen riders on the maiden voyage of the subway on October 27, 1904 that went from City Hall, past the Grand Central Terminal to Ninety-Sixth Street along Broadway. Jack Morgan also rode the subway, and George Baker also testified at the Pujo Hearings that he "sometimes patronize[d] the tunnel" that ran from Forty-Second Street and Madison down to Wall Street.[91] Several major trunk lines were completed by the early 1920s, when the automobile began solidifying its domination above ground.[92]

In the early 1900s and until the First World War, most of the New York Morgan partners lived in a cluster in an area known as Murray Hill, between Lexington and Madison Avenues and Thirty-Third and Thirty-Ninth Streets, which was an "older" fashionable neighborhood.[93] Not only did the New York partners live in relatively close geographic proximity to each other, they congregated around Pierpont Morgan at 219 Madison Avenue between Thirty-Sixth and Thirty-Seventh Streets. Morgan moved there in 1881 though his home, one of three brownstones on the block, had been built in 1853.[94] In 1900, with the exception of Charles Steele,[95] all of the New York partners lived within a four-block radius of Morgan's house between Thirty-Third and Thirty-Ninth Streets and Madison and Lexington Avenues.[96] The spatial distribution of residences in 1910 had similar patterns.[97] (See Figure 1.)

Just as a partner's family background, marriage and kinship ties, and residence spoke volumes about his respectability, identity, and his social capital, so did his other ties to society, such as his memberships in elite social clubs. According to Morgan's datebooks for the years 1899 and 1904–1912, about 10 percent of his activities directly involved club business or club activities. This may not appear to be much, but when we consider

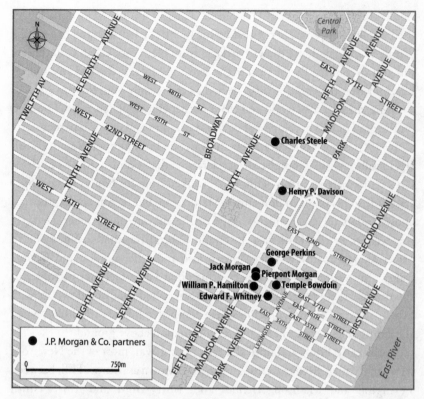

FIGURE I J. P. Morgan & Co. partners' residences, 1910

that a good percentage of his meetings involved the New York Central and Hudson River Railroad and the New Haven Railroad, which combined totaled 417 meetings (not including the secondary lines, about 20 percent) or the Metropolitan Museum of Art and the American Museum of Natural History, which combined totaled 204 meetings (about 10 percent), in comparison, his club activities were not insignificant.[98]

Social club membership was an important structural element that the Morgan partners had in common, particularly in the 1910s and 1920s. Modeled after the British social clubs, the purpose of the club system was to "ascribe status to its members."[99] Club membership has long been a mainstay in the organization of elite groups and New York in the late nineteenth and early twentieth centuries was no exception.[100] Social clubs in the nineteenth century were founded by the city's merchants and bankers to

PHOTO 7 Madison Avenue South from Corner of Thirty-Seventh Street, ca. 1910 (Homes of Pierpont and Jack Morgan), Museum of the City of New York, Photo Archive

"encourage concerted social action as much as to sustain business networks" as well as to "[enhance] their solidarity and their distinctiveness."[101] In network terms, club memberships are called affiliation ties; they reflect the way in which one's subjectivity is defined by being a member of a larger network.[102] If we were to look at the members of the eighteen banks included in the Scudder dataset for the Pujo Committee, we would find that fifty-three percent of the bankers represented were listed in the *Social Register, New York.* A small elite group, including George F. Baker, James Stillman, William K. Vanderbit of New York Central, and Henry Clay Frick, had more than eight clubs in common with Pierpont Morgan.[103]

Figure 2 includes a map of the 1910 partners' residences with nine of Pierpont Morgan's twenty-three clubs listed in the *Social Register* in that time. Though only thirty-nine percent of his clubs are shown, and Morgan belonged to more clubs than listed in the register, they include ones that Morgan partners, particularly the senior partners, frequented as members. The aggregate

FIGURE 2   J. P. Morgan & Co. partners' residences with sample of their social clubs, 1910

individual personal ties of the partners created institutional ties to elite social clubs, which, like their churches, had settled around their elite patrons uptown.[104] The location of private clubs and churches highlights the fact that the Morgan firm was an institution among other institutions with ties of its own. (See Figure 2.)

Social clubs carefully policed the admission of membership, the location of their houses, and the rules by which their members' interaction was governed. Admission was itself designed to be a remark on a person's character. Clubs were also hierarchical, with membership in the oldest and most exclusive clubs being the more prestigious. Some clubs limited the number of members. All of these elements enhanced both the status of being a member and the mutual interest created through membership.[105] Men, who belonged to the same clubs at the same time, were also able to measure the trustworthiness of other members, their adherence to norms, and their commitment to a wider community through their admission even if they did not interact as members of the club or did not have close personal ties. One thing that all private men's clubs had in common was they excluded women as members. For this reason, elite women founded clubs of their own. One example is the Colony Club, an elite women's club founded in 1903. (See Figure 2.) In 1910, Pierpont Morgan's wife, his daughters, and daughter-in-law were all members of the Colony Club. Anne Morgan was one of the founders and she was the first treasurer. (Pierpont Morgan served on the advisory commitee when the club was first organized, but he was not entirely happy about the club saying, "a woman's best and safest club is her home.")[106]

All clubs were private, but they were not secret societies.[107] Their activities were regularly reported in the press through club announcements, gossip, and the like. The *New York Times,* for example, had regular columns called "Doings in the Club World" and "Club News and Gossip," and society columns called "What is Doing in Society" and "Society News and Gossip," as did other newspapers like the *New York Tribune* ("Notes of Society" and "News of the Resorts").[108] Clubs were very much part of the urban landscape. The growth of clubs led to the creation of elite registries, such as the *Social Register,* which was first published in the United States in 1887 by Louis Keller, who aggregated the "visiting lists" of New York's elite and had been a publisher of a weekly society gossip magazine called *Town Topics: The Journal of Society.*[109]

Like private social clubs, the *Social Register* was modeled after British predecessors, such as *Who's Who,* first published in 1849.[110] Persons had to apply to be in the *Social Register,* and they had to be recommended by persons already listed, who were called "members." In this regard, it was similar to a social club itself. (In the Colony Club, non-members were initially referred to as "strangers.") Another registry, *Who's Who in America,* began publication in 1899.[111] In both the *Social Register* and *Who's Who,* members provided the information themselves. The combined listings provided a narrative of birth; family background, including parents, spouses, and children; race; religion; schooling; awards; clubs; domicile; and work. The *Social Register* was particularly significant in that a member was listed as the head of a family unit. Spouses were listed on the same line under the husband's name with the wife's maiden name in parentheses. Children were also listed in birth order with their educational affiliations. Women's clubs and junior clubs were also included. Thus, the *Social Register* data measured both an individual's and a family's social status.

The *Social Register* acted like a directory for the American elite. In 1900, when Pierpont Morgan's oldest daughter, Louisa, was engaged to marry Herbert L. Satterlee, Satterlee wrote his father saying that he was going to send a copy of the *Social Register,* "in which Mrs. Morgan & Louisa have checked all names to whom wedding invitations should be sent. . . ." He asked his father to go over it with his mother and mark down all the persons in blue (church invitations) or red (church and house invitations) whom they wanted invited from their side. Two days later, he followed up by writing his mother saying that he had express mailed the *Social Register* with a blue and a red pencil. Later, after his mother wrote him that there were people she might want to invite who were not in the *Social Register,* he told her to "Jot them down, from time to time, as they occur to you."[112] It had not occurred to him at first that there would be people outside the *Social Register* to invite to the wedding.

THE SIGNIFICANCE OF SOCIAL CLUBS

While it is clear that social clubs were important to the personal lives of the Morgan partners and their families, it does not answer the question of whether or not they had an impact on the structure of the partners' economic networks. It is a common assumption that clubs are important to business, but it is notoriously difficult to establish that business takes place within the clubs, precisely because the social and economic worlds of bankers are kept separate. Of course, certain key moments in the history of the Morgans have been tied to events in the club setting. The most important is the October 1894 meeting at the Metropolitan Club where the reorganization of the firm was determined, the first time all of the Philadelphia and New York partners were present in the same place at the same time. At a certain point during the Panic of 1907, as well, Morgan and other bankers met every night in a private dining room at the Union League Club to go over the events of the day.[113]

These meetings represent a deliberate usage of club space for the purpose of business, but clubs could also play a more subtle role in facilitating face-to-face interaction between businessmen. In December 1900, a critical moment in the founding of U.S. Steel took place when Charles M. Schwab, the president of Carnegie Steel, and Pierpont Morgan attended a dinner at the University Club in New York.[114] Their encounter led to a private meeting in Morgan's library after which Schwab arranged an outing at the St. Andrews Golf Club alone with Andrew Carnegie upon the suggestion of Carnegie's wife, Louise. In what is a well-known story, after a round of golf and lunch, Carnegie agreed to consider the sale of Carnegie Steel to Morgan.[115] These kinds of stories speak to the importance that clubs could play precisely because they were informal spaces.[116]

Anecdotal evidence aside, determining whether or not one's general activity at a club was important to one's business is a much more involved task.[117] During the Pujo Investigation, Untermyer confronted Henry Davison with the rumor that he and "the representatives of half a dozen or more banks in New York," including Francis L. Hine of First National Bank, Benjamin Strong of Bankers Trust, and Charles Sabin of Guaranty Trust, met regularly on Thursday afternoons at four o'clock for meetings at the Metropolitan Club. Davison categorically denied that any such meetings took place though he made a point of repeating the term "meeting" twice.[118]

Davison's testimony reflects how difficult it was to prove a direct relationship between social clubs and the world of finance precisely because the ostensible purpose of the private men's club was a social (not economic) space. Some clubs forbid the overt discussion of business, which was exactly the point. Trust between gentlemen was not based on transactions or self-interest but on the determination of a person's character. A club's admission of a member was an indirect affirmation of that character, one that was informally monitored by a community. The mention of business actually undermined the sanctity of that trust by suggesting that one's standing or one's relationships were founded on baser purposes.[119]

For these reasons, even though social clubs were (and are) assumed to be important to the world of business, actually establishing that this is the case is very difficult. In the case of the Morgans, to do so required investigating whether clubs were significant to the structure of the firm as an economic organization from a fundamentally empirical basis. By gathering substantial historical data on partnership capital, syndicate participations, interlocking directorates, and social club memberships, we asked the following question: Was a Morgan partner's social status outside the firm, as a measure of his social capital, important to his status within the firm? The answer is yes.

During its forty-five year history as a private partnership, the partners in the House of Morgan were strongly affiliated with the social elite regardless of the original background of the partners.[120] With regard to the American partners, if we look at the rate of social status of partners before and after they entered the firm, we find that the majority of Morgan partners were socially elite before they became partner, but they were even more so after they became partners. Sixty-eight percent were listed in the *Social Register* one year before they became partners, and 93 percent (thirty-eight of forty-one) of the partners were listed in the *Social Register* two years after they became partners. The only partners who were not listed in the *Social Register* after they became partner were those who became partner in 1939.[121]

Between 1906 and 1910, there were twenty partners in J. P. Morgan & Co., J. S. Morgan & Co. (later Morgan, Grenfell & Co), Drexel & Co., and Morgan, Harjes & Co.[122] Of these partners, fourteen were listed in the *Social Register* for New York and/or Philadelphia. All of the twelve American partners were listed in the *Social Register*. (Twelve were based in the United States, of which four were based in Philadelphia.) Only four overall were listed in *Who's Who* (Pierpont Morgan, Perkins, Steele, and Stotesbury). If we compare the incidence of social elite status among the Morgan partners to a sample of sixteen Morgan staff,[123] some who were highly regarded and worked at the firm for decades but who never made partner, we would find only two staff members were listed in the *Social Register* and only one before the First World War.[124]

In general, Morgan staff were much harder to identify and thus the sample cannot be considered definitive, but among men like Willard D. Straight, Frank H. McKnight (Henry P. Davison's brother-in-law), Leonhard A. Keyes, Martin Egan, J. A. M. de Sanchez, and Vernon Munroe, only Straight in the 1910s and Munroe in the 1920s and 1930s were listed in the *Social Register*.[125] The lack of promotion to partner was not a comment on their character. In other words, it did not have to do with the ability, character, or the loyalty of the aides. The partnership was just never within their realm of possibility.[126] The *Social Register* data suggest that this was most likely because the aides did not have the social capital necessary to become partner.[127]

The importance of social capital becomes more apparent when the relationship between a Morgan partner's club memberships is correlated with his economic capital: the percentage capital of the firm owned by that partner or the percentage of the firm's profits and losses to which a partner was liable. This percentage not only indicated the strength of his tie to the firm, it was a measure of his centrality within the firm and his status as a partner.[128] Private partnerships were hierarchical, like syndicates and private clubs. The more a partner was liable for the profits and losses of the firm, the more important he was to the firm. When Pierpont Morgan was alive, his ownership percentage dwarfed that of any other partner, from a "low" of 35 percent in 1894, 1899, and 1901 to a high of 42 percent in 1904, with an average of 38 percent between 1895 and 1913.[129] In comparison, the next two senior partners, Charles Steele and Edward T. Stotesbury, averaged around 12 to 14 percent at their peak.

Toward the end of a person's life, it was normal to see a partner cutting back on activities, including social clubs or firm activity.[130] As a partner's participation in the firm declined for reasons of health or age, so did his percentage capital in the firm and vice versa.[131] A statistical analysis must therefore measure more than the degree of activity of a particular partner over his lifetime, something more significant than a relationship with a person's normal life cycle. According to a study conducted by Pak and Halgin, a comparison between the average percentage capital of a Morgan partner within a five-year period and the partner's social club ties between 1895 and 1940 shows that the more clubs a Morgan partner in the American branches belonged to with other Morgan partners, the more likely he would become a senior partner in the future, meaning he was more likely to increase his percentage of the firm's capital in the years to come.[132]

Given that the partnership itself was hierarchical and a partner's percentage of the firm's capital was a reflection of his centrality within the firm, social clubs could thus be considered an indicator of a partner's future centrality within the firm. In other words, a member of the firm had to have the appropriate social relations in order to progress within the firm's hierarchy. Thus, clubs were not just about cohesion among the partners though strong ties to other partners through social clubs were rewarded. Clubs were also indicative of a partner's status in general and communication with the outside world.[133] Social capital was thus an important factor to being a Morgan partner, and aggregated, it was important to the firm's identity. This was in fact implicitly recognized by the world outside the firm. By 1926, when the *New York Herald Tribune* reported, "The biggest

New Year's honor that the financial world has to offer [was] a membership in the house of Morgan," *The World* reported requirements for the admission to the Morgan partnership were "exceptional ability and high social standing. . . ."[134]

The degree to which the Morgan partners were socially elite was unusual, but the fact that they were socially elite was not. In 1910, if we compare the percentage of socially elite members of banks of Morgan & Co.'s equivalent status, we would find that while 100 percent of J. P. Morgan & Co. and Drexel & Co. partners were listed in the *Social Register,* 69 percent of First National Bank directors and 68 percent of National City Bank directors between 1906 and 1910 were also listed in the *Social Register.*[135] These findings also hold true for the wider financial community. In 1912, eighty-one percent of the bankers in the Pujo dataset were listed in the *Social Register, Locater,* which meant that they were socially elite in their respective cities (mostly New York, Chicago, Boston, and Philadelphia). Of those 180 men, fifty-three percent were listed in the *Social Register, New York.*[136]

In order to place the findings in a broader time period, the social club memberships of the leading members of the Morgans' syndicate participants and associates were also studied. Based on circulars and letters inserted in the J.P. Morgan & Co. syndicate books, a list of forty-five firms, which included private firms, commercial banks, and trust companies, was created for the years 1900 until 1925. An average of twenty-three firms were studied for every five-year period. These firms had approximately thirty leading partners/presidents/chairmen of the boards during that time. Out of those men, an average of twenty-four were found in the *Social Register, New York* or eighty percent of the total for any given five-year period between 1900 and 1925.[137]

The social elite status of bankers seems to confirm the idea that the financial community was homogeneous, but this was not the case. In particular, the Morgans' social ties were distinct when compared to the German Jewish private banks of their economic stature like Kuhn, Loeb & Co.[138] Only 33 percent of partners in Kuhn, Loeb & Co. (Otto H. Kahn and Mortimer L. Schiff), 38 percent of partners in Speyer & Co. (James Speyer, Hans Winterfeldt, Charles H. Tweed), and 43 percent of partners in J. & W. Seligman & Co. (Henry, Isaac N. and Jefferson Seligman) were listed in the *Social Register, New York.*[139] Jacob H. Schiff was notably absent from the *Social Register* throughout his lifetime despite his stature within the financial community. (He was, however, listed in *Who's Who in America*.)

The Morgans and Kuhn, Loeb partners did have some clubs in common, but the type of club was very specific and the overlapping partners were extremely limited. Before 1930, only one partner, Mortimer Schiff, Jacob's son, belonged to any social club in which a majority of the Morgan partners were also members, and he only belonged to one: the New York Yacht Club. Neither Schiff nor Otto Kahn (who was the only other Kuhn, Loeb partner listed in the *Social Register* before 1935) were members of elite men's private clubs located in residential areas (that were not sports clubs), such as the Metropolitan, Union, Union League, or University Clubs. In fact, only one Kuhn, Loeb partner between 1895–1940 (Elisha Walker) was a member of the Metropolitan or University Clubs (and none in the Union or Union League Clubs) and that was not until the mid-1930s. The same applied to the only Kuhn, Loeb partner (Hugh Knowlton), who was a member of the Down Town Club (later called Down Town Association), the most elite men's luncheon club located in the business district in which senior Morgan partners were members throughout the early twentieth century. Both Walker and Knowlton were not Jewish, a point to which I will return.

By contrast, between 1895 and 1930, J.P. Morgan & Co. had substantial representation in all the top elite men's private clubs. Most J.P. Morgan & Co. partners, for example, were members of the Metropolitan Club and at the same time (Pierpont Morgan was one of the founders of the club). The only exceptions during any given five-year period between 1895 and 1930 were usually younger partners, all who eventually became members (with the single exception of E.F. Whitney). The percentage of Morgan partners in the Metropolitan Club dipped below fifty percent only after 1930. Even then, the most senior Morgan partners in the 1930s (Lamont, Jack Morgan, Leffingwell, and Steele) remained members in the club.

The Morgans' membership in the Metropolitan Club was significant not only because it tied the partners to each other, but also because it tied them to other influential members in the financial community. In every dataset noted above (the Pujo dataset of eighteen firms, the forty-five syndicate participant firms, the eight Anglo American and German Jewish banks), the Metropolitan Club was either the most central in the club network or among the top five clubs (meaning its members were among the most central and influential in the network in terms of social ties).[140]

From 1905 until approximately 1915, Mortimer Schiff and Otto Kahn had overlapping memberships with Morgan partners only in sports clubs (e.g., yacht, automobile, or whist) or downtown men's lunch clubs located in the business district. Mortimer Schiff and Morgan partner Henry Davison were both directors of the Recess Club, a men's lunch club founded in 1911, and the Kuhn, Loeb partners overlapped with several Morgan partners in the downtown men's business clubs, City Midday and India House. These ties have been interpreted as evidence of a "downtown meritocracy," and while this was true to a certain extent, there was some evidence of social separation even in the financial district. Schiff and Kahn were not, for example, members of the most elite businessman's luncheon club, the Down Town Club, while Morgan partners were. Most importantly, as we shall see, any perception of a meritocracy felt real largely because of the contrast to their lives uptown.[141]

Around 1915, Mortimer Schiff and Kahn began to overlap with several Morgan partners in civic, political, and country clubs, but again, they never overlapped in the most elite men's clubs in residential areas. And though university background became a commonality for the majority of the Morgan partners by the 1920s, the firms overlapped in terms of university background only by the mid-1930s when three Kuhn, Loeb partners were Yale graduates (including Mortimer's son, John), as were five Morgan partners. With the exception of Hugh Knowlton, who also went to Harvard Law, Kuhn, Loeb partners were not Harvard men, which also distinguished them from the Morgans and other elite private banks in New York and Boston. Moreover, at no point during the entire 1905–1940 period did any Kuhn, Loeb & Co. spouse belong to Colony, the elite women's club in which many Morgan partners' wives were members.[142]

The differences within the elite banking community in New York City were not emphasized during the government investigations into economic consolidation, such as the Pujo Hearings of 1912, which was more interested in documenting the collusion of elites. But when we study the diversity of the financial community with regard to social organization, we can better understand why it was so difficult to prove a conspiracy because of the way in which there were clusters of different groups that were largely socially separate. Given that the economic cooperation of different firms has often served as proof of the importance of economic self-interest, the assumption has been that social relations outside the financial community did not matter even if they were central to the internal organization of banks. As the Morgans' relationship with Kuhn, Loeb & Co. demonstrates, however, the situation was infinitely more complex. Interfirm relations, not just intrafirm relations, involved the close consideration of social interests and not the exclusion thereof.

## CHAPTER THREE

Anti-Semitism in Economic Networks

THE SOCIAL SEPARATION between J. P. Morgan & Co. and Kuhn, Loeb & Co. is particularly interesting given the fact that the banks had many structural and historical similarities.[1] Like J. P. Morgan & Co., Kuhn, Loeb & Co. was an unlimited liability private partnership, a merchant bank that channeled Europe's capital into American growth through a strong European network.[2] And like J. P. Morgan & Co., in the nineteenth century, Kuhn, Loeb & Co. was both subordinate in reputation (and capital) to the House of Rothschilds, the European banking family whose prestige and position they deeply coveted.[3]

In the American context, however, both banks held positions at the top of the banking hierarchy, and as leaders, they had the common concern of maintaining their position against less prestigious firms, who were always ready and willing to take their place, akin to their position vis-à-vis the Rothschilds and also Barings Brothers, a prestigious British merchant bank.[4] Both banks were also able to achieve their international and national prominence during a time of rapid and unprecedented growth in the American economy and infrastructure when there was little government regulation and a lack of centralized banking.[5] Both had senior partners with a strong sense of identity, conviction, and commitment to family, tradition, and conservative banking, who were the undisputed patriarchs of a centralized and hierarchically organized house.[6]

Kuhn, Loeb & Co. partner Otto Kahn once wrote, "It is said that as a man may be judged by the company he keeps so a company may be judged by the men it keeps."[7] Like the Morgans, Kuhn, Loeb were very careful about who they entrusted to be their partners. They also chose their partners from kinship networks but even more so because all the partners were tied to the same families. In 1895, 100 percent of Schiff's partners were related to another partner. Kuhn, Loeb did not admit a non-family member as partner until 1912.[8] The bank's kinship ties were not confined to intrafirm ties; they also extended to interfirm relations. Close social ties between partners and associates outside the firm through kinship offered a similar advantage in gaining information and monitoring and leveraging clients and collaborators.

Kuhn, Loeb & Co. shared multiple kinship ties with J. & W. Seligman & Co., another prestigious nineteenth-century American merchant banking house.[9] Isaac Newton Seligman, whom Schiff referred to as "Ike," was married to Guta Loeb, the daughter of Kuhn, Loeb & Co. founder Solomon Loeb.[10] Paul M. Warburg, another Kuhn, Loeb partner, married Loeb's daughter, Nina, so he, Seligman, and Schiff were all brothers-in-law. Paul's brother, Felix M. Warburg, also a Kuhn, Loeb partner, married Schiff's daughter, Frieda, making Paul Frieda's uncle and brother-in-law.[11]

Multiple family marriages were not unusual. Goldman Sachs & Co. did not have a non-family member until 1915 and Lehman Brothers not until 1924. The daughters of partners in Heidelbach & Ickelheimer were also married. Four partners in Hallgarten & Co. were connected by intermarriage.[12] James Stillman, the head of National City Bank, had two daughters who were married into the Rockefeller family. In 1895, his daughter Elsie married William G. Rockefeller of Standard Oil, the son of William Rockefeller and the nephew of John D. Rockefeller Sr., and William G. Rockefeller's brother, Percy A. Rockefeller, married Stillman's other daughter, Isabel, in 1901.[13]

Kinship was not the only method of creating ties between or within firms. Firms also shared ties through partner employment histories. J. P. Morgan & Co. recruited from banks with whom the firm had close

PHOTO 8 Jacob H. Schiff with family at Far View, Bar Harbor, Mount Desert Island, Maine (The Dorot Jewish Division, The New York Public Library, Astor, Lenox, and Tilden Foundations)

economic ties. Robert Bacon started at Lee, Higginson & Co., a Boston merchant bank. Henry P. Davison and Thomas W. Lamont were directors at First National Bank of New York before becoming Morgan partners.[14] Otto H. Kahn, who was married to Adelaide Wolff, the daughter of Kuhn, Loeb partner Abraham Wolff, started at Speyer & Co., a frequent Kuhn, Loeb & Co. collaborator.[15] This pattern of recruiting partners from firms with whom the bank had close ties persisted into the 1930s.[16]

Despite their structural and historical similarities, J. P. Morgan & Co. and its affiliated houses did not share kinship or partnership ties with Kuhn, Loeb & Co. or, for that matter, with J. & W. Seligman & Co., Speyer & Co., or any other German Jewish bank. Two more generations would pass before the social spheres of the two banks were connected by kinship ties.[17] As far as can be known, in their history as unlimited liability partnerships, J. P. Morgan & Co. and Kuhn, Loeb & Co. had only one direct tie by kinship and that was not until the 1930s.[18] They were fundamentally competitors; they performed essentially the same services and offered arguably the same level of service. Though the senior partners had a respectful relationship, they were not friends. Morgan and Schiff did not have, as one would call it, a close affective tie.[19]

As the social club data demonstrate, before the First World War, Morgan and Kuhn, Loeb partners generally did not patronize the same social, religious, or cultural clubs and associations. This social distance was also apparent in the geographic distance between the primary residences of the partners.[20] By the time J. P. Morgan & Co. was reorganized in 1895, Jacob Schiff lived relatively far uptown, some forty blocks away from the Morgan clique. [See Figure 3.] Given the significance of social elite affiliations to the world of J. P. Morgan and his partners, the exclusion of Jewish bankers and their geographic distance offer evidence of separate spheres. It is in this key area, that of social networks, that merchant banking networks did not overlap.

If relationship between Morgan and Schiff and that of their firms were characterized by social separation, social distance referred not just to the physical distance between the different banks but also the determination of difference itself, which was generally attributed to ethnic and religious background.[21] J. P. Morgan & Co. partners were all Protestant Christians like their senior partner. Founding partners were also from families who emigrated from Great Britain before the American Revolution, like Morgan, whose ancestor Miles Morgan arrived in 1638 from Wales.[22] Because of its history, J. P. Morgan & Co. was identified as an Anglo-American or Yankee house. Other prominent Yankee banks included Lee, Higginson & Co.; Kidder, Peabody & Co.; and Brown Brothers & Co.[23] Commercial banks First National and National City were also included in this category, even though Schiff was a director in National City between 1899 and 1914.[24]

Kuhn, Loeb & Co. partners were entirely Jewish. Though Kuhn, Loeb's partners were not equal in their observance, they shared Jewish and German origins.[25] In general, the partners also communicated with each other in German, and they had close ties to German investment houses with whom they also shared kinship ties, such as M. & M. Warburg & Co., which was led by Paul and Felix's brother Max Warburg.[26] With the exception of a few partners, most were also immigrants. For all these reasons, Kuhn, Loeb & Co. was referred to as a German Jewish bank. Other German American Jewish houses included Speyer & Co.; J. & W. Seligman & Co.; Heidelbach,

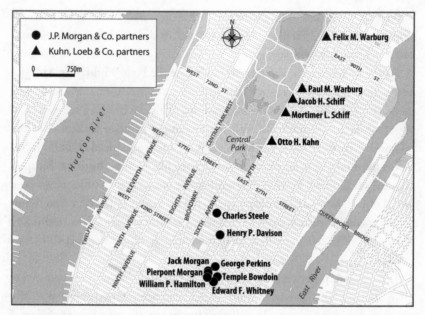

FIGURE 3 J. P. Morgan & Co. and Kuhn, Loeb & Co. partners' residences, 1910

Ickelheimer & Co.; Ladenburg Thalmann & Co.; Hallgarten & Co.; and L. von Hoffman & Co.[27]

Theoretically, social separation between firms (as compared to social separation within firms) could actually encourage interfirm collaboration. In network terms, a firm that operated only within a particular social circle inevitably limited its access to resources, capital, and information.[28] If different firms of equivalent status had access to different clients and sources of capital stemming from separate social spheres, collaboration would be an efficient use of resources and complement the firms' financial self-interest without the threat of competition. Client-investor-bank relations based on allegedly natural differences could also encourage collaboration by offering firms access to clients to whom they otherwise would not have ties or even the expectation of ties.

As the Morgans' relationship with Kuhn, Loeb & Co. demonstrates, however, history often diverges from theory. In reality, competition did not self-regulate. Financial efficiency was not the goal of all economic decisions. And without denying that financial self-interest can be an important motivator, social separation represented particular challenges for interfirm cooperation given the personal nature of investment banking.[29] If economic ties were not the primary way the firm communicated with its "friends," how did socially separate firms monitor each other? What kinds of leverage did they have? How did they access information about the other? Did they have other kinds of ties? Did they have different kinds of economic ties? What was the basis of their trust? In order to answer these questions, we must first turn to the reasons for why the firms were socially separate to begin with.

ANTI-SEMITISM BEFORE THE FIRST WORLD WAR

Kuhn, Loeb & Co. had a much higher percentage of kinship ties (almost double) than J. P. Morgan & Co. within the same time period and less diversity in terms of partner background. Thus the necessity of creating a common identification and internal cohesion through social clubs was not as structurally urgent. That was not, however, the primary reason why the incidence of common club membership was so much lower for Kuhn, Loeb & Co. and the other German Jewish banks. While not denying the significance of familial and cultural affiliations, social separation was not just the natural expression of cultural and religious differences. In the late nineteenth and early twentieth centuries, social separation was also the reflection of a negative reality that connected the history of the economic elite to that of other important historical trends of the period.[30]

The primary reason why Jewish and Yankee bankers did not socialize after hours and the reason why the incidence of social club membership was so much lower for German Jewish partners than their Anglo-American counterparts is that starting in the late nineteenth century, Anglo-American Protestant social elites and institutions discriminated against persons of Jewish background, making them unwelcome in social clubs, hotels and resorts, and the *Social Register*. During this time, Jews of all backgrounds and classes, including economic elites, found themselves excluded from institutions of higher learning and high society to an extent that had not existed before the 1880s. The result was referred to as the "five o'clock shadow" or the "nine-to-five relationship, which meant that [Jews] would have had close contact with gentile bankers and upper-class clients during the working house, but none afterward."[31]

One of the most notorious early incidents of elite anti-Semitism involved Joseph Seligman, the founder of the banking house J. & W. Seligman & Co. In the mid-nineteenth century, the House of Seligman was by far the most prestigious of the Jewish banks, with the possible exception of August Belmont & Co., who despite being the Rothschilds's American representative, did not embrace a Jewish identity.[32] The Seligmans were also tied to many if not all the prominent German Jewish families by marriage, including "the Lewisohns, the Lehmans, Kuhn, Loeb, and the Guggenheims."[33] Like Abraham Kuhn, Solomon Loeb, Philip Speyer, and August Belmont, Joseph Seligman was part of the earlier wave of German Jewish immigrants to the United States before the Civil War.[34]

Joseph Seligman (1819–1880) emigrated from Bavaria in 1837 and worked as a peddler in Pennsylvania before settling in the South. The family business eventually extended from San Francisco, New Orleans, and New York to the capitals of Europe, with a different brother (there were eight Seligman brothers and three sisters) and also their sons and brothers-in-law at different branches. (Joseph alone had five sons and four daughters.) The main house, J. & W. Seligman, which was founded in 1864, grew as a result of Seligman's efforts during the Civil War on behalf of the Republican Party. Joseph participated in a subscription with other merchants "to fit out New York's famous Seventh Regiment for active service" and later placed a large amount of U.S. government securities in Europe during the war. Through these activities, the firm became closely connected to the Republican Party and developed many political ties. Joseph's brother, Jesse Seligman, for example, was an old friend of Ulysses S. Grant.[35]

In 1877, Joseph and his family were refused admittance to the Grand Union Hotel in Saratoga, New York, on the grounds that they were Jewish or to use the term of the hotel, "Israelites." The reason given was that the hotel was losing business because Christians did not want to stay in the same place as Jews. The Seligman incident informally marked the beginning of widespread exclusion of Jews from hotels and resorts throughout the late nineteenth and early twentieth century.[36] Not only did this discrimination diminish the social capital of wealthy Jews, it was a clear example of the limits of their economic capital, in effect, a statement that there were some things that money could not buy because "Your money isn't welcome here."

For a man like Joseph Seligman, the changes were hard to bear. Some speculated that the incident led to his death three years later.[37] Unfortunately for the Seligman family, the Saratoga incident was not the only experience of anti-Semitism that they would publicly endure. In 1893, they again became the center of controversy when the Union League Club, a prestigious private men's club in New York, rejected Joseph's nephew, Theodore, for membership.

In New York society, different clubs had different reasons for their organization, and disagreements sometimes led to the formation of new clubs. Members of the St. Nicholas Society had to be descendants of settlers before the American Revolution. The Manhattan Club was a club for members of the Democratic Party and was founded in 1865. The Knickerbocker Club was formed in 1871 by members of the Union Club, the oldest private men's club in New York (f. 1836), who had wanted to limit the membership of the Union Club to only men "of Knickerbocker descent—from old established families of English and Dutch ancestry."[38] Both the Metropolitan Club, of which Pierpont Morgan was a founding member, and the Union League Club, of which Morgan had been a resident member since 1873, were also offshoots of the Union Club.[39]

The Union League Club was founded during the Civil War (f. 1863) because of a controversy around a member who had become a high-ranking Confederate official. When the member, Judah P. Benjamin, a former Democratic senator from Louisiana, was allowed to resign as opposed to being expelled from the club, other members protested by forming the Union League.[40] The new Articles of Association stated, "The condition of Membership shall be absolute and unqualified loyalty to the Government of the United States, and unwavering support of its efforts for the suppression of the Rebellion."[41] As bankers with close ties to the Republican Party, Joseph and two of his brothers, Jesse and William Seligman "were among the earliest members of the Union League Club." At the time of the incident, Jesse was a Vice-President of the club, a position he had held since 1879. He had been a member of the club since 1868.[42]

After Joseph died in 1880, Jesse became the head of the family firm. Jesse's son, Theodore, was not a partner in the bank. He was a graduate of Harvard University, Columbia Law School, and a member of the bar. He founded a law firm in 1888 with his cousins, Eugene and George Seligman.[43] When Theodore came of age, it was assumed that he would be accepted as a Union

League club member, meaning, his name would never have been submitted if the expectation were that he would be rejected. The consequences were simply too great, not only for the proposed member but also for his family. Being blackballed or expelled from a prestigious club meant being rejected from "other clubs and societies" and from the general "social life of the city's elite society" and could be "socially devastating."[44]

The Seligmans' assumptions of acceptance were justified given the fact that family ties were as common to social clubs as they were to banking houses. This was particularly true for those who were either founding members, in positions of governance, or had long histories with a club, as the Seligmans had. Multiple persons of the Morgan, Harriman, Roosevelt, Astor, Vanderbilt, and Rockefeller families were members of the same clubs (and at the same time).[45] As the Seligmans would discover, family ties could not, however, be taken for granted in firms or in clubs. Every generation had to affirm itself and decide the makeup of its members and identity. Social capital was not, contrary to popular assumption, directly transferable between generations or family members. Private clubs were also not synonymous with firms or kinship groups; they had their own rules and regulations, and they alone (or their admissions committees) chose their members. Despite the national stature of his family's firm and his family's history with the club, the Union League Club rejected Theodore for membership. According to Linton Wells, "When it came time to vote on Theodore's name, opposition to his election developed among the younger element in the club." The vote was 187 to 136. Wells writes, "Those who voted against him said they had nothing against him personally; they objected to his race."[46]

After Theodore was rejected because of his "race and religion" (in the words of Jesse Seligman), his father resigned. Pride, loyalty, and reputation dictated that he could not remain a member. *The Christian Advocate* editorialized, "Because he is a Jew, and for no other reason, Mr. THEODORE SELIGMAN was rejected. . . . There is no question but Mr. THEODORE SELIGMAN in every respect is superior in character and ability to a large number of those who voted against him, and no motive existed for it except the fact that he is a Jew."[47] (Capitalization in the original) When Jesse Seligman died the following year, his friends attributed the strain of the incident as playing a factor in his death.[48] Whether or not anti-Semitism had claimed another member of the Seligman family, after Jesse's death the only other Jewish member of the Union League Club, Edwin Einstein, resigned, citing the club's policy toward younger Jewish applicants.[49]

The Seligman/Union League incident was a very public example of the rise of anti-Semitism in the American elite during the late Gilded Age, but it was not unique. In 1910, the Metropolitan Club of Washington and the Union League Club of New York again came under fire again for restrictive admissions policies, which in the case of the Union League Club was directed against William Loeb Jr. (Loeb denied that he was Jewish. His parents were German immigrants.) Loeb was the Collector of the Port of New York and had been secretary to Theodore Roosevelt.[50] He had been recommended by Elihu Root (1845–1937), among others (Root was then a New York Senator), but was still rejected. *The New York Times* reported, "For years it has been an unwritten law of the club to exclude Jews."[51]

Pierpont Morgan was not immune to the social, cultural, and legal developments of the dominant society in which he was a prominent member. He had been a resident member of the Union League Club since 1873, and during the time of the Seligman incident, he did not register any protest. This is not because he was not interested in club life or admissions policies. Two years before the Seligman incident, he went as far as founding a rival club, The Metropolitan Club, in response to the Union Club's blackballing of his friend, John King, the president of the Erie Railroad Company, allegedly for lack of social etiquette.[52]

As the Union League Club early history demonstrates, however, discrimination against Jews was not consistent or a given. Before the late-nineteenth century, as Jesse and Joseph Seligmans' memberships attest, Jews were not thus excluded from prestigious private men's clubs.[53] Judah P. Benjamin, as well, the controversial member of the Union Club, was the son of Sephardic Jewish émigrés, who moved from the British West Indian colonies to the United States in the early nineteenth century.[54] The fact that Benjamin's ethno-religious background had not been a barrier to entry and his expulsion was due to his political beliefs is one example of how boundaries based on race, ethnicity, and religion were subject to change.

It bears repeating that the focus on ethno-racial difference is distinctly a story of the late nineteenth and early twentieth centuries, one that is even evident when we contrast J. P. Morgan & Co.'s history with that of its predecessor, Drexel, Morgan & Co. In the 1870s and 1880s, one of Morgan's partners was an Italian immigrant named Egisto P. Fabbri. Fabbri's father was from Florence and his mother was Russian. (His wife was English.) He came to the United States in 1854 and eventually founded Fabbri & Chauncey, a shipping company that specialized in South American business, with his brother Ernesto. Fabbri was known as a merchant with "extensive acquaintance and general popularity." In 1875 Pierpont Morgan asked him to join the firm as a partner in Drexel, Morgan & Co. He retired in 1881 to Florence and died in 1894.[55]

Fabbri's Italian background set him apart from all of the Morgan partners who joined J. P. Morgan & Co. after 1895 and were all native-born Americans from Anglo-American backgrounds, with the exception of Raymond Atkin and William Mitchell, who were Canadian. Even though he was exceptional in his own time, Fabbri's story reflects the extent to which the Gilded Age could be considered more open with regard to social background. His presence in Drexel, Morgan & Co. confirms impressions of the Morgans as being more meritocratic than its competitors, but more importantly, it testifies to the way in which criteria for inclusion was historically contingent. Religion was not always tied to one's ethnicity, race, or nationality (Fabbri was Episcopalian).[56]

The history of the Seligmans and the Union League Club shows how much had changed by the late nineteenth century and not for the better, despite the time being known as the Progressive era. This is not to say that the nineteenth century was a bastion of racial equality. No doubt, the rise of anti-Semitism drew on long-standing nativist and racist traditions and ideologies in American society. But the rise of anti-Semitism was also tied to changing immigration patterns that were by-products of American industrialization specific to the late nineteenth century.[57] Set within the larger conflict over the boundaries between whiteness and blackness, the diversification of American life and society disturbed many Americans, as evident in the rise of the science of eugenics, a resurgence of nativism, and an increase of violence and exclusionary legislation during this time.[58]

Between 1886 and 1916, a total of almost nineteen million immigrants arrived in the United States from Southern and Eastern Europe.[59] In the 1870s, after Russian Jews began immigrating to the United States in large numbers, fleeing the pogroms of Eastern Europe, Jews as a whole became increasingly characterized as outsiders, foreign, and different. Russian and Polish Jews were also referred to as "Orientals," which meant they were considered unassimilable. Congress reinforced this view by determining through the 1870 Naturalization Act that Asians, who were also referred to as Orientals or Asiatics, did not have the right to naturalize.[60] For European Jews, Orientalism referred to the Old-World view of Jews as outsiders. Jews, like Asians, were seen as stagnant, medieval, and foreign. Like African Americans and other racial minorities, they were characterized as intrusive and disruptive.[61]

During this time, Jews may have been classified as white insofar as they could naturalize as American citizens (though they had another option, which was to be classified as black). But the standards of whiteness in elite New York society did not directly coincide with the requirements of the state.[62] As *Plessy v. Ferguson* (1896) demonstrated so clearly, whiteness, like private property, was only meaningful in a structure of exclusion. If, as Noel Ignatiev has argued, whiteness is a social relation and not "a physical description," then in elite New York society, Jews were not white.[63]

By 1904, Morgan classified his and the British bank Barings's representative in the United States as the only "white firms in New York" and he declined to participate in an endeavor he thought "a little too Jewish."[64] This prejudice cannot be taken lightly. It reminds us that he, like other financial actors, was a social being, whose choices were historically specific and socially contingent. Recognizing this fact means acknowledging that economic actors feel and rationalize certain goals and rules as more important than financial gain, goals that could even go against their economic self-interest. Moreover, it also means that their efforts extend beyond the individual actor and involve a larger community.

If it was important for the identity of the Morgan bank to be associated with the institutions of the social elite, it was just as important for the identity of the bank in the twentieth century to be both an Anglo-American firm and a non-Jewish firm.[65] Even in the middle to late twentieth century, and even as the Morgan firm began to hire partners from outside their kin networks, they resisted accepting a partner of Jewish background. The Morgan bank did not have a Jewish director until 1963 (Lewis W. Bernard), and that was technically at Morgan Stanley & Co., a descendant of the bank that was formed in 1935. Morgan Guaranty, which was the product of the merger between J. P. Morgan & Co. and Guaranty Trust Co. in 1959, did not have a "high-ranking Jewish officer until the 1980s."[66] Kuhn, Loeb & Co., on the other hand, had its first non-Jewish partner, George W. Bovenizer, in 1928. Bovenizer, who was Baptist, immigrated to the United States from Ireland in 1880 with his family when he was an infant. He started with Kuhn, Loeb as an office boy in 1897.[67]

If the Morgan partners had ever directly expressed anti-Semitic views to the Kuhn, Loeb partners, it would have made it impossible for the firms to cooperate. Schiff, for example, would not do business with the Reading Railroad because of the public anti-Semitism of August Corbin, Reading's president. Schiff wrote Ernest Cassel, "Our self-respect forbids us to have anything to do with this man, able as he may be."[68] According to Naomi Cohen, Schiff also "refused invitations to dine at the University Club, announcing openly that he would not enter a place that barred Jews from membership" and he "and his friends consistently fought the rampant private discrimination of the early twentieth century that excluded Jews from business firms, hotels, private schools, and clubs."[69] He did not tolerate prejudice against Jews as different from and inferior to Christians in business or society.

Throughout his life, Schiff actively used the power of his social, economic, and symbolic capital to confront anti-Semitism in the United States and abroad. Kuhn, Loeb & Co.'s support of Japan during the Russo-Japanese War in 1904–1905, for example, was the result of Schiff's deep personal passion to undermine the Tsarist regime in Russia and its anti-Semitic policies, a fact that others, including the Morgans, readily acknowledged.[70] Not only did "Schiff's devotion to individual Jews and to Jewish causes [win] him the loyalty and admiration of the masses of Jews," his leadership in the Jewish communities in Europe and the United States was widely acknowledged and enhanced his influence and status at home and abroad.[71]

Schiff had his own social capital to protect, but it was not based on his association with elite Anglo-American social institutions. His social capital and reputation were based on his leadership among Jews, and he had a social community of his own, the German Jewish social and economic elite also referred to as "Our Crowd."[72] The members of "Our Crowd" were "wealthy, most were connected with the financial world; they went to the same clubs, attended the same synagogues, chose their friends and wives from within their own limited circle, were connected with the same philanthropic and communal activities, and displayed over their lifetime the same interest in German culture." They were an elite group "within but distinct from the larger society of New York City." Most importantly, they did not need to reference Anglo-American social institutions for their own standing and social capital. In fact, they would lose much by seeming to acquiesce to it in the context of discrimination.[73]

Given the nature of upper-class culture, the Morgan partners were not wont to be publicly anti-Semitic because the open expression of such views was considered crass and untoward.[74] Though Pierpont Morgan did not like Schiff personally, he respected him. When Morgan interacted with him face to face, as was a normal part of their business, he treated Schiff as though he was glad to see him.[75] That is not to say that the tension and threat of rupture ever really disappeared. While Schiff was the senior partner of Kuhn, Loeb & Co., however, the likelihood of these direct incidents was also considerably lower than for future generations. This is precisely because, unlike his son, Mortimer, or his partner, Otto Kahn, Jacob Schiff was not the kind of person who sought acceptance in Anglo-American Protestant dominated associations. Again, this was not because he feared rejection but because, as he wrote in 1914, "Personally I do not believe in the desirability of assimilation."[76]

THE SEPARATION OF THE SOCIAL AND ECONOMIC SPHERES

In 1898, Schiff had a series of correspondence with Bishop Henry Codman Potter (1835–1908), who was the diocesan bishop of New York and a close friend of Pierpont Morgan.[77] In the course of writing Schiff with regard to some business related to the Montefiore Home (a charity hospital that Schiff founded with other Jewish philanthropists to treat persons with chronic illnesses), Potter wrote Schiff a letter where he detailed his views of Jewish bankers. In the letter, Potter plainly stated that he had been told on good authority that the Jewish race was "the only race in Wall Street whose word is not as good as its bond, that is, among business men of recognized rank and character." In the same letter, he wrote Schiff that "the hostility to the Hebrew is because, in ordinary business and personal transactions, he is tricky and untrustworthy, and, unless held by a written agreement is sure to evade it and overreach the person with whom he is dealing." Potter concluded by writing, "I confess I am sometimes a little surprised at the resentment which Hebrews show to so-called Christian social exclusiveness."[78] Schiff was so angry that it took him a week to reply.

In his response, Schiff wrote Potter, "I did not trust myself to reply at once to your letter of the 11th inst., for its first reading amazed me, and I deemed it best not to reply until I should be able to do so in a more calm frame of mind." His letter to Potter, which has no reply in file, could barely maintain a cloak of civility. He wrote, ". . . What amazed me in your letter were the statements, which you so boldly make, as to the apparent reason for prejudice existing against our citizens of the Hebrew faith." After writing a long defense of the honor of the Jewish banker on Wall Street, his honesty, prestige, and credit, Schiff stated that he did agree with Potter on one point. He wrote, "As to your surprise at the resentment which Hebrews show to so-called Christian social exclusiveness, I am entirely one with you. That Jew and Gentile will socially not thoroughly mix is a natural result of the reluctance on the part of both to intermarriage, the uniting of the sexes in wedlock being, after all, the main stimulus to all social intercourse."[79]

Potter's correspondence with Schiff offers a sense of how pervasive anti-Semitic views were at that time. Like the controversies over social club membership, it also reflects the extent to which deliberate and sustained efforts were involved in preventing the social intercourse between Jews and Gentiles. Most importantly, as Schiff himself understood, it reminds us that the success of those efforts depended upon controlling the movements not just of men but of women as well. Like Pierpont Morgan, Schiff believed ardently in the right of patriarchy and closely monitored the lives of his children. Schiff's only daughter, Frieda, could not go out without a chaperone and college was never an option for her.[80] But as his correspondence with Potter suggests, Schiff's concerns were more than just those of an overprotective father. He was just as committed as Pierpont Morgan to keeping the social spheres of the two firms separate but for different reasons.[81]

Schiff did not encourage social intercourse because he felt deeply the clear subordination of Jewish culture and religion in American society. In a context of prejudice and discrimination, Schiff believed that Jewish and non-Jewish women and men had to be kept separate socially because such a union could only lead to the decline of Jewish culture and religion, not the other way around. In fact, Schiff's prediction did come true, at least in his own family. Despite his efforts, his own children (particularly Mortimer, who had a conflicted and difficult relationship with his father in general) and his grandchildren progressively became distant "from things Jewish."[82]

In addition to the reasons Schiff gave, there is, however, another possible explanation for why Jewish and non-Jewish women and men had to be kept separate. The imperative of separation lay not only in the possible future decline of Jewish culture and religion among Jewish youth, which so concerned Schiff, but in the more immediate issue of maintaining order in the economic and domestic spheres. It was not just the domestic sphere that was in danger; it was also the financial sphere. In other words, controlling the movement of women was significant because both heterosexual relations and homosocial relations depended upon it.

Consider that gentlemen bankers had to protect their reputation and social capital at all costs. Without their sense of pride and place, they could not engage as equals. How could gentlemen bankers do business when their social identities so clearly operated in the context of hierarchy and subordi-nation and given the context of racial discrimination, as anti-Semitism against Jews was then defined? Just beneath the surface of civility, negativity threatened the bonds of elite bankers. An eruption of conflict would not only break these ties and destabilize the alliances that kept order within the banking community. Even worse, it would also challenge the authority of those men within their domestic sphere over their wives and their children.

In this context, the absence of women is exactly what made them impor-tant. Without women, social interaction in the financial community did not carry the same implications as they did in the domestic sphere. Though the financial community did not invent patriarchy, the absence of women allowed for personal and social contact in the world of business without disturbing the social hierarchies and mores found in the society at large. Without the fear of miscegenation and social integration, men could interact as men without bringing up other negative issues and potential sources of conflict that threatened their masculinity, honor, and pride, and thus without disturbing the social distance that defined their identities and social capital. In other words, they could be gentlemen bankers.

As we have shown, women were critical participants in kinship ties and intermarriage in the domestic world of private bankers. In this part of their world, women were assumed to be present, and in fact, their cooperation, especially that of their wives and daughters, was absolutely necessary to main-tain the image of a conservative and respectable merchant bank. Kinship and marriage ties were also important to the structure of interfirm and intrafirm cohesion. Ties involving women also played a role in creating ties between firms. Because women were confined to the domestic sphere, however, it has been assumed that they did not have anything to do with the world downtown.

For the Morgans, this impression was supported by the fact that women were not even present as staff within the Morgan bank in the early twen-tieth century. According to Chernow, Morgan "was stoutly opposed to women employees, and he didn't discuss business with women, whom he saw as inhabiting a separate realm."[83] While the exclusion of women was not only found in business, it had an important meaning for the financial community where Jews were present in relative numbers and more importantly, in positions of equivalent status. As the social organization of Morgan's network demonstrates, the presence of Jews did not mean that they were completely integrated nor were their differences magically erased. And as we shall see, there were clear limits to this "downtown meritocracy" even in the evidence of financial cooperation.

When we look at the relationship between Yankee and Jewish men from their different perspectives, it becomes clear that they had different motivations even though the result was the same. From the perspective of the new generation of Morgan partners, segregation had to be established because their identities as Morgan partners depended upon it. In other words, their claim to an elite identity was not guaranteed. For this reason, it is not surprising that the rejection of Theodore Seligman from the Union League Club was blamed on younger members, who probably had more in common with men like Seligman than they did his father. If the two domestic and economic spheres had to be kept separate, it was precisely because they were in fact so closely intertwined—so much so that the separation extended beyond the domestic sphere into the realm of social clubs. Even in men's private clubs, where women were excluded completely, the Morgan partners could not interact socially with Jewish elite men because these were *social* spaces for men where their identities and status were being created and affirmed.

If we think of Morgan's network as a whole, with different layers of varying degrees of closeness, we can see in the ways that interaction of different groups was organized that cooperation was not simply a product of "good business." Social relations also served to organize economic relations and vice versa. Cooperation was therefore the result of an uneasy alliance between two communities, economic and social, that functioned as long as other conditions, limitations, and traditions supported its hierarchical structure, even though the result was to make it appear as if they were separate. What is so interesting is that though these boundaries involved an enormous amount of labor to maintain, they were completely taken for granted as the norm.

In light of their social distance, personal views, and the potential for conflict, the fact that Schiff and Morgan worked together at all seems a remarkable feat. Indeed the opposite is true. They found a way to work together in one part of their lives and then ignore each other in another despite the personal nature of investment banking precisely because of that separation.[84] Yet because the gendered nature of gentleman banking was taken for granted and because there was also evidence that Morgan bank and Kuhn, Loeb & Co. cooperated economically, it has always been assumed that Morgan's personal beliefs and social ties did not matter and that economic self-interest and class unity were the sole basis for their ties. In effect, the social and economic spheres were seen as operating under different rules and customs.[85]

For this reason, we find that their differences were not the focus, for example, of state investigations into the Money Trust, which were more interested in documenting their collusion or class unity. But while both firms accepted that the financial community and the society in which they worked were much more diverse than their own circles, they could not completely ignore the social separation that existed between the partners in the United States even within the world of business. This fact was evident in the history of their syndicate cooperation to which we now turn.

THE STRUCTURE OF ECONOMIC COOPERATION

In 1957, Barry E. Supple wrote an influential study on German Jewish bankers, which remains one of the standards on the subject. Regarding ethnic and religious differences, Supple wrote, "In the New York money market it was normally the financial standing, not the ethnic background, of a house, its credit and expertise, not its religion, which in the long run determined whom it would work with or who would engage its services."[86] In this regard, he was at one with Vincent Carosso, who wrote several decades later, "All of the prominent investment banking houses of the post-Civil War era, Jewish and non-Jewish alike, owed their position and influence to considerations that had little to do with religion or ethnic orientation."[87]

As Supple recognized, however, there was no study of how the social organization of German Jewish and Yankee bankers affected interfirm as opposed to intrafirm relations. We know that German Jewish banks "were not entirely insular in [their] business activities is equally clear from a brief study of available data on underwriting syndicates."[88] The same could be said of the Morgan firm. But as the history of the Morgan syndicates demonstrates, the Morgans did not cooperate with all of the participants equally in terms of frequency or amount. Within this world, Kuhn, Loeb & Co. was an important partner, though with certain limitations: it was important *because* it was a competitor and not in spite of the fact that it was a competitor.

The economic data itself do not indicate whether the two firms were socially separate because they were competitors or if they were competitors because they were socially separate. For that we must rely on the qualitative data above to theorize that given the makeup of both banks, the identity of the Morgan bank, and the historical context, the latter is the more likely history of origin. What the Morgan bank's syndicate data do show is that syndicate participation did not ignore social separation but accommodated for it. The key to understanding their relationship and cooperation is recognizing that Morgan's financial ties were tied to Kuhn, Loeb & Co. by a larger network of financial actors.

Kuhn, Loeb & Co.'s syndicate participation did not come close to that of First National Bank and National City Bank, who became and remained the Morgan bank's most important collaborators starting in the early twentieth century. First National and National City were commercial banks and distinct from the private investment banks in their greater access to funds, particularly for large syndicates. But even they were unique among the commercial banks as partners in Morgan's syndicates. For example, Deutsche Bank had a significant number of participations, but most were for the same client, the Northern Pacific Railway. This suggested that its relationship to Morgan was predicated on its ties to the client. First National Bank and National City Bank, in comparison, had regular collaborations on every group of the syndicate, offering, purchasing, and distributing.

Looking more closely at the banks' participation shows another subtle difference. As an individual, George F. Baker had participations in twenty-one syndicates for a personal total of almost $7 million (four were unknown because they were valued in shares). James Stillman personally participated in twenty-five syndicates for a total of almost $15 million (three were unknown because they were valued in shares).[89] Even though Jacob Schiff sat on the National City board, he had no individual participations in any of the Morgan firm's syndicates and neither did any of his partners.[90] Kuhn, Loeb & Co.'s participation increased dramatically after the Panic of 1907, making it unique among the German Jewish houses, not only with regards the Speyers but also J. & W. Seligman & Co. But this increase was not great relative to the participation of the other Yankee private banks (as opposed to the commercial banks), such as Kidder, Peabody & Co., a Boston based bank, which was an important Morgan collaborator.

Formally organized in 1865 by Henry P. Kidder, Francis H. Peabody, and his brother, Oliver W. Peabody, Kidder, Peabody began to reach prominence "during the railroad boom of the late 1870s." All three men were clerks in a Boston-based banking and brokerage house, J. E. Thayer & Brother, founded by John E. Thayer, the son of a Unitarian minister from Massachusetts and a "descendant of John Cotton, the seventeenth-century Massachusetts religious leader."[91] By 1886, the bank became the exclusive American agents of Baring Brothers & Co., London, "one of the world's most prestigious and influential private banking houses." A member of the Baring family, Thomas Baring, who was also the American representative of his family firm, became a partner that year though he was stationed in New York, where a branch had been opened 1868 under the leadership of George C. Magoun. (In 1891, the two firms, the Boston and the New York branch became two separate partnerships, Kidder, Peabody & Co. in Boston and Baring, Magoun & Co. in New York, though ties between the houses remained strong.)[92]

If we compare Kuhn, Loeb & Co.'s participation in J. P. Morgan & Co. syndicates only to other private banks, we find that it always ranked below Kidder, Peabody & Co., with the exception of 1905–1909, which was the period of the Panic of 1907.[93] (Baring, Magoun & Co.'s participations were counted separately, but a case could be made for aggregating the two.) For all other five-year periods up to 1929, Kidder, Peabody & Co. ranked higher than Kuhn, Loeb & Co. in terms of the amount of syndicate participation it received, and it was lower in terms of the number of participations it received. (The number of participations would even out when studied in the long term.) The average participation during a single five-year period during the entire forty-year period was much higher than for Kuhn, Loeb & Co. as well. (The unique number of clients does not seem to follow a consistent pattern, but they did not have a large variance.)

The data suggest that while Kuhn, Loeb & Co. was given relatively frequent participations in J. P. Morgan & Co.'s syndicates, the amount was not as high as the bank would allocate for one's "friends," who were within one's own social sphere and economic cluster. A comparison of the top five private firms who participated in Morgan's syndicates between 1895 and

1934, shows that all but Kuhn, Loeb & Co. were Yankee banks. Kuhn, Loeb & Co.'s total participation also trailed that of Kidder, Peabody & Co., the leader, by about 21 percent even though the number of participations and the number of unique clients was about the same. This is particularly significant also because Kuhn, Loeb & Co. most likely had more capital resources than Kidder, Peabody & Co. throughout this period.[94]

The hierarchy of J. P. Morgan & Co.'s syndicate network is interesting when compared with the firm's participation in the syndicates of other firms. Between 1895 and 1914, the total amount that Morgan's competitors had to divide (at par) was approximately $3.5 billion. J. P. Morgan & Co.'s portion was approximately $300 million (8.6 percent). Among the top banks, Kuhn, Loeb & Co. was by far the leader with seventy-eight. National City Bank gave fifty-seven and First National, thirty-one. Lee, Higginson & Co. and Kidder, Peabody & Co., two Yankee banks who ranked among the top ten private firms in J. P. Morgan & Co.'s syndicates, gave the bank only twenty-one and eleven, respectively. This suggests that their relationship to the Morgan firm was not based on their ability to bring new business/clients to the bank. (See Table 9.)

Table 9 Other Banks' Syndicates, 1894–1914

Name of Managing Bank	Total*	% of Total Given to JPM & Co.	# of Participations Given to JPM & Co.**	# of Participations Amount Unknown
Kuhn, Loeb & Co.	$1,440,000,000	4%	78	3
National City Bank	$694,000,000	10%	57	1
First National Bank (NY)	$223,000,000	21%	31	2
Lee, Higginson & Co.	$120,000,000	15%	21	0
Kidder, Peabody & Co.	$90,000,000	18%	11	1
Harvey, Fisk & Sons	$88,000,000	21%	19	5

* Rounded to the nearest million
** If the syndicate had co-managers, both were noted as having given a participation
Source: J. P. Morgan & Co. Syndicate Books, ARC 108–ARC 119, Pierpont Morgan Library (PML)

In addition to being the leader of the firms who gave J. P. Morgan & Co. syndicate participations, Kuhn, Loeb & Co. was the leader in terms of the total amount that it offered the Morgan bank as well. The percentage of the total amount of the syndicate that was offered to J. P. Morgan & Co., however, was relatively small (4 percent) in comparison to the percentage of the syndicates offered by First National Bank; Harvey Fisk & Sons; Lee, Higginson & Co.; Kidder, Peabody & Co.; and National City Bank. Unfortunately, due to lack of comparable data for Kuhn, Loeb & Co., we do not know what the percentage was of all the syndicates that Kuhn, Loeb & Co. offered, the percentage that they personally had to offer of the total amount of the issue, or how highly the bank ranked J. P. Morgan & Co. in its syndicates.[95]

Was J. P. Morgan & Co.'s collaboration with Kuhn, Loeb & Co. significant because its syndicates were more profitable and the Morgan bank needed to practice quid pro quo in order to enjoy the benefits?[96] Out of the 321 syndicates sponsored by other banks and firms, J. P. Morgan & Co. noted the profits and losses (including the commission as a syndicate member) for 251 of the deals, or 78 percent. The total profit of the syndicates with the information available was approximately $5.1 million, and the average profit was $20,472 with a high of $274,161.74 for a $4 million syndicate managed by Graves & Maxwell in 1914 for the Atlas Portland Cement Co. (J. P. Morgan & Co.'s portion was $1,934,000) to a loss of $268,313.51 for a $1.5 million syndicate co-managed by Kuhn, Loeb & Co. in 1912 for the Argentine Railway Co. (J. P. Morgan & Co.'s portion was $360,000).[97]

J. P. Morgan & Co. noted the profits and losses for seventy-one out of the seventy-eight syndicate participations it received and accepted from Kuhn, Loeb & Co. The total profit was $933,486.71 (18 percent of the total noted for all syndicates by others), but the average profit was $13,147, about 35 percent less than the average profits for the syndicates by other banks overall. Kuhn, Loeb's overall profits may have been below average due to the high-quality nature of the securities they underwrote, and the risk involved in those securities may have been lower than the average as well. But the data suggest that participation in Kuhn, Loeb & Co.'s syndicates was profitable primarily due to the frequency with which J. P. Morgan & Co. was invited to participate. Thus, frequency and consistency allowed the Morgans to share in a portion of the profits of their competitor, keep tabs on the competition, have access to a competitor's clients, and maintain the quid pro quo so essential to their economic relationship.

The syndicate data indicate that Kuhn, Loeb & Co. was a significant player within Morgan's financial network for several reasons. First, it was a formidable and important collaborator *because* it was a competitor and not in spite of the fact that it was a competitor. This fact is apparent in its participations in comparison to private banks within Morgan's economic cluster, such as Kidder, Peabody. Second, Kuhn, Loeb & Co. occupied a position at the highest level within the financial hierarchy for underwriting, making it unique among all private banks, which is apparent in the number of participations given to J. P. Morgan & Co. in comparison to those given by other banks. Third, like the Morgans, Kuhn, Loeb did not do business alone.

Kuhn, Loeb & Co.'s network, like the Morgans' network, involved a much larger community than Yankees and Jews, and they did not confine their relationships to other German Jews.[98] This fact is apparent through a brief look at the Kuhn, Loeb & Co.'s co-managers. Twenty-six of Kuhn, Loeb & Co.'s syndicates that Morgan & Co. were invited to participate in had co-managers, and an additional nine involved an international syndicate of banks, in which Kuhn, Loeb & Co. and J. P. Morgan & Co. were both members. Out of the twenty-six co-managed syndicates, two were with First National Bank and eleven were with National City Bank. The overlapping ties to National City Bank, which was more diverse in makeup than either firm, were also important given that this tie was a direct tie and to an important collaborator for both firms.

Yet while the syndicate data and the qualitative data on social separation between Kuhn, Loeb & Co. and J. P. Morgan & Co. before the First World War indicate that doing business did not require close social ties or kinship ties, that did not mean that it excluded the consideration of social concerns. Kuhn, Loeb & Co. and J. P. Morgan & Co.'s relationship was not predicated on kinship or close affective ties but on a different kind of proximity by being at the top of the banking hierarchy. The nature of Morgan and Kuhn's syndicate participation shows that the firms' relationship was based on a deep understanding of their social organization, not the exclusion thereof.

Studying the complexity of J. P. Morgan & Co. and Kuhn, Loeb & Co.'s relationship helps to explain in part how firms monitored one another and accessed information about each other even when in different communities. Given that their cooperation also shows the replication of social clusters within the financial community, however, it does not explain the origin of their trust. In other words, the presence of economic ties alone cannot explain how the banks could have come to a consensus to ignore their social differences outside the financial community given the personal nature of investment banking and the contradictory personal views of the senior partners; it only shows that they did.

UPTOWN AND DOWNTOWN: THE IMPORTANCE OF GENDER

The key to understanding Morgan's network thus lies in looking at it not only from the perspective of individual bankers or from the perspective of the financial community and their adherence to the gentlemen banker's code. Rather, what is necessary is the study of the syndicate community from a perspective of two communities, one uptown and one downtown. [See Figures 4 and 5.] It is not just that the residences of Jewish and Yankee bankers were separate uptown or that they were so closely situated downtown. The point is that the domestic space uptown was also completely separated from the world of business downtown. Looking at the map and the separation between their domestic and financial spaces asks us to think critically about why the informal code of conduct was referred to as a *gentlemen's* code.

The gender organization of the banks or the separation of the domestic world from the economic world of business was a critical structural factor that allowed for economic cooperation. But because it was so normative and because it seemed so stable, it has been completely ignored. Over the course of the early twentieth century, the increasing assimilation of American Jews of elite backgrounds and changes in women's position in society put pressure on these existing networks, but they did not dramatically alter social and economic hierarchies because they did not undermine the separation of a domestic and social sphere even when greater numbers of women began to move into the public sphere.

Thus, despite the fact that women gained greater political rights during the Progressive period, the presence of women in the public sphere did not greatly affect the organization of the Morgans' economic network. As we shall see in the case of women's peace groups in the postwar, this also had

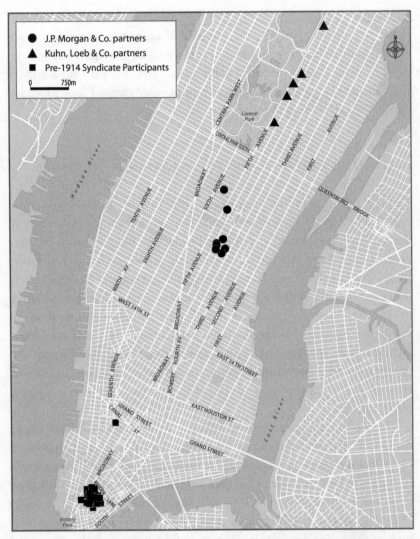

FIGURE 4 J. P. Morgan & Co. and Kuhn, Loeb & Co. partners' residences in 1910 with sample of downtown offices of J. P. Morgan & Co.'s syndicate participants, pre-1914

to do with the fact that any critique of gender segregation was complicated by the commitment of elite Jewish and Yankee women of Pierpont Morgan and Jacob Schiff's generation to social, racial, and class hierarchies.

Even those "who belong to someone else" had property of their own that they were also committed to protecting. Anglo-American elite women like

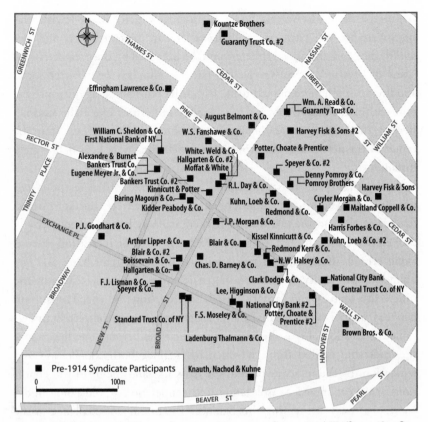

FIGURE 5 J. P. Morgan & Co. syndicate participant sample, pre-1914 (Different #'s reflect multiple office locations)

Fanny Morgan were just as deeply committed to retaining their social capital and preserving their own forms of social distance in the world uptown as were the men of their families. German Jewish elite women like Therese Schiff were just as invested to maintaining social and class boundaries, partly because their claims to an elite bourgeois status were always considered to be somewhat suspect in the context of anti-Semitism. Questions of difference and equality between the genders remained unresolved for women as a group, as did racial hierarchies between women.[99]

It is in this regard that the story of Belle Greene is most instructive. Her experience of passing as white reminds us that in the organization of the Morgan network, the gendered nature of the domestic and economic spheres was inseparable from American race relations, of which Yankee-Jewish relations were just one part. As we shall see later in the text, the boundaries *within* the Morgans' social sphere would be breached by the greater assimilation of Jews in the postwar period, but the boundary *between* the social and financial sphere remained firm, as did the prohibition against integration within the social sphere for racialized minorities like Belle Greene. Because this structure is not obvious, we need to look further away from the center of the network to the fringes where relations were kept deliberately distant.

Again, that is not to say that keeping stable and cordial relations was easy. It took an enormous amount of effort and there were constant threats. Economic elites in the late nineteenth century may have worked within a cooperative structure, but they also lived at a time of increasing discord along ethnic, religious, and racial lines, and the Morgan bank and the financial community were not immune to these historical trends. In the nineteenth century and early twentieth century, however, social separation between members of the financial community did not completely undermine the creation of trust between economic elites because conditions and the leadership existed through which to facilitate both cooperation and separation. By the interwar period, the networks and the historical conditions that encouraged consolidation and cooperation would come under enormous stress threatening this balance. The first major challenge to the stability of the banking community after Pierpont Morgan's death was the First World War.

## CHAPTER FOUR

Disrupting the Balance: The Great War

THOUGH SUBTLE CHANGES in the makeup and organization of the Morgan bank began before the First World War, they did not emerge as significant until after Pierpont Morgan's death. Like his father, Jack Morgan was a private man with a strong sense of responsibility and patrician values. He was raised in the same merchant banking traditions and his death in 1943, above all, signified the passing of that generation.[1] But during the interwar period, the Morgan firm began to move toward a more managerial model, which had much to do with Morgan's character, personality, and style.

The change in the senior leadership of the Morgan bank was apparent in the fact that the other partners addressed him as Jack while his father had only been called "Mr. Morgan" and was referred to as "J. P. M." or "The Senior." (Jack also referred to his father thusly when corresponding with his partners).[2] Even the new Morgan building, completed the year after Pierpont's death, made a statement of the bank's movement toward a modern era. With its clean lines and smaller size, it was a dramatic contrast to the Gilded Age style of the older Drexel building.

PHOTO 9 Drexel Building, J. P. Morgan & Co. offices, Broad and Wall Streets, New York City, ca. 1900–1906 (Library of Congress, Prints & Photographs Division, [reproduction number LC-D4–19583])

PHOTO 10 J. P. Morgan & Co. Building, Broad and Wall Streets, New York City, 1914
(Library of Congress, Prints & Photographs Division, [reproduction number LC-USZ62–124435])

Jack Morgan recognized his privileged status as his father and grand-father's heir, but being Pierpont Morgan's only son did not eliminate the necessity of his having to prove himself worthy of the title of "The Senior."[3] The pressure of being the heir to the House of Morgan was compounded by the fact that he did not have a close relationship with his father. Even after he became a partner, he was kept in the dark about key aspects of the business.[4] Before his marriage, Jack's closest relationship was with his mother, Fanny. Louisa, Jack's older sister, was their father's favorite child, and she remained Pierpont's companion until her marriage to Herbert Satterlee in 1900 at the relatively late age of thirty-four.[5]

Jack's sense of insecurity and melancholia faded somewhat after he got married in 1890 and started his own family. He met his wife, Jane Norton Grew (called Jessie), the daughter of a Boston merchant, while a student at Harvard. Jack Morgan's marriage differed dramatically from that of his parents. He and his wife were very close, and their relationship gave him a

PHOTO 11 Miss Elizabeth Haldane (wearing hat with white plume; sister of Viscount Haldane, Lord Chancellor and former British secretary of state for war), Judge (Jacob M.) Dickinson (carrying umbrella; former American secretary of war), and Jack Morgan at the Columbia Yacht Club, located at the foot of Eighty-Sixth Street, New York City, August 25, 1913 (Library of Congress, Prints & Photographs Division, [reproduction number LC-DIG-ggbain-14052])

sense of confidence, security, and acceptance.[6] Despite his father's dominant shadow, Morgan came into his own as a family man, a partner in the firm, and an economic leader. Morgan had to lead the firm at a time, however, when the expectations that the firm be responsive to the needs of the country were much higher and when the firm was less able to take on the leadership role internationally without the state's cooperation.[7] His greatest challenge came in the form of the First World War.

If Pierpont Morgan's time as senior partner marked the height of private banking at the Morgans, Jack Morgan's tenure told the story of private banking at a time of transition. The Great War was not just the starting point; it was also the driving force. The war changed everything from America's place in the world hierarchy of nation-states to the growth of American state power to the society at large, creating new expectations with regard to the moral and practical obligations of financial organizations and actors. Private banking was no exception.

Given the centrality of social relations to the economic network of the bank, the war created challenges for the Morgans in ways that were not entirely coherent. On the one hand, the experience and violence of the war and the fact that the war had been fueled by ethno-national differences made it more difficult to claim moral authority and social and economic leadership without an acknowledgment of democratic values, such as the "fundamental principle of equal opportunity" and the principle of individual freedom. On the other hand, a nationalist patriotism heightened by the strain of the war experience also gave less incentive for the partners to hide their preexisting prejudices specifically at a time when the bank was going through a generational transition.

Looking at the changes from the perspective of firms within the financial community, with the major economies of Europe in deep trouble, Anglo-American banks were less beholden to their European counterparts, even as they may still have deferred to them. German Jewish bankers were not completely abandoned by their friends and associates, and they were needed by their European associates more than ever given their American capital networks. But with Germany defeated, certain ties that had previously given German Jewish banks advantages became a liability. In the new world order, as the community and the structures that enabled the prominence of nineteenth century merchant banking traditions began to fade, Kuhn, Loeb & Co. partners lost substantial leverage because of the way in which ethno-cultural tensions in the United States characterized them as potential allies to the enemy.

Even though the Morgan partners did not cut their ties with German Jewish banks from the prewar period, they were already socially separate, and now they had more emotional and personal animosity toward their German Jewish counterparts, whom they resented for not being as fully committed to the Allied cause.[8] During and after the war, particularly in the 1920s, the Morgan partners, both in New York and in Europe, began to be more open and intense about establishing their differences and distance from Jews. Though their anti-Semitic attitudes have largely been attributed to the experience of the war with Germany, this is only part of the story.

By looking at the changes in the financial community in the context of internal changes within the Morgan bank, we will see how the rise of anti-German sentiment cannot entirely account for the rise of anti-Semitism among the partners, whose growth was also a response to the growing assimilation of Jews in the United States. In other words, the rise of intolerance, while clearly related to the anti-German and postwar fervor, is particularly interesting given the fact that the generation of partners who led the firms of Kuhn, Loeb & Co. and J. P. Morgan & Co. after the war had much more in common than any previous generation, socially and culturally.

THE GREAT WAR

Given its English identity and history and its ties to French and British networks, the House of Morgan was deeply committed to an Allied victory well before the United States entered the war. Though the majority of the American population was overwhelmingly isolationist,[9] for Jack Morgan, who had family in England, had lived there between 1898 and 1905, and spent months at his London home every year, "the war was a holy cause as well as a business opportunity."[10] In December 1914, the House of Morgan became the buying agent for the British and French governments, essentially "coordinating the vast and growing war purchases both countries were making in the United States. . . ." The effort was organized by Henry P. Davison and managed by Edward R. Stettinius, whom Thomas Lamont had recruited from the Diamond Match Company. In 1915, J. P. Morgan & Co. "offered the $500 million Anglo-French loan . . . the first of a total of $1.05 billion of such securities marketed between then and Jan. 1917."[11] While the Morgans had done considerable business with German banks before the war, those relations were put on hold.

Over the course of the War, the Morgan partners became extremely anti-German, a sentiment that was exacerbated by the fact that they were targeted for their pro-Ally activities, personally and as a firm.[12] One of the most dramatic and frightening incidents took place early on in the war. In 1915, a man named Frank Holt (a.k.a. Erich Muenter), an American of German descent who once taught German at Harvard and Cornell, tried to assassinate Jack Morgan at his home in Long Island. In front of the British ambassador, Sir Cecil Spring-Rice, the ambassador's wife, his wife Jessie, and with their children at home, Morgan was shot twice but survived.

According to Spring-Rice, Holt entered the home with two revolvers and a stick of dynamite and went searching for Morgan in a room where Morgan's children were playing. Holt was confronted by Jessie and the Morgans' butler, Henry Physick, before being seized and pummeled by Jack Morgan, who was shot in the ensuing struggle, once in the abdomen and once in the thigh. After being subdued by Morgan and his servants, Holt was arrested.[13] Holt told the police that his "motive was to try and influence Mr. Morgan to use his influence in the manufacture of ammunition in the United States and among millionaires who are financing the war loans, to have an embargo put on shipments of ammunition so as to relieve the American people from complicity in the deaths of the thousands of our European brothers."[14] He later committed suicide in prison.[15]

During and even after the war, the firm and the Morgan family continued to be a target of violence. In 1917, two German men were arrested for intending to bomb J. P. Morgan & Co.[16] In April 1920, Thomas W. Simpkin, a London-born printer, shot Dr. James Markoe, a close friend of the Morgan family, during services at St. George's Protestant Episcopal Church in Stuyvesant Square, where Pierpont Morgan had been a senior warden of the church (1885–1913) and a member of the vestry from 1868 until his death.[17] Simpkin, who had escaped from an asylum, had traveled to the United States to shoot Pierpont Morgan, who was of course already dead. He fired several shots, one that killed Markoe, and another, which almost hit Herbert Satterlee, Louisa Morgan's husband.[18] Dr. Karl Reiland, the rector of St. George's, who had been giving a sermon at the time, said in his account of the shooting that Markoe had been shot above the left eye. When it was determined that Markoe was dead, Reiland said, "Then I felt like killing the man because I thought he was some Bolshevik. I was relieved to learn that he was an insane and irresponsible person."[19]

If those events were not traumatic enough, the worst was yet to come. At noon on September 16, 1920, a bomb went off outside the Morgan offices, killing thirty-eight people including one Morgan employee (William Joyce, the son of Thomas Joyce, who was the clerk in charge of securities and had been with the firm for thirty-five years). Hundreds were wounded, including Jack Morgan's oldest son, Junius. It was never discovered who was responsible, though it was later determined that the bomb had been hidden in a horse-drawn wagon.[20] This torrent of unprecedented violence against the firm created an environment where the partners became even more inward facing, more suspicious of outsiders and the outside world, and increasingly more protective of Jack Morgan. After his home invasion, Morgan traveled with bodyguards, who were former marines, and had any persons of German or Austrian descent fired from Camp Uncas, his retreat in the Adirondacks.[21]

For Kuhn, Loeb & Co. and other German Jewish firms, the war was a time of terrible uncertainty and personal crisis. Emotionally and culturally tied to the country of their birth, Schiff and his partners were enormously conflicted about their proper relationship to Germany, and the partners' differences with regard to the war also created tension within the family partnership. Though American public sentiment leaned toward the Allied cause, Schiff could not. He did not hide his feelings from the public though he was much more open in his personal correspondence. In November 1914, he was quoted in the *New York Times* stating, "For many reasons my personal sympathies are with Germany. I cannot feel convinced that she has been the real aggressor. . . . Although I left Germany half a century ago, I would think as little of arraying myself against her, the country of my birth, in this, the moment of her struggle for existence, as of arraying myself against my parents."[22] He later wrote to Louis Wiley of *The Times,* "Germany, and least the Kaiser, are not the real instigators of this terrible conflict."[23]

Particularly in the first two years of the war, Schiff clearly wished for and expected to see a German victory. In 1914, he wrote to a colleague, "I have no fear that German civilization, German culture and German manhood cannot be downed."[24] Schiff also tried to warn Baron Korekiyo Takahashi, a close associate and the Minister of Finance for Japan, that if Japan got involved in the war, it could bankrupt them.[25] Later when Japan entered the war on the side of the Allies, it led to a "suspension" of formal relations between the bank and Japan. In December 1914, the *New York Times* reported that Schiff resigned from the Japan Society, "an organization of Americans and Japanese who endeavor to encourage friendly relations between the United States and Japan."[26] Schiff wrote Takahashi:

I am sure you will readily understand that while a state of war exists between Japan and Germany, my friendly relations with Japan as a whole must be suspended, but I have no desire whatsoever to interrupt the good, and in some instances, intimate relations I hold with you and other individual Japanese. As a native German, though I have been an American citizen for almost half a century, my sympathies are naturally with the country I have been born in and in which my forefathers have lived for many centuries.[27]

In 1915, Schiff repeated the sentiments that were quoted in the *New York Times,* when he wrote Lucien Wolf, the English journalist, "I would just as little think of turning against [Germany] in this hour of its struggle and peril, as I would turn against my own parents were their existence endangered" even though he also stated he had "no anti-English feeling" and that England had done more for the liberty of Jews than Germany.[28] While other partners, such as Jacob's son Mortimer and Otto Kahn, participated in loans made to the Allies as individuals (against his wishes), Schiff abstained, as did Kuhn, Loeb & Co. as a firm.[29]

Schiff's refusal to support the Allied cause did not only have to do with his attachment to Germany. It was also the consequence of his deep hatred for the Russian tsar, whom Schiff had "declared was the enemy of all mankind."[30] As long as Russia remained an ally to Great Britain and France, and as long as Russia persecuted Jews, Schiff could not bring himself to see the outcome of the war differently. When the House of Morgan gave Russia a $12 million credit, Schiff registered his protest with Jack Morgan as he had during the Russo-Japanese War when he "argued with the Morgans, albeit in vain, that doing business with Russia was financially as well as morally unsound."[31]

Throughout the war, the relations between Kuhn, Loeb and Morgan partners became increasingly fragile and tense. In May 1915, German submarines sank the British liner the *Lusitania,* which was traveling from New York to Liverpool. The ship was owned by the Cunard shipping company, the major rival of the International Merchant Marine (IMM), a giant shipping combination of British origin that Pierpont Morgan reorganized in 1902. The attack led to the deaths of more than a thousand people. In shock, Schiff went to see Jack Morgan at the Morgan offices to express his regrets and "apologize for his compatriots' behavior."[32] It was an unusual gesture for Schiff, not just because of the circumstances, but because most of the face-to-face correspondence between the two banks appears to have taken place between Mortimer or Otto Kahn and Jack Morgan or one of the other senior Morgan partners, as a sign of seniority and rank.[33] In what is a well-known story, Morgan rebuffed Schiff to his face, and Schiff left the office. Morgan's partners urged Morgan to rethink his actions, and he went to Kuhn, Loeb's office to apologize.[34] This pattern of a break and tense reconciliation was repeated throughout the war, testing the limits of the gentlemen's code.[35]

In 1916, the Morgans excluded Kuhn, Loeb & Co. from a syndicate for the Erie Railroad. Kuhn, Loeb partners retaliated by excluding the Morgans from a syndicate they were managing. Schiff wrote his partners, ". . . as far as Morgans are concerned to whom, with all friendship for them, we cannot offer participation in view the way they have ignored us in the Erie com. syndicate, without loosing (sic) our self-respect." Schiff was not entirely decided on whether or not to exclude Guaranty Trust Co. and Lee, Higginson & Co., who were allied with Morgan on the issue. But he suggested to his partners that they would have to strengthen their ties elsewhere.[36] Eventually, Mortimer met with Jack Morgan, who apologized and claimed he had known nothing about it. Relationships were restored but they remained fragile.[37]

That year, Jack Morgan told his grand-nephew, Henry Fairfield Osborn, who was the president of the American Museum of Natural History (AMNH),[38] that he would not attend any board meetings as long as Kuhn, Loeb partner Felix Warburg, who was Jacob Schiff's son-in-law and the first Jewish board member of the AMNH, was there. Morgan and his father had a long history with the AMNH, and they were major supporters of the museum, so his refusal to attend the board meetings was quite serious. He wrote Osborn, "I cannot stand the German Jews and will not see them or have anything to do with them. . . . In my opinion they have made themselves impossible as associates for any white people for all time. I am sorry to bother you but there it is." Morgan's characterization of German Jews as non-white people is indicative of the ways in which his prejudice against them was not merely ethno-national but also racial.[39]

If the hatred for Germany brought Anglo-American houses closer together, the war also created tensions within the German Jewish houses. Henry Goldman of Goldman Sachs, for example, was openly and publicly supportive of Germany, which created such a crisis for his firm that he was forced to resign in 1917.[40] Within Kuhn, Loeb & Co., the tension brought on by the war came to a head in 1916 when the firm received an invitation from M. & M. Warburg, a prestigious German investment house based in Hamburg, to sponsor an issue of German municipal bonds (also called the German Cities Loan). This offer would spark a huge crisis in the firm, such that Otto Kahn would write to his partners, "In the present instance our house is strongly and deeply divided."

THE GERMAN CITIES LOAN

Of Schiff's partners, Otto Hermann Kahn (1867–1934) was the most gregarious and colorful. Similar in temperament to Morgan partner Thomas W. Lamont, Kahn was outgoing, social, and ambitious. Born in Mannheim, Germany, Kahn was the son of a banker, who had immigrated to the United States in 1848 to escape political persecution. Bernhard Kahn, his father, naturalized as an American citizen but eventually returned to Germany where he married and raised a family. Otto Kahn was apprenticed in Germany and then later at Deutsche Bank in London, when he became a British subject. He moved to the United States in 1893 to take a position at Speyer & Co. and married Kuhn, Loeb partner Abraham Wolff's daughter, Adelaide (Addie), in 1896. The following year, he became a partner in Kuhn, Loeb & Co. His trajectory into the firm was thus similar to Schiff's, who joined the firm the year after he married Therese Loeb. Schiff did not like Kahn personally but accepted him as Wolff's son-in-law. Part of Schiff's impression of Kahn stemmed from their substantial differences in style and inclination.[41]

Kahn's lifestyle reflected the fact that he saw himself as a cosmopolitan person and a man of society. Kahn was one of the only two members of the firm listed in the *Social Register*. Kahn was proud to be Jewish, but he was also secular, and he spent much more time as a patron of the arts than he did observing religious customs.[42] (Kahn served on the Metropolitan Opera House board with Pierpont Morgan, whom Kahn regarded as being a bit prudish in his artistic tastes, limited by "inappropriate religiosity.")[43] When Mortimer Schiff was in Paris as an envoy for the YMCA, Mortimer wrote his wife, "Strictly entre nous, I am drawing as much as possible out of the purely Y.M.C.A. situation and devoting myself more particularly to 'schmoozing' with the more or less important people, as that is really more worth while. In other words, I am acting á la Kahn, which you always recommended." (Underline in original)[44] While Kahn's social ties and gregarious nature were no doubt assets to the firm in certain ways, they also meant that Kahn felt more deeply than Jacob Schiff the social exclusion against Jews by the Anglo-American elite. He did not believe in or desire social segregation, and he had more to lose socially and personally by appearing to assist Germany against the Allies.

The difficulty with the German Cities Loan had largely to do with the

PHOTO 12 Otto H. Kahn with his daughter, Margaret Kahn (center), and Beatrice Byrne, most likely daughter of lawyer James Byrne, first Catholic member of Harvard Corporation, date unknown (Library of Congress, Prints & Photographs Division, [reproduction number LC-DIG-ggbain-27736]) NOTE: Identification in original photo is labeled in the wrong order for Margaret Kahn and Beatrice Byrne.

source of the invitation. M. & M. Warburg, founded in 1798, was the family firm of Kuhn, Loeb & Co. partners Felix and Paul Warburg. (Paul, who was an economic adviser to Wilson, left the firm to join the Board of the Federal Reserve in 1913). Felix and Paul's brother, Max was the head of the bank, which had affiliates in Holland. The brothers (there were two other brothers, Fritz and Aby) were very close.[45] While Felix naturalized as an American citizen in 1900 and Paul naturalized in 1911, Max and their mother remained German subjects.[46] These ties and the fact that the business proposal had come from the Warburgs made the German loan a difficult one.[47] While Schiff and his son-in-law, Felix, were more inclined to take the business, Kahn and Mortimer were against it.[48]

In the fall of 1916, Kahn wrote the partners a long letter about the proposed German Cities Loan that illustrated the difficulties brought on by the war. The conflict combined many different social and economic issues: a consideration of public opinion with regard to the war, competition with the Morgans, long-term business strategy, and their responsibilities as a Jewish house. Kahn was deeply afraid of alienating their friends and associates, of becoming isolated, and even being labeled as seditious, but he was also aware of the ways in which the organization of the firm obligated him to act with the group or else retire from the firm, which he did not want to do. Kahn was enormously proud to be a member of the bank, which he felt was equal, if not superior to, the House of Morgan.[49] His objection to the German Cities Loan reflected the delicacy with which the consideration of any business involved the maintenance of networks, image, reputation, national loyalty, and self-respect.

In the letter, Kahn wrote that the "best public opinion" was against Germany and that all of their friends in the financial community (except Goldman Sachs) were also "against the militarist classes whose rule has brought Germany to her present plight . . ." He asked his partners, "Are we really called upon to be the one and only important financial house to put ourselves in conflict with the best prevailing public opinion in the land in which we live, a public opinion which is based upon no unworthy considerations, but upon the belief, rightly or wrongly, that the cause of France and England is the cause of justice, liberty, civilization and humanity?" Kahn argued that if the firm took on the proposed German loan, it would place them on the British Government's blacklist, which was of some concern given that he was still a British citizen at the time. (He naturalized as an

American citizen in 1917 during the war.) He also stated that being black-listed would "be damaging to our international relations for years to come" and also "have a certain measure of effect even upon relations here." He also tried to persuade the partners that by aiding Germany, they would "throw France . . . back into the hands of Morgans," meaning that alienating the Allies would allow the Morgans to monopolize business with the French after the war.

Kahn wrote that "if our duty and self-respect require it," they should not "shrink from this or any sacrifice," but he did not think that was the case in this instance. Moreover, he wrote, "Is it in the interest of the Jews in the allied countries that the only large house to finance a German loan abroad should be a Jewish house?" He was also afraid should "some submarine or other incident . . . in the course of the war lead to a breach between America and Germany," referring to the sinking of the *Lusitania* the year before. Kahn concluded by writing:

> I have no right to base an appeal on the personal ground that the conclusion of the German Cities loan would place me in the painful dilemma of either committing what is under the laws of the country which still has jurisdiction over me, a crime, an act which would probably make it impossible for me to set foot in England for years to come, or of retiring from a firm and associations in which I take great pride and great satisfaction, and to which I have contributed twenty years of work, whatever it may be worth.[50]

Kahn wrote directly to Schiff and made many of the same points, though he did not repeat the suggestion that he would leave the firm. He wrote, "If, however, the business is to be considered cold-bloodedly like any ordinary proposition," then the most important condition was that they "find one first-rate concern like the City Bank or the Guaranty Trust Company, or an influential house, like Kidder, Peabody & Co. or Lee, Higginson to undertake the business jointly. . . ."[51] Kahn understood that isolation would mean the end of the firm's predominance. Diversification of their networks and creation of alliances, specifically with top-tier Anglo-American banks, was critical if they were to survive the war and maintain their position.

Schiff's remarks were equally frank, writing Kahn, *"Man merkt die Absicht und wird verstimmt,"* or "One understands the intention and is displeased."[52] First, he wondered why Kahn had written him and in English, "notwithstanding the fact that our intercourse, both verbal and in correspondence, is most always in German." Schiff wrote Kahn, "As I see it, the partners are grouped thus: Mortimer's and [Jerome] Hanauer's views are about identical with your own; Felix, for motives which I am sure we all can understand, would much like to have a way found in which the proposition which has been made to us could be accepted and carried into effect." Schiff told Kahn he agreed with many of his views but that he felt that they had to "show Warburgs our good will." He argued that if they were going to continue in the line of "very strict neutrality," that the firm should also not consider engaging in "non-governmental French or English financing of magnitude." He ended the letter, *"Ci je suis, ci je reste,"* or "Here I am, Here I stay."[53] In the end, Schiff prevailed and he and Felix carried forward with their plans though the issue was eventually dropped because of opposition by the Federal Reserve Board against war financing.[54]

In the face of Schiff's opposition, Kahn's small compensation was a successful loan to French cities that he and Mortimer had been pursuing for the city of Paris since the summer of 1916, the French financing to which Schiff referred in his letter. The protocol observed in the course of completing the Paris issue is also an example of how the bank continued to adhere to the rules of the gentlemen's banker's code during the war. Kahn and Mortimer recognized the Morgans' prominent place in France, given the firm's role as the buying agent for the government. They wanted to keep relations with the Morgans cordial, and they did not take their relations lightly, but they also did not want to concede the whole of the country's business to the Morgans during or after the war.

Mortimer met with Jack Morgan to tell him that he had been in talks "with some French friends" about placing a loan in New York for Paris. Mortimer told Kahn that Jack Morgan "replied that he was much gratified and greatly appreciated that we should have come to him frankly about this," and said that the Morgans had not heard nor contemplated a loan for Paris.[55] To this news, Kahn replied, "I am delighted to learn that you have tackled the Paris loan idea, and that after your tactful interview with Jack Morgan, the road seems to be open."[56] Despite Schiff's request to maintain "strict neutrality," the Paris loan was already in the works. By October 2, 1916, only five days after Schiff sent Kahn his letter, Kahn wrote Mortimer a letter of congratulations "on the Paris business." Kahn was glad to do the Paris deal for the exact reasons he did not want to do the German Cities Loan. Kahn also claimed that the praise for the Paris loan was also "of satisfaction and relief that we have entered the field" and because "there was noticeable an undertone of resentment against the Morgan monopoly. . . ."[57]

The internal conflict within Kuhn, Loeb & Co. over the war was only resolved by external events: the overthrow of Tsar Nicholas II in Russia in February and March 1917 (the tsar abdicated on March 15, 1917) and the entry of the United States on the side of the Allies in April. For Schiff, the fall of the tsar was a monumental event.[58] He wrote his brother Philip that the Revolution was "almost greater than the freeing of our forefathers from Egyptian slavery."[59] After the February Revolution, Schiff wrote former Harvard president Charles Eliot a letter where he continued to express his love for Germany, but he distinguished the German people from the German government, whom he said had perpetrated "ruthless and inhuman acts."[60]

By June 1917, Kuhn, Loeb & Co., like other German Jewish firms, "threw their financial weight," not just emotional and ideological support, behind the United States, joining hands with a wide diversity of groups and individuals in the American war effort.[61] Whether or not they felt more pressure to demonstrate their patriotism, they embraced the American cause as Americans. They participated in a Red Cross Fund campaign, led by Morgan partner Henry P. Davison, to raise $110,000,000, an effort that was organized into teams with the amounts raised reported in the press.[62] Former Pujo counsel Samuel Untermyer was on the Executive Committee Team. Schiff was captain of Team 13, which included firms like Kuhn, Loeb, the Guggenheim Bros., Heidelbach Ickelheimer & Co., Hallgarten & Co., Goldman, Sachs & Co., and Lehman Bros. Jack Morgan was captain of Team 9, which was largely made up of individuals. Frank A. Vanderlip of National City was captain of Team 18.[63]

On October 25, 1917, a Liberty Loan parade took place in New York City. Starting at Washington Square Arch in Greenwich Village, a cadre of bankers with Jack Morgan at the center marched up Fifth Avenue to Central Park. Though Jacob Schiff was there, he did not walk in the front line. That place was taken by his son, Mortimer, who walked to Morgan's right, separated by Allen B. Forbes, president of Harris, Forbes & Co., a leading bond house.[64] Another Red Cross drive in May 1918 with a goal of $25,000,000 raised $4,500,000 on the first day from thirty-one teams, however, and it was led by captains such as Jacob Schiff, Jack Morgan, John D. Rockefeller Jr., Mrs. George F. Baker Jr., Daniel Guggenheim, Mrs. E. H. Harriman, and Mrs. W. K. Vanderbilt Jr.[65]

PHOTO 13 Bankers at Liberty Loan Parade, October 25, 1917, Washington Square Park, New York City (Library of Congress, Prints & Photographs Division, [reproduction number LC-DIG-ggbain-25574])

The Red Cross drives and other patriotic and charitable efforts were important ways for the financial community to create a sense of purpose and cohesion around the national cause. For members of the elite and upper classes it offered a way to reaffirm their leadership, but it also cemented their ties to the nation-state, which was already heightened by the experience of the war. Several of the Morgan partners had sons who served in the war, as did their associates, and they also suffered losses that were personal and devastating.[66] Morgan partner William Henry Porter lost his only son, Lieutenant James J. Porter; First National's George Baker lost a grandson, Avenel St. George, who was a lieutenant in the British First Life Guards; and Jacob Schiff lost a nephew, Mortimer H. Schiff, who was a captain in the British Army.[67] The devastation of war changed them and their families, as it did the world around them.

As the Red Cross team structure demonstrated, however, even nationalistic activities were still done within existing boundaries, and the competitive environment forecast that the tension between firms would persist after the war. Schiff did not live to see how much the war would change his firm, the world he knew, and the Germany he loved. He died in 1920, the year after the signing of the Treaty of Versailles. Schiff's death created an enormous void. Like Pierpont Morgan, Schiff had a critical, even domineering, presence in his house. The deaths of the seniors not only foretold changes in their firms' ability to act as leaders within a nation that had been changed by the experience of the war, a more pressing and immediate concern was the inevitable change in leadership within the banks themselves.

THE NEXT GENERATION

The First World War was a watershed moment, not only for how it changed the world but also because it marked a generational transition within the financial community. In 1912, the year of the Pujo Investigation, Pierpont Morgan was seventy-five years old. He died the following year, a month before his seventy-sixth birthday and a year before the start of the First World War. Schiff, who was ten years younger, died at the age of seventy-three in 1920. Thus, the senior partners of J. P. Morgan & Co. and Kuhn, Loeb & Co. died within a year or two of the start and end of the First World War, and they were not the only ones.

Like Morgan, George S. Bowdoin, Morgan's close friend and former partner, died in 1913. Associates and major financial leaders like Gardiner Martin Lane of Lee, Higginson & Co. died in 1914; Baron Nathan M. Rothschild of N. M. Rothschilds & Sons died in 1915 as did DeWitt Clinton Blair of Blair & Co.; James J. Hill of the Great Northern Railway and James Seligman of J. & W. Seligman & Co. died in 1916; Isaac Newton Seligman of J. & W. Seligman & Co. died in 1917; James Stillman of National City Bank and Luther Kountze of Kountze Bros. died in 1918; Morgan's former partner, Robert Bacon, Lee, Higginson & Co.'s senior partner, Henry Lee Higginson, and George C. Clark of Clark, Dodge & Co. all died in 1919; Levi P. Morton of Morton, Bliss & Co. died in 1920; and E. C. Converse of Bankers Trust died in 1921. Other notable financial and political figures also died in this period, including Andrew Carnegie, Henry Clay Frick, and Theodore Roosevelt, who all passed in 1919.[68]

The fact that J. P. Morgan & Co. and Kuhn, Loeb & Co. shared their loss of leadership with the community at large did not make it any easier. For J. P. Morgan & Co. and the Morgan houses in Philadelphia, London, and Paris, Pierpont Morgan's death came at a critical moment. Even though

Morgan had an heir of the same name, several factors made the leadership change particularly difficult. In the United States, the most obvious challenge was the war and the way in which the war led to the increased connectivity of the nation as a whole and the growth of national infrastructure. The state became a more forceful leader through the experience of managing the war, which created different circumstances for the Morgan bank in the postwar period.[69] This transformation was complicated by an international shift in power as the United States replaced Great Britain as the capital-lending nation of the world. International borders were realigned in the wake of the war, and Europe was in need of much assistance to reconstruct. These changes meant new opportunities but also new challenges for the Morgans.

For Kuhn, Loeb & Co., with Schiff gone, the spirit of the firm's acceptance of social separation began to fade as the leadership of the bank was assumed by partners with different inclinations. This was particularly true for Jacob's son and heir, Mortimer. For all of his life, Mortimer had lived under the domineering presence of his father with whom he had a close but conflicted relationship. According to his sister, Frieda, Mortimer was regularly "punished for various misdemeanors" as a child by his father, who was extremely autocratic in his parental style.[70] Frieda's memories evidence a measure of pathos for Mortimer, who appears to have accepted many of Jacob's decisions, trying vainly to live up to his father's standards, expectations, and achievements. Like Jack Morgan, who was under similar pressures, Mortimer did not shirk what he considered to be his responsibilities, including the preservation of his father's legacy, and he became well-respected as a financial leader in his own right. But unlike Jack Morgan, Mortimer did not find solace in his marriage. In 1900, he married Adele Neustadt, the daughter of Sigmund Neustadt, a partner in Hallgarten & Co., who was a close friend of Jacob and Therese Schiff. Mortimer and his wife had two children, but lived largely separate lives.[71]

Mortimer was close to his mother to whom he was devoted, but his father was the dominating figure in his life. Mortimer and Jacob Schiff clearly had elements of the classic cultural clash of immigrant families, however nontypical an immigrant Jacob Schiff was. Mortimer was American born and raised, and his attitudes toward the Allied loans and German Cities Loan clearly indicate that he did not have strong attachments to Germany, though he was apprenticed there for a time. Like his father, however,

PHOTO 14 Mortimer Schiff and his wife, Adele Neustadt Schiff, date unknown (Library of Congress, Prints & Photographs Division, [reproduction number LC-B2–1412–7])

Mortimer did not see a conflict between his Jewish religion and American identity. In his will, the two largest bequests were to the Federation for the Support of Jewish Philanthropic Societies in the City of New York and the Boy Scouts of America. After he died, Therese Schiff donated funds to the Boy Scouts to establish a training center for scout leaders in a memorial to her son.[72]

Mortimer had a different experience compared to Felix Warburg, who was his brother-in-law and partner. Growing up in Germany, Felix was the fourth son of five brothers and two sisters. By nature, he was outgoing and upbeat.[73] He and Frieda had fallen in love at a young age, and they married only after strenuous efforts to separate them. For one year, Jacob Schiff had Frieda and Felix correspond through letters, which he read, interpreted, and responded to. If not for the efforts of Ernest Cassel, who convinced him that Felix was a good match, Schiff may not have relented to the marriage. Felix had to leave Germany in order to marry Frieda, but he was never cowed by Schiff in the same way as Mortimer. Schiff, was, after all, not his father. Felix had many interests, but unlike his brother, Paul, who also married

PHOTO 15 Felix Warburg, Frieda Schiff Warburg, S. W. Rosendale (U.S. Attorney General), and Edward Warburg (the Warburgs' youngest son), date unknown (Library of Congress, Prints & Photographs Division, [reproduction number LC-DIG-ggbain-38909])

into the Kuhn, Loeb family and joined the firm, banking was not one of them. He did not devote much of his time to business affairs, though he became a senior partner at Kuhn, Loeb.[74]

With regard to their involvement in Jewish philanthropic works, however, the Schiffs and Warburgs had much in common. Felix and Mortimer continued to be heavily involved in Jewish philanthropic works after Jacob's death, but they differed with Jacob in their interpretation of Jewish integration.[75] They did not consider social assimilation to be necessarily contrary to their Jewish roots or religion, a view that was reflected in their choice of partners. By the 1920s, Kuhn, Loeb started to include partners, who were not Jewish, such as George W. Bovenizer, who was of Irish and Baptist background.[76] This change continued to the post-World War II period and reflected a larger trend for German Jewish banks in general.[77]

During the 1920s, the children of Kuhn, Loeb's senior partners also began to marry non-Jews. Paul M. Warburg's son, James, who graduated from Harvard in 1916, was the first of the third generation in the United States to marry someone who was not Jewish. He married Katherine Swift, the daughter of Samuel Swift, a music critic. All of Otto Kahn's children, who were baptized in the Episcopal Church, did not marry persons of Jewish faith. His daughter, Maud, married Major General Sir John Marriott of England in 1920. (She became Lady Marriott.) His son, Gilbert, married Anne Elizabeth Whelan in 1924. In 1928, his daughter, Margaret, married John Barry Ryan, the grandson of Thomas F. Ryan, the financier, who was Irish Roman Catholic. Kahn's son, Roger, married Hannah Williams in 1931.[78]

In 1923, Mortimer's daughter, Dorothy Schiff (1903–1989), converted to Episcopalianism after her first marriage to Richard Hall, who was not Jewish.[79] Though her "parents were not pleased" with Hall as a catch, they went along with the marriage. Dorothy was quoted as saying, "I don't know what would have happened if Grandpa Schiff had still been alive."[80] In 1934, Mortimer's son, John (1904–1987), who joined Kuhn, Loeb & Co. in 1929, married the granddaughter of George F. Baker of First National, Edith Baker. Theirs was the first significant link between the social circles of Kuhn, Loeb and the Morgans, a direct tie between George F. Baker and Jacob Schiff's families.

The fact that Dorothy met her first husband "at a dance in the Plaza Hotel" during her debut season, and the fact that John and Edith had been introduced through friends, indicated a much higher rate of social interaction between elite Jewish and non-Jewish men and women than had been possible in Jacob Schiff's generation or even Mortimer and Frieda's generation.[81] In 1918, when Paul Warburg's son was engaged to be married, Felix Warburg wrote, "Paul and Nina are very fond of the girl, as we all are, and while my father naturally would have strongly objected to his grandchild marrying a girl of the Christian faith, nowadays these things will happen."[82] By 1937, Warburg wrote to Stephen Wise, the rabbi and Jewish community leader, "I feel somewhat as my father felt in his time, when one of my brothers married out of his faith, and as I felt when the same thing happened to one of my boys—we objected and fought the decision and tried to prevent it, but once vis-à-vis of the fait accompli we made the best of it to achieve happiness for the parties most directly involved."[83]

In the 1920s, as Jews began to intermarry with Gentiles and with greater frequency, they stopped referring to themselves as a "race" as had once been the norm.[84] In the late nineteenth century, Jews did not classify themselves, for example, on their birth certificates or immigration forms as anything but white. For Jacob Schiff or Felix Warburg, who were naturalized Americans,

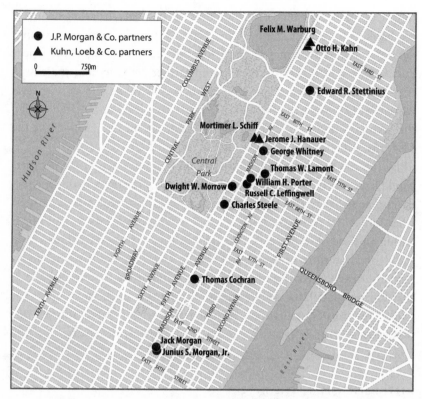

FIGURE 6 J. P. Morgan & Co. and Kuhn, Loeb & Co. partners' residences, 1925

whiteness was a necessary identity to gain American citizenship. But like Jacob Schiff, Jews in the late nineteenth century did not see this classification as contrary to calling themselves a Jewish race. This was not the case twenty years later.[85] By their grandchildren's generation, Jewish men and women were not inclined to use the word "race" to describe their differences from non-Jews, which they preferred to express as religious differences.[86] This was a significant shift; but while the definition of whiteness was expanded, the racial divide between whiteness and blackness remained firmly entrenched.

The greater assimilation of Jewish banking families can be observed in their spatial organization. [See Figure 6.] Between 1910 and 1940, the partners of J. P. Morgan & Co. and Kuhn, Loeb & Co. began to move increasingly uptown, with the exception of Jack Morgan and his son, Junius, whose city residences remained in their traditional family home in Murray Hill.[87]

In general, the geographic distribution of the bankers, including commercial bankers from First National and National City, became more similar not only because they moved closer together, concentrating in the Upper East Side, but also because they moved farther away, leaving the city as transportation and communication technology developed to allow greater movement. Many of the National City directors lived outside the city by the Second World War, and others had residences in Long Island like the Morgans, who had second homes in the suburbs.[88]

By the 1930s, the incoming generation of Kuhn, Loeb & Co. partners would have much more in common with their competitors than their predecessors, a change that was accelerated by a catastrophic loss of partners when almost all of Kuhn, Loeb & Co.'s senior partners died from illness within a period of seven years. Like their counterparts in the Morgan firm, the second and third generations of Jewish American bankers were largely native born and university educated. What is important to note, however, is that during the 1920s, despite the subtle changes in the makeup of the banks, the greater similarities did not translate into more affective ties between the firms. In fact, it led to a period of intense negativity.

ANTI-SEMITISM IN THE INTERWAR

The world that the second generation of Morgan partners inherited was one of increasing diversity and rancor, of hardening lines against ethnic groups. In the 1920s, the Morgan partners in general were more willing to embrace their identity in ethno-racial terms and worked harder to differentiate themselves socially from Jews and other groups, which may also have had to do with the fact that the work they did with elite Jewish banks actually increased in the first five years after the end of the First World War. In the post-World War I period, the partners of both Kuhn, Loeb & Co. and J. P. Morgan & Co. were from more varied backgrounds, they were not kin-related, and they were mostly university educated.

When we compare the partners of the two firms, they actually had more in common than the earlier generation of partners. Yet at a time when there was less to distinguish them and when there was greater diversity in their economic, political, and social networks, the firms retained separate and distinct identities. As time passed, the Morgans also passed down a history of themselves where the many similarities during Morgan and Schiff's time were not as well remembered and when their separation was taken for granted. In that narrative, the historical separation between Anglo-American and German Jewish existed because it was a natural reflection of a biological or cultural difference on the basis of race, religion, and ethnicity.[89]

In the immediate period following the First World War, Kuhn, Loeb & Co.'s percentage participation in J. P. Morgan & Co.'s syndicates actually increased relative to its previous participation and in comparison to other private banks (though not relative to the leaders, who remained First National Bank, National City Bank, and National City Co., National City Bank's securities affiliate). In the first few years after the Crash of 1929, Kuhn, Loeb's position within the Morgan syndicates was ranked even higher relative to other banks, though clearly external circumstances were involved. Significantly, this increase in participation was not due to a quid pro quo of receiving syndicate participations from Kuhn, Loeb & Co. Between 1920 and 1934, the total amount of syndicates offered by Kuhn, Loeb & Co. was about $262 million, about half of what it was even during the war ($498.6 million).

J. P. Morgan & Co.'s participation in Kuhn, Loeb & Co.'s syndicates totaled about $29.5 million during the war, while Schiff was still alive, with a total profit of about $322,000 and was about $14.4 million between 1920 and 1934, with a total profit of about $173,000. In comparison, between 1920 and 1924, Kuhn, Loeb & Co. received and accepted forty-one different participations from J. P. Morgan & Co. for a total of $158.85 million for sixteen different clients; 50 percent were major utilities, four, or 25 percent, were international governments, and three were railroads. Kuhn, Loeb & Co.'s participation in Morgan syndicates also reflected the change in the nature of Morgan's syndicates, where increasingly, the bank was doing business for industrial clients, utilities, and nation-states.[90]

As J. P. Morgan & Co. began to take on a greater role in representing American interests abroad, including in Germany, the Morgans also felt great pressure to put on a united front by including Kuhn, Loeb & Co., still the leading German American Jewish bank. Having also established a working relationship over a period of decades, Jack Morgan was enormously conflicted about respecting the traditions of the private banking community in the face of rising antipathies.[91] Major challenges included the rise of American nationalism and the United State's changing role in the new world order after the First World War. Both created new circumstances for both banks, forcing them to contend with the language of national unity and idealism that the sacrifices of the war demanded.

In 1924, for example, when J. P. Morgan & Co. was preparing to present a significant German bond issue also known as the Dawes Loan, American loans made to Germany that partially enabled German payments of World War I reparations,[92] the firm had to make a decision of who to include in the purchasing group and how to rank the syndicate members, who were organized in hierarchical tiers representing their reputation and influence. After Mortimer Schiff met with Lamont, telling him that he felt Kuhn, Loeb & Co. should be ranked in the first tier, Jack Morgan agreed to do so.[93] The continued participation of Kuhn, Loeb & Co. reflects the depth to which the existing separation of the social and economic spheres of the banks (as opposed to the separation within the social sphere) remained stable.[94]

Kuhn, Loeb would never be chosen to lead an "American" loan of great importance; that much was clear.[95] Their ethnic and religious identity and history also relegated them to a secondary status behind the Yankee bankers for reasons quite outside their control. The stories of how much business the bank lost as a result of the war should not be, however, exaggerated. Again, that is not to say that the process by which this stability was maintained was easy or simple. In 1927, Kuhn, Loeb & Co. offered J. P. Morgan & Co. a participation in a syndicate for the Baltimore & Ohio Railroad (B & O). The syndicate was with Speyer & Co. and National City Co. The offer was 10,000 shares out of 632,425 possible shares. J. P. Morgan & Co. declined to participate, but the way in which they did so was important. In a telephone conversation, Lamont and Mortimer Schiff agreed that the Morgans would not formally decline the invitation but that the letter "without being entered in [the Morgans'] correspondence register was returned to Mr. Lewis Strauss of Kuhn, Loeb & Co. in its original envelope just as received by us."[96]

The B & O episode demonstrates that the Morgans themselves had developed a relationship over the years with Kuhn, Loeb & Co., and they were committed to maintaining stability and the appearance of stability in the financial community, particularly at the apex level.[97] Both firms were tied to a larger community of financial collaborators, and they did not act unilaterally. Though Kuhn, Loeb & Co. received criticism from both sides of the Atlantic for their conflicted positions on the war, it was not abandoned by its clients or its associates, which in many ways speaks to the

diversity of its network and the importance of establishing long-term relationships with clients and collaborators.[98]

Particularly in the realm of international financing, Kuhn, Loeb & Co.
was able to leverage its past experience and relationships. It remained, for
example, a member of an elite group of banks involved with the Morgans in
South American financing (called informally the "South American Group").
It also remained a member of the American group of international banks
led by the Morgans in East Asian (Chinese and Japanese) financing along
with banks like Lee, Higginson & Co., known as the International Banking
Consortium to China (IBC). Membership in these organizations, which, as
we shall see, gained new meaning for the Morgans during the 1920s, also
helped to mitigate Kuhn, Loeb's loss of social capital in the postwar.[99]

The biggest difference in the firms' relations was in the qualitative nature
of the way in which the Morgans talked about Jews in the postwar period.
While the growth in the expression and vehemence of anti-Semitic expression
within the firm has been largely interpreted as a natural extension of the
Morgan partners' anti-German prejudices stemming from the war or the late
postwar hysteria over foreigners, immigrants, and Bolsheviks, this is only part
of the story.[100] If it was the critics of capitalism and foreigners that the Morgan
partners feared, this would not explain why they turned their prejudices
against their German Jewish counterparts, who were becoming more similar,
more "Americanized," less "foreign," and were certainly not anticapitalist.

In the ten years following the First World War, as Kuhn, Loeb partners
became more assimilated and as the banks' economic cooperation increased,
the Morgan partners also became more and not less expressive of anti-Semitic
prejudices. That German Jewish bankers continued to be seen as different
and inferior was not a comment on their ideology or their nationality. Most
of the second and third generation was American born. It was specifically
because they were Jewish and because they were becoming *less* separate
socially. It is important to note that while the critical separation between the
financial and social sphere remained intact, the decline in the separation
within the social or domestic sphere so disturbed the Morgans that anti-
Semitism also colored the Morgan partners' views of business outcomes,
which were now combined with anti-German antipathies.

Throughout the 1920s, the partners made negative comments about
doing business with Jews in ways that indicated they saw Jews as different,
inferior, and adversarial. For example, in May 1922, Herman Harjes told

Lamont that he had heard Otto Kahn was upset that Jack Morgan had been appointed to the Committee of Bankers, which was put together by the Reparation Commission to study the possibility of a loan to Germany. He wrote, "I continue to hear reports from different sides of the activity of the tribe in New York, which is trying to do all it can to hurt Jack and the firm."[101] He repeated the term "the tribe" in a followup letter to Lamont.[102] Lamont wrote him, "I am more than interested in all that you say in regard to the campaign of the Chosen People against the Christians and I can readily believe that it is all true."[103]

Later that month, Lamont wrote a letter to his partner George Whitney regarding business with Mortimer Schiff and other German Jewish bankers. Lamont told Whitney that he was upset that Mortimer, along with James Speyer and another banker, Rosen, pulled out of a pledge, possibly regarding Mexican business. Lamont wrote, "Now in my absence Schiff, Rosen and Speyer seem to have struck hands together and to be having a regular Old Testament love feast. You might show this to Jack Morgan, who I am afraid won't be a bit surprised, and in fact will be a little bit pleased as to his powers as a prophet."[104] Speyer apparently came around, but Jack Morgan wrote Lamont, "Do not, however, for any reason, let yourself be persuaded into the error of mistaking a change of mood for a change of character! The Ethiopian does not change his skin, although sometimes he makes a good servant; and a leopard does not change his spots, although he is in some places used for hunting. Undoubtedly the person in question saw that it would be to his advantage to behave decently to decent people in the hope of re-habilitating himself somewhat in the eyes of the world."[105]

It seems that Speyer's alleged efforts to rehabilitate himself did not work because later that year Morgan also referred to Speyer as a "Jewish-Hittite, German descended so-called American."[106] Morgan had had problems with James Speyer since the early twentieth century, when the Speyers were alleged to have poached on a deal with Cuba, among others. But his antipathies grew over time, were expressed in racialized language, and clearly became articulated with the more open expression of anti-Semitism within the firm.[107] In 1927, Lamont wrote Vivian H. Smith, a partner of Morgan Grenfell & Co., that J. P. Morgan & Co. advised Morgan, Harjes & Co. to refrain from doing business with a particular firm, "not because [the] institution was untrustworthy but because of generally third class make up. Its directorate almost wholly Jewish."[108]

Anti-Semitic views did not preclude the Morgan partners, even Jack Morgan, from interacting with persons of Jewish background, but close relationships were few and far between, more the exception than the rule, and usually with British Jews in positions of importance.[109] Perhaps it would be more accurate to say that interaction with individual Jews, such as Lord Reading (Rufus Daniel Isaacs, Viceroy of India, Special Ambassador the United States, and British Foreign Secretary [1860–1935]) or American journalist Walter Lippmann, did not prevent them from being anti-Semitic.[110] Now that the generation of Jacob Schiff had passed and the age of separation was beginning to wane, the greatest threat was to the undoing of the separate spheres, not between the world of finance and society, which remained intact, but within society where transgressions were negatively perceived as an implicit challenge to the exclusive identity upon which their social capital was built. For this reason we find that the partners made specific notations about interacting socially with people of Jewish background, particularly in places where they could not completely avoid social integration, such as on transatlantic passages.[111] Many of the references to Jews can be found on ship stationery.

In 1922, Jack Morgan wrote his mother on the way to Europe, "Fellow passengers are not very interesting as they are in very considerable part Jews and actress folk."[112] In 1924, he wrote her on another voyage, "This is only a line to tell you we are all right and having a really delightful voyage with no Jews and no one on board travelling with anyone else's wife." [Underline in the original][113] Lest we think that Jack Morgan was alone in his sentiments, in 1925, Charles F. Whigham, a Morgan Grenfell & Co. partner, wrote to Lamont from the *S.S. Olympic* on the way back to London, "So far we have had an uneventful trip but calm and cooler than New York. Not many people on board I know and the Jewish persuasion predominant. However the time has passed pleasantly enough. . . ."[114]

As their correspondence indicates, not only did the partners exhibit strong anti-Semitic attitudes, these sentiments emerged precisely when the social separation of the past was not observed. The correspondence also shows that there were some places where the Morgan partners could not completely exclude Jews. If anything, the exclusion of Jews was actually becoming more difficult to achieve despite the increase of prejudice, or rather, prejudice was increasing precisely because Jews were becoming more assimilated and also possibly because the numbers of assimilated and prosperous Jews had increased relative to the early twentieth century.[115]

In 1929 when Teddy Grenfell was up for reelection as a Member of Parliament, Jack Morgan wrote him, "How horrible that a Danish Jew should think that he could be a Member for the City while you are still willing to do it! If you need any funds for your election, draw on me for any amount you deem necessary."[116] By the late twentieth century, quite significantly, these attitudes took on an ahistorical, predetermined, normative quality, what contemporary observers would call "normal for their time." In 1979, Henry S. Morgan told Vincent Carosso that the "partners didn't like to do business with Ge-Jew houses, didn't like the way they did business; didn't like their Ge. Associations; also probably simply because were Jews." (Abbreviations in the original)[117]

The ways in which German Jews were coded as different and foreign is indicative of the particular challenges created after the war. During the interwar period, patriotic fervor combined with preexisting prejudices in a nativist movement called "Americanization" and gained support from the rise of the eugenics movement, a pseudo-scientific racism later embraced by Nazi Germany.[118] The sacrifices and experiences of the war created a stronger national identity, one that was ostensibly more inclusive and democratic, but one that was equally as exclusive, intolerant, and suspicious of differences, immigrants, and people referred to as "hyphenated Americans." What began to emerge was a different kind of American narrative, one that appeared to expand the definition of who could be an American yet also narrowed the definition of what belonging entailed. These changes paralleled those taking place in the House of Morgan.

In the 1920s, the presence of Jews and other minorities was considered a serious threat by the largely white male Protestant leadership to their social capital in another kind of private association, the university. By studying the Morgan partners' ties to institutions outside the world of finance like Harvard, we can observe the extent of their efforts to monitor the membership of institutions from which they gained their identity as individuals and as a firm. These non-economic ties demonstrate the extent to which they were part of a larger world, one that was at a time of transition. And in that space, as we shall see, they would have to contend with the new world order the war had made, one where the open expression of racism and anti-Semitism was determined to be incompatible with the assumption of national and international leadership.

## CHAPTER FIVE

The Significance of Social Ties: Harvard

THE FIRST DECADE after the First World War was a period of enormous growth for the Morgan bank, both in terms of the size and the scope of its organization. Between 1920 and 1929 the House of Morgan's American branches admitted more partners (fourteen) than they had during any ten-year period in the twentieth century before the Second World War. Three were admitted in 1920 alone, including Jack Morgan's son, Junius Spencer Morgan Jr., who represented the first of the third generation of the Morgan family in the firm.[1] In 1929, Junius was joined by his brother, Henry Sturgis Morgan, and four other partners, who were the sons or nephews of current or former partners. Eight of the new partners, however, had no prior kinship ties to the firm.[2] (See Table 10.)

During the early twentieth century, the Morgan bank began to adapt to the "process of transformation from the proprietary to the corporate form of capitalist property in the United States." Like other firms, the bank's American branches continued promoting men with family ties "while at the same time opening avenues to higher eminence and income to new families

Table 10 The House of Morgan American Partners, 1920–1940
(Refers to the date of entry into the partnership)

Name	Main Affiliation	Date of Birth	Date of Death	Date Became Partner in Newly Formed J. P. Morgan & Co./ Drexel & Co.*	Date Left Firm if Before Death
Elliot C. Bacon	JPM & Co.	1888	1924	1920	
Junius Spencer Morgan Jr.	JPM & Co.	1892	1960	1920	
George Whitney	JPM & Co.	1885	1963	1920	
Thomas S. Gates	Drexel & Co.	1893	1948	1921	1930
Russell C. Leffingwell	JPM & Co.	1878	1960	1923	
Arthur M. Anderson	JPM & Co.	1880	1966	1927	
Francis D. Bartow	JPM & Co.	1881	1945	1927	
William Ewing	JPM & Co.	1880	1965	1927	1935
Harold Stanley	JPM & Co.	1885	1963	1928	1935
Henry P. Davison Jr.	JPM & Co.	1898	1961	1929	
Thomas Stilwell Lamont	JPM & Co.	1899	1967	1929	
Henry Sturgis Morgan	JPM & Co.	1900	1982	1929	1935
Edward Hopkinson Jr.	Drexel & Co.	1885	1966	1929	
Thomas Newhall	Drexel & Co.	1876	1947	1929	1936
S. Parker Gilbert	JPM & Co.	1892	1938	1931	
Charles D. Dickey	Drexel & Co.	1893	1976	1932	
Henry C. Alexander	JPM & Co.	1902	1969	1939	
I. C. Raymond Atkin	JPM & Co.	1892	1957	1939	
William Arthur Mitchell	JPM & Co.	1892	1980	1939	

*Traditionally a partner's entry to a firm happened on the last day of the year. For example, 12/31/1899 is thus listed as 1900. Also refers to the date entered JPM & Co. (as opposed to only Drexel & Co.).

Source: "Articles of Partnership, 1894–1908" and "Articles of copartnership, J. P. Morgan & Co., 1916–1939," Morgan Firm Papers, ARC 1195, Boxes 1 and 5, PML. For sources of biographical information on individual partners, see Chapter 5 endnotes.

of middle and lower rank."[3] The new partners who entered the firm after the war came of age in the twentieth century, not in the late nineteenth century, and they carried with them different kinds of training and social expectations. Like the partners who joined in the 1910s, they were all native born and Christian, and they did not all come from socially elite backgrounds.[4] But most had little or no business experience before joining the firm, a marked contrast to partners who joined before the war.

What the younger generation of Morgan partners did have in common with each other, unlike the older Morgan partners, was their university education. Between 1895 and 1919, the House of Morgan's American branches, J. P. Morgan & Co. and Drexel & Co., had twenty-one different partners. Only seven were university graduates, or 33 percent.[5] Between 1920 and 1929, of fourteen new partners who entered the firm, eleven held a university degree (79 percent). Of the eleven, eight went to either Harvard or Yale (four to each school).[6] In 1920 alone, there were fifteen partners in the American branches and twelve (80 percent) were university graduates. In essence, a university education from an elite university became an informal requirement for partnership.[7] (See Table 11.)

Technically, the emphasis on education rather than kinship meant that men, who were not born of high social status, had a greater opportunity to enter the firm's partnership than previous generations, a path that was ostensibly based on individual abilities rather than familial or social connections.[8] Universities were hierarchical, but they were also supposedly "democratic," i.e., based on merit and not inheritance. Families could not guarantee the ascendance of ability or of public-minded heirs, but they did not have to because universities played that role. Like the corporation, which "'democratized' and nationalized previously segmented and hierarchic layers of the capitalist class" and "offered opportunities of social mobility for middle class people," the university represented a critical shift in the standardization and nationalization of social and economic mobility. It also represented the possibility of democratic self-realization that was so central to the narrative of American individualism.[9] For the Morgans, this change in the background of the partners confirmed their more outward-facing attitude, one that reflected the strength of American nationalism in the postwar.

While the Morgan bank began to move beyond the family-dominated model, there were important limitations.[10] Any democratization of the

Table 11 The House of Morgan American Partners, 1920–1940: Biographical Data
(Refers to the date of entry into the partnership)

Name	Family Tie to Another Partner (When Joined Firm)	Occupation of Father if Known	Religion if Known	Attended American University (Received BA or Higher Degree)	Occupation of Wife's Father if Known*
Elliot C. Bacon	Yes	Banker	Episcopalian	Yes	Banker & Senator
Junius Spencer Morgan Jr.	Yes	Banker	Episcopalian	Yes	Composer
George Whitney	Yes	Banker	Episcopalian	Yes	Banker & Secretary of State & Ambassador to France
Thomas S. Gates		President, Germantown Mutual Insurance Co.	Episcopalian	Yes	N/A/ N/A/ Lawyer
Russell C. Leffingwell		Businessman (Iron)	Episcopalian	Yes	Businessman (Iron)
Arthur M. Anderson		Bookkeeper & Clerk in bank	N/A		Educator
Francis D. Bartow		Insurance agent	Episcopalian		Businessman (Insurance)
William Ewing		Businessman (Dairy)	Episcopalian	Yes	N/A
Harold Stanley		Inventor	Episcopalian	Yes	N/A/Businessman

Name		Occupation	Religion		
Henry P. Davison Jr.	Yes	Banker	Episcopalian	Yes	Banker/N/A
Thomas Stilwell Lamont	Yes	Banker	Episcopalian	Yes	Manufacturer (Glass/Enamel)
Henry Sturgis Morgan	Yes	Banker	Episcopalian	Yes	Secretary of Navy
Edward Hopkinson Jr.		Lawyer	N/A	Yes	Railroad executive & Stock broker
Thomas Newhall		Sugar merchant & Purchasing agent, Penn RR	Episcopalian		Broker & Lawyer
S. Parker Gilbert		Coal Merchant & Politician	Episcopalian	Yes	Businessman
Charles D. Dickey		Banker	Episcopalian	Yes	Exporter
Henry C. Alexander		Feed store operator	Methodist	Yes	Engineer & Industrial executive
I. C. Raymond Atkin		Farmer	Episcopalian		Minister
William Arthur Mitchell		N/A	Presbyterian		Secretary (Auto Co.)

* Separation of different occupations with a slash refers to multiple marriages.
Source: For sources of biographical information on individual partners, see Chapter 5 endnotes.

Morgan bank had to contend with the identity and history that the partners had inherited. Every partner, including newer partners who benefited from having a more meritocratic path to partnership, was also deeply committed to perpetuating the firm's exclusive identity. If the Morgans were anxious about the increasing assimilation of previously segregated communities, their concern extended to the membership of the universities they attended, where their sons and future partners were now in attendance. Universities were spaces through which they, and by extension their firm, gained a sense of identity and social status, and universities were used as a way to indirectly vet new partners and create a basis for future cohesion. Thus, the Morgans had much at stake in the makeup and policies of those institutions.[11] For this reason, their desire to maintain and protect their networks from outsiders was strongly evident in these seemingly non-economic spaces beyond the immediate circles of their financial network.

Ties to universities posed a unique challenge, however, because unlike private clubs they had an educational mandate and national even international reputations to protect. When there were conflicts between the university's mission and the desire for exclusivity, problems could and did arise. That was the case in the early 1920s, when Jack Morgan and Thomas Lamont served on the Board of Overseers, a governing board of Harvard University. During that time, Harvard went through a public crisis over its discriminatory policies against black freshmen and Jewish applicants.[12]

The Harvard case demonstrates why the increase of prejudice against German Jews during the interwar period could not be explained by anti-German sentiment. It is also an example of new conditions the Morgans faced in the postwar. During this time, the Morgans were forced to confront a new nationalist rhetoric that challenged their exclusive tendencies, one that built on the values central to the American narrative of equal opportunity that was also heightened by the experience of the war. In response, the Morgans turned to the same networks, traditions, and ideals that formed the basis of their social capital and their elite identity in the world of finance.

CRIMSON

Jack Morgan was the first of his family to attend Harvard (Class of 1889).[13] His sons, Junius (Class of 1914) and Henry (Class of 1923), were also Harvard graduates. He was an active supporter of his alma mater as was Thomas W. Lamont (Class of 1892). Lamont was also emotionally identified with Harvard, though for slightly different reasons than Morgan. Before Lamont made his career as a partner at J. P. Morgan & Co., he was a humble minister's child growing up in the hills of New York State. His family's resources contrasted sharply with that of the "rich Presbyterians" in their Hudson Valley town. Lamont's social and economic origins were even more modest when compared to that of Morgan, who was a senior when Lamont was a freshman.[14]

Though the ministry had been the traditional position of prestige within American society, the relative standing of ministers declined as the country became more secular and the economy industrialized. Despite their lack of abundant monetary resources, however, the Lamonts were able to send Thomas's older brother, Hammond, to Phillips Exeter Academy and then to Harvard. Hammond, who became an editor of *The Nation* and died prematurely at the age of 45, was the first of the Lamont family to go to Harvard (Class of 1886). (Their father went to Union College.)[15]

Following in Hammond's footsteps, Lamont attended Exeter and then Harvard, where he began to accrue the social capital necessary to reach the apex of the financial world. Lamont worked as a tutor at Harvard, however, and he did not run in the same circles as Jack Morgan.[16] Much more than Morgan, Lamont personally understood what a Harvard education could mean for his future.[17] Phillips Exeter and Harvard represented Lamont's doorway to a world beyond the parsonage. During his lifetime, Lamont remained grateful and nurtured a strong attachment to both Exeter and Harvard, and he showed his appreciation by contributing financially and personally.[18] His three sons, Thomas S. Lamont (Class of 1921), Corliss Lamont (Class of 1924), and Austin Lamont (Class of 1927) were all Phillips Exeter and Harvard graduates.[19]

In the 1910s into the mid-1920s, Lamont and Jack Morgan served on the Board of Overseers, while their sons were students at the university. The Board of Overseers was an elected body of alumni, who counsel and advise the university on policy and teaching. Service on the board was an honor and a sign of great prestige and it brought together men from different areas of national life including finance, politics, and the arts. Other members of the board at that time included diplomat and banker William Cameron Forbes, Senator Henry Cabot Lodge, Franklin Delano Roosevelt, Governor-General of the Philippines Leonard Wood, journalist Ellery Sedgwick, Robert Bacon, and Lee, Higginson & Co. partners Jerome D. Greene and Francis Lee Higginson Jr., Henry Lee Higginson's nephew.[20]

Most of the older Morgan partners who attended Harvard, such as Robert Bacon, Jack Morgan, and Thomas Lamont, did so during the presidency of Charles W. Eliot (1834–1926; president, 1869–1909), who was a pioneer in the field of higher education and liberal arts.[21] Eliot defined a liberal education as freedom from the past and introduced the elective system to Harvard.[22] As a professor of chemistry and a scientist, Eliot was also one of the few Harvard presidents not trained in the ministry.[23] He was widely respected as an intellectual, and he cultivated a wide circle of friends and associates, including Jacob Schiff, with whom he had a friendly and respectful relationship.

Among the early generations of Kuhn, Loeb & Co. partners, university education was not common, but cases did exist. Therese Schiff's brother, James Loeb, for example, was a Harvard graduate (Class of 1888).[24] Mortimer Schiff had wanted to go to Harvard, but Jacob refused to send him, being wary of its "many temptations."[25] (Mortimer's son, John, went to Yale [Class of 1925].)[26] Three out of four of Felix and Frieda Warburg's male children, Jacob Schiff's grandchildren, however, did go to Harvard: Frederick M. Warburg, Class of 1919, who later joined Kuhn, Loeb & Co. in 1931; Gerald F. Warburg, Class of 1923; and Edward M. M. Warburg, Class of 1930.[27]

Even though Jacob Schiff refused to send Mortimer to Harvard, Eliot's views on religious tolerance particularly endeared him to Schiff. Compulsory religious worship was one of the reasons why Schiff did not send Mortimer to Groton, an Episcopalian school founded in 1884 by Rev. Endicott Peabody, whose father, Samuel, had been a partner at J. S. Morgan & Co., the House of Morgan's London branch. (Peabody's daughter married Morgan partner Henry P. Davison's son, F. Trubee.)[28] Schiff had asked Peabody to exempt Mortimer from attending Christian services, should Mortimer attend the school, and Peabody refused.[29] Given that Peabody was an Episcopal priest and founded the school to foster "manly Christian character,"[30] it would appear that Peabody's decision was a foregone conclusion, but Schiff did not believe that religion or education should be interpreted so narrowly. More importantly, he did not see that placing limits on religion was a refutation of religion. As evidence of his confidence in Eliot, whose ideas were more similar to his own, Schiff donated $250,000 to Harvard to found the Semitic Museum in 1899. He also sponsored an undergraduate essay prize "on the work and achievements of the Jewish people" by the Menorah Society, an undergraduate club at Harvard.[31]

When Eliot retired in 1909, he was succeeded by Abbot Lawrence Lowell (1856–1943; president, 1909–1933; a graduate of Harvard, Class of 1877, and Harvard Law School, Class of 1880), who was quite different in inclination and style from his predecessor.[32] Lowell was the son of a financier and the descendant of a prominent Boston Brahmin family. Trained as a lawyer, Lowell practiced for many years before becoming a professor of government at Harvard in 1897. When he became president of Harvard in 1909, one of his priorities was to reduce social class segregation at the university. In theory, Lowell's goal was to further the ideals of Harvard in keeping with the changing expectations to democratize national leadership and training. In order to accomplish his goal, Lowell instituted a policy that required all freshmen to reside in the same dormitories after 1915.[33] His plan was similar to one proposed by Woodrow Wilson at Princeton University and based on the models of Oxford and Cambridge Universities in England.[34]

Lowell's decision to require freshmen to reside in the same dormitories had one important exception, which would become the centerpiece of a larger crisis at Harvard in the early 1920s. All freshmen were required to live in the dorms except African American freshmen, who were excluded.[35] Lowell's actions instigated a flurry of criticism, and the case received a considerable amount of attention in the American press and abroad.[36] In the contemporary historical record, the segregation of black freshmen has been called "the most notorious single example of racism at Harvard."[37] Critics at the time compared Harvard's policies to the actions of German militarists and the Ku Klux Klan.[38] If Harvard had been a school for the Ku Klux Klan, its segregation policy would probably not have received much notice. The contradiction between Harvard's reputation as a place of liberal and higher education and its support of racial segregation made its policies extremely controversial.[39]

Because Harvard was so prominent a university, the segregation case attracted national and international attention. In 1922, the British Foreign Office noted in its annual report for the United States that Harvard University was continuing "to study the much-vexed question of the desirability of admitting negroes as undergraduates." The report observed "the subject has aroused heated comment in the press" and that the issue was also complicated by concurrent "allegations of anti-Semitic as well as anti-negro discrimination on the part of the university authorities."[40] The Foreign Office was referring to the fact that Lowell added further fuel to the fire in 1922 by attempting to limit the number of Jewish students accepted at Harvard.

Jewish freshmen made up 21.5 percent of Harvard's incoming class, or 150 of 658 students, that year. This was compared to 7 percent, or 36 of 511 students, in 1900.[41] Like black students, Jewish students who made it to Harvard were excluded from social, athletic, and cultural organizations. For many non-Jewish alumni, this segregation was thought to be the natural outcome of the individual freedom of students to choose their own companions and social partners, social associations and preferences that could not be dictated. Lowell argued that Jews should be excluded because they were too insular even though he also argued that they should be excluded because Harvard alumni clubs could not recruit members due to the presence of relatively large numbers of Jews.[42]

At the time, supporters of Jewish students and black students at Harvard did not link their struggles. Black segregation at Harvard was seen as becoming a controversy, "despite their small numbers . . ." in contrast to the anxiety created by large numbers of Jewish students.[43] The relatively small number of black freshmen was one reason why several key members of the Board of Overseers, including Lamont, were critical of Lowell. They believed black segregation should not have been an issue since they assumed that those African Americans who could academically merit a Harvard education would be naturally small. But they also supported a quota to exclude Jewish students, who by their academic merit could have gained admittance to Harvard if not for a policy of discrimination.[44] Theoretically, politically, and morally, the Jewish quota and black segregation together demonstrate a prevailing assumption that Harvard as an institution should be led by and populated with white, Anglo-Saxon, Protestant men, a belief that was echoed in the policies of other elite institutions like Cornell, Yale, and Princeton.[45]

As we have seen, the Morgan partners implicitly understood that they were part of a larger world from which they drew their social capital. In both the economic and social spheres and in both the private and public spheres of their world, they supported exclusive policies on the basis of ethnic, racial, and religious identity. Changes in the postwar challenged these hierarchies which, like President Lowell, they did not take well. In March 1920, Jack Morgan personally wrote Lowell that he wanted the membership of Harvard Corporation, the main governing body of the university, to be restricted to "Protestant Christians."[46] Morgan wrote Lowell, "I think I ought to say that I believe there is a strong feeling among the Overseers that the nominee should by no means be a Jew or a Roman Catholic, although, naturally, the feeling in regard to the latter is less than regard to the former. . . . The Jew is always a Jew first and an American second, and the Roman Catholic, I fear, too often a Papist first and an American second."[47]

Morgan's reference to Jews may have been influenced by the fact that the Board of Overseers (presumably also without his support) elected its first Jewish Board of Overseers member, Judge Julian Mack, in 1919.[48] With regard to the reference of the "Roman Catholic," most likely Morgan was writing about the vacancy in the Harvard Corporation created by the death of Henry Lee Higginson the year before. In April 1920, despite Morgan's protests, Harvard Corporation elected its first Roman Catholic member, James Byrne (1857–1942; Class of 1877; Harvard Law Class of 1882), a New York lawyer.[49] When these kinds of views were privately held, either personally or within Harvard's governing bodies, there was little outsiders could do, partly because they had no direct knowledge of the internal events of private institutions. The problem arose when the issues became more publicly known because of the way these beliefs contradicted other traditions that were identified as central to the memory and identity of the university by many of its alumni and by a wider public.

SEGREGATION AT HARVARD

In 1921, Professor Albert Bushnell Hart, a professor of history and government at Harvard, and Harvard alumni from *The Nation* began to write letters to President Lowell questioning "the freshman dormitory color bar and the possibility of total exclusion of black men from Harvard College."[50]

Hart came from an antislavery family and had a history of championing the
rights of African Americans. He was a trustee of Howard University, which
was founded in 1867 to train black clergymen and teachers.[51] Hart was
similar to another Harvard alum who was deeply critical of Lowell's policies, Moorfield Storey (Class of 1866, Harvard Law Class of 1869). Storey
was a highly respected Boston lawyer and a former member of the Board of
Overseers. He started his career as the private secretary to Charles Sumner
(Class of 1830), the antislavery and abolitionist Republican senator.[52] Like
Hart, Storey had a history of working for civil rights for African Americans.
He was the first president of the National Association for the Advancement
of Colored People (NAACP), which was established in 1909.[53]

The NAACP's members had ties to other progressive organizations,
whose members were involved with the Harvard segregation case, including
the *Nation,* which became another cluster in the network of anti-Lowell
alumni.[54] At the time of the Harvard crisis, the *Nation* was owned by
Oswald Garrison Villard, the grandson of famed abolitionist, William
Lloyd Garrison, the publisher of the antislavery newspaper, the *Liberator.*
Villard was also one of the NAACP's founders.[55] Both the NAACP staff
and the *Nation* staff would play an important role in putting the pressure on
Lowell and organizing alumni against his segregation policy.

In 1922, Moorfield Storey and William Channing Gannett, the Unitarian Minister and abolitionist, organized a petition or "Memorial" to
send to Lowell and Harvard Corporation protesting the exclusion and treatment of African American students.[56] Gannett's son, Lewis S. Gannett,[57]
was an associate editor at the *Nation.* He and other editors, such as Ernest
Gruening,[58] worked on the petition. It was eventually signed by 143 alumni
and included a range of graduates from the Class of 1850 to the Class of
1920.[59] They included: Edward Waldo Emerson (Class of 1866), the son of
Ralph Waldo Emerson, and Rev. Francis G. Peabody (Class of 1869), who
was also Charles Eliot's brother-in-law and the son of Rev. Ephraim Peabody (the Unitarian minister; no direct relation to Groton's Rev. Endicott
Peabody).[60]

Writing to the petitioners, supportive Harvard alumni voiced a number
of consistent themes.[61] They included the history of New England or Massachusetts with regard to the Civil War, their own personal experiences and
personal family history with regard to African Americans, the reputation of

Harvard as an institution of higher learning, Harvard's reputation as a liberal American institution, and the general appeal to both progressive and nationalist sentiment. The persistent mention of New England and the Civil War demonstrated how important the memory of the Civil War was to the self-representation of Harvard, which was reflected in the antislavery background of many of the most ardent protesters. As with the war and the fight against slavery, the struggle against segregation and discrimination at Harvard could not avoid the moral question, what the graduates called "justice."[62]

Until 1923, much of this conversation took place within Harvard communities. Then, in January 1923, Lowell personally rejected the request of Roscoe Conkling Bruce (Class of 1902) to place his son Roscoe Conkling Bruce Jr. in the freshman dormitory.[63] The son of Blanche K. Bruce, the first black United States Senator (Mississippi), Bruce had a distinguished career at Harvard.[64] He was elected to Phi Beta Kappa, was class orator, and graduated magna cum laude. He went on to be the head of the academic department of the Tuskegee Institute and then had a long tenure as superintendent of schools for African Americans in Washington.[65]

Lowell wrote Bruce, ". . . 'In the Freshman Halls, where residence is compulsory, we have felt from the beginning the necessity of not including colored men. . . . .I am sure you will understand why, from the beginning, we have not thought it possible to compel men of different races to reside together.' "[66] After Bruce received Lowell's negative reply, he wrote Lowell:

> I have lived and labored in the South so long since my graduation from Harvard College over twenty years ago, that despite the newspapers, I had fondly cherished the illusion that, step by step with the unquestionable growth of liberal sentiment in the Southern States as a whole, New England was enriching rather than impoverishing her heritage. The policy of compulsory residence in the Freshman Halls is costly indeed if it is the thing that constrains Harvard to enter open-eyed and brusque upon a policy of racial discrimination. . . . [67]

W. E. B. Du Bois, the editor of the NAACP's the *Crisis,* would later write, "Imagine, my masters, six decades after emancipation, a slave's grandson [Bruce] teaching the ABC of democracy to the Puritan head of Harvard!"[68]

Bruce took Lowell's letter to the press, making the case public for the first time. A torrent of negative press began against Harvard. Newspapers carried the issue on the front page.[69] Lambasting Harvard for duplicity, the *Boston Herald* editorialized on January 15, 1923: "Once more Harvard learns the disadvantage of a reputation for equality of right higher than she really wishes to maintain. . . . Why not face this question honestly and squarely, and either keep all negroes out of Harvard, admitting we have discarded our principles and have drawn the color lines, or allow them to come and, at least officially, treat them without discrimination."[70] The media also connected Harvard's case to German militarism and lynching. Other letters to newspapers referenced the Ku Klux Klan.[71]

Numerous and passionate, Lowell's critics had the moral high ground, but significantly, they were not organized as a cohesive network. Though members of different progressive organizations and publications, such as the *Nation* and the NAACP, overlapped in terms of personnel and ideological commonalities, structurally and institutionally, they acted as largely separate organizations. More importantly, the Harvard alumni attached to these organizations did not have key support on the governing bodies of the university even though several members of the Board of Overseers were not happy with Lowell. Franklin Delano Roosevelt, who was an Overseer at the time, wrote to colleague R. S. Wallace, " 'It seems a pity that the matter ever came up in this way. There were certainly many colored students in Cambridge when we were there and no question ever arose.' "[72] Roosevelt may have been critical of Lowell, but the board as a whole was not eager to challenge Lowell directly. One exception was Julian Mack, the first Jewish person to serve on the board in Harvard's history.

Julian W. Mack was a judge in the United States Circuit Court in New York. He was also "past president of the first American Jewish Congress (1918–19)" and "former head of the Zionist Organization of America."[73] Like Jacob Schiff, Mack was not only Jewish, he identified his interests as a Jew and he was friends with many prominent Jews of similar mindset and inclination. He had a close ideological ally in the form of Felix Frankfurter, the Harvard Law professor, whom Lowell disliked immensely.

In June 1922, former Harvard president Charles W. Eliot wrote to Jerome D. Greene (1874–1959; Class of 1896), another Board of Overseers member, about a meeting he had with Frankfurter and Mack at his home. Eliot said that Mack believed that the Board of Overseers sympathized with his views regarding the treatment and exclusion of Jews. Eliot wanted to know if Greene felt the same. Greene wrote Eliot that members of the Board of Overseers had racial antagonisms but that they understood after Judge Mack had made statements to the board, "the great seriousness and delicacy of adopting any course which the Jews would have a right to complain of on grounds of racial or religious discrimination."[74] As a dissenting Board of Overseers member, Greene, like Mack, was also an exception on the board, but for different reasons. He represented many Harvard alumni who believed that President Lowell's policies damaged Harvard's reputation and went against Harvard's creed.

Jerome D. Greene was a partner of Lee, Higginson & Co., the Boston Brahmin merchant house founded in 1848,[75] whose namesake George Cabot Lee was the father-in-law to Theodore Roosevelt. Lee, Higginson's senior partner before the war, Henry Lee Higginson, was close friends with Pierpont Morgan.[76] Lee, Higginson & Co. was not as strong a banking house as the Morgans, but it was considered a prestigious, old-stock Anglo-American house, and it did a considerable amount of business with the Morgans. Though it was largely a regional (Boston) firm, Lee, Higginson opened a New York office in 1906 where Greene was based.[77]

Morgan partner Thomas Lamont and Greene were acquaintances, not close friends, but they had certain similarities. Like Lamont, Greene was the son of a clergyman though he had much more experience abroad. Greene's parents, Rev. Daniel Crosby Greene and Mary Jane Forbes Greene, were Christian missionaries in Japan under the auspices of the American Board of Commissioners for Foreign Missions of the Congregational Church. Greene was born in Japan and lived there until he was thirteen years old. He moved to the United States to attend high school, after which he entered Harvard.[78] Though their father went to Dartmouth, Greene's brothers, Evarts (who became a professor of history at Columbia University) and Roger (who joined the U.S. diplomatic corps), were also Harvard graduates.[79] Like Lamont and Jack Morgan, Greene had a son, Jerome Crosby Greene, who was also a student at Harvard at the time of the controversy.[80]

Like Lamont, Greene also began his career outside of business and then eventually became an investment banker. Greene's earliest positions were actually with Harvard. Having served as Charles W. Eliot's secretary, Greene's strong personal and professional ties to Harvard and to Eliot explain in part why he was so disturbed by Lowell's actions. In 1910, he entered the world of philanthropy and administration, a relatively new field, when he joined the Rockefeller Institute and the Rockefeller Foundation. Greene and Lamont had a lot of social and professional interests in common given their positions in investment banking, including relationships to organizations involved in U.S.-Japan relations.[81]

Greene had written to Lamont to ask if he would support a special meeting of the board. He wrote, "This is the second time this year that [Lowell] has in the eyes of the public committed the University to a definite position on a matter of policy gravely affecting the responsibility of the Governing Boards."[82] Greene's views on segregation were specific to Harvard's reputation and to the rules and procedures of the university. He believed that Lowell had exceeded his institutional authority at the expense of the board.[83] Greene also believed, unlike Lowell, that negative publicity had already begun to affect the university and could not be avoided.[84]

Lamont had been well aware of the antisegregation petition that had been circulating among the alumni, but he did not become engaged until after the issue went public some months later. He was also aware of the controversy regarding Jewish applicants and had correspondence directly with Lowell about the subject. In September 1922, Lowell had written Lamont saying that there was no important business for the Board of Overseers meetings "unless Judge Mack starts a discussion on the question of the Jews."[85] His correspondence with Greene on the Harvard case is particularly interesting because it offers a rare view of what he thought about the segregation crisis.

Though Lamont had definite views on Jews, he took little to no interest in issues pertaining to African Americans. References to persons of African descent are infrequent and scattered throughout correspondence in his vast archive, unlike, for example, the views of Morgan staff member Martin Egan, who worked closely with Lamont and whose private correspondence with friends inside and outside the firm contains significant examples of derogatory language with regard to persons of African (and Asian) descent.[86] Lamont's references to persons of African descent are far from frequent, but those that remain suggest that he did not disagree with Egan's views.

In 1927, Lamont went to Haiti, and he took the time to characterize the people by their color, even in limited diary entries, comparing "dingy little town of darkies" with "friendly and light colored natives."[87] In 1942, he was asked to comment on a special issue of the magazine *Survey Graphic,* titled *Color: Unfinished Business of Democracy: the New World, Negroes U.S.A., the Old World,* and he wrote Morgan staff member Vernon Munroe, "Do you want to glance through this copy of the Survey Graphic, which I used to support rather liberally, and tell me whether all this darkey business is justi-fied, or whether Paul Kellogg [the editor of *Survey Graphic*] has gone off the deep end on it?"[88]

The fact that Lamont used the word "darkey" to describe a series of doc-uments and articles on equality between the races indicates that he did not believe in racial equality or social integration.[89] Though both references post-date the Harvard case, it is not unreasonable to assume that he held similar views during his lifetime, particularly given that he made the latter comment during the Second World War when the Nazis had made overt racism extremely unpopular, if not a completely untenable. That Lamont did not use this language as a Board of Overseers member to address the issue of black segregation suggests he already understood this to be the case in the early 1920s. His strategy offers further evidence that he understood maintaining his reputation, and by extension that of the Morgan firm, required a specific kind of discourse in the postwar.

When Greene wrote to Lamont to ask him about his views of Lowell's actions, Lamont's response consisted of two main points. He believed that the principle of equality had to be upheld when things were made public. However, he did not agree that there should be or would have been a problem due to the small numbers of black students at Harvard. He wrote Greene that he thought "the whole episode as most unfortunate," but he did not support the special board meeting. He suggested that they take no action and wait for newspaper talk to die out. He agreed with Greene that Lowell had overstepped his boundaries writing, "Now that the question has been raised, it must of course come before the governing boards for their consid-eration, and unless I receive far more light than I have at present, I should certainly vote against any formal discrimination in the freshman dormito-ries against negroes."

But Lamont's primary concern was that "question that need never have come up at all, and I am vexed that it should have come up." He wrote Greene:

It would appear that out of the seven or eight hundred freshman entering college each year, two or three hundred must room outside the freshman dormitories. It would appear to me, therefore, quite natural that generally the one or two negroes that are in every freshman class would find themselves in the outside crowd, which would mean no discrimination directed against the negro personally and the adoption of no principle discriminating against him.

Lamont denied that this was a "camouflage," saying that it was not his intention. He wrote, "If the matter ever came down to one principle, I think that we would have to take a stand."[90] Lamont thus appreciated the way in which the principle of equality had to be upheld, but he also felt that it did not have to actually be practiced; given the assumption that the numbers of black freshmen would remain minimal, social segregation could be practiced informally and individually without the university having to make a formal statement. The entire episode could be avoided by giving black freshmen reasons other than their race, such as the lack of space, thereby achieving the same result without the unpleasant controversy.

The position of African American students and alumni at Harvard as part of the "outside crowd," to use Lamont's words, demonstrates what was really at stake during the segregation controversy. It also shows why it is important to analyze the Morgan network broadly and to look beyond the Morgans' closest circles. Without a consideration of the larger networks at play, we cannot understand the limits of a policy of equal opportunity based on the principle of *individual* merit. In other words, equal opportunity was not just about individuals, it was also about communities and networks.

Like Lowell's other critics, Harvard's African American alumni were not an entirely cohesive group, institutionally or individually. Among them, they had many personal differences.[91] Given the fact, however, that the African American community was entirely united in their opposition to the substance and the method of Harvard's segregation policy, what was more significant with regard to African American alumni was their lack of representation on the Board of Overseers and the lack of close ties to board members and influential alumni. These included lack of ties to alumni who were critical of Lowell's plans like Greene, who wrote Charles Eliot that he did not want to associate with Moorefield Storey or the NAACP, "the negrophile group with which Mr. Storey is associated."[92]

The social distance between African American alumni and the decision-making alumni of the university was a structural issue, one that was the result of racial segregation during and after Harvard. In their own experience, African American alumni knew that it was not enough to have the opportunity to attend Harvard. The benefit of a Harvard education was measured by the potential it held for an individual in his life after the university, one that could tie him to social and economic networks beyond what he might have inherited personally. Thus, the greatest benefit of a Harvard education would accrue to those who had complete access to the social benefits of Harvard education, without which "the most complete opportunity for education," of which Lowell spoke, was not attainable. This was what the segregation case at Harvard meant, and W. E. B. Du Bois offers an instructive example.

THE IMPORTANCE OF SOCIAL TIES

As the first African American Ph.D. graduate from Harvard and the editor of the *Crisis,* William Edward Burghardt Du Bois (1868–1963; AB 1890; AM 1891; PhD 1895) had a national reputation as a leading intellectual voice on American race relations. Born in Massachusetts, Du Bois distinguished himself academically at a young age. He attended Fisk University, graduating in 1888, and then entered Harvard as a junior. After completing his undergraduate and master's degree at Harvard, Du Bois spent two years at the University of Berlin and returned to Harvard to complete his doctorate. His thesis was on the African slave trade in America. Du Bois taught at various universities, eventually settling at Atlanta University before he joined the staff of the NAACP in 1909–1910. By the time of the Harvard segregation crisis, Du Bois had authored several books, including *Souls of Black Folk* (1903), his study on African Americans in American society and on race in America, where he famously declared ". . . the problem of the Twentieth Century is the problem of the color line."[93]

Despite Du Bois's prominence as a Harvard alumnus and as an African American scholar and intellectual, his name was not on the original petition organized by Storey and others.[94] In fact, the petitioners' initial letter to Du Bois was originally misdirected to a Dr. Eugene F. Du Bois (Class of 1903), an alum who was in favor of the exclusion. In the initial letter, Du Bois was not asked to sign but to make suggestions on three enclosed letters to Lowell; to general graduates; and to Norwood Penrose Hallowell (Class of 1897), a Board of Overseers member, who was also a partner in Lee, Higginson & Co. and whose father had served as a colonel in the Massachusetts 54th Regiment during the Civil War. The fact that several of the original peti-tioners did not initially know Du Bois's first name or his graduation year is significant. It explains in part the way in which the university would even-tually "resolve" the issue through rhetorical proclamations of equality and tolerance.[95]

Du Bois's distance from the center of decision-making power in the case is an indication that the personal views and concerns of African American alumni were not central to the outcomes or discussions of the segregation case at Harvard. That Du Bois had merited admittance to Harvard was not in question. What was at stake was the extent to which he had the same opportunities to which Greene referred. Du Bois's relationship to other non-African American alumni involved in the segregation case was one defined by marginalization, which started when he was a student at Harvard, an experience he himself described as being "in Harvard but not of it."[96] His interaction with other classmates at Harvard was confined to the classroom, which he described as "merely civil in the lecture hall."[97] In other words, Du Bois was clearly in the "outside crowd," to use Lamont's term.

Du Bois actually attended Harvard at the same time as Lamont (AB 1892), and they took one class together in 1890–1891: "English 12–Composition."[98] Members of Lamont's social circle, such as Jeremiah Smith Jr. (Class of 1892; Harvard Law 1895),[99] a diplomat and lawyer who had been Lamont's classmate at Exeter, and Norman Hapgood (Class of 1890; Harvard Law 1893),[100] who wrote on the *Crimson* with Lamont, also took some of the same courses with Du Bois while students at Harvard.[101] Du Bois must have stood out in class. He was one of the very few African American students, who had been admitted to Harvard by that time.[102]

Whether or not they noticed Du Bois, there is no indication that Lamont or other men in his social circle interacted with him during or after their time at school.[103] The common educational link was not enough to create a tie, affective or otherwise. Harvard's education afforded different kinds of benefits depending on the ties and connections one could make, ties that were not determined by individual freedom, even though they appeared to be the result of individual choice. It is understandable, therefore, why

Lamont believed a formal policy of segregation was unnecessary. The same results could have been carried out by the informal practices of administrators and students as was done during his time at Harvard.

This context explains in part why Du Bois was not able to take a leadership role in the university's decision-making process on the issue of segregation.[104] Without an institutional presence and with limited ties to white alumni, Du Bois, like other African American alumni, had to rely on the leadership of others to make the case on behalf of African Americans.[105] Though the petitioners considered the possibility in early February 1923 of nominating Roscoe Bruce to the Board of Overseers, even Storey did not think it was a good idea.[106] While Storey believed that "in the near future the colored people should have a representative on the board," he thought it would only increase a negative response.[107] Du Bois wrote, "I suppose that we are practically compelled to follow Mr. Storey's advice since we should sorely need his support in any such movement."[108] Ultimately, the Board of Overseers did not have a member of African American descent until 1959, and Harvard Corporation did not until 2001.[109]

As Greene predicted, however, the issue did not go away until a decision was made by the governing bodies of the university. By the spring of 1923, the university community and the public attention moved the board closer to having a vote on Lowell's policies. The Committee on Methods of Sifting Candidates for Admission concluded its investigation, and in its final report, recommended ". . . that in the administration of rules for admission Harvard College maintain its traditional policy of freedom from discrimination on grounds of race or religion."[110] The faculty voted to adopt the report. The outcome of the segregation case was very similar.

In March 1923, Harvard Corporation voted to undo the segregation policy of the freshman dormitories. In April 1923, the Board of Overseers voted unanimously to "comply with the faculty committee's report recommending the abandonment of Harvard's exclusionary policies."[111] The board's executive committee, which included Lamont, submitted a report to the board that stated: "The following acts of the Board are deserving of note. . . . Votes that the rules as to residence in the Freshman Dormitories and admission to the College be applied without discrimination on grounds of race or religion. . . ."[112] The same year, Jack Morgan received an honorary degree from Harvard.

PRIVATE ASSOCIATIONS AND INEQUALITY

While the conclusion of the segregation case appeared to be a success for the petitioners and for African American and Jewish students, the reality was much more complicated. The *Harvard Crimson* reported that in addition to the fact that the board voted "negroes will not be excluded from the Freshman Halls by reason of their color," the board also voted "that men of the white and colored races not be compelled to live and eat in the same dormitory if they object to members of the other race."[113] In other words, the board did not uphold the ideal of racial equality as much as it upheld the right of the individual, including the right of the individual to discriminate on the basis of assumed racial inferiority. By the right of individual freedom, they meant that black students would be free to apply to live in the dorm (without any guarantee of being granted a space) and white students would be free to choose to discriminate against them.

As in business and society, the justification for maintaining inequalities based on racial differences at Harvard was the right of private association. In effect, the position of the university was to not interfere in private behavior, which remained distinct from the public or institutional policies of the college. The same structure of private versus public associations and the right to private property that was so important to the outcome of the Money Trust Investigation also enabled the continuation of the status quo at Harvard. The significance is clear. Institutions like Harvard, which practiced segregation but did not want to admit to doing so overtly, offered implicit support for the structure of separate spheres that was so important to elite bankers like the Morgans and in ways were also tied to the individual's ability to practice his right to private association. The outcome of the Harvard case demonstrated the limits of making community through ideology or publicity alone. Unless the issue of social segregation was directly addressed, African American and Jewish American alumni would continue to find themselves separate and unequal. Without changing the structure of social networks, ideological rhetoric served to hide or evade discriminatory policies and intentions and to maintain pre-existing hierarchies.

Despite pronouncements of Harvard's commitment to equality, the institutionalization of discrimination at Harvard was not deterred. With regard to Jewish applicants, in January 1926, the Board of Overseers amended admission standards that could be selectively used to exclude Jews without naming them, such as requiring photo identification, a practice that often led to excluding non-Jews.[114] Starting in 1930, Lowell's administration also began a quota system against Jews, which reduced their enrollment to about 10 to 15 percent of the incoming class from 25 to 27 percent.[115] The fear that the expectation of merit would not be enough to keep Harvard's student body white and Protestant was addressed through methods and standards seemingly unrelated to race, which made them that much more difficult to identify and publicly criticize.[116]

The policies at Harvard, including the informal policies of the university's social clubs and the like, did not change much until after the Second World War and then much later in the twentieth century.[117] Between 1890 and 1940, only about 160 African American students matriculated from Harvard College.[118] African American students at Harvard numbered about five or six per year until the 1960s.[119] Ultimately, the Harvard case demonstrates that the actualization of democratic principles, such as individual merit and equal opportunity, was greatly limited by the structure of existing networks inherited from the pre-World War I period and by the ways in which rights and opportunities were seen as the property of individuals. These exclusive policies were not limited to Harvard and also applied to elite schools such as Princeton and Yale.[120] As Jerome Greene told Abby Rockefeller (Mrs. John D. Rockefeller Jr.), albeit in an effort to show that Harvard was not unique, "No negro can get into Princeton and no negro can live in a Yale dormitory or play on a Yale team."[121]

Lamont remained on the Board of Overseers until 1925, and he continued to be an active and prominent alumnus. He was deeply committed to Harvard, an institution that had been his entrée to his position in society. He also remained committed to keeping Harvard closed to those whose association and proximity threatened his social capital. But the fact that he could not do so openly was a testament to the changes in the conditions and expectations of his world. Lamont also knew that the controversy over social equality was not confined to Harvard. As we shall see, the same structure of separate spheres had a particular significance in the area of foreign and diplomatic policy and affected the Morgans' work as international bankers. That is because the Morgans' relationship with the empire of Japan, an important client, gave the issue of racial equality greater urgency and made it a diplomatic concern during the interwar period.

## CHAPTER SIX

Complex International Alliances: Japan

AS HIS ROLE in the Harvard segregation case demonstrated, Thomas Lamont was adept at dealing with unpleasant contradictions. In the 1920s, during the same time as the Harvard case, his skills were also put to the test on the international stage as the Morgan firm became more deeply involved in American foreign policy interests in the aftermath of the First World War. Lamont was not only exceptionally well suited for the postwar world, he embraced his role as the bank's most public face. More than a journalist or a banker, Lamont was truly a "diplomat" at heart. When he died in 1948, the *New York Times* reported, "Associates remember Mr. Lamont best as a man with a gift for friendship."[1]

Lamont's prominent position as the public face of the Morgan firm was made possible by two interrelated factors. The first was the character and style of his senior partner. Jack Morgan considered his participation in the politics of international finance an enormous burden, a necessary responsibility that he would not shirk but did not relish.[2] While Morgan remained the undisputed senior partner during his lifetime, his experience during and after the First World War further deepened his sense of isolation from the outside world, which was compounded by the death of his mother in

1924 and his wife in 1925. By nature shy and aloof, Morgan remained a private person known intimately only by his children, partners, and close circle of friends and family, shunning publicity and social interaction with outsiders.

Morgan's personal style accelerated changes in the organization and makeup of the firm in the postwar period. As the firm embraced a broader definition of belonging, partners did not have to be of the manor born but could assume the mantle of Morgan through identification with elite institutions. In effect there was a greater opportunity for men of a different class to become partners as long as the criteria for partners remained exclusive along the lines of religion, race, and gender. This newfound democratic spirit also had other important limitations. Despite the fact that Lamont's percentage ownership of the partnership was second only to Jack Morgan, he was not the heir to the throne, so to speak, which was Morgan's place as the namesake of the firm. He was the "ambassador," or Morgan's representative, a sign of the firm's transition to a more managerial model.[3]

Though Lamont celebrated his humble beginnings, he was deeply ambitious and coveted a greater role for himself in national and international affairs. His first autobiography was titled *My Boyhood in a Parsonage* (1946), but his second (posthumous) autobiography was titled *Across World Frontiers* (1951).[4] If Lamont embraced his role as Morgan's ambassador, it was not only because he respected and cared for his senior partner. It was also because he believed his position in the firm and his relationship to the Morgan name could provide him and his heirs an entrée to a world of power and importance far beyond that of the parsonage, and unlike Morgan, he welcomed all its possibilities. In this regard, he was similar to other members of the Morgan bank, whether staff members like Martin Egan, who had unfulfilled aspirations to become the governor general of the Philippines, or partners like Dwight Morrow, who left the firm in 1927 to become the American ambassador to Mexico.[5]

America's place in the changing international context enabled men like Lamont to imagine a role far beyond the borders of the United States. His international work on behalf of the bank involved him in negotiations with many different countries from Germany to Mexico to China. During the 1920s, Lamont also became the Morgan bank's primary representative with Japan, a relationship that gave him enormous personal prestige and conferred upon him "expert" status on Far Eastern affairs.[6] Lamont respected Japan as a serious political and economic player, and he was enamored with the esteem afforded by being an international diplomat of sorts. His "expert" status on Asia is particularly interesting, however, given that Lamont had very limited experience with Asian affairs and even less contact with Asian people. Like Jews and African Americans, Lamont saw Japanese as inherently different and foreign. He and his partners frequently used the term "Japs" in private correspondence, which was not something they did in the presence of Japanese.[7]

The issues related to German Jewish bankers, whom the Morgans supplanted as Japan's primary banker, are echoed in the narrative of the Morgans' ties with Japan, but they also speak to the ways in which private banking at the Morgan firm were changing in the postwar period. Their relationship with Japan, in particular, demonstrates how the conditions under which the Morgans pursued their work were affected by America's rise to world power and the rise of state power. They also resonate with the issues raised by the Harvard case, such as the need to publicly acknowledge the pressure for national unity and also to claim the moral high ground as leaders in an international context and in the area of race relations.

As the leading international bankers of the world's leading power and with Japan as their client, the Morgans could not openly espouse racial discrimination and segregation even though they were deeply committed to those structures in their own communities. How they managed this conflict was an important statement about how much the conditions of their business had changed as national and international circumstances shifted the balance of power.

UNSEATING KUHN, LOEB

As an international bank, the Morgan firm's client base had always been diverse, but before the First World War, the scope of its business with Japan was limited by the strong and proprietary relationship that Kuhn, Loeb & Co. had as Japan's American banker. In 1904 alone, Kuhn, Loeb & Co.'s sales for the Japanese government amounted to £11,000,000 or approximately $53,460,000.[8] In total, Kuhn, Loeb & Co. made five loans for Japan during the Russo-Japanese War, of which "the American share of the five loans combined amounted to over $196 million, a sum that was said to set a record for large-volume financing before World War I."[9]

Jacob Schiff had such close ties with Baron Korekiyo Takahashi (1854–1936),[10] the vice-governor of the Bank of Japan and later the Japanese minister of finance and premier, that Takahashi's fifteen-year-old daughter, Wakiko, lived with Schiff and his wife in New York for three years (1906–1909).[11] Takahashi met Schiff at a dinner in London in 1904 after he had been sent abroad as Japan's financial commissioner. He spent the better part of three years in Europe and the United States in order to raise money for the Japanese war effort. His life-long friendship with Schiff started as a union of common interests against Russia.[12]

Takahashi had initially hoped to enlist Pierpont Morgan to Japan's cause, but he found Morgan to be unfriendly and rude.[13] Pierpont's seeming disregard for and disinterest in Japan's business left open the field for his rival. While in New York in 1905, Takahashi told his associate Kentaro Kaneko, the brother-in-law of Takuma Dan, a financier and representative of the Mitsui industrial conglomerate, "Kuhn, Loeb is strong enough to prevent any mischief that might come from Morgan."[14] In 1906, after the Russo-Japanese War, Schiff was invited by the Japanese government to visit Japan, where he met central financial and political leaders, including the Japanese emperor, who "presented [him] with the Order of the Rising Sun." It was at the conclusion of that trip that Wakiko accompanied Schiff, whom she later referred to as "Uncle," and his wife, Therese, to New York to live and study in the United States.[15] After she returned to Japan, Wakiko stayed in touch with the Schiffs and she eventually moved to London with her husband, Toshikata Ōkubo, a member of the Yokohama Specie Bank and the son of Toshimichi Ōkubo, a Japanese statesman, who was one of the founders of modern Japan.[16]

As long as Kuhn, Loeb & Co. retained their proprietary right as Japan's bank, J. P. Morgan & Co. could not poach Kuhn, Loeb's client without violating their informal code of conduct.[17] Kuhn, Loeb & Co.'s break with Japan over its alliance with Russia and Jacob Schiff's death in 1920 offered the Morgans the opportunity to begin anew with Japan, now the dominant power in East Asia.[18] By the early 1920s, the Morgans made critical steps toward replacing Kuhn, Loeb & Co. as Japan's leading foreign bank, which also served as an example of how the German Jewish bank had lost some of its prestige during the First World War. In effect, the Morgans were able to leverage not only their position as the Allies' banker, they were also able to leverage their social status as Anglo-American elite bankers in order to supplant Kuhn, Loeb's proprietary rights.

PHOTO 16 Viscount Korekiyo Takahashi, date and place unknown (Library of Congress, Prints & Photographs Division, [reproduction number LC-DIG-ggbain-34576])

Morgan's first major offering ($150 million) for Japan took place in 1924 after the Great Tokyo Earthquake of 1923.[19] Kuhn, Loeb was invited to participate on the loan as a syndicate manager along with National City and First National Bank to "soothe ruffled feelings," but Lamont told Teddy Grenfell that he had suggested to the Japanese that they inform Kuhn, Loeb & Co. that they had chosen the Morgans to take on the loan in order to secure "co-operation throughout the entire American investment public." The implication, of course, was that Kuhn, Loeb & Co. could not.[20] On all of the Japanese syndicates, which included loans to the cities of Yokohama and Tokyo, Kuhn, Loeb & Co. remained a co-manager, listed before National City Bank and First National Bank, but always second to J. P. Morgan & Co. Between 1924 and 1931, J. P. Morgan & Co. "floated bond issues totaling $263 million for Japanese borrowers . . . the largest amount for any country outside Europe."[21]

By depriving Kuhn, Loeb of its special status with Japan, the Morgans, led by Lamont, added immeasurably to their reputation, but the new alliance also brought them into an unfamiliar territory. Unlike Schiff, who had allied with Japan to defeat Russia during the Russo-Japanese War because of the anti-Semitic policies of the Russian Tsar, the Morgans did not have an ideological basis for comprehending the particular interests of its client with regard to race politics. If anything, their personal commitment to racial and social exclusivity worked against their understanding the interests of their client. Through their relationship with Japan, they learned quickly that their international ties required as much fluency in progressive racial rhetoric as did domestic relations in the postwar period. The Morgans had to modify their views if they wanted to do business with Japan because the priorities of their client extended far beyond the profit motive.

JAPAN AND RACIAL EQUALITY

Japan's need for capital stemmed from a long history of nation-building. Before 1868, Japan was a preindustrial country and subordinated to the United States and Western European powers in a manner to which China, its primary competitor in East Asia, had also been subjected.[22] Starting in the late nineteenth century, Japan sought to establish its own empire in East Asia, which it saw as the only way of undoing unequal treaties with the other powers.[23] Japan's expansion was pursued and justified in the context of American and European imperialism. Its rationale was that Japan had to secure the East Asian region to protect the area from western imperialists.

In 1904, Japan went to war with Russia over territory in Manchuria and Korea. The outcome of the Russo-Japanese War, which was widely seen as a race war between a white and non-white nation, shocked the world. Japan's defeat of Russia made it the world's only non-white imperial nation. Following the war, the other imperial powers, including the United States, agreed to recognize Japan's claims to Korea. In 1905, Korea was made a protectorate of Japan. In 1910, it was formally annexed as a Japanese colony. That same year, Japan gained tariff autonomy from the imperial powers.[24]

After the Russo-Japanese War, the American government became sensitive to the way in which anti-Asian discrimination in the United States strained U.S.-Japanese relations. Since the late nineteenth-century, Japan had been unhappy with American discriminatory policies based on race, particularly with regard to immigration. In 1907, President Theodore Roosevelt and Elihu Root, his secretary of state, also convinced the San Francisco Board of Education that it would not be in the national interest to segregate Japanese

American children in public schools.[25] The same year, Roosevelt reached an important informal agreement with Japan where the United States agreed not to pass exclusionary legislation barring the immigration of Japanese to the United States and the Japanese government agreed to restrict emigration to the United States. This pact became known as "the Gentleman's Agreement."[26]

As is becoming more and more apparent, the definition of "gentlemen" appears to have meant the observance of separate spheres of influence. As was the case with the social and economic spheres of private bankers, however, the divisions between the separate spheres of influence in the national and international spheres were also subject to change and could be disturbed. Despite Roosevelt's efforts, which the Japanese government watched closely, the executive branch of the American government was not successful in stemming anti-Asian legislation and agitation in the United States at the local and state levels.[27] In the post-World War I period, Japan's unhappiness grew as nativist groups in the United States rallied the legislative bodies against Asian immigration using the term "aliens ineligible for citizenship," which was essentially a code for persons of Asian descent.[28]

After the First World War, Japan felt it was in a stronger position to negotiate for its interests, having sided with the Allies early on in the war.[29] During the Paris Peace conference, the Japanese delegation led by Baron Nobuaki Makino and Sutemi Chinda, the Japanese ambassador to London, twice attempted to pass an amendment to be included in the League of Nations covenant on the issue of racial equality.[30] At the conference, Makino stated that Japan could not join the League of Nations if it was not an equal party with the other nations. He stated, "No Asiatic nation could be happy in the League of Nations in which sharp racial discrimination is maintained."[31]

By bringing up the issue of the existence of racial discrimination, Japan had created a difficult situation. The French delegation representative Léon Bourgeois called the racial equality clause an "indispensable principle of justice." Prime Minister Vittorio Orlando of Italy argued that the issue should not have been raised at all but that it had to be supported because it had been made public.[32] Postwar era nationalism could not openly advocate racial discrimination even if it was widely practiced. Ultimately, though the racial equality clause was passed by a majority of league representatives, it was not included in the covenant. President Wilson, who was not a progressive on race issues, wanted to shelve the issue and was able to defeat the proposal by requiring the ruling to be unanimous.[33]

Though the Japanese were unsuccessful in their immediate goal, they managed to place the issue of racial equality on an international stage. They used this pulpit to critique American and European imperialism in Asia and racial discrimination in the United States and the British colonies. In a reversal of roles, Japan appeared to capture the moral high ground and gained many allies by presenting itself as the champion of the colored races.[34] W. E. B. Du Bois, for example, became an ardent "apologist for Japan."[35] African American views of Japan were not completely supportive, however. Prominent African American critics included A. Philip Randolph and Adam Clayton Powell Sr., who argued that Japan, like the other imperial nations, was capitalist and working together at the expense of nations like India, China, and Egypt.[36]

THE 1924 IMMIGRATION ACT

Japan's push for an international racial equality clause, while clearly self-serving, is an important example of how the conditions under which the Morgans pursued their work had changed in the aftermath of the First World War and how the bank was pushed to become more public-facing and acknowledge outside interests. The fact that the new conditions dealt with the issue of race was also very unusual for the Morgans, but these concerns had to be addressed if they were to maintain good relations with their client. It also meant some compromise and skill given the Morgans' own views on racial inequality.

Japan's push for a racial equality clause was the context in which the showdown over the United States's 1924 Immigration Act took place. American opposition centered on arguments that Japan's proposal was purely strategic. Opponents argued that Japan's clause was an attack on American sovereignty. "Racial equality," they argued, meant "the right to immigrate," and thus was contrary to the right of a nation-state to determine its own immigration laws.[37] Coming five years after the failure of the racial equality clause at the Paris Peace Conference, and after numerous other incidents like the passage of the Alien Land Law, the proposal for an exclusionary immigration act deliberately aimed at Japanese became a serious domestic and foreign policy issue.[38] The fact that American immigration policies were an enormously contentious issue between the United States and Japan was not lost on the House of Morgan.

Between 1923 and 1924, Lamont made "considerable efforts" to persuade Congress not to pass legislation excluding Japanese immigration.[39] Like most supporters of the Japanese quota, Lamont did not believe in increasing Japanese immigration to the United States. His basic argument was that an exclusion act was unnecessary because the Japanese government would follow the Gentleman's Agreement to restrict immigration on its own.[40] He believed that the desired results could be achieved through private actions and agreements rather than public policy statements. The parallels to his strategy in the Harvard segregation case, and to the organization of separate spheres in the banking community, are particular striking.

In October 1922, Viscount Eiichi Shibusawa, a leading Japanese financier and diplomat, wrote Lamont he was "deeply concerned" about the issue of Japanese immigration to Hawai'i and California. He wrote, "To me the Japanese American friendship can never be firmly established unless the question is definitely solved for the mutual satisfaction." Lamont told Shibusawa that he would do what he could to further "friendly relations" between the United States and Japan. Shibusawa wrote, "To enlist the interests of gentlemen like your good self for this important and grave subject is a might upset to the forces, which have been in the operation thus far. I shall certainly count you as one of our foremost friends."[41]

Like Lamont, other bankers and diplomats proposed throughout the interwar period that the Japanese government and Japanese public opinion could be placated by the utilization of a quota. Jerome Greene of Lee, Higginson & Co. had the same opinion as did members of the diplomatic service who served in Japan, including Roland S. Morris, Cyrus E. Woods, and W. Cameron Forbes, who were the U.S. ambassadors to Japan in the 1920s and 1930s. Members of the U.S. State Department were also wary of both domestic and foreign policy fallout from any action by Congress. They classified the issue of Japanese immigration to the United States and the status of Japanese nationals and their American children in the United States as foreign policy concerns.[42]

Lamont, Greene, Forbes, and others argued that Japan's negative "feelings" generated by exclusionary acts would damage foreign relations. They were afraid of the clear statement of racial discrimination, which they felt could only serve to antagonize Japan.[43] They were not, however, interested in increasing Japanese immigration to the United States. Their goal was to find a way to prevent Japanese immigration and avoid insulting the Japanese government.[44] In essence, the debate revolved around the method of exclusion rather than a critique of exclusion itself. Neither side wanted to see a large influx of Japanese immigration to the United States. They shared the same opinion voiced by Theodore Roosevelt, who wrote then-president Taft in 1910, "Our vital interest is to keep the Japanese out of our country, and at the same time to preserve the goodwill of Japan."[45] The question was how to keep the spheres separate and maintain a compromise given that Congress seemed determined to insult Japan by waving the flag of white supremacy under the veneer of self-sovereignty and congressional jurisdiction.[46]

Lamont's involvement in the 1924 act demonstrated his continuing adaptation to the international circumstances and, in particular, his learning curve regarding the significance of race relations in the world of international finance. It also displays the diversity of the actors putting pressure on him and the bank. In addition to the barriers created by the long history of anti-Asian agitation in the United States, J. P. Morgan & Co. had little influence with the congressional members on the House Committee on Immigration and Naturalization and the Senate Foreign Relations Committee, most of whom were from midwestern and western states and had constituencies historically hostile to eastern money interests. It is important to recognize, however, that the Morgans did not want to increase Japanese immigration to the United States any more than the Senate and House committee members. Their differences were in how to handle the exclusion.

Despite their efforts and those of other interested parties, bankers, missionaries, and the State Department, the Immigration Act was passed on May 26, 1924.[47] Also called the Johnson-Reed Act, the law placed a quota on the number of people who could enter the United States based on a 2 percent calculation of the number of people already residing in the United States of that ethnicity or country of origin. The law also specified that countries with "aliens ineligible for citizenship" were not even eligible for the 2 percent quota. Because Asians were the only group specifically determined to be ineligible for citizenship, the 1924 act excluded them entirely. Given that Chinese had already been excluded by the 1882 Chinese Exclusion Act, the 1924 act was clearly designed specifically to exclude Japanese.

The 1924 act put Japan on par with China, something Japan had actively tried to avoid with the Gentleman's Agreement of 1907.[48]

The reaction of Japan and the Japanese was immediate and severe. The Japanese press, for example, "predicted an inevitable race war."[49] Lamont wrote Dr. Takuma Dan, "Of course we have all been much distressed here over the unfortunate outcome of affairs at Washington, but we hope that you and other men of like position in Japan will not misunderstand the situation. It would be a great mistake to assume that the discourteous manner adopted by Congress in handling the immigration matter reflects the feelings of a great majority of the American people."[50] Dr. Dan responded to Lamont, "I confess . . . that there exist among our people keen disappointment and wide spread feelings of recentment [sic]."[51] Lamont and Jerome Greene signed a cable with the International Society to the American-Japanese Society in Tokyo, which was published in the *New York Times* that stated, "We deeply deplore any such expressions, and we give assurances that in our opinion they do not represent the real feeling of the American people."[52]

Conversations about the effect of the Immigration Act would continue for the next decade.[53] And Lamont would continue to advocate on behalf of the Japanese government into the 1930s.[54] In December 1930, W. Cameron Forbes, then the ambassador to Japan, wrote to Lamont, "If the wording of that law (exclusion) could be changed in a way that would not affect very much the number of people coming in, it could still be done in such a way as to soothe the wounded sentiments of the Japanese people and hurt no one."[55] Lamont answered, "It would end the last real difficulty in our relations if the Japanese could be put upon the quota for even a minimum number annually."[56]

By the late 1930s, as Japan began increasing military actions in China, Lamont and the other supporters of the Japanese quota were forced to disavow their ties to Japan, but they argued that American immigration policy had been a major factor in straining Japanese-American relations, implying that the path to war could have been avoided.[57] Whether or not a quota would have changed the tenor of Japanese-American relations in the 1920s, the primary reason why Japan went to war against China in the 1930s was its firm commitment to empire building in China. In that effort, the House of Morgan was also Japan's willing ally. And surprisingly, with regard to those particular endeavors, they also had active and broad support within multiple branches of the American government.

THE MONEY TRUST AND AMERICAN FOREIGN POLICY

While the Morgans had distant and often antagonistic relationships with congressional leaders, they received support from the legislative as well as the executive and federal branches of the American government in one important area of their business—loans that furthered American interests and expansion abroad. Their relations with the American nation-state were, in other words, extremely complex. Starting in the 1910s, institutional support took the form of legislation that exempted businesses from existing antitrust procedures and legislation in the context of foreign trade. Significantly, this support crossed party lines.[58] Even the passage of the Federal Reserve Act in 1913, a major reform, allowed American commercial banks, such as National City Bank, a strong Morgan ally, to set up bank branches abroad and was a pre-World War I indicator of the consensus to exempt overseas expansion from antitrust legislation.

In 1919, after the American government discontinued any government-to-government loans, Congress passed the Edge Act, whose purpose was to provide easier access to long-term capital for financing projects in the reconstruction of Europe. Other institutional efforts to encourage overseas expansion for the purpose of competing globally with other imperial powers included the passage of the Webb-Pomerene Act (1918) which "primarily exempted export trade associations from those provisions of the Sherman Anti-Trust Act that forbid combinations in restraint of trade; it also relaxed the Clayton Act's (1914) strictures on acquiring part or all of the stock of another corporation."[59] Legislation also gave the State Department methods to circumvent congressional oversight and control of international loans through the use of contracts whereby the chief justice of the Supreme Court or the secretary of state was named arbiter in the case of loan default.[60]

As early as 1912, policies were already in place through which the U.S. government sanctioned "private" contracts, while the contractual nature of the agreement allowed loans to remain private and out of public view. Building on the foundation created by Taft and others, the Wilson, Harding, Coolidge, and Hoover administrations of the postwar period threw their support behind private business interests abroad. Constrained by the liberal ideals of limited government but wanting to promote free enterprise and the expansion of American interests, this alliance between private capital and American state interests was called "dollar diplomacy."

Despite the lack of overt support for military aggression, dollar diplomacy was no less assertive in pushing American interests abroad. Its practice was also closely entangled with an ideology of "modern, commercial civilization" through which the debtor nation would learn "modern" and "scientific" policies that included "gold-standard currency stabilization, central banking, strict accounting practices, and administrative rationalization."[61] Fundamentally, it meant that the United States used debt as a way to force its interests on less powerful countries in Asia, Latin America, and the Caribbean. A central part of the "cooperative ethic of the 1920s," dollar diplomacy also fundamentally affirmed the structure and values of private relations that were at the heart of the business community. In 1919, Charles Evans Hughes, who later became Harding and Coolidge's secretary of state (1921–1925), stated at the Union League Club in New York that he believed private informal ties based on shared interests and "firm friendships" were the best way to create cooperation in international relations.[62] Four years later, while he was secretary of state, Hughes stated, "It is not the policy of our Government to make loans to other governments, and the needed capital, if it is to be supplied at all, must be supplied by private organizations."[63]

By the 1920s, the relationship between private business and government was not only well established, it could draw from a community of men, who were personally inclined and institutionally situated to realize its cooperative vision. Though mapping the ties between capital and state institutions is a project that must be considered in greater detail elsewhere, even a general overview of the Morgans' formal social club ties with state actors before the Second World War shows that though the majority of American government officials were not members of the same social clubs as the Morgans and other private bankers, certain positions consistently drew from a community of men with whom leading private bankers had greater similarity in terms of social background and elite identification. This was particularly true for positions dealing with American foreign policy, such as the Department of State and the diplomatic service.[64] Without an appreciation of the larger ideological and empirical networks in play, it would be difficult to understand how the Morgans could have cooperative relations with the American state in the realm of foreign policy given the hostility it faced by certain sectors and members of the American government. One example of this cooperative alliance was the Morgans' quasi-governmental role with regard to U.S.-Japan and U.S.-China relations.

During the interwar period, the Morgans served as the leading American bank of the American group of the International Banking Consortium to China (IBC) at the behest of the American government.[65] In many ways the IBC's collaborative and hierarchical structure mimicked that of the banking syndicate. What made the IBC unique was that its private structure had the backing of the state. In 1909, Jacob Schiff wrote to railroad magnate Edward Harriman regarding the First Chinese Consortium (there were two consortium, one in 1909 and one in 1919), "I feel it but right for those who, like you and me and Morgans, who occupy prominent positions, [to] do something to vouchsafe American preponderance and influence in the Far East."[66] Having a structure of cooperation already in place within the financial community, banks that shared similar ideological attitudes with the Morgan firm regarding the necessity and benefits of imperial expansion were able to combine their efforts.

Though the ostensible purpose of the IBC was to lend money to China for development of its national infrastructure (in particular, its railways), the Morgans believed, as did German Jewish American bankers and the leading British bankers and policy-makers, that their interests could only be protected in China by a strong Japanese power amenable to American and British interests.[67] (The Morgans' British branch, Morgan, Grenfell & Co., was a member of the British banking group of the IBC, which was led by the Hongkong Shanghai Banking Corporation.)[68] Within the American group, banks, who were Morgan competitors, including those outside of New York, such as Chicago Continental and Commercial Trust and Savings bank,[69] were willing to work within the reality of spheres of interest under Morgan's leadership. Given the Morgans' ties to Japan, this also meant working with Japan.[70] Thus, for most of its history, the IBC did not lend money to China. Instead, it gave substantial support for the expansion of Japanese empire in China by refusing to lend money to China until the nationalist government paid loans that China had received under its predecessor, the Manchu dynasty, which had been overthrown in 1911.[71]

The importance of this banking alliance centers on the fact that the banks and the practices so deeply criticized during the Pujo Hearings in the United States were encouraged if and when they were used to expand American corporate and political interests abroad, even if it meant undermining the sovereignty of other countries like China. Thus, even though the American government was highly antagonistic to the Japanese government with

PHOTO 17 Official Representatives at Organization Meeting, International Consortium for China, October 15, 1920, the New York Chamber of Commerce (Sitting at the head of the table: Mortimer Schiff, Thomas W. Lamont, Sir Charles Addis, head of the British Group), Thomas W. Lamont Collection. Baker Library Historical Collections, Harvard Business School (HBS)

Full list in order starting from left, front row first:

1. Frederick W. Stevens, new American Group Representative at Peking
2. Frederick W. Allen, Lee, Higginson & Co.
3. Georges Picot, French delegate
4. Charles E. Mitchell, Pres., National City Bank
5. Rene Thion de la Chaume, French delegate
6. John Jay Abbott, Vice Pres., Continental & Commercial Trust and Savings Bank
7. Burnett Walker, Vice Pres., Guaranty Company (for Guaranty Trust Co. of NY)
8. Henri Mazot, French Group
9. Mortimer L. Schiff, Kuhn, Loeb & Co.
10. Thomas W. Lamont, Chairman, American Group, J. P. Morgan & Co.
11. Sir Charles Addis, Chairman, British Group, Hongkong Shanghai Banking Corporation
12. Kimpei Takeuchi, Japanese delegate
13. W. E. Leveson, British Secretary of Conference
14. Sydney F. Mayers, British delegate
15. R. Ichinomiya, Japanese delegate
16. R. C. Witt, British Group
17. Albert H. Wiggin, Chairman, Chase National Bank of NY
18. Malcolm D. Simpson, Secretary, American Group
19. J. Ross Tilford, American Secretary of Conference

regard to the issue of immigration, they were willing to look the other way in the case of China, implicitly sanctioning the Morgans' relationship to the Japanese empire.

In 1921, Lamont, President Warren G. Harding, Secretary of State Charles Evans Hughes, Secretary of the Treasury Andrew W. Mellon, Secretary of Commerce Herbert Hoover, and other banking representatives reached an agreement that private bankers would consult with the State Department on any future loans so that the government could "express itself regarding them." Jack Morgan wrote President Harding in June 1921 to confirm this agreement.[72] The Morgans remained the head of the IBC until the Second World War, and in the post-World War I period, Lamont was the bank's main representative in East Asian finance. Their relationship with Japan was pursued in the context of this informal alliance with American state interests.

As the United States's position changed among the world powers, the boundaries between private and public spheres took on greater meaning because of the ways in which the state's ties to private capital supported American imperial interests abroad. But with Japan as a client, the Morgans also had other interests with which they had to contend. Over time, Japan became increasingly less amenable to American interests, particularly in China. By the 1930s, Japan's interests in China became so all encompassing that its rejection of the separate spheres of influence would destroy the structure of compromise with the United States it had cultivated since the turn of the century. But before that catastrophe could realign the Morgans' ties to Japan, the firm's proximity to its client would put them in conflict with other interests in the United States, ones that would emerge from within their own social sphere.

THE SOUTH MANCHURIAN RAILWAY LOAN OF 1927

The Morgans' relationships with American, British, and Japanese state interests did not escape the notice of a wider public. During the interwar period, the Morgans were severely criticized by groups within the society at large for their role in supporting Japanese empire in China. Utilizing the language of national sovereignty, numerous individuals and organizations challenged both the practice of American dollar diplomacy and the Morgans' right to conduct business for foreign governments. As these critics tried to insert themselves in the Morgans' sphere through the realm of politics, a unique voice emerged among the detractors, that of women.

Though women were excluded from the financial world, their political activities and ties to peace and reform organizations posed a singular challenge and were further evidence of the changing conditions of private banking in the interwar period. Not only did these constituencies put pressure on the Morgans to be more responsive to American public interests, they called attention to the fact that the Morgans' work could not be defined only in economic terms. A clear example is the controversy over an attempted loan to Japan's South Manchurian Railway (SMR).

The SMR was part of the spoils that Japan won in the Russo-Japanese War, along with the Liaotung peninsula.[73] It was not just a railroad. It was an enterprise that included warehouses, schools, hospitals, public utility companies, hotels, stores, restaurants, a research branch, revenue collection, importation of Japanese civilian labor, and a military branch.[74] In short, the SMR was a Japanese government owned and operated "corporation" and the material embodiment of the Japanese government's colonial enterprise in China.[75] In 1910 Theodore Roosevelt wrote Taft, "How vital Manchuria is to Japan, and how impossible that she should submit to much outside interference therein, may be gathered from the fact . . . that she is laying down triple lines of track from her coast bases to Mukden."[76]

In 1927, the Morgan firm entered into negotiations with the Japanese government to refinance the maturing obligations on the SMR and to finance improvements for the railway, something that the firm had been asked to undertake by the Bank of Japan since 1922.[77] The proposed Morgan SMR issue was for "$30,000,000 approximately . . . the bonds to be guaranteed, principal and interest, by the Imperial Japanese Government. . . . Proceeds of the loan were to be devoted about 60% to refunding purposes and 40% to improvements."[78] The amount was eventually increased to $40 million.[79] The co-managers of the loan syndicate were First National Bank, National City Bank, and Kuhn, Loeb & Co.

Lamont's main contact in Japan was Junnosuke Inouye (1869–1932, General Director, Bank of Japan, 1919–1923, 1927–1928, Japan's Minister of Finance, 1923, 1929–1931).[80] Inouye (also spelled Inoue) was a graduate of the law faculty of the Imperial University in Tokyo (1895). In 1896 he joined the Bank of Japan and was sent abroad to study, living in London from 1908 to 1911. He became the president of the Yokohama Specie Bank, which he joined in 1911, and became governor of the Bank of Japan in 1919.[81] He served as finance minister three different terms in his career, the first starting in 1923. In 1927, when the SMR negotiations began, he was governor of the Bank of Japan under Korekiyo Takahashi, then the finance minister.[82] Lamont wrote to his partners during his trip, "Inouye speaks the same financial language as . . . all of us. I have never found him to deviate from a straight line. I have confidence in his statements."[83]

If Japan and Inouye also counted on Lamont and J. P. Morgan & Co. to identify with their interests, Lamont did not disappoint them.[84] In January 1928, even after the uproar over the SMR loan was in full swing, Lamont wrote to Inouye, "I am not exaggerating when I say that from start to finish we have desired to serve the legitimate purposes of our good client, the Japanese government."[85] Lamont had much at stake with regard to the loan both inside and outside his firm. In 1921, Lamont wrote, "When any one of us partners in J.P.M & Co. goes abroad he is under the instructions of the House [of Morgan], that is to say, all the partners at home. Very likely his partners never send him one word of instructions; they give him the widest possible discretion."[86] This also meant that the partners depended entirely upon him, and his own personal stature within the firm was at stake. "None of us is independent," he said.[87]

The Morgan bank wanted to do business with Japan and the partners relied on Lamont to make it work.[88] For the other partners, the financial guarantee was one of the most attractive aspects of working with the Japanese. Cabling Lamont in Tokyo, they wrote, "As a matter of fact in considering this loan we have given very little thought to the Manchurian political questions involved, relying as we do on the [Japanese government] guarantee."[89] Lamont knew, however, the loan to Japan would be controversial such that he consistently denied that he had gone to Japan with the purpose or intention of making a loan to the Japanese government.[90] As he himself said, "Capital is timid and most investors are not free from the influence of a statement that a proposed operation is likely to produce international misunderstandings."[91] Despite the risks, Lamont was anxious to work with Japan not just because of the potential for profit but because of the prestige it offered the bank and him personally.

When Lamont went to Japan to negotiate the SMR loan, he was accom-

panied by Morgan staff member Martin Egan and Jeremiah Smith Jr., his
former classmate at Harvard. Both had also accompanied him to the Paris
Conference and on his first trip to Japan in 1920. In addition to being one
of his closest friends, Smith was also Lamont's legal adviser in Japan.[92] In
mid-August 1927, Lamont wrote Smith:

> Kengo Mori tells me, whether justified or not, that in Japan I have come
> gradually to be looked upon as their country's best friend in America, and he
> thinks it advantageous from both Japan's and America's points of view that
> I should make this brief visit there. In like manner you would come to be
> regarded, I feel sure, from the further contacts that you would form in addi-
> tion to those you have already formed in Japan, as a friend, fair and well
> disposed toward Japan.

Lamont claimed that Smith's work for the League of Nations would be
greatly enhanced by the contacts that he could develop in Japan. He wrote,
"You would be in a position to handle the Japanese as no one else would."[93]
Lamont kept his personal observations about the potential gain from Japanese business in close confidence. In a draft of a letter to Oswald Garrison
Villard, Lamont wrote that Jeremiah Smith went with him to Tokyo because
he "was in bad health" and his "doctor had recommended a sea trip."[94]

Throughout his negotiations with Japan, Lamont believed that he could
somehow control Japanese foreign policy. High-ranking Japanese officials,
American merchants and representatives, and J. P. Morgan & Co. staff and
executives encouraged this perception.[95] Lamont was not entirely unique in
having great confidence in his cultural understanding of Asian people and
in his ability to influence Japanese foreign policy, but he continued to have
great confidence in his abilities to influence Japan well into the 1930s despite
the fact that most of the advice he gave the Japanese was ignored.[96] He was
unable to grasp that Japan had a history of which he was mostly ignorant,
one that had demonstrated an absolute dedication to empire that emerged
from a critique of western colonialism and racism.

Lamont's trip was widely reported and caused great speculation as to its
purpose.[97] By 1927, the SMR's significance was already being debated in
the American public.[98] In November 1927, the *New York Times* reported
that Lamont had begun negotiations for a $40 million loan to the SMR
with a Japanese government guarantee.[99] For weeks, the *Times* and other

PHOTO 18 Thomas W. Lamont and Jeremiah Smith Jr. at the Meiji Shrine, Japan, October 4, 1927, The Queens Borough Public Library, Archives, New York Herald-Tribune Photo Morgue. (Image courtesy of Thomas W. Lamont Collection. Baker Library Historical Collections, Harvard Business School)

newspapers reported on the Chinese protests against the loan and published editorials denouncing the loan. For example, an article stated:

> Persistent rumors since the recent visit to Japan of Thomas W. Lamont of J. P. Morgan & Co. concerning the alleged intention of Morgan interests to advance large loans to the South Manchuria Railway resulted today in a group of influential Chinese financiers and business men sending a cable to the Chinese Minister at Washington [Alfred Sze] requesting him to present their resolution opposing such loans to Secretary [of State Frank] Kellogg and the American people. The resolution asserts that the South Manchuria Railway is an 'imperialistic Japanese political and economic instrument,' and declares that the line is not a commercial enterprise but one used by Japan to promote her aggressive policy in Manchuria and Mongolia.[100]

On December 1, 1927, the Chinese Ministry of Foreign Affairs telegraphed the U.S. State Department to declare its opposition to the SMR loan. The State Department's commercial attaché in China, Julean Arnold, called the telegram "an excellent, comprehensive statement of the feelings of the Chinese on this subject." It stated that the Chinese people were deeply alarmed about reports of the loan and thought it to have the complete backing of the U.S. government. It also stated:

> It is well known to the world and to none better than the American Government that that Railway is not a mere industrial enterprise but the symbol and instrument of alien domination over a large and rich portion of Chinese territory. . . . [101]

Other newspaper reports also connected the SMR loan to Japan's imperialistic policy and implied that the State Department had approved the Morgan loan.[102] Even articles critical of China announced, "It is hard to divorce finance from politics in the Far East."[103] These reports were not confined to the Chinese government or American newspapers.[104]

After Lamont returned from Japan, his friend Mrs. Julia Ellsworth Ford (1859–1950) contacted his wife, Florence, to say that she had read about the Morgan loan. Lamont had been friends and business associates with Mrs. Ford's husband, Simeon Ford,[105] a hotel proprietor and financier. (Mr. Ford had also been a director of Columbia Bank and Manhattan Life Insurance Company.) Julia Ford was a "socialite, arts collector and patron, and author of children's books," who "presided over a salon" in New York. Like the

Lamonts, who had strong personal interests in the arts, Ford had a wide circle of friends in the literary world. She was close enough to Lamont that they had together written the introduction of a book by the artist George Frederick Watts at the turn of the century.[106] Ford also had ties to Lamont's wife, Florence, with whom she served on the board of directors of the China Society of America, an organization founded in 1911 to "promote friendly relations between the United States and China" and to encourage "a correct knowledge of the ideals, culture, and progress of the two nations." One of the society's principles was the "undivided territorial and political sovereignty of China."[107]

Ford was a member of a larger American peace movement, which "led by women, clergymen, and students disillusioned by the experience of World War I . . . boasted twelve million adherents and an audience of between forty five and sixty million people" in the 1930s.[108] She exemplified the position of peace progressives and pro-China sympathizers, who argued that the SMR loan violated Chinese national unity and sovereignty and allied U.S. finance and policy with British and Japanese imperialism.[109] Ford was also associated with the American Committee for Justice in China, an organization in which Harvard president A. Lawrence Lowell was a prominent member. The organization was extremely critical of Japanese imperialism in China.[110] Around the same time as Ford's correspondence with Lamont and his wife, the committee sent out a newsletter headlined "The Manchurian Loan." It stated:

> A new issue has arisen to disturb our relations with China through press reports that J. P. Morgan & Co. are considering a loan to the Southern Man-churian Railway. . . . Newspaper reports have announced a conference on this matter between one of the partners of the Morgan firm and officials of the State Department. . . . The Morgan firm refuses either to confirm or deny the reports. There is no doubt, however, that there is under consider-ation a possible loan of 30 million dollars . . . the loan being guaranteed by the Imperial Government of Japan.[111]

The committee's official position as stated in a letter to the State Depart-ment was that the SMR loan "cannot be divorced from political conse-quences." The attack on the opacity of private business by groups like the committee echoed the critique of the Pujo Hearings, but the force of their argument derived from the experience of the First World War and the value placed on national sovereignty.

In many ways, Ford's role in pushing the issue of Chinese sovereignty is an example of the ways in which the conditions of private banking had changed and were changing in the interwar period. Under the mantle of self-determination, numerous individuals and groups found a voice to speak on the Morgans' private deals and relationships. A significant portion of this group was made up of white women. Though women, even elite white women, continued to be excluded from the financial world, their work within the political arena threatened to disturb the boundaries between the domestic and business spheres of private bankers so essential to the structure and balance of their community. In other words, their critique directly challenged bankers in the world outside of finance, in the society from which they gained their social capital and where their closest personal ties, that of their family members, were also made and sustained.

For this reason, it is significant that Ford wrote directly to Florence Lamont. In her letter, Ford wrote Florence, "I hear that through Morgan & Company Tom has arranged for a loan of $40,000,000 to the Japanese government to help strengthen the Japanese hold of the Manchurian railway, and a newspaper report confirms it." Asking Florence if the report was true, she said, "It will make the ultimate recovery of Manchuria by a United China the more difficult, won't it, and American finance will be lined up with British and Japanese imperialism to defeat Chinese aspirations. Poor China!"[112]

As a member of the China Society board, Florence must have been aware of the political controversies with regard to Chinese sovereignty. While China lacked the political power of Japan, it had long held an important place in the American imagination as an ancient civilization and a potential marketplace for the surplus of American industrialization. Ford's letter implied that the Morgans were undermining official American policy in China, which theoretically rejected the idea of separate spheres of influence (also called the Open Door). Even worse, it insinuated that these choices were morally indefensible, which threatened the Lamonts' social capital. The controversy put Florence in a difficult situation and she referred Ford to her husband, but she also implied that Ford was ignorant of many aspects of the loan. In a more explicit tone, Ford replied to Florence's letter stating, "An extension of the Manchurian Railway by Japan in China's land against the will of the Chinese people, as far as I can learn, can only lead to trouble between China and the United States (through the loan) and China and Japan, as China has threatened."[113]

Even before he received Ford's letter from Florence, Lamont had started a private letter-writing campaign to influential individuals in the State Department and the media to press his case.[114] Not wanting to seem as if the firm of which he was leading partner was supporting the Japanese empire in China and potential violence in East Asia, Lamont wrote Ford, "I did not go out to Japan on any loan or any other business whatsoever." In a letter marked "strictly personal," Lamont wrote Ford, "I think all you people are getting unduly excited about South Manchuria." He consistently held to this line of defense, despite the fact that internal documents from J. P. Morgan & Co. and correspondence with Japanese officials said otherwise.[115] Lamont defended the supposedly nonexistent loan by arguing that any loan, if there were one, would be perfectly appropriate under the existing lease of the SMR. Mobilizing a nationalistic argument, Lamont later wrote Ford:

> Suppose, for instance, that the Railway desires to buy some American steel rails. I don't suppose that for a minute you would say it was the province of the steel companies in the United States to refuse to steel the rails for cash. Yet you do say that bankers ought not to arrange so that the road can buy the rails on time instead of for cash. To tell the truth, I can't see very much difference between the two,—can you?[116]

In effect, Lamont tried to appeal to a nationalistic populist sentiment of jobs for Americans, greater American prosperity based on an international market for American goods, which he saw as a way to justify the SMR loan. Lamont also told Ford that the Chinese were better off having Japan in Manchuria because the Chinese were incapable of ruling themselves. He said that any opposition to a possible SMR loan was the result of Chinese propaganda "so as to attract sympathy to themselves and cover up the fact that they are utterly failing to show the slightest capacity for organized government," a persistent accusation he made against the Chinese.[117] In a letter to Undersecretary of State R. E. Olds, Lamont also accused the Chinese of instigating the tension with the Japanese by building competing railway lines with the SMR, actions that were allegedly prohibited by previous treaties signed by the two countries. Though the Chinese rejected the validity of those treaties, their views were ignored.[118]

In response to Lamont's arguments, Ford wrote him, "The financial affairs of the South Manchurian Railway cannot be divorced from the

Japanese government policies in Manchuria. (The 50% government ownership and the official status of the railway chief executives are two of many reasons for such a statement.)" Ford's concern was that American ownership of SMR bonds would be an "American endorsement of the Japanese aims and aspirations in Manchuria." According to Ford, "Such endorsement may be worth far more to the Japanese than the proceeds of the loan. The widespread ownership of such bonds throughout the United States would unquestionably be of material assistance to the Japanese in influencing American opinion regarding any controversy as to Manchuria."[119]

The implication was clear. If a private bank like the Morgans lent money to the Japanese government, it would become in effect an American endorsement of Japanese imperial policies in Asia and a threat to American interests. If lending money to the SMR was lending money to Japan to further their empire in China against the will of the Chinese people, this could only lead to war. War with China and Japan could involve the United States at a later date, possibly dragging the United States into another war at the cost of American lives.[120] By invoking the specter of the Great War and by utilizing the language of national security, Ford like other peace progressives had created a space in the public sphere to speak on the affairs of private bankers and she was not alone with regard to her concerns or strategies.

In January 1928, the Women's International League wrote a letter to Lamont stating that they were very concerned about the "rumors of a projected loan to Japan in connection with the Manchurian railway." Dorothy Detzer, the executive secretary, wrote Lamont, "It is because such a financial transaction, while in a sense private business, affects more or less directly the whole people of the United States that we venture to lay our point of view before you."[121] The Women's International League for Peace and Freedom (WILPF) was founded after the First World War by Jane Addams and other leaders, including Emily Balch Greene (1867–1961), a former professor at Wellesley, who had been a staff member of the *Nation* since 1919.[122] Though Addams was criticized during the war for her pacifism, she was connected to many influential individuals and groups and continued to be revered in certain circles.[123]

In 1924, the Women's International League and other anti-imperialists launched a campaign to prevent the participation of U.S. government agencies in what they characterized as private financial arrangements between American citizens and foreign sovereign governments, including supervision of such arrangements.[124] The Women's International League argued that private loans had to be more transparent because of their potential impact on the nation as a whole. Like Ford, their strategy specifically challenged the legitimacy and boundaries of private business.

The spring before Lamont went to Japan, the Women's International League had actually started a campaign on Chinese women and the political situation in China. In March 1927, the Women's International League proposed a "strong resolution" on China to be sent internationally. It stated:

> Believing that China has the right to be considered a sovereign state, the Executive Committee of the W.I.L. urges the governments concerned: 1) to continue conciliatory methods for settlement of all points of difference between China and other countries with a view to concluding treaties based on justice and equality. 2) to oppose in every way the use or threat of military or naval intervention.[125]

Addams stated that the executive committee found that the resolution was not strong enough and hoped for something "more drastic" to create further discussion and public opinion regarding China.[126] The Women's International League was interested not only in the "question of national sovereignty" but also in China itself.[127]

The national board of the league met in January 1928, after which they sent a letter to Lamont stating that they were concerned about the "rumors of a projected loan to Japan in connection with the Manchurian railway." They told Lamont "their feeling for the Japanese government and the people of Japan is most cordial and their regret to see such a loan of American funds is based on their conviction that it will complicate the relations of Japan as well as of the United States with the people of China." The league said that "regardless of the real character and purpose of such a loan," it could only lead to conflict and misunderstanding.[128] The league was careful to state that the SMR loan, while ostensibly a private business matter, reflected on the American financial policy in China.

Ford had already written to Addams, among others, about the SMR loan and asked her to sign a petition against the loan while informing Addams that she had written to Lamont, "who is a dear friend of mine." She hoped, "dear Jane Addams you will stand by me." Addams also knew Lamont personally through other organizations related to international affairs; they both served on the executive committee of the China Famine Relief Fund to which Lamont had been appointed by Woodrow Wilson as chairman.

Lamont and Addams had also served on the national council executive committee of the Foreign Policy Association (FPA), an organization founded in 1918 to "consider the role that the United States might play in the post-war world." (Lamont and his wife, Florence, were active in the FPA). Though the FPA had also held a meeting earlier in the month where leading members spoke out against the Manchurian Loan, Addams felt uncomfortable about signing the petition, and she wrote Ford, "I have a great deal of confidence in Mr. Lamont and his attitude towards International Affairs." She said she "would like to have a few days to go into the matter . . ."[129]

After receiving Ford's letter, Addams then contacted Lamont's sister, Lucy Lamont Gavit (1867–1941), who was married to John Palmer Gavit (1868–1954), a journalist, who served as associate editor and was vice-president of Survey Associates, the publisher of *Survey Graphic*.[130] (Addams was also a cooperating member of Survey Associates). Repeating the sentiments she wrote Ford, Addams told Lucy that she had not signed the petition "because of my confidence in Mr. Lamont," but she asked Lucy if she could send her some material on the issue. Addams enclosed not only Ford's letter, but also a letter from Emily Balch, who had said she would be pleased if Addams would sign the petition. Lucy sent the Ford letter to Addams as well as Miss Balch's letter to Lamont.[131]

After receiving Lucy's letters, Lamont wrote his son, Thomas S. Lamont, who also worked at J. P. Morgan & Co., "Jane Addams has quite a wide circle of influence . . . and I would like to have something said to her."[132] Lucy urged him to do so as soon as possible, writing him that Addams was an important person "worth setting straight about this matter."[133] Like his sister and wife, Lamont did not want it to appear as if J. P. Morgan & Co. was supporting Japanese empire in China, potential violence in East Asia, and the loss of American lives.[134] The fact that he received these letters through his sister and wife was even more disturbing because it threatened his and his family's standing in the personal and private sphere that was normally kept separate from the Morgans' business.

In a strategy that echoed the tactics of the Harvard segregation case, Lamont acted upon the belief that the public appearance of the loan could be separated from its private intention. Thus he proposed to Inouye to delay the loan until the publicity around it died down. He cabled Inouye, "We think the best course for both you and us to adopt at this moment would be to say absolutely nothing, either in the negative or the affirmative, as to our plans for this loan, letting the newspapers and the Chinese blow off steam, and the matter would soon die down. . . . For your information National City Bank, Kuhn, Loeb & Company and First National all join us in this recommendation."[135]

Lamont also suggested reducing the loan to $20 million to cover only the refunding of the loan, as opposed to refunding and expansion of the railway. He wrote that it would "enable us to state publicly that the proceeds of this particular issue are purely for refunding purposes."[136] Lamont's strategy echoed the spirit of Jack Morgan's decision to abandon interlocking directorates before the passage of the Clayton Anti-Trust Act. As they did then, the Morgans were willing to make concessions about the public nature of their work in order to protect their private ability to conduct their business as they saw fit. Thus, though the SMR loan did not go through in the planned manner, efforts to support Japan were not abandoned.[137] During the same period, the Morgans also co-managed a $20,640,000 loan to the City of Tokio in 1927 with Kuhn, Loeb & Co., National City Bank, First National Bank, and Yokohama Specie Bank. In 1930, the same syndicate managers led a $71 million loan to the Imperial Japanese Government.[138]

Lamont's response to outside criticism around the SMR loan demonstrates that they were enough to warrant a response to safeguard the firm's image, but they were not enough to change the firm's actual policies.[139] Like Harvard African American alumni, peace progressives could claim the moral high ground, but they did not have the necessary networks or information to uncover or confront the strategy of evasion directly.[140] Thus, they were unable to challenge Lamont's tactics within the private economic sphere of international bankers. While numerous and passionate, their position in the network of international and national politics and finance determined that their protests would be made and would remain in the public sphere of politics as opposed to the private sphere of finance.

Though women peace progressives were not exactly members of the "outside crowd," their ties to the networks of private bankers were also limited by the fact that they were to women were both segregated from that business and closely aligned with the interests of their family members.[141] And as Jane Addams' letter to Ford demonstrated, they were not able, nor did they necessarily want to undermine the social capital of their friends, either the men or women, in the private domestic or social spheres either. In mid-January 1928, Julia Ellsworth Ford also informed Addams, "There has been so much opposition to and protest against the Manchurian loan from Chinese and Americans that every indication points to its not going through. As Mr. and Mrs. Lamont are very old friends of mind, I am very happy about it personally, as it makes the open letter unnecessary."[142]

In the long run, the interaction with peace progressives did push the Morgans to recognize the extent to which their work created broader interested constituencies. But one has to consider the possibility that the reformers were also successful in making the activities of private bankers more difficult to detect. In essence, they affirmed the division between public and private spheres of activity, and as long as the public activities of the firm appeared to conform to national interests, the private activities of the firm remained hidden and unchallenged. In the case of Japan, only Japan's own actions would force the Morgans to disavow their client, but for the exact reasons that peace progressives feared.

THE BREAK WITH JAPAN

Soon after the SMR loan debacle, the Japanese government began an even greater penetration into mainland China. In April 1928, the Japanese government dispatched troops to Shantung, calling it "self-protection" for Japanese residents in China.[143] China's nationalist government saw the activities as a violation of their territorial sovereignty and a "hostile position against the whole Chinese race which position is also against the dictates of justice and humanity."[144] In September 1931, the Japanese government invaded Manchuria, claiming that the Chinese troops provoked an attack on the SMR and put "hundreds of thousands of Japanese residents . . . in jeopardy" and that they had the right to self-defense.[145] In fact, the Japanese military themselves provoked the SMR incident and in 1932 established the state of Manchukuo with a puppet ruler, Pu-yi (1906–1967), the heir to the Manchu dynasty.[146]

During this period, the Morgans continued to lend money to Japan. In 1930, the firm made "a loan to the Imperial Government for debt refunding in 1930 and a guaranteed loan in June 1931 to the Taiwan Electric Company. Morgan had also organized a $25 million bank credit to the Yokohama Specie Bank for currency stabilization as Japan prepared to return to the gold standard in 1930."[147] In 1932, J. P. Morgan & Co. advanced ¥127 million to the Yokohama Specie Bank for a short-term loan. That loan was made in November 1931 after the September invasion of China.[148] The degree to which Lamont and the Morgans believed their relationship to Japan was important is evident in the fact that Lamont continued his campaign of persuasion of key officials and persons in the United States into the 1930s, producing propaganda for Japan. His main concession was that he avoided doing so publicly.[149]

In 1929, according to an internal Morgan memorandum written by Martin Egan, Japanese Consul General Renzo Sawada asked Lamont "if he might feel free to rely on the firm for information and counsel and Mr. Lamont assured him that he could."[150] In 1931, Lamont told the Japanese government that he could not be a direct publicity agent for the Japanese. Instead he edited material regarding the SMR for the Japanese and suggested that they issue the statement with Lamont's changes, while he arranged for it to get publicity in the United States.[151] In this manner, Lamont tried to maintain the bank's support for Japan but keep it from being in the public eye and therefore from provoking the kind of negative attention of the SMR loan.[152]

As American relations with Japan deteriorated, however, the bank's support for Japan continued to be a publicity problem.[153] In December 1934, Egan sent a letter to Ambassador Hiroshi Saito (1887–1939) from Lamont asking Saito to review a June 30, 1934, article called "Morgan & Company and the Japanese 'Hands-Off' Doctrine" published in the *China Weekly Review*. The article called "the New York banking house of Morgan and Company . . . the silent partner in Japan's 'hands-off' declaration." The article singled out Lamont, saying that the Japanese newspapers quoted him as not only supporting Japanese militarism in China but also declaring "that any future investments in China *must rest on the necessary condition that the Nanking Government will honor all its existing loans.*" (Italics in the original) Lamont had in fact made these arguments repeatedly through the IBC.[154]

Though there is some speculation about exactly when Lamont's "love affair" with Japan ended, when it did, Lamont came to deeply regret the relationship.[155] After right-wing nationalists assassinated Junnosuke Inouye in February 1932, Baron Takuma Dan in March 1932, and Viscount Korekiyo Takahashi in 1936, the Morgans' ties with Japan began to come completely undone.[156] By September 1937, Japan invaded China with great brutality, bloodshed, and violence.[157] Two weeks later, President Roosevelt made a speech where he talked about "the epidemic of world lawlessness" that was spreading like a disease.[158] Having supported Japan in its imperial endeavors for more than two decades, the Morgans were forced to disavow their ties. They understood their reputation could not survive affiliation with a state that clearly rejected democratic ideals in ways that were so contrary to American interests in Asia. This break with Japan reminds us that not all relationships are good ones, and that they are also subject to change.

The ways in which Lamont and the other Morgan partners responded to the events in Japan demonstrate that they took seriously how these associations could affect their reputation. In September 1937, Thomas S. Lamont, Lamont's son, wrote a letter for Junius Spencer Morgan, Jack Morgan's son, to send to E. J. M. Dickson, a doctor and a Presbyterian missionary who had worked in China and was affiliated with the Chinese Medical Board of the Rockefeller Foundation. The letter said, "You and I and all my associates evidently feel probably the same way about the horror of the character of warfare waged by Japan. So far as we are concerned in this office, we are of course a purely private firm. We are lending no money to any phase of Japanese activity, nor have we done so for some years past."[159]

That month, Lamont wrote E. Araki of the Bank of Japan that he could not attend a luncheon to welcome Araki's successor. Lamont said, ". . . quite without reference to whether the Chinese have been on their side at fault or not in many particulars, nevertheless, as you know, the whole civilized world is aghast at these bombings by the Japanese military of innocent non-combatants."[160] Lamont forwarded his correspondence to Martin Egan saying that he had "attempted to spank the Japs a bit."[161] Egan replied, "It seems to me that if they get enough of this stuff it must make an impression upon them."[162]

In December 1937, Lamont also wrote personally to Abby Rockefeller to deny that the Morgan firm was financing the Japanese government. Calling rumors "that fantastic tale," he wrote, "I hardly have to tell you there is not the slightest foundation for it. We have not loaned a dollar to the Japanese Government for years." Lamont went on to blame the military for the Japanese government's aggression in China, saying he felt sorry for the "Liberal element in Japan."[163] Given the importance of the SMR to Japan's foreign policy, and given the high-ranking nature of figures like Inouye, it is difficult to see how it was possible to separate Inouye and others from Japan's imperialistic policies. But given the manner in which Inouye died, it made it easier for the Morgans to convince themselves that they had not been aiding and abetting war in Asia.[164]

Perhaps because the Morgans knew that they had previously professed great friendship with Japan and, more importantly, as Leffingwell had written to Lamont, that they had been a "banker for Japan with heavy responsibility to the holders of Japanese bonds which we sold," the partners remained hopeful that the United States would not go to war with Japan.[165] On November 13, 1941, Lamont wrote Walter Lippmann, "Will you forgive me if I do not altogether agree with your statement this morning that a crisis had been reached in the relations between our country and Japan? . . . Only I wish to God Frank Knox [secretary of the Navy] would let [Cordell] Hull [secretary of state] make the speeches on our foreign relations and not continue quite needlessly and uselessly to bait Japan with provocative statements."[166] Three weeks later, on December 7, 1941, Japan attacked Pearl Harbor, and on December 8 the United States entered the Second World War. On Christmas Eve Lamont wrote Leffingwell that he hesitated "even to mention the subject of the Far East after my fatuous confidence that the Japs would not dare attack us."[167]

For the Morgan firm, the road leading up the war was one that was fraught with tension, not only because of its relationship to Japan, but also because by the mid-1930s, the partners were forced to testify again to Congress in what became known as the Nye Investigation, or the Senate Munitions inquiry, which was spearheaded by the Women's International League. Though the League and other Morgan critics had not been successful in directly preventing the Morgans from financing Japan's empire in China, they were able to provoke a response from the bank by challenging the legitimacy and boundaries of the Morgans' private business by appealing to national interests. And though they were mostly successful in reaffirming the limits of public intervention, external circumstances would feed new life into their critique of private banking. Unfortunately for the Morgans, the national spectacle of the Nye Investigation was only one of the many challenges the bank would face in the 1930s, not the least of which was the partial collapse of world capitalism, the onset of the Great Depression, and another politician named Roosevelt.

## CHAPTER SEVEN

The End of Private
Banking at the Morgans

IN 1938, JACK Morgan wrote to his youngest son, Henry, about a nightmare he had that was so vivid he had to write it down. Morgan "saw and heard [President Franklin Roosevelt] giving a fireside chat. [Roosevelt] said he had determined to pay no more attention to Congress but to tell the people in fireside chats what he had decided on as legislation. These statements would thereafter have the force of law." In the nightmare, "the question of monopolies had had intensive study by [Roosevelt] when off on his fishing holiday. . . . He had solved it by this plan:—Any business which did more than 4% of the business of its sort should hereafter be required to take out a Federal license. A condition of this license would be that the President should appoint a director." Morgan dreamed that Roosevelt's director would be given final control over every decision made by the board of that business. He ended his letter, "Please do not let this idea get public or it might give [Roosevelt] a suggestion for something he hasn't yet thought of, and so prove to be prophetic!"[1]

By the time Jack Morgan was writing to his son, Henry was no longer a partner of J. P. Morgan & Co. Three years earlier, he left the firm to become a partner in a new investment bank, Morgan Stanley & Co., with Harold Stanley and William Ewing, who had also been Morgan partners.[2] This break from the family firm was made not by choice but by necessity in the new political climate that had given rise to Roosevelt's administration and was giving Jack Morgan his nightmares. In 1933 Congress passed the Glass-Steagall Act, which mandated the separation of commercial and investment banking. By choosing to remain a commercial bank, J. P. Morgan & Co. was forced to stop their investment bank activities. Because Henry was only thirty-five years old at the time and the younger of the two Morgan sons, it was reasonable to assume that Morgan, Stanley would act as an investment proxy for J. P. Morgan & Co. Other investment houses like Kuhn, Loeb & Co., which gave up its deposit business entirely, saw the formation of Morgan Stanley as a subterfuge to circumvent the law.

At the time, the creation of Morgan Stanley may have appeared to be a largely cosmetic one, but it was nevertheless an important sign of how the conditions of private banking had changed and also the most dramatic example of the depth of the external pressures facing the banking community during the 1930s. Fueled by the Crash of 1929 and the suffering of the Great Depression, the popular perception of integrated power and privilege found new life. With confidence in the business community at its nadir, political momentum brought about increased legislative scrutiny on the banking community. In 1932, the Senate began an investigation into the practices of the securities business and stock exchanges called the Gray-Pecora Investigation or the Pecora Hearings. Once again, the banking community was at the center of the inquiries.

The return of the Money Trust issue accelerated the realization of a transition at the Morgans, which had started after the First World War but was hastened by the enormous pressures that attacked them from all sides. Immediately following the Pecora Hearings was a Senate investigation on the munitions industry called the Nye investigation (1934–1936).[3] The munitions industry hearings serve as a key example of how the controversy over the existence of the Money Trust was different from that which predated the First World War because of the international dimensions. During the Nye investigation, the Morgans were accused of consolidating economic power and undermining the economic stability of the nation. They were also accused of involving the United States in international conflicts for their own economic benefit, a particularly inflammatory accusation given the rise of fascism in Europe and Asia. If the experience of the First World War served as a constant reminder of the potential consequences of the actions of the banking community, the context of political and economic stability in Europe and Asia gave them greater meaning and a sense of urgency.

In the wake of the Crash of 1929, Roosevelt's New Deal also created significant changes in the expectations of government at a time when the reputation of the banking community was severely damaged and the banks themselves were under siege from external and internal pressures. During this time, the Morgan bank went through major formal structural changes that reflected an ideological shift with regard to its relationship to American national interests and its views on anti-Semitism. Together these changes required not only new relationships and alliances, they also necessitated a re-interpretation of the separate spheres that defined their business structure and would mark the end of private banking at the Morgans.

THE CRASH

Part of the reason why the Great Depression was such a shock was because it followed a period of rapid economic and social change. It is either ironic or logical that a time symbolized by "easy living" and "booze and money" was also a period when Prohibition was the law.[4] The 1920s also hid the terrible "gap between the ideal and the reality" of American capitalism and American prosperity.[5] By October 1929, business had already begun to slow down. Overall, the economy evidenced a structural weakness: insufficient demand, i.e., not the lack of desire to consume but the lack of ability to pay, or a dramatic economic inequality.[6]

As the economy began to contract and banks began to fail, the vast majority of Americans had no savings and little safety net, which caused great suffering. In September 1931, Great Britain went off the gold standard, the centerpiece of the ideology of sound money. By this time, the signs that the Depression was more serious were inescapable.[7] In 1933, conservative estimates reckoned that 25 percent of the workforce was unemployed, though the number was probably as high as one-third of the labor force.[8] By the time Franklin Delano Roosevelt (1882–1945) began his first term as president, more than one-third of all American banks had either gone out of business or were absorbed by other banking institutions.[9]

The lines within the financial community were also being reorganized as firms merged and others disappeared under the weight of the Depression. Harvey Fisk & Sons, which had once been one of the Morgan's largest allies in the distribution of bonds, ceased to be listed in the banking directorates after 1930.[10] Other syndicate participants, such as Kountze Brothers, suspended in 1931.[11] P.J. Goodhart & Co. closed in 1933.[12] Perhaps the most dramatic suspension was the dissolution of Lee, Higginson & Co., which had been a major syndicate partner for the Morgans, ranking seventh for 1895–1934 among all syndicate participants and third among private bankers. (See Table 4.) In 1932, Lee, Higginson & Co. went bankrupt in a scandal involving one of their clients, Ivar Kreuger, also known as the Swedish Match king.

Raised near Kalmar, Sweden, Ivar Kreuger was the son of a factory manager. His family business was match production, which the Swedes had revolutionized in terms of safety and efficiency. Trained as a civil engineer in Stockholm, Kreuger worked in the United States and in South Africa. In 1907, he founded the Swedish Match Company. By the early 1920s, Sweden was the world's "leading exporter of matches" and Kreuger's company "made two-thirds of all matches used in the world."[13] With the assistance of American capital and the banking house of Lee, Higginson & Co., Kreuger tried to secure a worldwide monopoly on the production and distribution of matches through "a series of highly speculative financial operations." Unfortunately for Lee, Higginson & Co., "the assets and profits recorded for the business were largely fictitious."[14]

In 1932, Kreuger, who once said, "Everything in life is founded on confidence," committed suicide in Paris. After his death, Lee, Higginson & Co. admitted that the firm had taken his word with regard to his holdings and had not investigated the actual state of affairs of his company because of their confidence in his reputation and integrity.[15] Having put its own reputation on the line, the Kreuger scandal destroyed the venerable bank.[16] As Higginson partner Jerome Greene searched for another job, he wrote a series of letters to his associates trying to explain the Kreuger scandal and his and his partners' involvement in it.[17] He left banking permanently and took a teaching job abroad (in international relations) in Wales, eventually returning to the United States to become secretary of Harvard Corporation.

Lee, Higginson & Co. was not the only elite Yankee bank to be shaken to its core. Kidder, Peabody & Co., the Morgans' number one private banking syndicate partner, found itself on the brink of bankruptcy in 1930, and its survival was due largely to the Morgans. On top of the stock market crash, Kidder, Peabody & Co. was destabilized by the death and retirement of five partners in the late 1920s and lack of effective leadership. Because of their strong personal and professional ties to the bank, the Morgans decided to come to the bank's rescue by organizing "a revolving credit of $10 million" from New York and Boston banks. Kidder, Peabody itself raised $5 million in loans from friends, banks and individuals, who included Kuhn, Loeb & Co.'s Mortimer Schiff.

Even though Kidder, Peabody continued to lose money and was soon in need of more funds, the Morgan bank did not abandon it. The bank's name and reputation being "its greatest assets," the Morgans guided the sale of Kidder, Peabody to other Boston banking families, who included Edwin S. Webster Sr.; Edwin S. Webster Jr., Webster Sr.'s son, of Stone & Webster; Chandler Hovey, Webster Sr.'s brother-in-law, of Chandler Hovey & Co.; and Albert H. Gordon, who was a staff member at Goldman, Sachs.[18] Kidder, Peabody's personal ties to the Morgans proved to be *their* greatest assets, as they were given a lifeline that others were denied. The fact that the association with the Morgans enhanced their social capital was not lost on the new owners. During the negotiations, Gordon wrote to Webster Sr., "Incidentally, we are slowly making the grade socially. Yesterday for the first time [Jack] Morgan invited us to tea on our way out of the almost daily conference."[19]

In 1931, the new Kidder, Peabody entered into negotiations to merge with Kissell, Kinnicutt & Co., a firm founded in 1906, which was also on the verge of bankruptcy. While Kissell, Kinnicutt was not one of the Morgans' top syndicate partners in terms of overall total amount, it had a respectable standing with the firm.[20] G. Herman Kinnicutt, who was the senior partner of the bank, was a graduate of Harvard (Class of 1898) and started his banking career at J. P. Morgan & Co. before leaving to strike out on his own. Upon the suggestion of Morgan partner George Whitney (Robert Bacon's son-in-law and E. F. Whitney's nephew), the two banks merged in 1932.[21]

Kidder, Peabody & Co. and Kissel, Kinnicutt & Co. were not the only banks to merge during the Depression. Other Morgan syndicate participants went through a series of mergers, such as National Bank of Commerce and

Guaranty Trust in 1929.[22] Equitable Trust Co. of New York merged with Chase National Bank and Interstate Trust Company in 1930.[23] E.A. Harriman & Co. merged with Brown Brothers & Co. in 1931.[24] While a certain amount of business change was to be expected, this was an unusual time of uncertainty and scandal as the banking community anxiously observed the solvency of their competitors and collaborators. For Kuhn, Loeb & Co., in particular, the 1930s were an extremely difficult time, a period of devastating generational change that effectively ended their participation in the story of the Morgan network before the Second World War.

ANTI-SEMITISM IN THE 1930S

If the pressures of the Great Depression were not enough, Kuhn, Loeb & Co. lost all of its senior partners in the 1930s, mostly due to sudden illness. The first to pass was Mortimer Schiff, who died suddenly at his home from heart disease in 1931. Mortimer was only fifty-four years old, almost twenty years younger than his father at the time of his death.[25] Felix Warburg wrote to his brother Max with the news and details of Mortimer's death, "As the lines grow thinner, the remaining partners have to fill in the holes left by predecessors and carry on, but at the moment I feel naturally as if, during my connection with the firm, we have lost too many partners through death, two Messrs. Wolff, Solomon Loeb, Louis Heinsheimer and now father Schiff and son."[26] The following year, their brother Paul Warburg also died from illness.[27] Only Jerome Hanauer, who was the first non-family member to join the firm, left voluntarily in 1933. (He died in 1938). To the great regret of the partners, Hanauer left while Otto Kahn was also ill.[28] The following year, in 1934, Kahn died of a heart attack at the age of sixty-seven in his office. The *New York Times* reported in the byline, "Wall Street is Shocked-Morgan and Lamont Hurry to Office."[29]

The Morgan partners were concerned about what the deaths of the partners would mean to the future of Kuhn, Loeb & Co.[30] In 1932, Thomas Lamont wrote Jack Morgan that he had met with Elisha Walker, who had accepted an invitation to join Kuhn, Loeb & Co. Lamont wrote, "With the death of Mortimer L. Schiff a little over a year ago, with the continued ill-health of Otto Kahn who is reported as stating that he never expects to be very active in the firm's affairs again, with the withdrawal on 31st December of Jerome Hanaeur who has for twenty years been the wheel horse of the firm the juniors are left almost completely in charge with the exception of Felix Warburg who has never been over active."[31] Between 1925 and 1935, Kuhn, Loeb & Co. added nine new partners, only three of whom represented the third generation of family members: Gilbert H. Kahn (Otto's son), John M. Schiff (Mortimer's son), and Frederick M. Warburg (Felix's son). Kuhn, Loeb & Co. was becoming less of a family -dominated firm, but that was not unusual. What was disturbing was the lack of senior leadership at Kuhn, Loeb at a critical time. The same factors had almost led to the demise of Kidder, Peabody.[32]

Lamont and Morgan worried that Kuhn, Loeb & Co.'s decline would undermine the hierarchy and the organization of the financial community, which had remained relatively stable for the last four decades and was now under enormous stress from multiple external challenges including the Depression, an extremely hostile Congress, and the ascension of Franklin Roosevelt. Lamont wrote, "From our point of view it is important that Kuhn Loeb & Co should not drop to the status of a third-rate power so to speak." Lamont did not put much stock into Elisha Walker as being able to make a bold statement about the firm's future. He wrote, "[Walker] is competent but not a great pillar of strength." Still, he told Morgan in a cable, "We hope that the loss in personnel which the firm is apparently suffering will not give you undue concern (Stop) We are informed on excellent authority that the financial position of the firm continues unquestioned."[33]

Felix Warburg was the only remaining senior partner at Kuhn, Loeb from the pre-World War I period, but he did not live long enough to prove his ability to take the firm through a difficult transition. He died three years after Kahn in 1937. Some of Warburg's associates believed that his death was caused by the strain of his many endeavors, which he freely admitted took up more of his time and interest than banking. He had been deeply involved in a number of Jewish and non-Jewish charities and philanthropic efforts.[34] Starting in 1933, Warburg had been put under doctor's orders for "spasms in the heart region" to cut back on work, including his activities on behalf of Jews in Germany under the Nazi regime.[35]

Warburg's work demonstrated that he had serious concerns, ones that other German Jewish banks shared in the 1930s. He, like many of his associates, was deeply troubled by the ominous signs in Germany and the devastating rise of the Nazi Party and Hitler, whom Otto Kahn called "the enemy of humanity."[36] Unfortunately for Warburg and others concerned about the Jewish refugee situation in Europe, the same immigration laws that had exacerbated tension between the United States and Japan during the 1920s made it difficult if not impossible to relieve Jewish suffering as thousands attempted to flee Nazi Germany's advance across Europe.[37] A year after Felix Warburg's death, the Nazi regime forced Max Warburg to leave his family's firm, M. & M. Warburg & Co., and he fled to the United States. The firm became Brinckmann, Wirtz & Co. in 1941.[38]

If the rise of the Nazis was a sign of the terrible devastation that would befall Europe's Jewish communities and Europe in general, it was also a gamechanger for the Morgan partners, if not in their actual sentiment toward Jews (because they continued to have negative attitudes toward Jews), but in the way in which they publicly addressed anti-Semitism.[39] During the 1930s, it became increasingly less acceptable to express racist and anti-Semitic views. This had to do in part with the fact that to express those views in public violated the private/public divide that allowed for these views to go unchecked in private life, but it was also a result of the way in which the Nazis' ardent support for white supremacy delegitimized their claims to moral superiority. By the late 1930s, the Morgans' conversion to the public espousal of support for racial tolerance was more or less complete.

In December 1938, Lamont wrote to his son Thomas S. Lamont about a letter his son was going to write to Theodore Roosevelt Jr. about the issue of anti-Semitism.[40] Lamont suggested his son write the following:

We—all of us—are strongly against any intolerance in this or in any other country, especially in our own country. But there are certain instances of intolerance that are sporadic and are derived from special causes. Anti-Semitism at the present moment is one of them. I, TSL, want to do every-thing I can to offset even casual and sporadic instances of intolerance, but I think that the more we get together and the more hullabaloo we raise about anti-Semitism the more we create in the minds of the public the idea that there must indeed be something behind the whole situation that causes anti-Semitism and they begin to exaggerate the dangers of Jewry and do an injus-tice to the very cause that they want to help.[41]

Lamont's response is entirely consistent with his position on Harvard's discriminatory policies, and he would make the same argument later about how talking about racial inequality only made things worse for African Americans.[42] But his overt recognition of the existence of discrimination against Jews was a marked departure for him, and he was not the only member of the firm to take on the mantle of tolerance. Morgan partner Russell Leffingwell was even more extreme in his rhetoric, linking tolerance to Christianity, liberty, and American nationalism.

In 1939, Leffingwell wrote Lamont suggestions for a speech or letter on anti-Semitism that stated the United States had to be a "land of liberty" for Jews as much as Christians and cautioned "we Protestants" from becoming "arrogant, intolerant, unfriendly and unhelpful to our fellow men and fellow citizens of a different race." He wrote:

> If there is any such thing among us as anti-Semitism let us pluck it out. . . .
> Let us remember that we, or our ancestors, came over three hundred years
> ago or more . . . to escape religious or social or economic disadvantages in
> Europe. We, or our ancestors, found here a land of opportunity and of lib-
> erty. What shall it profit us if we seek to deny the enjoyment of this land of
> liberty and opportunity to our fellow men of any race?

Leffingwell even suggested that Lamont use a quote from First Corinthians chapter 13, verse 3: "And though I bestow all my goods to feed the poor, and though I give my body to be burned, and have not charity (which is love), it profiteth me nothing."[43]

Meanwhile, Leffingwell had written just two years earlier to Jack Morgan that he went on a "dull leisurely and extremely restful Caribbean cruise" and that "the company was largely oriental and we were consequently spared all social effort, which was just what we wanted." [NOTE: 'Oriental' meaning Jewish not Asian.][44] Lest we think Leffingwell had quickly changed his mind in two years time, in January 1942, he also wrote Lamont:

> Like France we have been softened and sapped by the Jews, the pacifists, the
> Communists and by incompetence in high places. When I say Jews I mean
> those brilliantly able people who are instinctively and constitutionally
> destructive in their relation with Government. They never could create or
> govern or defend a country of their own for themselves. Their brilliant minds
> are essentially sadistic and destructive.[45]

Leffingwell clearly had strong prejudices, but he was just as strategic and self-righteous about his rhetoric on tolerance as Lamont. In December 1940, he wrote an extremely effusive letter to Franklin Delano Roosevelt advising him to sway public opinion by announcing "that you conceive yourself to be President of the whole people, and that as such you recognize no differences of race, creed, color or party; no difference between capital, labor and management; no difference between your friends and your opponents. That you are the leader of the whole people, and that you dedicate yourself anew to the cause of democracy against autocracy, or freedom against despotism, of the peaceful and law-abiding against the aggressors." Leffingwell added as a postscript, "Tom [Lamont] has read this and suggests adding a word of aid to China, very popular cause."[46]

GENERATIONAL CHANGE: NEW AND OLD CHALLENGES

Whether the particular stress of the plight of Jews hastened the deaths of Kuhn, Loeb & Co.'s partners, the House of Morgan was not immune to changes either. During the 1930s, both internal and external pressures created pressures on the House of Morgan's leadership. By the mid-1930s, Jack Morgan was getting older and had already started to reduce his load at the firm. In 1937, soon after George F. Baker of First National Bank died, Morgan suffered a heart attack, which prevented him from attending the coronation of King George in England. (It was actually probably the only thing that would have prevented him from going. He had anxiously procured an invitation through the Morgan London partners and had ordered a new suit and shoes to be made for the occasion).[47] Edward Stotesbury, the senior Morgan partner in Philadelphia, who had been a partner in the original reorganization of the Morgan firm in 1895, passed away in May 1938. Charles Whigham, a senior Morgan Grenfell partner in London, died in a riding accident in February of that year.[48]

Other partner losses included Thomas Cochran, who died in 1936 after not being active for about four years. Horatio Lloyd, another Philadelphia senior partner, died in 1937.[49] S. Parker Gilbert, a New York partner, died in 1938.[50] Benjamin Joy, a partner at Morgan et. Cie., withdrew from the firm in 1934.[51] Teddy Grenfell, the senior partner in London, had also suffered some health-related reverses, and his involvement declined after 1935. (He died in 1941).[52] Charles Steele, who was such a senior partner in the early part of the twentieth century that he alone shared an office space with Pierpont Morgan, had started to reduce his activity in 1923 and more so in 1932 after the death of his wife, Nannie. He died in 1939.[53]

Partnership changes were to some extent to be expected given the natural cycle of life. During the 1930s, J. P. Morgan & Co. and Drexel & Co. also accepted or promoted five new partners, Morgan, Grenfell & Co., Ltd. four new partner/directors, and Morgan, Harjes & Co. three new partners.[54] So while the deaths and retirements of the 1930s began a transfer of leadership within the firm and were a drain on the firm's capital, they were not the only reason the 1930s was a period of great challenge for the Morgan bank. During this time, they were faced with new challenges and revisited by old ones, which would continue to change the conditions of their business. As Morgan's nightmare intimated, great external pressure also came from the return of the Money Trust.

In the early 1930s, Brandeis was still a force to be reckoned with, perhaps more so given his status on the Supreme Court. In 1932, he republished his book, *Other People's Money*, which summarized his arguments from twenty years previous about the existence of the Money Trust. Ever vigilant, Lamont wrote to Norman Hapgood arguing that the book was based on statistics put together by the Pujo Committee in 1912, which he said were inaccurate. In a more generous portrayal, most likely given Brandeis's elevated position of power, Lamont told Hapgood that Brandeis had been duped.[55] Leffingwell had a less generous reading of Brandeis. He later wrote Lamont that Brandeis and Felix Frankfurter were "responsible for the clauses in the Glass Bill directed against private bankers, as well as for the [1934] Securities Act." He told Lamont, "The Jews do not forget. They are relentless."[56]

The 1930s put Lamont's publicity skills to the test as he dealt with old and new challenges. As was his usual refrain, Lamont said a money trust, "in my own view never existed and does not exist today." Lamont argued that the public needed experts to translate the value of securities for them and bankers were "the most convenient expert."[57] At the same time that Lamont was writing to Hapgood, the whole question of the banker's expert status and his supposedly dispassionate and professional knowledge and advice was being put under an unfriendly microscope. The previous month, the Senate had begun an investigation into the securities business.

The purpose of the Senate hearings, which were initiated during the Hoover administration, was to understand the origins of the Crash of 1929. After the prosecutors began to uncover significant evidence of spectacular malfeasance, the hearings became part of a much larger reform movement that eventually led to the creation of the Securities Exchange Commission (1934). The hearings also gave rise to another Morgan adversary for whom they were named. After Samuel Untermyer turned down the job, the position of the bank's nemesis was occupied by Ferdinand Pecora, the lead counsel.[58]

THE MONEY TRUST RETURNS: THE PECORA HEARINGS

Like Samuel Untermyer, Ferdinand Pecora (1882–1971) was a progressive Democrat, a New Yorker, and a graduate of City College. Sicilian by birth, Pecora immigrated to the United States with his family at the age of five. He graduated from New York Law School in 1906 and served as the assistant district attorney of New York (1918–1930).[59] In 1912, he became friends with Bainbridge Colby, who later served as Secretary of State under Woodrow Wilson. Pecora began his job as lead prosecutor in 1933 after Colby and others recommended him to Senator Peter Norbeck (R-SD), who was the chairman of the Senate Banking and Currency Committee.[60] Initially, President Hoover, Congress, and later President Roosevelt saw the investigation as limited in scope. Pecora's investigation changed all that.[61] The hearings made Pecora famous, and in 1939 he published a book about his experience titled, *Wall Street Under Oath: The Story of Our Modern Money Changers.*[62] Like Untermyer, Pecora was no favorite of the Morgan firm. Jack Morgan referred to him as a "dirty little wop."[63]

Pecora's investigation was dramatically effective because it uncovered significant examples of malfeasance in the financial community involving some of its most prestigious names. The first firm to come under fire was Halsey, Stuart & Co., who had been the principal bankers for businessman and industrialist Samuel Insull. Insull was born in London, the son of a clergyman. He immigrated to the United States in 1881. Insull worked as Thomas Edison's personal assistant and later became vice-president of General Electric, Edison's company, which J. P. Morgan & Co. reorganized in 1892. That year Insull also became president of Chicago Edison Company, which he expanded into a major public utility provider in the Midwest through a complicated structure of holding companies. By 1932, Insull had distributed in excess of $2.6 billion worth of securities in his various holding companies. After the Crash, Insull's companies went into bankruptcy.

During the hearings, Pecora questioned Harold L. Stuart, the head of Halsey, Stuart, about how they had marketed Insull's bonds. The revelations were astounding. Stuart revealed that the firm had written radio broadcasts and hired a professor at the University of Chicago to deliver them as investment education on an hour-long radio program that the firm had also secretly financed. The firm's partners had also sold securities in Insull's companies to clients without letting their clients know that the firm had a large investment in those companies or that the firm's partners were also members of that corporation. While their actions were not illegal, they were clearly unethical and represented a conflict of interest. For his part, Insull tried to escape prosecution by going to Europe. He was found off the coast of Turkey and faced trial for mail fraud and embezzlement, among other charges, but was acquitted. He left the United States and died in Paris in 1938.[64]

The next bank to come under fire during the Pecora Hearings was National City Co., the security affiliate of National City Bank of New York, one of the Morgan firm's strongest and most important collaborators. National City Co. was at the time "the nation's largest investment banking house."[65] Though it was only founded in 1911, National City Co. was the second top syndicate partner for J. P. Morgan & Co. between 1895 and 1934. Its total of over $1.6 billion with 391 participations for 110 unique clients was only surpassed by First National Bank of New York, which had a total participation of $2.17 billion and 709 participations. (First National had 189 unique clients.) (See Table 4.)

If we think of National City Bank and National City Co. as basically acting in concert, which the hearings found they did do, and sum their participations in the Morgans' syndicates, their total (more than $2.5 billion) exceeds that of First National Bank and for approximately the same number of participations (737).[66] Between 1920 and 1934, National City Co. outpaced First National Bank in Morgan's syndicates in total amount and number of participations. In other words, it was Morgan's top syndicate partner, which made the revelations against the affiliate extremely problematic.

National City Co.'s abuses were so excessive that Charles E. Mitchell, who was the chairman of the board for National City Bank and National City Co., was not only forced to resign from the bank, he narrowly avoided going to jail for income tax evasion and had to pay a large fine. During the investigation it was revealed that not only had National City Co. sold securities and bonds without informing investors about the "pertinent facts concerning the qualities of the securities recommended," it had done so knowing that the quality in some cases was extremely poor. Not only did National City Bank use its affiliate to evade the law and participate in stock speculation and stock pools, National City Co. had also traded on the stock of its parent company to manipulate its stock price. National City also used its affiliate to keep National City Bank's losses off their books and hide it from their stockholders.[67]

If those abuses were not shocking enough, it was also revealed that Mitchell and other executives "voted themselves huge annual bonuses, not reported in annual statements" and that they saw themselves as, in Mitchell's own words, "'partners in a private banking or investment firm'," and not as the "employees of a corporation and responsible to its stockholders" they really were. Then came the revelation that Mitchell and other executives practiced accounting deceptions in order to avoid paying income taxes. In 1929, Mitchell sold tens of thousands of shares in National City Bank to his wife. On paper, he incurred a loss about $2.8 million, which he counted against his income though the shares and the money had clearly been kept within the family.[68]

Two days after National City Bank's actions were brought to the light of day, Franklin Delano Roosevelt assumed the U.S. presidency. Invoking the language of the New Testament, Roosevelt declared in his inaugural address:

> Practices of the unscrupulous money changers stand indicted in the court of public opinion, rejected by the hearts and minds of men. . . . Faced by failure of credit they have proposed only the lending of more money. Stripped of the lure of profit by which to induce our people to follow their false leadership, they have resorted to exhortations, pleading tearfully for restored confidence. They know only the rules of a generation of self-seekers. They have no vision, and when there is no vision the people perish. The money changers have fled their high seats in the temple of our civilization. We may now restore that temple to the ancient truths.[69]

Because of the revelations, the Pecora Hearings were extended. About two months later, the second phase of the Pecora Investigation began. The first person called to testify on the world of private banking was Jack Morgan as the head of J. P. Morgan & Co.[70]

Given the stature of the Morgan bank and the previous testimony of their associates, Pecora later noted, "Public interest in [Morgan's] appearance was almost hysterically intense." He stated, "Not for a generation, not since the elder Morgan had been examined in the Pujo Committee investigation of 1912, had the public been permitted a clear view of the man whom everybody acknowledged as a world figure."[71] Reporters rushed in and out of the courtroom to post their stories, and the senators of the subcommittee would hardly let Pecora get a question in edgewise. They argued not only with Pecora but also amongst themselves, also taking it upon themselves to question Morgan directly.[72] As a result, as the hearings progressed, they had little of the control and order that characterized the Pujo Investigation.

During the course of the hearings, Jack Morgan, who was by all accounts a sensitive person, was subjected to some of the worst public humiliations of his life, including a moment when a press agent for Ringling Brothers Circus brought a dwarf, Lya Graf, into the court room while Morgan was giving testimony. During a break, the agent had Ms. Graf put on Morgan's lap to his great surprise (he at first thought she was a child) and to the excitement and glee of the court reporters. In the midst of this "circus," as Senator Glass had called it, the inner workings of the bank were again exposed to the harsh light of public condemnation.[73]

The Morgans were not found to have engaged in the same kinds of abuses as National City Co., but their association with National City did not encourage confidence in their judgment or friendships. The committee was especially interested in the fact that Morgan and his partners were shown to have offered stocks to a special list of friends or a "preferred list" at special prices that included former president Calvin Coolidge. The most harmful publicity to the firm, however, was the revelation that the partners had not paid any income tax during 1931 and 1932. In 1930, they claimed a more than $20 million loss on capital after having reevaluated their securities holdings on the occasion of the entry of two new partners.[74]

As his father had done during the Pujo Hearings, Jack Morgan defended his firm's practices and testified that the values of the firm were held to a higher standard than the pursuit of economic profit. He told the committee that private bankers were ruled by the ancient code of conduct that was not determined by laws but by a strong tradition based on character and integrity. Referring to the private banker as a "national asset," he spoke of credit as "a private banker's 'most valuable possession . . . the result of years of fair and honorable dealing and, while it may be quickly lost, once lost cannot be restored for a long time, if ever.' "[75]

To many observers, Jack Morgan's testimony seemed just as self-serving as his father's, perhaps even more so because it was made during the depths of the Depression after significant malfeasance had been exposed within the banking community. Even though the Morgans were a private unlimited liability partnership, "risking their own money and doing their own work" as Morgan called it, they were frequent collaborators with commercial banks and trust companies that did receive deposits from the general public. These connections made them vulnerable to the charge that they were in fact playing with "other people's money," not just their own.[76]

Critics also portrayed Morgan and the firm as living in the nineteenth century, with outdated modes of doing business, both secretive and aristocratic.[77] The partners took great offense at any portrayal of Jack Morgan and the bank as out of touch at a time of great national suffering. They understood that respect and confidence for the banking community was badly damaged by the many scandals brought to light by the Pecora Hearings, but they believed that economic crises were the handiwork of unscrupulous individuals with low morals and poor character, who were unable to "self-regulate" (to use a contemporary term) or "second, third, and fourth class bankers."[78] Unfortunately for the Morgans, some of those unscrupulous individuals were found to be members of their own inner circle.

In 1938, George Whitney's younger brother Richard Whitney (1888–1974), the former head of the New York Stock Exchange, was convicted of embezzlement and sent to Sing Sing prison.[79] The Morgans were somewhat tarnished by the association, having loaned substantial sums of money to Whitney since 1931. They had also made their own investigation of his finances as early as 1934. By 1937, Richard admitted his embezzlement to his brother, George, who in turn turned to Lamont for assistance. Not reporting Richard implicated them in his crimes, but they tried to deal with it privately. When their efforts failed, Whitney was exposed and George Whitney and Lamont had to testify to their role at a Securities and Exchange Commission hearing, where their primary defense was that they had only done what a brother or friend would do.[80]

Given examples like Mitchell, Insull, Kreuger, and Whitney, the Morgans were not completely against some regulation of the securities industry, which was inevitable considering the kinds of abuses that were revealed.

They were not as understanding, however, about the direct attacks on the firm's reputation that continued throughout the 1930s. In the decade before the Second World War, and as conflicts began to heat up in Asia, Europe, and Africa, the critique of money power became intertwined with an intense public scrutiny of private banking loans to foreign countries. Soon after the senate hearings, Jack Morgan and the firm faced an even more serious threat from critics that labeled them "merchants of death."

THE SPECTER OF WAR

In 1934, H. C. Engelbrecht, the former editor of the *World Tomorrow* and F. C. Hanighen, a journalist, published a book called *Merchants of Death: A Study of the International Armament Industry.*[81] Born in Chicago, Engelbrecht was a graduate of the University of Chicago (B.A./M.A.) and Columbia University (Ph.D., history).[82] Hanighen was born in Nebraska, graduated from Harvard University, and worked as a foreign correspondent for the *New York Evening Post* and the *New York Times.* Their book, *Merchants of Death,* was a history of armaments-making and profiteering. It was a best-seller and a Book-of-the-Month Club choice in 1934.[83]

At several key points in their book, Engelbrecht and Hanighen singled out the Morgan bank for dealing in and profiting from the sale of arms. Starting with a story about Pierpont Morgan having sold (defective) arms during the Civil War, they wrote with regard to the First World War, "It is the Morgan group of corporation clients and banks which dominates the American arms industry."[84] *Merchants of Death* was basically a publicity nightmare for the Morgans—a direct challenge to their reputation and character—and it foretold more serious things to come.

Soon after the Pecora Hearings, the Senate began the Senate Munitions Hearings, which were later named after Republican Senator Gerald P. Nye (1892–1971). Born in Wisconsin, Nye graduated from high school at the age of nineteen and embarked on a career in journalism in the footsteps of his father, who was a newspaper publisher. Both Nye and his father were deeply influenced by Robert M. LaFollette, the progressive governor of Wisconsin. In 1926, Nye was elected to the U.S. Senate after having served one year as a replacement for Senator Edwin F. Ladd, who had died in office. Nye's constituent base was rural western farmers. As a champion of agrarian interests, Nye was particularly critical of "urban business interests." His interest in American policy started during the First World War when he became convinced "that foreign ventures were designed more to line the pockets of eastern business and financial interests than to guard American freedom."[85]

Nye had been asked to initiate the munitions investigation by Dorothy Detzer, the executive secretary of the Women's International League, which had been lobbying with other peace groups for an official government inquiry since 1932. Though she was turned down by the Senate Committee on Banking and Currency and the National Recovery Administration, Detzer was able to create an alliance with Nye. Her success spoke to the networks of women reformers and peace groups within the world of politics and also to the broad appeal of their ideological stance.[86] The purpose of the Nye investigation was to show that special interests including "munitions manufacturers, shipbuilders, and financiers" were responsible for pushing the United States into the First World War for the purpose of making money at the expense of the lives of American soldiers.[87] The investigation, which President Roosevelt endorsed, is the clearest example of how the international context changed the debate over financial reform in the post-World War I period.

The Nye investigation claimed that if the economic self-interest of those who might profit from war were reduced, a greater consideration of moral interest would be made in domestic and foreign affairs.[88] Because the Morgan firm had been the buying agent for Great Britain and France during the First World War and because they had been a marketer of British bonds to the American public prior to the war, critics singled them out for having created an implicit commitment between American investors and the outcome of the war. Under this logic, America's best interest was to see the Allies win and see American military power put to that purpose. In addition to being accused of unpatriotic actions, the partners were also charged with morally reprehensible behavior, the encouragement of war for the purpose of profiteering.[89]

The Morgan partners were extremely unhappy with the tenor and the objective of the Nye Hearings. Their character was at stake, and after the Pecora Hearings, they were already on the defensive. At the start of the investigation, the bank's lawyers "demanded certificates of good character" of the investigators of the Munitions Committee before they testified. In response, Stephen Raushenbush, the leading prosecutor of the Nye investigation, suggested that the Morgan partners be asked to provide certificates of character as well.[90] Things only got worse when Nye was quoted as saying, "If the Morgans and other bankers must go in for their share of another war, then, for heaven's sake, let them join the Foreign Legion." The Morgan partners were horrified at the rhetoric used. They responded, "To what lengths is it permissible for a United States senator, about to preside at a semi-judicial inquiry . . . to go? How far will public opinion endorse his endeavor to prejudice opinion beforehand, to declare that the case is already closed? Such procedure, we submit, is unfair, un-American, indecent."[91]

In 1935, Jack Morgan suggested to Lamont that the firm sue both Senator Nye and Oswald Garrison Villard, the editor of the *Nation,* for libel. Morgan wrote Lamont:

> The fact is that I am so tired of letting attacks on our character and on the morality of our conduct go without any reply that I am beginning to think it is unwise not to say something that would indicate to the public that there is something to be said on the other side and that they had better wait and hear both sides before making up their own minds. I fear that the public will get the diea [sic] that we have no answer and that therefore the facts are true.[92]

The partners were particularly angry with Villard's review of former Secretary of State Robert Lansing's book, *War Memoirs.* Villard had written that Lansing and the Morgan firm pushed the United States into war to retrieve money loaned abroad. He referred to the Morgans as the "American traitors."[93]

The fact that these attacks were taken seriously is reflected in the efforts of the partners' family members, who were most likely questioned about the firm's activities as they had been during the SMR controversy and also felt compelled to defend the firm. Florence, Lamont's wife, wrote to Robert Nichols, the British poet, "I don't pretend to know very much about the business of Tom's firm, either in America nor in England, but I do know this: that they are absolutely and irrevocably opposed to having any interest in a business that might be construed as having to do with munitions or armament. They have been subject to a very unjust attack along this very line without any basis for the attack."[94]

Ultimately, the Nye committee could not prove a direct cause and effect between munitions makers and the United States's entry into the First World War, but "Nye and his associates were persuaded nonetheless that opportunities for economic gain had encouraged armament races and agitation that led to war." Though the investigation did not result in any direct legislation, the widespread isolationist sentiment, heightened by fears stemming from the Italo-Ethiopian War, was reflected in the passage of the Neutrality Acts, 1935–1937, one of whose sponsors was Senator Nye.[95]

TNEC AND THE LIMITS OF GOVERNMENT REGULATION

After the munitions investigation concluded in 1936, the Morgan bank had little time to catch its breath before talk started of another government investigation on the concentration of economic power. In April 1938, after the economy suffered a setback in the recession of 1937, President Roosevelt proposed to Congress the Temporary National Economic Committee (TNEC), an investigation on monopoly. When Roosevelt first proposed the commission, he was particularly concerned with "banker control of industry," believing "interlocking financial controls . . . have not given the stability they promised."[96] During his fireside chat on June 24, 1938, he presented the TNEC to the American people as "a fact-finding commission . . . to find the necessary facts for any intelligent legislation on monopoly, on price-fixing, and on the relationship between big business and medium-sized business and little business."[97]

The TNEC Hearings were chaired by "an antimonopoly New Dealer, the Senator Joseph O'Mahoney of Wyoming."[98] The hearings lasted from December 1938 until March 1941.[99] It produced a mountain of information, and during the hearings it was revealed that between "January 1, 1934, to June 30, 1939, the country's thirty-eight leading investment houses managed $7.3 billion of bond issues, of which $1.3 billion received top-quality rating. Not a single investment house outside of New York City managed one of these first-grade issues. . . . One firm alone, Morgan Stanley, accounted for 65 percent of the entire amount."[100]

If taken into consideration that Morgan Stanley actually started business little "more than eighteen months after the beginning of [this period], its share of the top-quality managements would have been 81 percent." A similar study was done with regard to syndicate participations, and it was found that in the same period, "the country's eight leading investment houses, all but one located in New York City, retained for themselves underwriting participations averaging 86 percent of the group's total originations." Because they were able to demonstrate serious evidence of economic concentration, the hearings did little to dispel the popular perception of economic collusion. But significantly, they did not end with concrete results outside of recommendations for the "enforcement of antitrust laws."[101]

Scholars argue that the TNEC represented a shift in New Deal policy for Roosevelt, who was facing extensive push back on his domestic policies after the 1937 economic slowdown and the Supreme Court packing debacle. Though Roosevelt was certainly constrained to act on TNEC's findings by domestic politics, the outcome of the hearings was also an example of how money power investigations had changed in the post-World War I period and how they were limited both by existing business-government relations and by forces outside their control. The most ominous were the developing international crises, which cast a shadow over the TNEC Hearings even before they started.[102]

By March 1936, Germany had already occupied the Rhineland, and by May of that year, Italy had sent Emperor Haile Selaissie into exile. In July 1937, the Sino-Japanese War had begun and by December 1937, Japan had perpetrated a massacre in Nanking, China. The spring before the start of the hearings, Germany had annexed Austria, and in November 1938, thousands of Jewish businesses and synagogues were burned and attacked in Germany. While the TNEC Hearings were still taking place, Britain and France declared war on Germany. The final report was submitted only about nine months before Japan attacked Pearl Harbor. Its antitrust recommendations were largely forgotten as the United States prepared for war.[103]

Ironically, though the Morgans' international ties made them a target of mistrust, the same ties also protected them somewhat from direct intervention. Having fostered the activities of private American bankers in the international sphere, the American government had an implicit stake in protecting their interests, even while the money trust investigations continued. There is no question that the Nye and TNEC Investigations were deeply unpleasant for the Morgans, who, as we shall see, were forced to adapt to their circumstances to safeguard their reputation and capital. But in the long term, their position in larger institutional networks, which was not entirely of their own making, meant they were supported by interests even they considered to be hostile. This included President Roosevelt, who was himself very critical of the Morgans' activities abroad. In December 1934, Roosevelt had written Henry Morgenthau, "China has been the Mecca of the people whom I have called the 'money changers in the Temple' . . . They are still in absolute control. It will take many years and possibly several revolutions to eliminate them."[104]

While the war effort certainly made the critique of big business less likely, Roosevelt's support for private enterprise, capitalism, and individualism was not new or politically expedient. The son of a "wealthy upstate New York landowner," whose family had its roots in mercantile trade, Roosevelt had more in common with Jack Morgan in terms of family background than any other president, save Theodore Roosevelt, his distant relative.[105] He was not anti-capitalist or even anti-imperialist. During Wilson's administration, when he served as assistant secretary of the navy, Roosevelt had been a big supporter of American intervention in Latin America and the Caribbean.[106] In a fireside chat in 1937, Roosevelt stated, "We are already studying how to strengthen our antitrust laws in order to end monopoly—not to hurt but to free the legitimate business of the nation." Like Brandeis, he was concerned about the right to "individual enterprise," which he did see as confined to the borders of the United States.[107]

As Jack Morgan's letter to Henry suggests, the similarities in their background did not endear Roosevelt to the Morgan family or the firm. The Morgans certainly did not approve of his New Deal for the American people, and they were unhappy with the imposition of government power in general. In the same letter Jack Morgan wrote about his Roosevelt nightmare, he also wrote regarding Morgan Stanley's placing of an issue, "But what a nuisance to have to wait for governmental authorizations all the time!"[108] Complain as they did, over the two decades since the Pujo Hearings, the Morgans had also been developing strategies and relationships to adapt to these pressures and changing national circumstances. Even before the outbreak of the Second World War, their efforts focused on challenging the idea that private bankers could not be trusted to serve the interests of others.

THE BANKER AS PUBLIC SERVANT

When Jack Morgan testified at the Pecora Hearings about the traditions and values of private bankers, he was not being evasive when he said there were things more important to him and his firm than money. Though the partners' request for character references by the Nye committee was extreme, it reflected their determination to protect their reputation and their prestige. As we have seen, the definitions and meaning of that reputation were not exactly as they portrayed them to be and the relationships that it entailed were also much broader than they themselves acknowledged, but a bank's reputation remained the source of all things.

Over the course of the interwar period, through their experiences inside and outside the financial world, the Morgans came to understand that their reputation also depended upon their adherence to the norms of national discourse. By June 1934, Lamont wrote a confidential memorandum to his partners on "J. P. Morgan & Co. and Their Relations to the Public." In it he stated, "We are a private firm of merchants. . . . And as private merchants there is no theoretical reason why we should have public relations." But Lamont went on to say, ". . . practically we have such relations, and they are inevitable and proper because of the nature and importance of the firm's transactions." The Morgans could no longer protect themselves simply by claiming their legal status as private bankers. Nor, as Lamont's memorandum indicated, would they try.

Instead, the Morgans made a concerted decision to advertise their public service and charitable work believing that the "individual activities of firm members in certain conspicuous directions" proved the firm's patriotism and sense of civic duty. Lamont detailed the partners' activities he felt should be highlighted:

> The repute gained by the Morgans, senior and junior, as magnificent patrons of the arts, letters, charities, etc. The service of Robert Bacon as Assistant Secretary and for a brief period as Secretary of State. The public service of R.C.L. [Leffingwell] in the Treasury and of S.P.G. [S. Parker Gilbert] in the Treasury and in Germany—even though these services preceded their entry into the firm. H.P.D.'s [Henry P. Davison] work in the American Red Cross during the war. J.P.M.'s [Jack Morgan] service on the Bankers' Committee re. Reparations in 1922. His service on the Young Committee in

1929. T.W.L.'s [Thomas W. Lamont] ditto and in other lesser capacities. Activity of many firm members on educational boards and charitable foundations.[109]

The Morgans' embrace of an identity of the private banker as a public servant was a significant shift from its nineteenth-century past. Ironically, it was also made possible by the American nationalism to which the firm was now resigned and even embraced. In other words, by the postwar period, the Morgans realized that concessions to national discourse did not fundamentally challenge the separate spheres model that was so important to the traditions and practices of gentlemen banking. To the contrary, accepting the nationalism of their time, particularly given America's changing position in the world, was actually essential if the Morgans wanted to protect the private nature of their work and associations. From the 1930s and into the postwar period, this shift in identity was clearly articulated by the younger generation of Morgan partners such as Russell C. Leffingwell.

Russell Cornell Leffingwell (1878–1960) was born and raised in New York. His father was an executive in his mother's family's iron business. He attended Yonkers Military School, Halsey School (both private schools), and Yale University (BA, 1899). After college, he went to law school at Columbia Law School (L.L.B., 1902), where he was editor of the *Columbia Law Review*. His first job after law school was at Guthrie, Cravath & Henderson (1902). He made partner in 1907. When the First World War broke out, Leffingwell volunteered for military service, but his senior partner, Paul Cravath, recommended him to then Secretary of Treasury William McAdoo. Leffingwell was the Assistant Secretary of Treasury from 1917 to 1920 under Secretaries of Treasury McAdoo and Carter Glass. After the war, Leffingwell returned to his former law firm, which was renamed Cravath, Henderson, Leffingwell, & de Gersdorff (1920). He left the firm to become a Morgan partner in 1923.[110]

Leffingwell was one of the few partners in the Morgan firm, if not the only partner, who was not an avowed Republican Party supporter. He had known Franklin D. Roosevelt for several decades, and though they did not always agree, they were friends.[111] These ties, and his government experience, distinguished him from previous generations of Morgan partners, which did not go unnoticed.[112] When he became a partner, the *New York*

Times reported, "Newest Morgan Partner Won Fame in War Loans: Leffing-well, as Assistant Secretary of the Treasury, Virtually in Charge of the Floating of the Government's Vast Bond Issues."[113] Other partners, who represented this important shift in the background and training of Morgan partners in the postwar, included S. Parker Gilbert, who had been Leffing-well's colleague at the Department of Treasury.

The son of a New Jersey politician, Seymour Parker Gilbert (1892–1938) was a graduate of Rutgers University (B.A., 1912) and Harvard Law School (L.L. B., 1915). Before he joined the Department of the Treasury, Gilbert had also been a member of Leffingwell's firm (then called Cravath & Hen-derson). Like Leffingwell, he served at the Department of Treasury during the Wilson years. Gilbert had an even more extensive and prominent career as a government man and was considered something of a prodigy. In 1924, at the age of thirty two, Gilbert was appointed the agent general for repara-tion payments under the Dawes Plan, and his work brought him recogni-tion that led to the Morgan partnership in 1931. (Gilbert was only with the firm for seven years. He died while still a partner at the age of forty-five from cardio-nephritis).[114]

The Morgans were not the only bank to recognize the utility of recruiting partners with government experience and contacts. In 1921, Kuhn, Loeb & Co. invited Sir William Wiseman, a British national with considerable gov-ernment experience (covert and overt) to join the firm. Wiseman made partner in 1929.[115] That year Kuhn, Loeb also promoted Lewis Strauss, Jerome Hanauer's son-in-law, who had been with the firm since 1919 and had worked as secretary for Herbert Hoover, who was a close friend.[116] Like the Morgans, these partners were important resources for the bank and their ties to the government represented potential lines of communication between the banks and the state.[117]

Within the context of the Morgan bank's history, Leffingwell is particu-larly significant because he ascended to the most senior position of the Morgan bank after Lamont's death in 1948, a rise in the firm's hierarchy that itself reflected the firm's willingness to embrace the identity of the banker as public servant. Like Lamont, Leffingwell became deeply invested in the history of the bank and in protecting the reputation of the firm and its founders.[118] Most importantly, he helped to articulate what would become the postwar identity for the bank: the idea of the Morgans as the bastion of "social order."

Time and again, Leffingwell argued that any attack on the Morgan firm was "an attack on our social order . . . because [J. P. Morgan & Co. was] the best and most conspicuous exponents of the social order." After the Pecora Hearings, he stated, "The more serious people behind the attack are only against J. P. Morgan & Co. because they conceive it to be necessary in order to destroy the social order and substitute their own, to destroy also the power and repute of J. P. Morgan & Co. precisely because they (J.P.M. & Co.) are good, able, wise, and admired and envied." [Cross out in the original][119] Leffingwell repeated these arguments well into the war years.

In 1940, he wrote to lawyer Morris Ernst that "the foundation of such power of influence as J. P. Morgan & Co. had and have . . . is not in wealth, but in the personal distinction of the Morgans themselves and of the part- ners they have associated with them from time to time. It is character, ability, diligence, and hard work, not bigness that have made and do make the Morgans." Echoing the arguments made by Pierpont and Jack Morgan at the Pujo and Pecora Hearings, he argued that power "based on char- acter and the personal distinction of the partners and the confidence of the community . . . need not be feared. It has not a proprietary right. It is not something people own. Reputation, character, good will, confidence, these things vanish like a dream if the men who had had them cease to be worthy of them."[120]

Like Lamont, Leffingwell wanted others to know "how many of the Morgan partners during or after the period of membership in the firm took an active part in public life."[121] He placed great emphasis on how the firm was presented and how the history of the firm was remembered. In 1944, he discussed with Lamont how to defend Pierpont Morgan's memory from critics stating, "I do not think [an article written by Professor Gras] ade- quately appreciates the immense value to this country of the elder Morgan's job in reorganizing the railroads after the disaster of the 'Nineties, in ratio- nalizing our industrial organization at the end of the 'Nineties and the beginning of the twentieth century, and in saving us from disaster in 1907. . . . Morgan's leadership was constructive and indispensable."[122] In the modern version of the Morgan's firm history as told by Leffingwell and other partners, the bank and its founder had always been guided by a desire to greater the public good.

While Pierpont Morgan knew that the fortunes of his firm were closely tied to that of the American nation-state, the narrative of the private banker as *public* servant was a marked departure from the way in which he would have expressed the purpose and responsibilities of private banking in his time. That is not to say that Morgan did not think of himself as patriotic or that he did not think of himself as an American with duties beyond his firm to city and country. Rather, it is a comment on the context in which he worked as a private banker and the traditions and networks to which he felt obligated. In his world, the idea of the private banker as a public servant would have implied a relationship with the American state that did not yet exist. Moreover, it would have assumed a relationship to an American society and to a nation not subordinate to European political and economic networks.

In the modern narrative of the bank, however, those historical differences were largely forgotten. In death, Pierpont Morgan could play a role irrespective of his views or choices as an individual. Freed from the boundaries of a certain time and place, Morgan became the embodiment of the bank as representative of economic stability and social order.[123] Over the course of the twentieth century, the Morgan partners repeated this story so persistently that it became a dominant narrative of the firm's own history: the history that it told to itself about itself. An internal Morgan bank memo stated on the eve of the Second World War, "There is no conflict between our duty to the public and our duty to investors. . . . The firm's record as bankers is also measure of our service to the public."[124]

The bank's identity as public servant is significant because it demonstrated that by the Second World War, the Morgans realized that they did not have to remain a private bank in order to protect the fundamental nature of their work. In a world characterized by the growth of American state power and nationalism, they found that that they could continue their traditions and practices and "the free and automatic conduct of business."[125] In fact, private bankers had much to gain by having the formal backing of their government and their network could be made that much more formidable by their willingness to embrace nation-state interests as their own.

Writing the History of Networks

IN FEBRUARY 1940, Jack Morgan announced that J. P. Morgan & Co. was leaving the private unlimited liability partnership structure to become a limited liability corporation. Though Morgan told his friends that the decision was made in order to safeguard the bank's capital from taxes and the death of senior partners, this was only part of the story.[1] Without denying that economic considerations were important, J. P. Morgan & Co.'s formal break with its nineteenth-century merchant banking roots was of enormous practical and symbolic significance. While the bank had abandoned investment banking in 1935 in direct response to federal legislation, the decision to become a corporation was made independently of government mandate. The question is how and why the Morgans came to that decision given that it meant they would no longer be able to claim their business was beyond the scope of public scrutiny.

If the decision to incorporate was the result of a long history of changes in the field of private banking that stemmed largely from the growth of state power and American nationalism, the irony is that the Morgans' willingness to concede national interests was also enabled by the American state. In other words, over time, the Morgans had been forced to acknowledge that private business had public consequences, but they were also able to reaffirm the boundaries of outside intervention. Key structures remained in place without which their business would not have been able to function. The most important of these were the distinction between private versus public spheres of activity and the separation of the economic and social spheres of bankers.

The Morgans' power did not stem from having the exact same interests as other powerful actors, such as the state or their competitors. As we saw, there were many times when their interests diverged and to such an extent that they produced serious consequences for the firm. While certain areas of government were closer to the center of the Morgans' network, important sectors of the state were also beholden to other constituencies, who were able to use the politics of national interests to intervene in their business or at least make it more difficult. The realm of politics was a particularly fraught area of uncertainty for the Morgans, enough so that they tried to adapt in ways that affected their choice of new partners.

If the state assisted the Morgans in maintaining or growing their influence over time, it was not because they were involved in a conspiracy. In fact, their cooperation was much more complex and much stronger than any alliance that they could have deliberately designed. The history of the bank demonstrates that even when their interests were not the same and even if their personnel did not directly overlap, state-business relations were not necessarily at odds. That is because the state had an invested interest and commitment to a society in which the Morgans were also deeply embedded and from whose hierarchies they gained meaning and social status. If the transition of the firm to a more public identity was part of an internal evolution that led to the end of private banking at the Morgans, the Morgans were willing and able to allow more transparency and public accommodation in their business world precisely because the most important structural boundaries remained intact.

It is important to remember that in the late nineteenth century, Pierpont Morgan and his partners considered their personal relationships and those of the bank in the economic sphere to be entirely private, but even they took for granted that the most private of relations, such as marriage and other contractual relations, were sanctioned by or monitored by state institutions. In other words, they were concerned about the degree and character of the state's regulation of individual rights, but they did not assume that individual rights and freedoms meant the absence of state power. Even in the world of business, though the Morgans were unhappy with certain kinds of state regulation, they did not imagine or desire a world guided only by the "free market."

During the Pujo Hearings, the Morgans did not claim that as private individuals they were not beholden to the laws of the nation. To the contrary, they often cited the law as their protection for keeping their work private. Their main concern was that their right to conduct business be respected not only in the public spaces of business, politics, and the market, but also in the private spaces of the firm, the club, the school, and the home. They argued that transparency was unnecessary because their character as men of honor assured the nation and the American people of their honesty as private merchants. And they claimed the bonds of their community and the desire to protect their reputation were greater enforcers of conduct than any formal regulation could bring to bear.

In the early twentieth century, this desire to keep their business private was so paramount that the Morgans abandoned ties they thought were controversial in order to avoid public scrutiny. As we saw, early on in his tenure as the bank's senior partner, Jack Morgan sacrificed formal economic ties, such as interlocking directorates or stockholding interests, rather than accept public examination of the firm's business and associations. Then, by mid-century, Morgan and his partners were not only willing to make their business dealings more transparent, they were willing to sacrifice the very structure of private banking itself. In order to understand this, we must look not only at what changed; we must look at what stayed the same.

By the Second World War, the Morgans abandoned private banking because they did not need to remain a private bank to safeguard the foundations of their business. Even though the balance of power had clearly shifted in the state's favor, they found that their associations were protected from state inquiry in ways that did not even require the active participation of private bankers. Over the course of the twentieth century, private bankers became more willing to acknowledge that the economic sphere was a public place in which consequences were created beyond the boundaries of private firms. But as the state succeeded in expanding their power within the economic and public spheres, it also reaffirmed the existence of separate social and private spheres even within the world of finance.

Thus when Jack Morgan testified at the Pecora Hearings stating, "No law could prevent anyone from discussing problems with, and seeking advice from, friends in whose judgment he has a confidence which is the result of years of experience and cooperation,"[2] he had almost unconditional support on this point. Even during the Great Depression, when conditions were exponentially worse and the reputation of bankers was at its nadir, these relationships remained beyond the scope of government regulation.[3] Unless private associations, which were viewed as part of an individual's private property, involved economic transactions used for illegitimate business activities like the evasion of taxable income, they were seen outside the purview of the state and protected by the right to privacy. Not surprisingly, the legislation that emerged from government hearings was subject to the same limitations. While transparency did increase in certain areas like the issuance of securities, American business remained quite opaque with regard to personal relationships, which were considered to be protected by one's individual rights.[4]

The value placed on the right to private property and the right to privacy was significant, not because the law had the final say or because it had historical precedent, but because it was part of an ongoing negotiation over the values and structures that defined economic interaction in American society at that time.[5] As this book has tried to demonstrate, these values were not determined only by economic factors; the role of non-economic relations must be studied in order to understand the structure of economic networks. The point is not to make an argument for why the state should or should not have monitored personal associations of private bankers in either the economic or social, public or private spheres. The point is to question the origin of the separation itself. The consensus around it has volumes to say about the society in which private bankers lived and what the source of their power could be, but unfortunately, that is not the way the history of the Morgans has been told.

Contemporary studies of the Morgans' economic power have made much use of the data generated by the Pujo and Pecora Hearings, but like their predecessors, they largely focus on economic ties and view their personal and social ties as immaterial. As this book demonstrates, it is critical to have a broader understanding of the bank's relationships, without which these kinds of differences and connections would be extremely difficult to identify, if only because they were so normalized. By aggregating and studying the larger structure of the Morgans' network, we can see the Morgans as dynamic and complex historical actors, who had a particular place in a network of national and international relations and who were not exempt from the social and economic inequalities that divided their society. In fact they were deeply committed to them because of the way in which social hierarchies were central to their own identity and elite status. And they were tied to them because social relationships, culture, and context had a profound influence on the workings of business enterprise in their time.

While the focus on the social organization of private bankers, in particular their gendered and racialized nature, distinguishes this book from other texts on the Morgan bank and other studies on investment banking, the point is not to increase the number of relationships studied as if to say that a complete understanding of the Morgan network would be more accurate by simply studying more of their ties. In other words, the text does not argue that the Morgans' story is missing a consideration of race, gender, or empire, which if added to existing studies would make them complete. Even though new stories certainly provide a different perspective on the bank's history, the larger point is that studying history as connections and relationships goes beyond the traditional contribution of social history of illuminating the motivation or intention of historical actors. It does not ignore the importance of studying cause and effect nor does it simply increase the volume of historical evidence. Rather, it changes the ways in which that evidence is interpreted and linked.

Historians have traditionally been limited by the desire to find direct causes, and therefore, ignore chains of evidence whose connections are indirect, weak, or absent. In particular, the historical profession has had difficulty dealing with the issue of *absence* and has had to draw on the insight of other fields to understand that even in an empirical discipline, what is not there can often be as important as what is there. History, which only studies actors and not their connections, implicitly mobilizes a set of values and beliefs that speaks to the persistence of an older model of history as a rational, linear development, one that unfortunately focuses on the conclusions and separates historical questions into discrete spheres of study.

If economics is not driven by some natural law or market mechanism and is rather the outcome of human agency, the practice of separating the study of economic and social spheres is highly problematic even if the historical actors themselves saw this separation as natural and inevitable, which was exactly the point.[6] When studied together, economic relationships and social ties often contradict the expectations of how relationships are generally assumed to work. They are not all positive, productive, direct, or present. They do not conform to direct causal relationships or develop in a rational manner. They evolve such that actors cannot predict the consequences of their actions even when they provide unambiguous accounts of their intentions and desires. In other words, the choices individual historical actors make involve and affect the multiple networks of which they are members even if they themselves treat and see those networks as separate.

As we saw in the case of the Morgans, the diversity and complexity of their relationships attest to the fact that the separation between their economic and the social worlds was not natural but historical. By highlighting the importance of relationships, the book has endeavored to demonstrate that the Morgans' power, their name and reputation, was created not by an individual or a family but by a community, that it was not just economic but social, and that it was possible, not in spite of the diversity of its network but because of it. In the case of the Morgans, this meant studying relationships that they themselves did not acknowledge, which again was exactly the point. Thus, one goal of the book has been to focus on studying the origin and history of that separation, to situate it within its historical context, and to understand its significance.

With regard to the Morgans' relationship to other banks within the financial community, such as Kuhn, Loeb & Co., the unspoken agreement to maintain separate social spheres and avoid open conflict was critical. Without the common commitment to separate the domestic sphere of the home from the public sphere of business, economic cooperation between the firms, which required personal interaction, would have been extremely difficult if not impossible. Because of their record of economic cooperation, however, the narrative of the social conflict within the financial community has largely been ignored, as have the details of the specific nature of their economic ties. The significance of their social relations remains suppressed by the assumption that the end result, which tells a narrative of economic self-interest, is the most important aspect of their story. Knowing how a story ends, however, is not the same as knowing the story.

Having been defined by a private and cooperative structure of gentlemen banking for four decades, questions remained as to how the Morgans would meet internal and external challenges under the public model. In 1943, three years after J. P. Morgan & Co. was incorporated, Jack Morgan died. As the only partner to have been a member of the bank during the entire period it was a private partnership, his death, as much as the formal conversion to a public corporation, signaled the end of an era for gentlemen banking at the Morgans. For the first time in its history, the House of Morgan proceeded without a J. P. Morgan at the helm, an identifiable leader and figure, who served as the physical link with the firm's foundation.

Yet even in death, J. P. Morgan continued to play an important role in the identity of the Morgan bank, which had come to be defined by a narrative of two modern institutions, the individual and the nation-state. His personal history became an important counter-narrative to the portrayal of the Morgans as a threat to American individualism, equal opportunity, and democracy. Separated from the physical body of a living person (both father and son), Morgan came to represent the highest level of individual and national achievement. His history became the story of a great man, whose legacy set the foundations for the growth of American finance and the American nation. As this book has demonstrated, the creation of this identity and narrative was actually the consequence of a long history and substantial effort of many historical actors, including those far removed from the world of private bankers.

Though the postwar history of the Morgan bank is beyond the scope of the present book, one thing is clear. That trust is so important to the functioning of business is the first clue that a bank, whether a private partnership or a public corporation, is a part of a broader social, political, and cultural world from which it gains its meaning and purpose. A bank's history is not an anonymous story of the movement of capital. It is not the genealogy of a person or a family. It is more than a story of formal economic relations. A history of a bank tells a story of a community that speaks to social, political, and cultural values and structures of a time. Any study of the financial world would do well to look at its relationships, define them broadly, and listen to the story that they tell.

Notes

INTRODUCTION

    1. *Money Trust Investigation: Investigation of Financial and Monetary Conditions in the United States Under House Resolutions 429 and 504 Before a Subcommittee of the Committee on Banking and Currency,* Parts 1–29 (Washington, DC: Government Printing Office, 1913). (Hereafter referred to as the "Money Trust Investigation.") Morgan's testimony can be found in *Money Trust Investigation,* Part 15, 1081–1083, 1050–1052. See also "Money Monopoly an Impossibility, Morgan Asserts," *The New York Times,* December 20, 1912. (Hereafter: *The New York Times* is abbreviated *NYT*). "Morgan Reveals Business of Firm," *NYT,* December 19, 1912. See also Vincent Carosso, *Investment Banking in America: A History* (Cambridge, MA: Harvard University Press, 1970); Robert H. Wiebe, "The House of Morgan and the Executive, 1905–1913," *The American Historical Review* 65:1 (Oct. 1959): 49–60.

    2. *Stock Exchange Practices: Hearings Before the Committee on Banking and Currency, United States Senate, 73rd Congress, First Session on S.Res. 84 (72nd Congress) A Resolution to Investigate Practices of Stock Exchanges with Respect to the Buying and Selling and the Borrowing and Lending of Listed Securities and S.Res.56 (73rd Congress) A Resolution to Investigate the Matter of Banking Operations and Practices, the Issuance*

and Sale of Securities, and the Trading Therein, Part I, May 23, 24, 25, 1933 (Washington: Government Printing Office, 1934). (Hereafter referred to as the "Pecora Hearings.")

3. Pecora Hearings, Part I, 6. See also letter from JPM Jr. to E. C. Grenfell, Jan. 16, 1925, Morgan Grenfell papers, Box 9C, Folder: Dec. 1906–Sept. 1914, Deutsche Bank AG Archives. (Hereafter: DBAG)

4. Alan D. Morrison and William J. Wilhelm Jr., *Investment Banking: Institutions, Politics and Law* (New York: Oxford University Press, 2007): 15; Vincent P. Carosso, *The Morgans: Private International Bankers, 1854–1913* (Cambridge, MA: Harvard University Press, 1987): 7–11.

5. As Ronald Burt writes, "The value of a relationship is not defined inside the relationship; it is defined by the social context around the relationship." Ronald S. Burt, *Brokerage & Closure: An Introduction to Social Capital* (New York: Oxford University Press, 2005): 11.

6. The concept of "embeddedness" was introduced by Karl Polanyi and can also be defined as being "socially situated." Fundamentally, it means that economic actions are situated in the social structure and that the social structure is composed of a series of "ongoing inter-personal networks." Richard Swedberg and Mark Granovetter, "Introduction to the Second Edition," in Mark Granovetter and Richard Swedberg, eds., *The Sociology of Economic Life,* 2nd edition (Boulder, CO: Westview, 2001): 1–9. As Mintz and Schwartz also write, "No social actors, however powerful, are completely or even substantially unconstrained." Beth Mintz and Michael Schwartz, *The Power Structure of American Business* (Chicago: University of Chicago Press, 1985): 58. Martin Sklar also made this point about capitalism, "a mode of production and a set of social relations." Martin J. Sklar, *The Corporate Reconstruction of American Capitalism, 1890–1916: The Market, The Law, and Politics* (New York: Cambridge University Press, 1988): 3–4, 11–12, 83.

7. As quoted in Peter Burke, *History and Social Theory* (Malden, MA: Polity Press, 2005): 153.

8. There are, of course, exceptions, without which this book would not have been possible. A representative example of an excellent, empirically based study of economic elites in their social context (in the United States) is John N. Ingham, *The Iron Barons: A Social Analysis of an American Urban Elite, 1874–1965* (Westport, CT: Greenwood Press, 1978). Ingham also references work such as William Miller, ed., *Men in Business: Essays on the Historical Role of the Entrepreneur* (New York: Harper & Row, 1952).

9. A very small sample of the literature on the Morgans, which does not even include all the biographies of the Morgans or the partners: Lewis S. Corey, *The House of Morgan: A Social Biography of the Masters of Money* (New York: Grosset and Dunlop, 1930); Frederick Lewis Allen, *The Great Pierpont Morgan* (New York: Harper & Brothers, 1949); George Wheeler, *Pierpont Morgan and Friends: The*

Anatomy of a Myth (Englewood Cliffs: Prentice-Hall, Inc., 1973); John Douglas Forbes, *J. P. Morgan, Jr. 1867–1943* (Charlottesville: University Press of Virginia, 1981); Vincent Carosso, "The Morgan Houses: The Seniors, Their Partners, and Their Aides," in Joseph R. Frese, S.J. and Jacob Judd, eds., *American Industrialization, Economic Expansion and the Law* (Tarrytown, New York: Sleepy Hollow Press, 1981); Carosso, *The Morgans;* Kathleen Burk, *Morgan, Grenfell 1838–1988: The Biography of a Merchant Bank* (New York: Oxford University Press, 1989); Ron Chernow, *The House of Morgan: An American Banking Dynasty and the Rise of Modern Finance* (New York: Touchstone, 1990); Jean Strouse, *Morgan: American Financier* (New York: Perennial, 2000); Martin Horn, *Britain, France, and the Financing of the First World War* (Montreal: McGill-Queen's University Press, 2002).

10. Within the literature on trust, there has been an effort to differentiate between trust and trustworthiness, but they are largely studied as concepts rather than as reflective of relationships. That is not to say that work on trust deals only in abstract terms, but even if research compares definitions of trust in different societies or at particular moments in time, that does not mean it deals with the dynamic issue of change over time, which is critical for understanding trust as a relationship. Again, this is in part a disciplinary issue. Exceptions include Avner Greif, "Reputation and Coalitions in Medieval Trade: Evidence on the Maghribi Traders," *The Journal of Economic History,* vol. 49, no. 4 (December 1989): 857–882, which studies the role of reputation and trust in an uncertain environment. See also Elinor Ostrom, *Governing the Commons: The Evolution of Institutions for Collective Action* (New York: Cambridge University Press, 1990).

11. With the possible exception of a firm, J. Pierpont Morgan & Co., which Morgan organized in 1862 with his cousin, James J. Goodwin and closed in 1864, the text considers J. P. Morgan & Co. (Hereafter: JPM & Co.) to be a new firm organized in 1895 with J. P. Morgan as the founding and senior partner. See Carosso, *The Morgans,* 91–107.

12. The House of Morgan was an international merchant bank and had four different branches, JPM & Co. in New York, Drexel & Co. in Philadelphia, Morgan, Harjes & Co./Morgan & Cie. in Paris, and J. S. Morgan & Co./Morgan, Grenfell & Co. in London. In this text, all the branches are discussed but the focus is primarily on the American partners and context. For a study of bankers and their society in the British context, which includes the British branch of the Morgan house, see Youssef Cassis, *City Bankers: 1890–1914* (New York: Cambridge University Press, 1994): 6–7.

13. Note: This text primarily focuses on the Morgans' relationships with their collaborators or other banks as opposed to their clients. For work that studies the Morgans from the perspective of the client, see Miguel Cantillo Simon, "The Rise and Fall of Bank Control in the United States 1890–1939," *American Economic Review,* vol. 88, no. 5 (1988): 1077–1093; Carlos Ramirez, "Did J. P. Morgan's Men

Add Liquidity? Corporate Investment, Cash Flow, and Financial Structure at the Turn of the Century," *Journal of Finance,* vol. 50, no. 2 (1995): 661–678; J. Bradford De Long, "Did J. P. Morgan's Men Add Value? An Economist's Perspective on Financial Capitalism" in Peter Temin, ed., *Inside the Business Enterprise: Historical Perspectives on the Use of Information* (Chicago: University of Chicago Press, 1991): 205–249; J. Bradford De Long, "J. P. Morgan and His Money Trust," *Wilson Quarterly* 16:4 (Fall 1992): 16–30; Leslie Hannah, "What Did Morgan's Men Really Do?" University of Tokyo, Dept. of Economics, Working Paper, http://www.e.u-tokyo.ac.jp/cirje/research/03research 02dp.html (January 2007); Carola Frydman, Eric Hilt, and Lily Y. Zhou, "The Panic of 1907: JP Morgan, Trust Companies, and the Impact of the Financial Crisis," NBER working paper, February 2012.

14. The text draws specifically on the insights of the field of Social Network Analysis (SNA), a subfield of sociology, which has made enormous advancements, theoretically and technologically, in the last thirty years. SNA uses mathematical theory to aggregate, organize, and visually map relationships. For related examples of work in SNA that deal with topics relevant to this book, including the social organization of elites and business, see Alain Degenne and Michel Forsé, *Introducing Social Networks* (London: SAGE Publications, 1999): 3; Bonnie H. Erickson, "Culture, Class, and Connections," *American Journal of Sociology* 102:1 (July 1996): 217–251; Mark S. Mizruchi, "Similarity of Political Behavior Among Large American Corporations," *American Journal of Sociology* 95:2 (Sept. 1989): 401–424; James S. Coleman, "Social Capital in the Creation of Human Capital," *American Journal of Sociology,* vol. 94 supplement (1988): S95–S120; Donald Palmer, Roger Friedland, and Jitendra V. Singh, "The Ties that Bind: Organizational and Class Bases of Stability in a Corporate Interlock Network," *American Sociological Review* 51:6 (Dec. 1986): 781–796; Richard D. Alba and Gwen Moore, "Elite Social Circles," *Applied Network Analysis: A Methodological Introduction,* ed. Ronald S. Burt and Michael J. Minor (Beverly Hills: Sage Publications, 1983): 245–261.

15. See C. Wright Mills, *The Power Elite* (New York: Oxford University Press, 1956); E. Digby Baltzell, *The Protestant Establishment: Aristocracy & Caste in America* (New York: Random House, 1964); Thomas R. Dye, *Who's Running America? Institutional Leadership in the United States* (Englewood Cliffs: Prentice-Hall, Inc., 1976); G. William Domhoff, *Who Rules America? Power, Politics & Social Change,* 5th edition (New York: McGraw Hill, 2006). For work that focuses more on the diversity of economic elites, but in a more contemporary period, see Richard Zweigenhaft and G. William Domhoff, *Jews in the Protestant Establishment* (New York: Praeger, 1982); Richard Zweigenhaft and G. William Domhoff, *Blacks in the White Establishment? A Study of Race and Class in America* (New Haven: Yale University Press, 1991); Richard Zweigenhaft and G. William Domhoff, *Diversity in the Power Elite: Have Women and Minorities Reached the Top?* (New Haven: Yale University Press, 1998); Richard Zweigenhaft and G. William Domhoff, *Diversity in the Power Elite: How it*

Happened, Why it Matters (New York: Rowman & Littlefield Publishers, Inc., 2006).

16. The Morgan bank was the direct descendant of several other American and European houses, including George Peabody & Co., Drexel, Morgan & Co., Drexel, Harjes & Co. Their earlier histories are discussed at length in Carosso, *The Morgans;* Kathleen Burk, *Morgan, Grenfell 1838–1988.*

17. For a study of the financial community in New York during the Gilded Age, see Sven Beckert, *The Monied Metropolis: New York City and the Consolidation of the American Bourgeoisie, 1850–1896* (New York: Cambridge University Press, 2003).

18. The focus on the post-1895 period also resonates with the particular history of the Morgan bank. Before the death of his father, Junius Spencer Morgan (1813–1890), Pierpont Morgan was not the senior partner of the House of Morgan and did not even have any official ties to the London house. Until Anthony J. Drexel (1826–1893) died in 1893, Pierpont also retained his title as the secondary partner in the firm of Drexel, Morgan & Co., whose founding was also engineered by his father in 1871. While Morgan was actively involved in the business of the other Morgan houses, the founding of JPM & Co. in 1895 marked a new era in the history of the House of Morgan entirely under the leadership of Pierpont Morgan. That this story is one endemic to the twentieth century is also evident in the fact that a central narrative in the history of their network is the Morgans' relationship with the American nation-state. It is no accident, for example, that JPM & Co.'s "first great undertaking," which cemented Pierpont Morgan's status as one of the world's premiere private bankers, was the gold sale for the American government in February 1895. Carosso, *The Morgans,* 276, 307.

19. Michael J. Hogan, *Informal Entente: The Private Structure of Cooperation in Anglo-American Economic Diplomacy, 1918–1928* (Chicago: Imprint Publications, 1991): 1; Alfred E. Eckes Jr. and Thomas W. Zeiler, *Globalization and the American Century* (New York: Cambridge University Press, 2003): 48.

20. There is no historical monograph about Kuhn, Loeb & Co.'s business outside of two histories published by the company in the mid-twentieth century. See Kuhn, Loeb & Co., *Investment Banking Through Four Generations* (New York: Kuhn, Loeb & Co., 1955); Kuhn, Loeb & Co., *A Century of Investment Banking* (New York: Kuhn, Loeb & Co., 1967).

In 1977, Kuhn, Loeb & Co. merged with Lehman Brothers (f. 1850) to become Lehman Kuhn, Loeb Inc. The bank's foreign division was called Kuhn Loeb Lehman Brothers International. In 1984, when the firm merged with American Express to become Shearson Lehman Brothers, Kuhn, Loeb's name was dropped entirely. Lehman Brothers was "spun off" from American Express in 1994 and went back to its original name. It was liquidated in 2008 after suffering heavy losses in the subprime mortgage crisis. "Lehman, and Kuhn, Loeb to Merge," *NYT,* Nov. 29, 1977; "Shearson, Lehman Sign Agreement," *NYT,* Apr. 20, 1984.

21. Naomi W. Cohen, *Jacob H. Schiff: A Study in American Jewish Leadership* (Hanover: Brandeis University Press, 1999): 3–9. See also Cyrus Adler, *Jacob H. Schiff: His Life and Letters,* vols. 1 & 2 (New York: Doubleday, Doran and Co., 1928).

22. For a discussion of Kuhn, Loeb's international network, see Priscilla M. Roberts, "A Conflict of Loyalties: Kuhn, Loeb and Company and the First World War, 1914–1917" in *Studies in the American Jewish Experience II,* ed. Jacob R. Marcus and Abraham J. Peck (New York: University Press of America, 1984): 4–5.

23. Vincent Carosso and Richard Sylla, "U.S. Banks in International Finance" in Rondo Cameron and V. I. Boykin, *International Banking 1870–1914* (New York: Oxford University Press, 1991): 7–8, 18–20. Roberta Allbert Dayer, *Bankers and Diplomats in China, 1971–1925: The Anglo-American Relationship* (New York: Frank Cass and Company Limited, 1981): 61.

During the early years of the Wilson administration, the bank was forced to withdraw from the IBC. After the war, however, Wilson approved the reorganization of a second IBC. JPM & Co. was the leading American bank of the American group of both consortia. For a much more detailed discussion of the Morgan bank's involvement in China before the First World War, see Carosso, *The Morgans,* 550–578. For the period during the war until 1925, see Dayer, *Bankers and Diplomats;* Arthur N. Young (Financial Adviser to China, 1929–1947), *China's Nation-Building Effort, 1927–1937: The Financial and Economic Record* (Palo Alto: Hoover Institution Press, Stanford University, 1971). See also for studies of dollar diplomacy before the Second World War, Emily S. Rosenberg, *Spreading the American Dream: American Economic and Cultural Expansion, 1890–1945* (New York: Hill and Wang, 1982) and *Financial Missionaries to the World: The Politics and Culture of Dollar Diplomacy, 1900–1930* (Cambridge: Harvard University Press, 1999).

The Hukuang Railway was to go from the city of Hankow (Wuhan) on the Yang Tze River in central China to the city of Canton in southern China. "A Review of the Interests of the United States Government and its Nationals in Financial Questions in China," undated without an author, most likely 1919, Stanley Hornbeck Papers, Box 51, Folder: China: American Interests In, Hoover Institution Archives (Hereafter: HIA); Young, *China's Nation-Building,* 129; Extract from Moody's Government and Municipal Manual, last edition, issued as of January 1, 1936, July 3, 1936, Arthur N. Young Papers, Box 22, Folder: Hukuang, From May 1 to July 31, 1936, HIA. See also Young, *China's Nation-Building,* 24; Cyrus Adler, *Jacob H. Schiff,* 251–259; Rosenberg, *Financial Missionaries,* 2.

24. Cohen, *Jacob H. Schiff,* 38.

25. W. G. Beasley, *Japanese Imperialism, 1894–1945* (New York: Clarendon Press, 1987): 2, 14; Paul A. Varg, *New England and Foreign Relations, 1789–1850* (Hanover, NH: University Press of New England, 1983): 6; Rosenberg, *Spreading the American Dream,* 26; Joan Hoff Wilson, *American Business & Foreign Policy, 1920–33* (Boston: Beacon Press, 1973): 215, 201; Dayer, *Bankers and Diplomats,* 49. For Jacob

Schiff's views on Chinese territorial integrity and Japanese imperialism, see Cohen, *Jacob H. Schiff*, 34.

26. "A Review of the Interests of the United States Government and its Nationals in Financial Questions in China," undated without an author, most likely 1919, Stanley Hornbeck Papers, Box 51, Folder: China: American Interests In, HIA; Young, *China's Nation-Building*, 129. For cooperation between the House of Morgan and National City Bank, see Carl P. Parrini, *Heir to Empire: United States Economic Diplomacy 1916–1923* (Pittsburgh, PA: University of Pittsburg Press, 1969): 55.

27. First National Bank of New York and National City Bank merged in 1955 to become the First National City Bank of New York, a predecessor to the modern-day Citibank (1976). National City Bank of New York was founded in 1812 as City Bank of New York. It changed its name in 1865 when it became a national bank and received a federal charter. National City Bank was the largest bank in the United States after 1894. It was the first national bank to establish correspondent branches overseas (1914). By 1939, National City was the world's largest bank. "National City Bank Merger with First National Slated," *NYT,* Mar. 2, 1955. In 1962, the bank was renamed First National City Bank. In 1968, First National City Bank Corporation, a bank holding company, was created. It changed its name to Citicorp in 1974. In 1976, the "First National City Bank [became] Citibank, N.A. (for National Association)" http://www.citigroup.com/citi/corporate/history/citibank.htm (June 14, 2010). For a map of all the multiple organizations that merged to become the modern-day Citibank, see http://www.citibank.com/citi/corporate/history/citibank.htm (Sept. 28, 2011).

28. Edward M. Lamont, *The Ambassador From Wall Street: The Story of Thomas W. Lamont, J. P. Morgan's Chief Executive* (New York: Madison Books, 1994): 210. See for exceptions in literature: Vincent P. Carosso, "A Financial Elite: New York's German-Jewish Investment Bankers," *American Jewish Historical Quarterly (1961–1978),* vol. 66, no. 1–4 (Sept. 1976–1977): 80; Barry E. Supple, "A Business Elite: German-Jewish Financiers in Nineteenth-Century New York," *Business History Review,* vol. 31 (Summer 1957): 171; Carosso, *Investment Banking in America,* 452.

29. Though the common practice is to call German Jewish banks as such, a more accurate, albeit unwieldy, description would be German Jewish-American banks. In this text the term "German Jewish" refers to "German Jewish American" banks.

30. In a seminal network study, Mark Granovetter argued that highly cohesive networks are actually disadvantaged by the structure of their network from accessing personnel, ideas, information, and influence. The idea is that if an individual or organization is only tied to other individuals or organizations who are similar, then those individuals or organizations will tend to have the same kinds of ties or connections. Therefore, a tightly cohesive community can actually reduce its viability and life span by cutting itself off from weak ties, which can provide ideas, information, and resources not found within a given network and that could be the key factors to

innovation. Structurally then, there is a problem with creating cohesion based on homogeneity. While effective in forming the in-group identity, cohesion based on homogeneity could actually decrease the value of the organization particularly as other sectors increase in scope and scale. Mark Granovetter, "The Strength of Weak Ties," *American Journal of Sociology*, vol. 78 (May 1973): 1360–1380; Granovetter, "The Strength of Weak Ties: A Network Theory Revisited," *Sociological Theory*, vol. 1 (1983): 201–223. See also Mark Granovetter, *Getting a Job: A Study of Contacts and Careers* (Chicago: University of Chicago Press, 1995) and Burt, *Brokerage & Closure*, 3–57. For excellent studies that look at economic leadership and decentralized networks in a historical context, see John F. Padgett and Christopher K. Ansell, "Robust Action and the Rise of the Medici," *American Journal of Sociology* 98:6 (May 1993): 1259–1319; Emily Erikson and Peter Bearman, "Malfeasance and the Foundations for Global Trade: The Structure of English Trade in the East Indies, 1601–1833," *American Journal of Sociology*, vol. 112, no. 1 (July 2006): 195–230.

31. See Carosso, *Investment Banking in America*, 152.

I. GENTLEMEN BANKING BEFORE 1914

1. George Peabody & Co. was founded in 1851 though there were earlier iterations of the bank. Born in Massachussetts, Peabody [1795–1869] established himself in Baltimore before moving to London. He had lived in London since 1837. Junius Morgan became a partner in the firm in 1854. http://www.peabodyevents.library. jhu.edu/history.html and http://www.themorgan.org/about/historyMore.asp?id=1.

For an extensive biography of Pierpont Morgan, see Jean Strouse, *Morgan: American Financier* (New York: Perennial, 2000).

2. Drexel & Co. severed ties with JPM & Co. in 1940 to pursue investment banking. In the post-1940 era, Drexel & Co. joined with Harriman, Ripley & Co. (1966), became Drexel Firestone (1970), and then Drexel, Burnham & Lambert (1973) after merging with Burnham & Co., which was founded in 1935 by I. W. Burnham II (1909–2002). Charles R. Geisst, *The Last Partnerships: Inside the Great Wall Street Money Dynasties* (New York: McGraw-Hill, 2001): 261.

3. In 1933, because JPM & Co. could not remain "principal shareholders and executive officers of a British company with unlimited liability," Morgan, Grenfell & Co. became a limited liability company, Morgan Grenfell & Co., Ltd. "All of the London partners became directors and managing directors." Morgan, Grenfell & Co. formally separated from JPM & Co., Drexel & Co., and Morgan et Cie. Morgan, Grenfell & Co. is included in the Morgan network after 1933 because ties between the banks through the individual partners/directors remained strong, at least until the merger between Guaranty Trust and JPM & Co. in 1959. In May 1981, Morgan, Guaranty & Co. sold its remaining shares in Morgan, Grenfell & Co. In 1989, Morgan, Grenfell & Co. merged with Deutsche Bank. See Kathleen Burk, *Morgan,*

Grenfell 1838–1988: The Biography of a Merchant Bank (New York: Oxford University Press, 1989): 102, 157–158, 190, 246–255, 257.

4. Morgan et Cie. remained the Paris branch of JPM & Co. In 1963 Morgan et Cie. was reopened in Paris as "a Morgan Guaranty overseas subsidiary in alliance with London's Morgan Grenfell and two Dutch investment banking houses." In 1967, it became Morgan & Cie., International under the joint effort of Morgan, Guaranty and Morgan, Stanley. "France: Morgan's Return," *Time,* Jan. 18, 1963; "Company History," http://www.morganstanley.com/company/history.html (Aug. 12, 2010).

5. For JPM & Co.'s partnership agreements, see "Articles of Partnership, 1894–1908" and "Articles of copartnership, J. P. Morgan & Co., 1916–1939," Morgan Firm papers, ARC 1195, Boxes 1 and 5, Pierpont Morgan Library (Hereafter: PML). J. S. Morgan & Co., later Morgan, Grenfell & Co., and Morgan, Harjes & Co., later Morgan et Cie., had separate partnership agreements. See Records of the Morgan firms, Box 5, Folder: Articles of copartnership, 1893, Folder: Articles of copartnership, 1907–9, Folder: Articles of copartnership, 1927–1928, Box 6, Folder: Articles of copartnership, 1931, Folder: Articles of copartnership, 1932–33, Folder: Articles of copartnership, 1934, Folder: Articles of copartnership, 1937, Folder: Articles of copartnership, 1941; Box 3, Folder: Articles of Co-partnership: J. S. Morgan & Co., 1882–1884; Folder: Articles of Co-partnership: J. S. Morgan & Co., 1885–1889; Folder: Articles of Co-partnership: J. S. Morgan & Co., 1898–1899. See also Burk, *Morgan, Grenfell 1838–1988,* 62.

6. This held true for the entire period in which the Morgans were a private partnership. See letter from E. C. Grenfell to JPM Jr., Sept. 5, 1914, E. C. Grenfell papers, Box 9C, Folder: Dec. 1906–Sept. 1914, Deutsche Bank AG Archives. (Hereafter: DBAG)

7. Vincent P. Carosso, *The Morgans: Private International Bankers, 1854–1913* (Cambridge, MA: Harvard University Press, 1987): 12; Stanley Chapman, *The Rise of Merchant Banking* (Boston: George Allen & Unwin, 1984): 2.

8. Morrison and Wilhelm Jr. refer to this as reputational capital. Alan D. Morrison and William J. Wilhelm Jr., *Investment Banking: Institutions, Politics and Law* (New York: Oxford University Press, 2007): 15. See also Carosso, *The Morgans,* 7–11.

9. This does not include the First Bank of the United States and the Second Bank of the United States and refers largely to the post-Civil War era. For a discussion of the United States in comparison to that of other financial systems, see Richard Sylla, Richard Tilly, and Gabriel Tortella, *The State, the Financial System, and Economic Modernization* (New York: Cambridge University Press, 1999); Allan H. Meltzer, *A History of the Federal Reserve, vol. 1: 1913–1951* (Chicago: University of Chicago Press, 2003).

10. See Vincent Carosso and Richard Sylla, "U.S. Banks in International Finance," in Rondo Cameron and V. I. Boykin, *International Banking 1870–1914* (New York:

Oxford University Press, 1991): 53; Leslie Hannah, "J. P. Morgan in London and New York before 1914," *Business History Review,* 85 (Spring 2011): 113–150.

11. Vincent Carosso, "The Wall Street Money Trust from Pujo to Medina," *Business History Review,* vol. 47, no. 4 (Winter 1973): 421–437; Vincent P. Carosso, "A Financial Elite: New York's German-Jewish Investment Bankers," *American Jewish Historical Quarterly (1961–1978),* vol. 66, no. 1–4 (Sept. 1976–1977): 82–83.

12. When First National Bank was first organized, for example, "it dealt almost exclusively in Government Bonds." It did not invest heavily in non-government bonds until after 1901. *Money Trust Investigation,* Part 26, 2024.

13. Morgan partner Robert Bacon was a director in National City from 1896 to 1903. George Perkins was a director from 1900 to 1912. Jack Morgan was a director from 1909 to 1914. Harold van B. Cleveland and Thomas F. Huertas, *Citibank, 1812–1970* (Cambridge, MA: Harvard University Press, 1985): 311–317.

14. The national banking laws of 1863 and 1864 also created a reserve-city and central-reserve-city banking system whereby a pyramid structure of bank deposits was created and most deposits flowed into the reserves of large national banks based in New York City. Carosso and Sylla, "U.S. Banks in International Finance," 54, 68–70.

15. Vincent P. Carosso, *Investment Banking in America: A History* (Cambridge, MA: Harvard University Press, 1970): 51–52.

16. Carosso, *Investment Banking in America,* 53, 55–56.

17. See letter from Jacob H. Schiff (Hereafter: JHS) to Robert Fleming, Mar. 1, 1897, Jacob H. Schiff papers (Hereafter: JHS papers), MS 456, Box 437, Folder 5, American Jewish Archives (Hereafter AJA); Letter to Robert Fleming from JHS, JHS, MS 456, Box 437, Folder 10, June 26, 1903; Letter to Robert Fleming from JHS, Mar. 29, 1904, JHS, MS 456, Box 437, Folder 11, AJA.

18. See also Carosso, "A Financial Elite," 80; Barry E. Supple, "A Business Elite: German-Jewish Financiers in Nineteenth-Century New York," *Business History Review,* vol. 31 (Summer 1957): 171; Carosso, *Investment Banking in America,* 63, 452; Samuel L. Hayes III, A. Michael Spence, David Van Praag Marks, *Competition in the Investment Banking Industry* (Cambridge, MA: Harvard University Press, 1983): 5–20.

19. JPM had 139 purchases between 1894 and 1914, 136 of them had the amounts listed with an approximate total of $432 million. The total sum of purchases that the Morgan firm undertook was about 10 percent of the total amount of syndicates it sponsored and less than a third (31 percent) of the amount that it took of syndicates themselves in the same period. Unless otherwise noted, all of the information on Morgan syndicates comes from J. P. Morgan & Co. Syndicate Books, ARC 108–ARC 119, PML.

Brief background on the syndicate translation: JPM & Co. left twelve syndicate books, which are very large ledgers, handwritten with pages of documents (usually typewritten) bound into each book. Every deal in those books was put into an Excel file and coded according to the type of deal, the type of client, whether it had a comanager, if it was syndicated by JPM & Co., the total amount that JPM & Co. had to subdivide, the profit and loss if noted, and the year, among other details. Every single syndicate participant was noted for every syndicate and given a separate Excel file with the name of the deal, the year, and the amount. The amounts that the Morgans kept for each branch in the House (JPM, JSM, etc.) was also kept in a separate file and coded. All the totals were then aggregated and later parsed into five-year intervals. If the deal originated from another bank and was offered to the Morgans, that was noted in another file called "Other," which had the name of the deal, the name of the originating bank, the total amount of the deal, the amount given to JPM & Co. and the other Morgan houses, the profit if noted, and the year. If the profits or totals were listed in British pounds, they were converted into U.S. dollars according to the gold standard exchange rate at that time (approximately $4.86 to the pound) and included in the total. See Milton Friedman and Anna Jacobson Schwartz, *A Monetary History of the United States, 1867–1960* (Princeton, NJ: Princeton University Press, 1971): 85. (Thanks to Mary Tone Rodgers for this reference.) If the amount of the deal or the participation or the profit was listed in any other currency or in shares of stock, it was not included and noted.

20. For JPM & Co.'s syndicates between 1894 and 1914, the percentage that had the profits and losses noted was 71 percent. The average percentage of all the deals JPM & Co. initiated (including more than syndicates), which had the profits and losses listed, was about 52 percent for the same period. As time passed, the bank became more systematic in noting its profits in its syndicate books. By 1910–1914, 90 percent of the syndicates had the profits listed.

21. This amount includes multiple transactions (origination or managing, purchasing, banking, selling, distributing groups) made for the same deal and cannot be considered relative to the total syndicate amount. The total amount for 214 of the transactions (approximately 4 percent of the total 5,424) was either unknown or could not be converted easily (stocks, etc.).

22. This figure was probably higher because there were 17 syndicate participations of a total 321 (the number is higher than the above because some syndicate participations included multiple transactions, for example, when JPM & Co. took part in another bank's buying and selling syndicates) where the total amounts that the other party had to organize were unknown. Of the 321, 70 (or 22 percent), did not have their profits and losses listed for the period in question. (They might have the total profits listed for the deal, which might have ended five to ten years later, but those numbers were not included.) For the deals that did have the profits and losses noted, the aggregate total was approximately $5.1 million for 1894–1914. For about 6 percent of those deals (25 of 411 separate transactions), JPM & Co.'s exact participation amount was unknown.

23. For the period between 1915 and 1934, JPM & Co. noted approximately 929 deals, the total amount of which (not including that which was given by other banks) was over $11.7 billion. Of that total, 491 were deals that JPM & Co. initiated and

involved the participation of another bank, or 53 percent of the total. In other words, for the entire 1894–1934 period as indicated by its syndicate books, the vast majority of JPM & Co.'s business involved cooperation with another bank, firm, individual, etc. Syndicate participations given to JPM & Co. by another bank were 279, or 30 percent of the total. Aggregated, the 770 deals account for 83 percent of all the deals that JPM & Co. listed in their syndicate books. Other deals not included in the above were purchases or sales, for example, which the Morgan bank made on behalf of a client or for its own account.

24. Carosso, *Investment Banking in America,* 63; Hayes, Spence, Marks, *Competition in the Investment Banking Industry,* 5–6.

25. Hayes, Spence, Marks, *Competition in the Investment Banking Industry,* 5–17.

26. Letter from JHS to Robert Fleming, June 21, 1898, JHS, MS 456, Box 437, Folder 6, AJA; Hayes, Spence, Marks, *Competition in the Investment Banking Industry,* 14–15.

27. Hayes, Spence, Marks, *Competition in the Investment Banking Industry,* 5–17.

28. Private banks and commercial banks of Morgan's stature also held to this code. See Cleveland and Huertas, *Citibank, 1812–1970,* 33. Clients were not always as cooperative. See for example letter to Otto H. Kahn (Hereafter: OHK) from Victor Morawetz, Jan. 10, 1902, letter to Victor Morawetz from JHS, Jan. 13, 1902, letter to JHS from Victor Morawetz, Jan. 14, 1902, JHS papers, MS 456, Box 437, Folder 9; Letter to OHK from Victor Morawetz, Jan. 10, 1902, Letter from JHS to Victor Morawetz, Jan. 13, 1902 and reply from Victor Morawetz, Jan. 4, 1902, JHS papers, MS 456, Box 437/9, AJA.

29. When a bank broke that code, it could be banned from syndicate participation for decades, even permanently. One example is Speyer & Co., a prominent international banking house, which was effectively banned from the Morgans' syndicates after 1905.

Speyer & Co. was originally called Philip Speyer & Co. and was founded in 1845 by Philip Speyer, the descendant of a prestigious Frankfurt banking family. Speyer immigrated to the United States from Germany in 1837. He was thus one of the earlier waves of German Jewish immigrants. When he died in 1876, the name of the bank was changed to Speyer & Co. Its European affiliates included Speyer Bros. of London and Lazard Speyer-Ellissen of Frankfurt. James Speyer (1861–1941), Philip's nephew, became the senior partner in 1899. He was American born and a native New Yorker. Speyer's wife, Ellen Prince Lowery, who died in 1921, was not Jewish. (They did not have any children.) When James Speyer retired from the firm in 1939, he decided to close it rather than let his name continue with the remaining partners. "James Speyer, 80, Dies Here," *NYT,* Nov. 1, 1941; "Speyer & Co.," 1935, James Speyer papers, Reel #2, Manuscripts and Archives Division. The New York Public Library. Astor, Lenox, and Tilden Foundations. (Hereafter: NYPL); "James Speyer Plans to Retire," *Citizen Register,* June 14, 1939, James Speyer papers, Reel #6, NYPL.

In 1904, when Jack Morgan was living in London and working at J.S. Morgan & Co., the bank had a falling out with Speyers over an issue with Cuba. Though the lead banks were Kuhn, Loeb and National City, the deal had been initiated by Lord Revelstoke of Baring Bros., who had strong working ties to the Morgan London branch. When Revelstoke decided to postpone the business for external reasons, Speyers, led by London-based Edgar Speyer, took up the opportunity to do it. Morgan's London partner, Clinton Dawkins wrote Jack Morgan, "We had been the victim of Speyers." Letter from Clinton Dawkins to Jack Morgan, Feb. 16, 1904, Morgan Grenfell & Co. papers, MS 21, 800, 2, Guildhall Library. See also Philip Ziegler, *The Sixth Great Power: Barings, 1762–1929* (London: William Collins Sons & Co. Ltd., 1988): 303–304.

Speyer & Co. continued to work with Kuhn, Loeb & Co. and as comanagers on syndicates in which JPM & Co. participated, but the firm was excluded from taking a participation in the Morgans' syndicates after this period. Before this time, they had a more significant participation in the syndicates than Kuhn, Loeb. This does not mean, however, that Speyer & Co. did not expect to take part if a portion was given to it by Kuhn, Loeb & Co., but if that was the case and in how many cases and if the Morgans knew is unknown. As years progressed, Speyer & Co.'s relations with Kuhn, Loeb also became frayed. By 1909, Kuhn, Loeb joined with J. P. Morgan & Co., National City, and First National to create a North American group to cooperate on issues, which included Cuba. Carosso writes, ". . . all four usually joined together to oppose Speyer & Co., the most determined of their rivals for leadership of international accounts." Carosso, *The Morgans,* 591.

30. Pecora Hearings, Part I, 3–4.

31. See for Jacob Schiff's views with regard to his firm's "moral responsibility" for the notes they sell, letter to the Kuhn, Loeb & Co. papers "Dear Friends" from JHS, Mar. 29, 1915, JHS papers, MS 456, 444/4a, AJA. See also Cyrus Adler, *Jacob H. Schiff: His Life and Letters,* vols. 1 & 2 (Garden City, New York: Doubleday, Doran & Co., 1928): 121, 126, 128, 159. See also for the Morgans' views, letter from JPM Jr. to E. C. Grenfell, Jan. 16, 1925, Morgan Grenfell papers, Box 9C, Folder: Dec. 1906–Sept. 1914, DBAG.

32. "F. Augustus Heinze, Mine Owner, Dead," *NYT,* Nov. 5, 1914; David Fettig, "F. Augustus Heinze and the Panic of 1907," The Federal Reserve Bank of Minneapolis, Aug. 1989 (http://www.minneapolisfed.org/publications_papers/pub_display .cfm?id=3807) (Mar. 22, 2010).

33. Carosso, *The Morgans,* 537–538.

34. "C. T. Barney Dies, A Suicide," *NYT,* Nov. 15, 1907.

35. See *Money Trust Investigation,* Part 7, 631. For another more detailed perspective on the origins of the panic with regard to federal gold policy and based on Friedman and Schwartz, *Monetary History,* see Cleveland and Huertas, *Citibank, 1812–1970,* 51–53.

36. Ron Chernow, *The House of Morgan: An American Banking Dynasty and the Rise of Modern Finance* (New York: Touchstone, 1990): 121.

37. "Copy of memorandum the Panic of 1907 written by George W. Perkins and sent to Henry P. Davison. Sent to H.L.S. [Pierpont Morgan's son-in-law] and sent to G.W.P. Jr. Jan. 4, 1921." Herbert L. Satterlee papers (Hereafter: HLS), ARC 1219, Box 12, Folder 2, PML.

Pierpont Morgan also had meetings for the Corsair Dining Club and the Whist Club at Sherry's, and he had meals there often. J. P. Morgan Sr.'s datebooks, Pierpont Morgan papers, ARC 1196, Box 28, PML; "Sherry's," *NYT*, June 11, 1926; Morgan's daughter Juliet's wedding in 1894 was catered by Louis Sherry, the owner of Sherry's, as was his daughter Louisa's wedding in 1900. Strouse, *Morgan: American Financier,* 332, 389.

Sherry's was originally located on Thirty-Eighth Street and Sixth Avenue. It closed in 1919 due to Prohibition. "Louis Sherry Dies; Famous Caterer," *NYT*, June 10, 1926. It was later reopened and reorganized in the late 1920s and closed in the 1950s. It was also said that Louis Sherry catered Pierpont Morgan's funeral in 1913. Virginia Lee Warren, "A New Day of Elegance for Sherry's," *NYT*, July 24, 1966.

38. Strong came from a family of bankers and merchants. His father was a railroad manager. His father-in-law, E. C. Converse, was also a prominent banker. Converse was the chairman of the board of Bankers Trust, the president of Liberty National Bank, and the head of Astor Trust Co. Strong became president of Bankers Trust in January 1914 and was appointed the governor of the Federal Reserve Bank of New York in October 1914. Katherine Converse was Strong's second wife. They married in 1907 and divorced in 1920. After Strong's first wife, Margaret LeBoutillier, committed suicide in 1905, the Davisons took in Strong's three children. Chernow, *House of Morgan,* 182; "Benjamin Strong Dies at 81," *NYT*, Nov. 7, 1915; "Benjamin Strong, Banker, Dies at 56," *NYT*, Oct. 17, 1928; "E. C. Converse Dies of Heart Disease," *NYT*, Apr. 5, 1921; Michael V. Namorato, "Strong, Benjamin"; http://www.anb.org/articles/06/06–00635.html; *American National Biography Online* Feb. 2000. (June 28, 2012).

39. "An extract from the notes made by Benjamin Strong concerning his friendship and relations with Henry P. Davison. These notes loaned to H.L.S. by T.W.L., Feb. 1, 1929," HLS papers, ARC 1219, Box 12, Folder 2, PML.

40. "Copy of memorandum the Panic of 1907 written by George W. Perkins and sent to Henry P. Davison. Sent to H.L.S. and sent to G.W.P. Jr. Jan. 4, 1921." HLS papers, ARC 1219, Box 12, Folder 2, PML.

41. "An extract from the notes made by Benjamin Strong concerning his friendship and relations with Henry P. Davison. These notes loaned to H.L.S. by T.W.L., Feb. 1, 1929." HLS papers, ARC 1219, Box 12, Folder 2, PML.

42. "An extract from the notes made by Benjamin Strong concerning his friend-

ship and relations with Henry P. Davison. These notes loaned to H.L.S. by T.W.L., Feb. 1, 1929." HLS papers, ARC 1219, Box 12, Folder 2, PML.

43. Carosso, *The Morgans,* 535–547.

44. See also testimony of Walter Frew, President, Corn Exchange Bank, *Money Trust Investigation,* Part 7, 599.

45. "Business: All Paths Unite!" *Time,* Mar. 26, 1934.

46. Baker was also one of the original investors in the First National Bank. Baker eventually broke with the Thompson interests, who left First National and founded Chase National Bank (f. 1877), named in honor of Salmon P. Chase, former secretary of treasury. Baker retired from the bank's presidency in 1909 and became chairman of the board. Sue C. Patrick. "Baker, George Fisher"; http://www.anb.org/articles/10/10–00079.html; *American National Biography Online* Feb. 2000 (Dec. 1, 2010). See also Sheridan A. Logan, *George F. Baker and His Bank: 1840–1955: A Double Biography* (New York: The George F. Baker Trust, 1981).

47. As quoted in Carosso, *The Morgans,* 452.

48. Cleveland and Huertas, *Citibank, 1812–1970,* 34. Stillman's father's partner, William Woodward, had a brother named James Woodward, who was the president of Hanover National Bank during the panic. James Woodward was also an important ally of Stillman's. See also Milton Berman, "Stillman, James"; http://www.anb.org/articles/10/10–01589.html; *American National Biography Online* Feb. 2000. (Dec. 1, 2010).

49. Between 1895 and 1899, National City Bank participated in seven of J.P Morgan & Co.'s syndicates, all for different clients for an approximate total participation of $12 million. First National had thirteen participations with nine unique clients for a total of about $8.2 million. (For one, the amount was unknown.) In the following five-year period, First National Bank began to take the lead with thirty-eight participations for twenty unique clients for a total of $61 million (one was unknown), while National City had twelve participations for nine unique clients for a total of $34.5 million. During the next five-year period, which included the Panic of 1907, 1905–1909, First National Bank jumped to sixty-two participations for thirty-one unique clients for a total of almost $117 million, almost double the previous five-year period total, while National City moved up to thirty-nine participations for twenty-six unique clients for a total of $83 million. In the next five-year period before the First World War, the total for both banks would almost triple, and during this period, National City Bank also began to take a slight lead. National City Bank had 151 participations for fifty-six unique clients for a total of $365 million, and First National had 153 participations for fifty-eight unique clients for a total of $358 million (four were unknown for each bank). See also Baker's testimony, *Money Trust Investigation,* Part 20, 1467. Untermyer also made a point of noticing this change in the bank's relationships during the Pujo Hearings. *Money Trust Investigation,* Part 26, 2030.

50. *Money Trust Investigation,* Part 25, 1853–1854. See also letter from J. Pierpont Morgan to Hon. George B. McClellan, Mayor of the City of New York, Sept. 6, 1907, *Money Trust Investigation,* Part 26, 2126.

51. "J. Pierpont Morgan a Bank in Human Form," *NYT,* Nov. 10, 1907. See also John Moody, "The Masters of Capital in America," *McClure's Magazine,* vol. 36, no. 1 (November 1910): 3–24.

52. Carosso, *The Morgans,* 536, 546; "Steel Report Blames Morgan: Calls 1907 Panic Artificial and Says Roosevelt Aided Corporation," *NYT,* Aug. 3, 1912.

53. *Money Trust Investigation,* Part 1, 3–4.

54. "Arsene P. Pujo, 78, Ex-Congressman," *NYT,* Jan. 1, 1940.

55. Quoted in Louis D. Brandeis, *Other People's Money and How the Bankers Use It* (New York: Frederick A. Stokes Company, 1914): 1.

56. Cables from JPM Jr. to JPM Sr., Jan. 11, 1913 and Jan. 15, 1913, JPM Jr. papers, ARC 1216, Box 32, Folder 7, PML.

57. "Samuel Untermyer Dead in his 82nd Year," *NYT,* Mar. 17, 1940.

58. "Maurice Untermyer Dead," *NYT,* Dec. 30, 1908.

59. "Louis Marshall Dies Abroad at 73," *NYT,* Sept. 12, 1929; Herbert Alpert, *Louis Marshall, 1856–1929: A Life Devoted to Justice and Judaism* (New York: iUniverse, Inc., 2008): 212–213.

60. "T. L. Herrmann Dies Suddenly," *NYT,* Dec. 25, 1925.

61. Alvin Untermyer Dead at 80," *NYT,* Sept. 21, 1963.

62. "Slush Fund Data Given in Secret by Untermyer," *NYT,* Oct. 25, 1924.

63. "Death of Mr. Guggenheimer," *NYT,* Sept. 13, 1907; "Samuel Untermyer Dead in his 82nd Year," *NYT,* Mar. 17, 1940.

64. Samuel Untermyer, "Is there a Money Trust? An Address Delivered before the Finance Forum in the City of New York, Dec. 27th 1911," Thomas W. Lamont (Hereafter: TWL) papers, Box 210–17, Baker Library Historical Collections, Harvard Business School. (Hereafter: HBS).

65. "Samuel Untermyer Dead in his 82nd Year," *NYT,* Mar. 17, 1940.

66. "Trust the Real Issue, Samuel Untermyer Says," *NYT,* Nov. 4, 1904.

67. "Samuel Untermyer Dead in his 82nd Year," *NYT,* Mar. 17, 1940.

68. Untermyer's clubs included the American Bar Association, the New York State Bar Association, Lawyers, National Arts, Lotos, and the Automobile Club of America. "Samuel Untermyer Dead in his 82nd Year," *NYT,* Mar. 17, 1940.

69. Even bankers agreed to this point. See letter from Frank A. Vanderlip to James Stillman, Jan. 24, 1913, Frank A. Vanderlip papers (hereafter FAV), Box B-1–5, Rare Book and Manuscript Library, Columbia University. (Hereafter: RBML).

70. The witness was Frank K. Sturgis of Strong, Sturgis & Co., a past president of the New York Stock Exchange and a member of the governing committee. *Money Trust Investigation,* Part 10, 812.

NOTES TO PAGES 29–31

71. *Money Trust Investigation,* Part 1, 18; Part 2, 125, 144, 164; Part 3, 207, 209, 219; Part 4, 294, 298, 306; Part 7, 554, 579; Part 8, 638, Part 22, 1603, 1633.

72. Cable from Thomas W. Lamont, Charles Steele, and JPM Jr. to Henry P. Davison, May 23, 1912, JPM Jr. papers, ARC 1216, Box 32, Folder 7, PML. See also TWL papers, Box 210–18 on the Money Trust on investigating Pujo and Untemeyer through business dealings. Includes information that was received about Pujo trying to get a Senate seat in Louisiana in letter to JPM & Co. from Gilbert H. Montague and Lynn H. Dirkings, Feb. 11, 1912, TWL papers, Box 210–18, HBS. Lamont and several Morgan staff prepared for the Pujo trial in an office above the Bankers Trust building in 1912. Interview with TWL and Frederick Lewis Allen, July 22, 1947, Bounded book titled "Morgan," Box 13, Frederick Lewis Allen (Hereafter: FLA) papers, Manuscripts and Archives, Library of Congress (Hereafter: LOC).

73. Memorandum for Henry P. Davison from TWL, "Publicity Matters," June 24, 1912, TWL papers, Box 125–10, HBS.

74. John Douglas Forbes, *J. P. Morgan, Jr. 1867–1943* (Charlottesville: University Press of Virginia, 1981): 73. See also for similar sentiment during the Pecora Investigation on the securities business, memorandum to TWL from Russell C. Leffingwell (hereafter RCL), Oct. 6, 1934, Russell C. Leffingwell papers, MS 1030, Box 4, Folder 96, Manuscripts and Archives, Yale University Library. (Hereafter: YUL).

75. Samuel Untermyer, "Is There a Money Trust? An Address Delivered before the Finance Forum in the City of New York, Dec. 27th 1911," TWL papers, Box 210–217, HBS.

76. *Money Trust Investigation,* Part 2, 164; Part 3, 213; Part 10, 760, 810–811; Part 12, 900; Part 14, 1006; Part 20, 1428. See typical response from Congressman Pujo, *Money Trust Investigation,* Part 1, 56.

77. *Money Trust Investigation,* Part 15, 1068.

78. Untermyer made these comments after Morgan's death in March 1913, but he also made similar comments in 1911. As quoted in Strouse, *Morgan: American Financier,* 15.

79. "Pujo Now Questions Big Wall St. Banks," *NYT,* Dec. 8, 1912.

80. Rockefeller was eventually deposed on Jekyll Island, but he testified only as to his inability to testify. *Money Trust Investigation,* Part 14, 971–974, 978–979, 1008–1010; Part 17, 1300–1301; Part 22, 1575–1580; Part 27, 2141–2145. See also "Mr. Rockefeller Fails to Fool Inquisitor," *San Jose (CA) Times,* Jan. 8, 1913; "Will Verify Rockefeller Ill Health," *Wheeling (WV) Register,* Jan. 8, 1913, Samuel Untermyer papers, MS 251, Series D, Box 38, Scrapbooks, pgs. 2–3, AJA. Other bankers were critical of his actions. See letter to James Stillman from Frank A. Vanderlip, Jan. 4, 1913, FAV papers, Box B-1–5, RBML.

81. *Money Trust Investigation,* Part 2, 95; Part 7, 505; Part 12, 926; Part 18, 1290–1294.

82. To see how the eighteen financial institutions and 152 corporations were chosen, see *Money Trust Investigation,* Part 14, 980–1003. See also Exhibits No. 243 and 244, Feb. 25, 1913 for two diagrams of affiliations between the Morgans and other bankers and their clients.

83. For a contemporary study, see William G. Roy, "The Unfolding of the Interlocking Directorate Structure of the United States," *American Sociological Review* 48:2 (April 1983): 249.

84. *Money Trust Investigation,* Part 15, 1058.

85. *Money Trust Investigation,* Part 15, 1023–1025.

86. See for example, Untermyer's confrontations with A. B. Hepburn, President, Chase National Bank, Frederick Lewisohn, partner, Lewisohn Brothers, and George Henry, partner, William Saloman & Co. *Money Trust Investigation,* Parts 13, 18.

87. *Money Trust Investigation,* Part 15, 1071–1073.

88. *Money Trust Investigation,* Part 20, 1444; "Baker Admits Peril to Nation in Bank Control," *NYT,* Jan. 11, 1913.

89. Letter to George F. Baker from Edward Tuck, March 1, 1913, Baker Family papers, Box 1, Folder: GFB Sr. Correspondence, 1913–1914, HBS. This letter is cited in Sheridan Logan's biography of Baker and First National Bank, but it has been heavily redacted (i.e., missing sections including "pettifogging Jew"). Some of the words have also been altered. See Sheridan Logan, *George F. Baker and His Bank,* 159.

90. Fisher Ames Baker (1837–1919) was George F. Baker's father's younger brother. Though Fisher was George's uncle, they were only about three years apart and they were raised together by George's grandmother (Fisher's mother). Fisher and George were extremely close. Fisher was a graduate of Dartmouth College (BA 1859) and later studied law in Albany. After he died, George Baker donated a memorial library to Dartmouth in his uncle's name. "Col. Fisher A. Baker Dies," *NYT,* May 31, 1919; "George F. Baker Gives Dartmouth $100,000," *NYT,* Jan. 19, 1925; "George F. Baker Gives Another $1,000,000 For Memorial Library at Dartmouth College," *NYT,* Feb. 5, 1930; "Says G. F. Baker Gave Library to Dartmouth," *NYT,* Nov. 4, 1926.

91. See for example, *Money Trust Investigation,* Part 20, 1434.

92. *Money Trust Investigation,* Part 21, 1525–1526.

93. Cables from JPM Jr. to JPM Sr., Jan. 11, 1913 and Jan. 15, 1913, JPM Jr. papers, ARC 1216, Box 32, Folder 7, PML.

94. See also H. P. Davison's testimony, *Money Trust Investigation,* Part 26, 1968, 1973, 1983. See also for similar testimony by Francis Hine, president, First National Bank, *Money Trust Investigation,* Part 26, 2034–2035.

95. Carosso, *The Morgans,* 12; *Money Trust Investigation,* Part 20, 1442–1445; Robert T. Swaine, *The Cravath Firm and Its Predecessors, 1819–1948,* vol. 2 (New

York: Ad Press, Ltd., 1948): 99–104. See also letter to James Stillman from Frank A. Vanderlip, Jan. 17, 1913, FAV papers, Box B-1-5, RBML.

96. *Money Trust Investigation,* Part 23, 1676, 1661–1694.

97. *Money Trust Investigation,* Part 23, 1671, 1684–1685, 1691–1693. See also Cleveland and Huertas, *Citibank, 1812–1970,* 347.

98. Cable from JPM Jr. to J. P. Morgan, Jan. 17, 1913, JPM Jr. papers, ARC 1216, Box 32, PML.

99. Letter to Hon. A. J. Pujo from TWL, December 18, 1912, TWL papers, Box 210–19, HBS.

100. Letter to James Stillman from JPM Jr., Mar. 12, 1913, JPM Jr. papers, Letterpress Book #11, PML. See also letter from Frank A. Vanderlip to James Stillman, Jan. 24, 1913 and Mar. 8, 1913, FAV papers, Box B-1-5, RBML.

101. As quoted in Carosso, *The Morgans,* 641–642.

102. Letter from FAV to James Stillman, Apr. 4, 1913, FAV papers, Box B-1-5, RBML. See also quoted in Strouse, *Morgan: American Financier,* 681 and Martin J. Sklar, *The Corporate Reconstruction of American Capitalism, 1890–1916: The Market, The Law, and Politics* (New York: Cambridge University Press, 1988): 16. Jacob Schiff echoed these sentiments when he wrote to Ernest Cassel, "Now that [Morgan] has passed away we shall feel in New York what he has been and how much we have lost in him." As quoted in Cyrus Adler, *Jacob H. Schiff,* vol. 1, 179.

103. *Our Documents: 100 Milestone Documents from the National Archives* (New York: Oxford University Press, 1995): 69–73.

104. Untitled document with a handwritten "AP" and edits by TWL, undated but most likely 1914, TWL papers, Box 110–1, HBS.

"The Clayton Antitrust Act," http://www.stolaf.edu/people/becker/antitrust /statutes/clayton.html (Mar. 20, 2010) The Clayton Antitrust Act also banned banker's directorships on the boards of railroads. See also Carola Frydman and Eric Hilt, "Predators or Watchdogs? Corporate Boards in the Age of Finance Capitalism," NBER paper, August 2010.

According to Frank Vanderlip, Jack Morgan had been considering this move since at least September 1913. See letter to James Stillman from FAV, Sept. 27, 1913, FAV papers, Box B-1-5, RBML.

105. Philippa Strum, *Louis D. Brandeis: Justice for the People* (New York: Schocken Books, 1984): 234–235.

106. Chernow, *House of Morgan,* 181.

107. In 1906, after an investigation into the insurance industry, the New York state legislature passed a law stating that life insurance companies could not "[underwrite] the purchase or sale of securities" or "[invest] in corporate stock and collateral trust bonds," which meant that they could no longer participate in private banking syndicates as underwriters. The Hepburn Act, which was passed in June 1906,

"authorized the Interstate Commerce Commission to fix just and reasonable maximum rates for railroads." Carosso, *The Morgans*, 533–534.

This did not, however, stop insurance companies from purchasing securities privately from the Morgan bank. Between 1913 and 1932, for example, the Metropolitan Life Insurance Company made sixty-five purchases from Morgan syndicates for an aggregate total of more that $61 million; Mutual Life Insurance Co. made fifteen purchases between 1906 and 1932 for a total of $17.5 million; New York Life Insurance Company made fifteen purchases between 1906 and 1931 for a total of $20.7 million; Prudential Life Insurance Co. made twenty-seven purchases between 1914 and 1926 for $22.76 million. There were many others with smaller amounts as well.

108. Cable to J. P. Morgan from Herman Harjes, Dec. 24, 1913, and cable to J. P. Morgan from E. C. Grenfell, Dec. 24, 1913, TWL papers, Box 110–1, HBS; Untitled document, undated but most likely 1914, TWL papers, Box 110–1, HBS.

109. As quoted in Forbes, *J. P. Morgan, Jr.*, 72. For original see letter to James Stillman from JPM Jr., Mar. 12, 1913, JPM Jr. papers, ARC 1196, Letterpress Book #11, page 59, PML.

110. Vanderlip was reporting on a conversation he had with Henry Davison. Letter to James Stillman from FAV, Mar. 28, 1913, FAV papers, Box B-1–5, RBML. See also letter to James Stillman from FAV, Sept. 27, 1913, FAV papers, Box B-1–5, RBML.

111. Vanderlip was reporting on a conversation he had with Morgan. Letter to James Stillman from FAV, May 2, 1913, FAV papers, Box B-1–5, RBML. Stillman, however, did not want Morgan to sell National City stocks, but more likely because he was concerned about the bank stocks themselves and not the relationships.

112. Letter to George F. Baker Jr. from Benjamin Strong Jr., Jan. 14, 1914, Baker Family papers, Box 9, Folder: GFB Jr. Correspondence 1913–1931, HBS. Strong had just become president of Bankers Trust, succeeding his father-in-law, E. C. Converse. "Benjamin Strong, Banker, Dies at 56," *NYT*, Oct. 17, 1928.

113. A number of studies have asked the question from the perspective of the client, as opposed to the banker, and asked whether or not the loss of the Morgan partners as directors had a negative impact on the companies themselves. See Miguel Cantillo Simon, "The Rise and Fall of Bank Control in the United States 1890–1939," *American Economic Review*, vol. 88, no. 5 (1988): 1077–1093; Carlos Ramirez, "Did J. P. Morgan's Men Add Liquidity? Corporate Investment, Cash Flow, and Financial Structure at the Turn of the Century," *Journal of Finance*, vol. 50, no. 2 (1995): 661–678; J. Bradford De Long, "Did J. P. Morgan's Men Add Value? An Economist's Perspective on Financial Capitalism" in Peter Temin, ed., *Inside the Business Enterprise: Historical Perspectives on the Use of Information* (Chicago: University of Chicago Press, 1991): 205–249; J. Bradford De Long, "J. P. Morgan and His Money Trust," *Wilson Quarterly* 16:4 (Fall 1992): 16–30; Leslie Hannah, "What Did Morgan's Men Really Do?" University of Tokyo, Dept. of Economics, Working

Paper, http://www.e.u-tokyo.ac.jp/cirje/research/03research 02dp.html (January 2007); Carola Frydman, Eric Hilt, and Lily Y. Zhou, "The Panic of 1907: JP Morgan, Trust Companies, and the Impact of the Financial Crisis," NBER working paper, February 2012. For a study that also looks at the question of the role of interlocking directorships and includes the Morgans but uses a much broader database, see Frydman and Hilt, "Predators or Watchdogs?"

114. See Susie J. Pak and Daniel S. Halgin, "The Significance of Social Clubs: Syndicates, Interlocking Directorates, and the Network of J. P. Morgan," paper presented, International Network for Social Network Analysis (INSNA) annual conference, March 2012. By combining the study of the retirement of directorships and the social clubs of the Morgan partners, Pak and Halgin asked the following questions: "Do the social club memberships of the firm's partners indicate a pattern as to the decisions for why certain individual partners retired from some firms and not others? Do they indicate that the Morgan partners leveraged their social ties in the face of impending government regulation of their economic ties?"

Pak and Halgin studied all the directorships of all Morgan partners in 1912, the year of the Pujo Hearings, not just the five Morgan partners whose retirements were announced. In 1912, the eleven Morgan partners held directorships on 215 different companies of which they were able to collect the complete board memberships of 189 companies (88 percent) from sources such as *The Manual of Statistics: Stock Exchange Handbook*, vol. 34 (New York: Manual of Statistics Co.), *The Directory of Directors in the City of New York* (New York: The Directory of Directors Company, 1911–12), *Moody's Manual of Railroads and Corporation Securities*, vol. 13 (New York: Moody Manual Company, 1912), and *The Trow (formerly Wilson's) Copartnership and Corporation Directory of the Boroughs of Manhattan and the Bronx, City of New York* (New York: Trow Directory, Printing & Bookbinding Co., 1912). They determined that Morgan partners were affiliated with 1,557 other directors through board ties. To determine social affiliations, they collected the complete social club memberships of the eleven Morgan partners and the 1,557 directors. 51 percent of the directors were listed in the *Social Register, Locater*, 29 percent were listed in the *Social Register, New York*, and 12 percent in the *Social Register, Philadelphia*. Their results from a regression analysis indicate that Morgan partners were more likely to leave the boards of companies in which they had multiple connections to other members through social club ties in 1912.

Pak and Halgin also analyzed the change in social club overlaps of the board members five years later in 1917, and they studied the social elite status of the directors and partners of the top eighteen national banking institutions as identified by the Pujo statistician (18 financial institutions and 152 corporations) to place the 1912 Morgan directorships in a wider context. Using the Pujo dataset, they also looked to see if the directors and partners in the largest and most important banking institutions in the United States in this period were also socially elite, and they studied the relationship between social club membership and participation in the Morgans' syndicates. They found that "both board and social overlaps had independent relationships with an individual or firm's involvement with JPM & Co. Those with greater board overlaps and social overlaps with the Morgan partners obtained the greatest amount of syndicate participation over time."

115. This is also different from the discussion of how an individual's right to property and ownership has changed due to the separation of ownership and control or from the proliferation of securities ownership, what has also been called investor or shareholder democracy. See Adolf A. Berle and Gardiner C. Means, *The Modern Corporation & Private Property*, 11th ed., (New Brunswick, NJ: Transaction Publishers, 2010); William G. Roy, *Socializing Capital: The Rise of the Large Corporation in America* (Princeton, NJ: Princeton University Press, 1997); Julia C. Ott, *When Wall Street Met Main Street: The Quest for an Investors' Democracy* (Cambridge, MA: Harvard University Press, 2011).

116. Strum, *Louis D. Brandeis*, 1–29.

117. Thanks to John Kleeberg for bringing this point to my attention. Melvin Urofsky, *Louis D. Brandeis: A Life* (New York: Pantheon, 2009): 181–200; Henry Lee Staples and Alpeus T. Mason, *The Fall of a Railroad Empire: Brandeis and the New Haven Merger* (Syracuse, NY: Syracuse University Press, 1947); Richard M. Abrams, "Brandeis and the New Haven-Boston & Main Merger Battled Revisited," *Business History Review*, no. 36 (Winter 1962): 408–430; Chernow, *House of Morgan*, 149.

118. Chernow, *House of Morgan*, 176–177.

119. Between November 22, 1913, and January 17, 1914, Brandeis's articles included: "Breaking the Money Trust" (Nov. 22, 1913), "The Endless Chain: Interlocking Directorates" (Dec. 6, 1913), and "The Inefficiency of Oligarchs" (Jan. 17, 1914). Louis D. Brandeis, *Other People's Money and How the Bankers Use It* (New York: Frederick A. Stokes Company, 1914).

120. Hapgood had written for the *Harvard Crimson* with Lamont. He was also a very good friend of Brandeis and a Democrat by political affiliation. Melvin I. Urofsky and David W. Levy, *The Family Letters of Louis D. Brandeis* (Norman, OK: University of Oklahoma Press, 2002): 148f. "The Hapgood Relationship" also labeled "The Brandeis Talk," undated document but probably Dec. 1913, TWL papers, Box 84–16, HBS.

121. S. Sloan Colt, *44 Years in American Banking, 1903–1947* (New York: The Newcomen Society of England American Branch, 1947): 9; Edward M. Lamont, *The Ambassador From Wall Street: The Story of Thomas W. Lamont, J. P. Morgan's Chief Executive* (New York: Madison Books, 1994): 35.

122. Lamont, *Ambassador From Wall Street*, 40–42.

123. Chernow, *House of Morgan*, 179.

124. Lamont, *Ambassador From Wall Street*, 5–6, 57; Chernow, *House of Morgan*, 180.

125. Others present at the conversation included Hapgood and Colonel E. M. House, Woodrow Wilson's close friend and associate. "The Hapgood Relationship" also labeled "The Brandeis Talk," undated document but probably Dec. 1913, TWL papers, Box 84–16, HBS.

Between 1911 and 1915, seven of eleven American Morgan partners were members of the University Club of New York. See *Social Register, New York* for those years and James Waddel Alexander, *A History of the University Club of New York, 1865–1915* (New York: Charles Scribner & Sons, 1915). Brandeis was not a member. His membership in New York City clubs was limited to the Harvard Club. He was a member of three clubs in Boston: Union, Union Boat, and Exchange. *Social Register, Boston* (New York: Social Register Association, 1912): 24.

126. See Carosso, *Investment Banking in America,* 145–148; Carosso, "The Wall Street Money Trust from Pujo to Medina," 421.

127. "The Hapgood Relationship" also labeled "The Brandeis Talk," undated document but probably Dec. 1913, TWL papers, Box 84–16, HBS.

128. See also Philip Cullis, "The Limits of Progressivism: Louis Brandeis, Democracy and the Corporation," *Journal of American Studies,* 30 (1996): 381–404.

129. Oliviero Bergamini, "Public and Private in the Thought of the New Republic Progressive Intellectuals," in *Public and Private in American History: States, Family, Subjectivity in the Twentieth Century,* ed. R. Baritono, D. Frezza, A. Lorini, M. Vaudagna, and E. Vezzosi (Torino: Otto editore, 2003): 57–84.

For the study of private property in a more legal and philosophical disciplinary context, see Terry L. Anderson and Fred S. McChesney, eds., *Property Rights: Cooperation, Conflict, and Law* (Princeton, NJ: Princeton University Press, 2003); Matthew H. Kramer, *John Locke and the Origins of Private Property: Philosophical Exploration of Individualism, Community, and Equality* (New York: Cambridge University Press, 2004); Jeremy Waldron, *The Right to Private Property* (Oxford: Clarendon Press, 1988).

130. See also Bergamini, "Public and Private," 69.

131. Brandeis, *Other People's Money and How the Bankers Use It,* 4.

132. To the extent that theories of bank control emphasize direct, prolonged intervention, their understanding of bank control differs from the work of other theorists that emphasize "structural hegemony" and not "strategic control." See Beth Mintz and Michael Schwartz, *The Power Structure of American Business* (Chicago: University of Chicago Press, 1985): 1–44.

133. Louis D. Brandeis and Samuel D. Warren, "The Right to Privacy," *Harvard Law Review,* vol. 4, no. 5 (1890).

134. Susan S. Gallagher, "The Right to Privacy," University of Massachusetts, Lowell http://faculty.uml.edu/sgallagher/harvard_law_review.htm (May 13, 2010).

135. Strum, *Louis D. Brandeis,* 330, 334.

136. See Cheryl Harris, "Whiteness as Property," *Harvard Law Review* 106.8 (June 1993): 1712.

137. "Plessy v. Ferguson, 163 U.S. 537 (1896)," http://caselaw.lp.findlaw.com /scripts/getcase.pl?court=US&vol=163&invol=537 (May 27, 2010).

138. Bergamini, "Public and Private," 69, 72.

139. A. J. Glass, "Negro on Wall Street—An Expanding Role," *New York Herald Tribune,* Aug. 20, 1916, Vincent P. Carosso papers, ARC 1214, Box 29, PML. See Gregory S. Bell, *In the Black: A History of African Americans on Wall Street* (New York: John Wiley & Sons, 2002).

2. THE SOCIAL WORLD OF PRIVATE BANKERS

1. "Richard T. Greener: The First Black Harvard College Graduate: For Good Government & Urban Politics," in Werner Sollers, et al., *Blacks at Harvard: A Documentary History of African-American Experience at Harvard and Radcliffe* (New York: New York University Press, 1993): 40–41.

2. "Belle da Costa Greene, 1879–1950," Pierpont Morgan Library (Hereafter: PML).

3. "Belle da Costa Greene, 1879–1950," PML. See letter to J. P. Morgan from Belle Greene, Feb. 11, 1913, John Pierpont Morgan Papers, ARC 1196, Box 7, PML.

4. Jean Strouse, *Morgan: American Financier* (New York: Perennial, 2000): 509–517, 530. For a full-length biography of Belle Greene, see Heidi Ardizzone, *An Illuminated Life: Belle da Costa Greene's Journey from Prejudice to Privilege* (New York: W.W. Norton & Company, 2007).

5. Ardizzone, *Illuminated Life,* 441. See also "Belle da Costa Greene, 1879–1950," PML.

6. "Education: Belle of the Books," *Time,* Apr. 11, 1949. Thanks to Sharon La Cruise for this reference.

7. Ron Chernow, *The House of Morgan: An American Banking Dynasty and the Rise of Modern Finance* (New York: Touchstone, 1990): 116–117.

8. Letter to J. P. Morgan from Belle Greene, Feb. 11, 1913, John Pierpont Morgan Papers, ARC 1196, Box 7, PML.

9. Quoted in Strouse, *Morgan: American Financier,* 681.

10. Chernow, *House of Morgan,* 170, 171, 602.

11. Social capital is referred to here as a person's social relations, through which resources and information are accessed, and includes a person's social status. See Pamela Walker Laird, *Pull: Networking and Success since Benjamin Franklin* (Cambridge, MA: Harvard University Press, 2006): 11–50; Alejandro Portes, "Social Capital: Its Origins and Applications in Modern Sociology," *Annual Review of Sociology,* vol. 24 (1988): 3; Pierre Bourdieu, "The Forms of Capital," in Mark Gra-

novetter and Richard Swedberg, eds., *The Sociology of Economic Life*, Second Edition (Boulder, CO: Westview Press, 2001): 102–104; Nan Lin, *Social Capital: A Theory of Social Structure and Action* (New York: Cambridge University Press, 2001): xi, 19–25; John Field, *Social Capital* (New York: Routledge, 2003): 1–43.

12. Barry E. Supple, "A Business Elite: German-Jewish Financiers in Nineteenth-Century New York," *Business History Review*, vol. 31 (Summer 1957): 170.

13. In this regard, merchant banks in the United States and England were identical. Youssef Cassis, *City Bankers: 1890–1914* (New York: Cambridge University Press, 1994): 31; Alan D. Morrison and William J. Wilhelm Jr., *Investment Banking: Institutions, Politics and Law* (New York: Oxford University Press, 2007): 15–16.

14. Morrison and Wilhelm Jr. note that limited liability was largely prohibited in England "by the Bubble Act of 1720, but in a business like merchanting where so little was contractible, the partnership form may well have been optimal anyway." Morrison and Wilhelm Jr., *Investment Banking*, 114–115. See also Oscar Handlin and Mary F. Handlin, "Origins of the American Business Corporation," *Journal of Economic History*, vol. 5, no. 1 (May 1945): 5–6, 9–12.

15. Kathleen Burk, *Morgan, Grenfell, 1838–1988: The Biography of a Merchant Bank* (New York: Oxford University Press, 1989): 43.

16. Stanley Chapman, *The Rise of the Merchant Banking* (London: George Allen Unwin, 1984): 2–3. For a classic study on social networks and kinship ties, see John F. Padgett and Christopher K. Ansell, "Robust Action and the Rise of the Medici, 1400–1434," *American Journal of Sociology*, vol. 98, no. 6. (May, 1993): 1259–1319. Though there were other historical differences, American and European networks were similar to those found in China, Japan, and, later, South Korea with regard to the prominence of family as a structural component. See Sherman Cochran, *Encountering Chinese Networks: Western, Japanese, and Chinese Corporations in China, 1880–1937* (Los Angeles: University of California Press, 2000): 117–146; Shibagaki Kazuo, "The Early History of the Zaibatsu," *The Developing Economies*, vol. 4, no. 4, 1965 (online publication: March 2007): 535–566; Sangjin Yoo and Sang M. Lee, "Management Style and Practice of Korean Chaebols," *California Management Review*, vol. 29, no. 4 (Summer 1987): 95–110.

17. Vincent P. Carosso, "A Financial Elite: New York's German-Jewish Investment Bankers," *American Jewish Historical Quarterly (1961–1978)*, vol. 66, no. 1–4 (Sept. 1976–1977): 77; Supple, "A Business Elite," 168. See also Andrea Colli, *The History of Family Business, 1850–2000* (New York: Cambridge University Press, 2001).

18. Morrison and Wilhelm Jr., *Investment Banking*, 115.

19. Supple, "A Business Elite," 168–170.

20. Pierre Boudieu, *Outline of a Theory of Practice* (New York: Cambridge University Press, 1997): 33–34.

21. Of the seventeen men who were partners or made partners/directors in J. S. Morgan & Co./Morgan, Grenfell & Co. between 1895 and 1940, including Pierpont Morgan and Jack Morgan, nine (or 53 percent) had kinship ties to another partner in the firm (eight when they joined the firm). They were: JPM, JPM Jr., Walter Hayes Burns, Walter Spencer Morgan Burns (Burns's son), Edward Charles Grenfell (Lord St. Just) and his cousin Vivian Hugh Smith (Lord Bicester). Later, Randal Hugh Vivian Smith (Second Lord Bicester, Vivian Smith's son) joined the partnership, as did Francis James Rennell Rodd (Vivian Smith's son-in-law), and William Edward (the 2nd Viscount Harcourt), who was the grandson of Walter Hayes Burns and the great-grandson of J. S. Morgan. Post-1940 directors with family connections included Hon. Stephen Gordon Catto, the son of Sir Thomas Sivewright Catto (First Lord Catto and Morgan, Grenfell & Co. partner), and John Ernest Harley Collins, the son-in-law of Randal Hugh Vivian Smith. See Morgan Grenfell Co. Ltd., *George Peabody & Co., J. S. Morgan & Co., Morgan Grenfell & Co.* (London: Morgan Grenfell & Co., 1958).

22. Of the thirteen men who were partners in Morgan, Harjes & Co./Morgan et. Cie. between 1895 and 1940, including Pierpont Morgan and Jack Morgan, seven (or 54 percent) had kinship ties to another partner (six when they became partners). In the early period, they were JPM, JPM Jr., John Harjes, John Harjes Jr., and Herman Harjes. Very little information is available in the Morgan archives about John Harjes Jr., but he is listed separately from his father in the partnership agreement for Morgan, Harjes & Co. in the early period. After Herman Harjes's death in 1926, John Ridgely Carter and, later, his son, Benjamin Carter, formed the primary kinship tie.

23. Vincent Carosso, "The Morgan Houses: The Seniors, Their Partners, and Their Aides," in Joseph R. Frese, S.J. and Jacob Judd, eds., *American Industrialization, Economic Expansion and the Law* (Tarrytown, New York: Sleepy Hollow Press, 1981): 2–15.

For Drexel Family: "Anthony J. Drexel Is Dead," *NYT,* July 1, 1893; "John R. Drexel, 72, Dies in Paris Home," *NYT,* May 19, 1935; "James W. Paul, Jr., Financier Is Dead," *Public Ledger Philadelphia,* Sept. 26, 1908; "James W. Paul Stricken," *NYT,* Sept. 26, 1908; "Special to The New York Times," *NYT,* Sept. 26, 1908.

For Wright and Robinson family: "Wright, James Hood," *The National Cyclopaedia of American Biography,* vol. 33 (New York: James T. White & Co., 1947): 443; "Will of James Hood Wright," *NYT,* Nov. 21, 1894; "Wright Will Contested," *NYT,* Jan. 29, 1895; "Weddings in Philadelphia," *NYT,* Mar. 2, 1881; "Society Topics of the Week," *NYT,* Jan. 1, 1893; "The Late Edward Moore Robinson," *Public Ledger Philadelphia,* Jan. 6, 1910; "Edward M. Robinson Dead," *NYT,* Jan. 5, 1910; "Society Topics of The Week," *NYT,* Jan. 1, 1893; "Weddings in Philadelphia," *NYT,* Jan. 1, 1893; "Morgan Partners' Estate," *NYT,* Feb. 26, 1913; *Sugar,* vol. 20, no. 1 (January 1918): 145; "Robinson," *NYT,* Dec. 31, 1909.

For the Bowdoin family: "George S. Bowdoin Dead," *NYT,* Dec. 17, 1913; "Temple Bowdoin Dead," *NYT,* Dec. 3, 1914; "Bowdoin's Estate Goes to His Family," *NYT,* Jan. 17, 1914; Hon. Robert Bacon, "George Sullivan Bowdoin: An Appreciation," *The New York Genealogical and Biographical Record,* vol. 45, no. 2 (New York, April 1914): 7; Miss Georgina Schuyler, "George Sullivan Bowdoin: A Sketch of His Life," *The New York Genealogical and Biographical Record,* vol. 45, no. 2 (New York, April 1914): 106–108; Hopper Striker Mott, "George Sullivan Bowdoin: His Ancestry—Single Line of Descent," *New York Genealogical and Biographical Record,* vol. 45, no. 2 (New York, April 1914): 109; Temple Prime, *Some Account of the Bowdoin Family,* 2nd ed. (New York: The De Vinne Press, 1894).

For W. Pierson Hamilton: Hamilton's father, William Gaston Hamilton, was "the last surviving grandson of Alexander Hamilton." "William Gaston Hamilton," *NYT,* Jan. 24, 1913. See also "Hamilton Heir Files $750,000 Will Suit," *NYT,* June 3, 1915; "W. P. Hamilton, 81, Retired Financier," *NYT,* May 9, 1950; "Mrs. W. P. Hamilton," *NYT,* Sept. 12, 1941; "Hamilton, William Pierson," *Who Was Who in America,* vol. 3 (Chicago: A.N. Marquis Co., 1966): 363; "Theodosia S. Carlin," National Archives and Records Administration (NARA), Washington DC; Passport Applications, Jan. 2, 1906–Mar. 31, 1925; Collection Number; *ARC Identifier 583830/ MLR Number A1 534;* NARA Series: M1490; Roll #: 2401; "Theodosia G. Sisson," "New Jersey Births and Christenings, 1660–1931." Index. FamilySearch, Salt Lake City, Utah, 2009, 2010; "Charles G. Sisson," Year: *1880;* Census Place: *Harrington, Bergen, New Jersey;* Roll: *771;* Family History Film: *1254771;* Page: *294A;* Enumeration District: *004;* Image: *0109;* Year: *1880;* Census Place: *Saint Paul, Ramsey, Minnesota;* Roll: *630;* Family History Film: *1254630;* Page: *250A;* Enumeration District: *013;* Image: *0501;* Tenth Census of the United States, 1880. Records of the Bureau of the Census, Record Group 29. National Archives, Washington, DC (Hereafter: RG and NARA).

24. For Charles H. Coster: Walter Barrett, *The Old Merchants of New York City,* vol. 2 (New York: Thomas R. Knox & Co., 1885): 190–198; Daniel Van Pelt, *Leslie's History of the Greater New York: Encyclopedia of New York Biography and Genealogy,* vol. 3 (New York: Arkell Publishing Co., 1898): 162–163; Albro Martin, Bradley University, "Charles Henry Coster 24 July 1852–13 Mar. 1900," Vincent P. Carosso Papers, ARC 1214, Box 13, PML. See also "Charles Henry Coster," *NYT,* Mar. 14, 1900; "Mrs. Annie E. Claiborne Pell," *NYT,* Nov. 3, 1916; "The Man Whose Specialty was Reorganization of Railroads," *Wall Street Journal,* Feb. 4, 1911; "News of the Railroads," *NYT,* Mar. 18, 1900; "Funeral of C. H. Coster," *NYT,* Mar. 17, 1900; "C. H. Coster Weds in Florence, Italy," *NYT,* Feb. 11, 1926; "Charles H. Coster," *NYT,* Apr. 5, 1977; "Clarence Pell," Year: *1860;* Census Place: *New York Ward 21 District 2, New York, New York;* Roll: *M653_819;* Page: *1207;* Image: *616;* Family History Library Film: *803819.* 1860 U.S. census, population schedule, NARA; John Frederick Dorman, *Claiborne of Virginia* (Baltimore, MD: Gateway Press, 1995).

For J. P. Morgan's family: "Morgan's Body Here Wrapped in Flag," *NYT,* Apr. 12, 1913; "$3,000,000 to Each Child and $1,000,000 to Mrs. Morgan," *NYT,* Apr. 20, 1913; "State Appraises Morgan Riches at $78,149,024," *NYT,* July 29, 1916; "J. P. Morgan Dies, Victim of Stroke at Florida Resort," *NYT,* Mar. 13, 1943; "Full Text of the Will of J. Pierpont Morgan," *NYT,* Apr. 20, 1913; "Mrs. Morgan Left Estate to Family," *NYT,* Aug. 29, 1925.

For Walter Burns and family: "Banker Walter Burns Dead," *NYT,* Nov. 24, 1897; "Americans at Two Funerals," *NYT,* Nov. 28, 1897; "Special to NYT," *NYT,* Sept. 26, 1908; "Names Harcourt an Heir," *NYT,* Aug. 25, 1919; "Tribute to Walter Burns," *NYT,* Dec. 28, 1929.

For George C. Thomas: "George C. Thomas," *NYT,* Apr. 22, 1909; "G. C. Thomas to Retire from Drexel & Co.," *NYT,* Nov. 6, 1904; "Thomas, George Clifford," *The National Cyclopaedia of American Biography,* vol. 15 (New York: James T. White & Co., 1914): 193–194; "Thomas, George Clifford," *The National Cyclopaedia of American Biography,* vol. 36 (New York: James T. White & Co., 1950): 431–432; "George C. Thomas's Useful Life Ends," *Public Ledger,* Apr. 22, 1909.

For Charles Steele: "Steele, Charles," *The National Cyclopaedia of American Biography,* vol. 14 (New York: James T. White & Co., 1943): 77–78; "Notables Attend Steele Services," *NYT,* Aug. 8, 1939; "Steele Estate Put at $29,498,373 Net," *NYT,* Feb. 5, 1941; "Rev. Dr. J. N. Steele Dies," *NYT,* Aug. 24, 1916; "$5,000,000 in Gifts Left by Steele," *NYT,* Aug. 11, 1939.

Charles Steele's wife's father, S. B. French, was a well-known financier and a close friend of Pierpont Morgan. "Mrs. Steele Wed to Opera Singer," *NYT,* Sept. 24, 1930; "Mrs. Steele Left $340,000 In Gifts," *NYT,* Dec. 28, 1932; "Five Debutantes Bow to Society," *NYT,* Nov. 28, 1912; "Mrs. Charles Steele," *NYT,* Dec. 19, 1932; "Obtains Divorce in Paris," *NYT,* Oct. 10, 1920; "Society at Home and Abroad," *NYT,* Feb. 20, 1910; "Seth Barton French Dead," *NYT,* Feb. 18, 1910; "George B. French, A Retired Broker," *NYT,* July 19, 1937; "W. B. French Suicide at Santa Fe, N.M.," *NYT,* Feb. 2, 1928; "Two Fashionable Weddings," *NYT,* Apr. 22, 1885; "Diana Bird is Wed to A. P. Osborn Jr.," *NYT,* Oct. 19, 1944.

25. For Arthur E. Newbold: "Dallas, George Mifflin," http://bioguide.congress .gov/scripts/biodisplay.pl?index=d000011 (July 9, 2012); Mark O. Hatfield, with the Senate Historical Office. *Vice Presidents of the United States, 1789–1993* (Washington, DC: U.S. Government Printing Office, 1997): 151–161; "A. E. Newbold, Banker, Dies Suddenly at 61," *NYT,* June 11, 1920; Arthur E. Newbold Jr., Banking Figure, 58," *NYT,* Sept. 4, 1946; Rev. S. F. Hotchkin, *The Bristol Pike* (Philadelphia: George W. Jacobs & Co., 1893): 356–357; "Miss Widener Engaged," *NYT,* Feb. 3, 1912; "Miss E. E. Widener Weds," *NYT,* June 20, 1912; "Eleanor W. Dixon Becomes Engaged," *NYT,* Nov. 11, 1937; "Sues Fitz Eugene Dixon," *NYT,* Sept. 30, 1936; "A. J. Dallas Dixon of Harvard 1870," *NYT,* June 10, 1948; Lewis Keen and Trudy

Keen, *A Brief History of Fort Washington, Pennsylvania: From Farmland to Suburb* (Charleston, SC: The History Press, 2006): 27.

26. For Robert Bacon: "Col. Bacon Dies in Hospital," *NYT,* May 30, 1919; Calvin D. Davis. "Bacon, Robert"; http://anb.org/articles/06/06-00017.html; *American National Biography* Online Feb. 2000. (July 13, 2008); "Two Fashionable Weddings," *NYT,* Oct. 11, 1883.

27. "William B. Bacon." *NYT,* Feb. 14, 1906. "Bacon, Robert," *Who's Who in New York City and State,* ed. John W. Leonard, 3rd edition (New York: Hamersly, 1907): 51.

28. "Charles Steele" and "Isaac Nevett Steele," *The National Cyclopaedia of American Biography,* vol. 14 (New York: James T. White & Co., 1910): 77-78.

29. In all the branches, the sons of previous partners began to enter the firm in the 1920s and 1930s, but the overall percentage of kinship ties did not exceed 40 percent after the war. It remained in the 30 percent range up to the Second World War.

30. The one partner in the original partnership agreement of 1895 whose background followed this narrative was Edward T. Stotesbury, the head of Drexel & Co. Stotesbury's father was a sugar refiner, but he worked his way up through the firm, starting as a clerk. "E. T. Stotesbury, Financier, Is Dead," *NYT,* May 17, 1938; "Mrs. J. K. Mitchell; Was a Stotesbury," *NYT,* Oct. 15, 1950; "Mitchell's Wife Starts for Home," *NYT,* Mar. 26, 1923; Lionel Atwill Wed to Mrs. MacArthur," *NYT,* June 8, 1930; "Mrs. Stotesbury Social Figure, Dies," *NYT,* May 24, 1946; "A Correction: Mrs. E. T. Stotesbury Denies That She Discharged 62 Servants," *NYT,* June 17, 1938; "Palm Beach Scene of Book Week Tea," *NYT,* Feb. 13, 1940; "Stotesbury Case Pact," *NYT,* Dec. 25, 1946; "New Yacht Launched for E. T. Stotesbury," *NYT,* Nov. 16, 1930; James H. Graebner. "Stotesbury, Edward Townsend"; http://www.anb.org/articles/10/10-01596.html; American National Biography Online Feb. 2000. (July 13, 2008); "Stotesbury, Edward Townsend," *Dictionary of American Biography,* Supplement 2 (New York: Charles Scribner's Sons, 1958): 634-635; "Stotesbury, Edward Townsend," *Who Was Who in America,* vol. 1 (Chicago: A.N. Marquis Co., 1943): 1194; Horace Mather Lippincott, *A Narrative of Chestnut Hill, Philadelphia, with some account of Springfield, Whitemarsh and Cheltenham Townships in Montgomery County, Pennsylvania* (Jenkintown, 1948): 113, 146-162; Horace Mather Lippincott, "Edward T. Stotesbury," *Old York Road Historical Society Bulletin,* vol. 6 (1942): 3-23.

31. Thomas W. Lamont (Hereafter: TWL), *My Boyhood in a Parsonage: Some Brief Sketches of American Life toward the Close of the Last Century* (New York: Harper & Brothers, 1946). See also TWL's biography of his senior partner, Henry Pomeroy Davison, whom he describes as being a small-town boy who made his way in the world to become a success. Thomas W. Lamont, *Henry P. Davison—The Record of A Useful Life* (New York: Harper & Brothers, 1933).

32. "Thomas W. Lamont, Banker, Dies at 77 in Florida Home," *NYT*, Feb. 3, 1948; "Lamont Succeeds to Morgan's Post," *NYT*, Mar. 18, 1943; "Lamont Will Gives $9,535,000 To Help Education, Charity," *NYT*, Feb. 11, 1948; "Lamont Funeral to be Saturday," *NYT*, Feb. 4, 1948; "Mrs. Lamont Left 3 Million to Seven Women's Colleges," *NYT*, Jan. 3, 1953; "Lamont, Thomas William," *The National Cyclopaedia of American Biography*, vol. 41 (New York: James T. White & Co., 1956): 6–8; "Wilbur Fisk Corliss," Class of Sixty-Three, Williams College, 1863–1903, Fortieth Year Report (Boston: Thomas Todd, Printer, 1903); "Wilbur F. Corliss Dead," *NYT*, Jan. 29, 1928; "John Henry Coon Dead," *NYT*, Jan. 18, 1916; "In the Business World," *NYT*, May 27, 1913.

33. Pierpont Morgan, for example, did not go to an American university. He studied at the University of Gottingen in Germany, but like other men of his generation and class, he went to public school (Hartford Public School and later English High School in Boston, which were public in the American sense and not public in the British sense of being a private school) and received most of his training through apprenticeships with firms with whom his father had close ties.

34. For Thomas Cochran: "Thomas Cochran, Financier, is Dead," *NYT*, Oct. 30, 1936; "Cochran, Thomas," *The National Cyclopaedia of American Biography*, vol. 27 (New York: James T. White & Co., 1939): 368–369; "Cochran, Thomas," *Who's Who in New York*, ed. Frank R. Holmes, 8th edition (New York: Who's Who Publications, 1924): 270–271; "Wins Partnership in J. P. Morgan & Co.," *NYT*, Dec. 18, 1916; "Thomas Cochran," *Quarter-Century Record Class of 1894 Yale College*, ed. Frank Dwight (New Haven: 1922): 115–117; "Allen Griffin," Year: *1880;* Census Place: *Flatbush, Ulster, New York;* Roll: *940;* Family History Film: *1254940;* Page: *289B;* Enumeration District: *155;* Image: *0580;* Year: *1880;* Census Place: *Saint Paul, Ramsey, Minnesota;* Roll: *630;* Family History Film: *1254630;* Page: *250A;* Enumeration District: *013;* Image: *0501;* Tenth Census of the United States, 1880. Records of the Bureau of the Census, RG 29, NARA.

35. John A. Garraty, *Right-Hand Man: The Life of George W. Perkins* (New York: Harper & Brothers, 1957): 5–7; William C. Fitzgibbon, "Book of the Times," *NYT*, Sept. 1, 1960; "Edward R. Perkins Dead," *NYT*, Jan. 19, 1912; "G. W. Perkins Will Leaves to Family $10,000,000 Estate," *NYT*, June 23, 1920; "G. W. Perkins Estate Put at $6,008,081," *NYT*, Mar. 1, 1922; "George W. Perkins Jr. to Wed Miss Merck," *NYT*, Nov. 12, 1921.

36. For Horatio G. Lloyd: "Horatio Lloyd, 70, Financier, Is Dead," *NYT*, Jan. 22, 1937; "Horatio G. Lloyd, Noted Financier, Dies After Stroke," *Philadelphia Inquirer*, Jan. 22, 1937; "Morgan Takes in a New Partner," *NYT*, Dec. 31, 1911; "Lloyd, Horatio Gates," *Who Was Who in America*, vol. 1 (Chicago: A.N. Marquis Co., 1943): 737; "Miss Wadsworth a Bride," *NYT*, June 17, 1950; "H. G. Lloyd Left $3,363,339," *NYT*, May 7, 1937; "Financial Leaders at Lloyd Funeral," *NYT*, Jan. 24, 1937; "Horatio G. Lloyd," Year: *1880;* Census Place: *Camden, Camden, New Jersey;*

Roll: *774;* Family History Film: *1254774;* Page: *209D;* Enumeration District: *047;* Image: *0061.* Tenth Census of the United States, 1880. Records of the Bureau of the Census, RG 29, NARA; "A Day's Wedding; Lloyd-Wingate," *NYT,* May 7, 1897; "Gen. Wingate Rests in Prospect Park," *NYT,* Mar. 25, 1926; "Wedding is Planned By Prudence Lloyd," *NYT,* May 20, 1962; "Janis Devereux Marries George Lloyd," *NYT,* June 29, 1986.

For William H. Porter: "W. H. Porter Dead; Stricken in Street," *NYT,* Dec. 1, 1926; "Porter, William Henry," *Who Was Who in America,* vol. 1 (Chicago: Marquis Who's Who, 1943): 985; "Throng of Notables Mourns W. H. Porter," *NYT,* Dec. 4, 1926; Jan Albers, "A Capsule History of Porter Hospital," www.portermedical.org /history.html (Apr. 2, 2008); "Mrs. Porter Dead, Welfare Worker," *NYT,* May 25, 1934; "James Jackson," Year: *1880;* Census Place: *New York City, New York, New York;* Roll: *897;* Family History Film: *1254897;* Page: *124B;* Enumeration District: *618;* Image: *0251.* Tenth Census of the United States, 1880. Records of the Bureau of the Census, RG 29, NARA.

37. "Morrow, Dwight Whitney," *The National Cyclopaedia of American Biography,* vol. 23 (New York: James T. White & Co., 1933): 10–12; "Morrow Won Fame in Only Four Years," *NYT,* Oct. 6, 1931; Stephen A. Schuker, "Morrow, Dwight Whitney"; http://www.anb.org/articles/10/10–01179.html; American National Biography Online Feb. 2000. (July 13, 2008)

38. For Edward Stettinius: John Douglas Forbes, *Stettinius, Sr.: Portrait of a Morgan Partner* (Charlottesville: University Press of Virginia, 1974): 1–4; "Stettinius, Edward Reilly," *Who's Who in New York,* ed. Frank R. Holmes, 8th edition (New York: Who's Who Publications, 1924): 1186. "Stettinius's Will Leaves All to Wife," *NYT,* Sept. 16, 1935; "Stettinius, 49, Dies of Heart Ailment," *NYT,* Nov. 1, 1949; "Mrs. Stettinius, Widow of Banker," *NYT,* Dec. 6, 1938; Robert James Maddox. "Stettinius, Edward Reilly"; http://www.anb.org/articles/06/06–00624.html; American National Biography Online Feb. 2000. (July 13, 2008); Papers of Richard Watkins Carrington, Accession #2705, Special Collections Dept., University of Virginia Library, Charlottesville, VA tp://ead.lib.virginia.edu/vivaxtf/view?docId=uva-sc /viu01404.xml] (July 15, 2012)

39. For Henry P. Davison: John Moody, "The House of Morgan," *The Independent,* Dec. 22, 1910, 1380–1386; E. J. Edwards, "The New House of J. P. Morgan & Co.," *NYT,* Apr. 20, 1913; "Davison Leaves $4,500,000 to Son," *NYT,* May 12, 1922; "H. P. Davison Dies As Surgeons End Second Operation," *NYT,* May 7, 1922; "Davison's Life Story Reads Like Fiction," *NYT,* May 7, 1922; "H. P. Davison Left $7,408,952 Estate," *NYT,* Mar. 12, 1925; "Mrs. Henry P. Davison, 90, Dies; Long a Leader of Society on L.I.," *NYT,* Feb. 1, 1962; Harriet Trubee Garlick, *History of the Trubee Family* (Bridgeport, CT: Marigold Publishing Co., 1894); Lamont, *Henry P. Davison: Record of a Useful Life,* 15; "Davison, Henry Pomeroy," *Dictionary of American Biography,* vol. 3 (New York: Charles Scribner's Sons, 1929):

148–149; "Davison, Henry Pomeroy," *The National Cyclopaedia of American Biography*, vol. 20 (New York: James T. White & Co., 1929): 88–89; Chernow, *House of Morgan*, 143; *The Federal Reporter*, vol. 55 (St. Paul: West Publishing Co., 1888): 652.

40. Vincent P. Carosso, *The Morgans: Private International Bankers, 1854–1913* (Cambridge, MA: Harvard University Press, 1987): 307. Though National City was a commercial national bank, Frank Vanderlip's experience as president of National City under James Stillman, who was chairman of the board, gives credence to this argument. Stillman was a majority shareholder of the bank and he refused to share his stockholding interests with Vanderlip or to help him to acquire National City shares that were offered to him by Jack Morgan. After this break, relations between the two men were never the same. A highly capable and ambitious banker, Vanderlip eventually left the bank because he was denied the possibility of promotion and greater investment in National City. Stillman's son, James A. Stillman, who was a member of the bank and was considered to be Stillman's heir, also wanted Vanderlip to leave after Stillman's death. See Cleveland and Huertas, *Citibank, 1812–1970*, 90–94. See for Vanderlip, Larry Schweikart. "Vanderlip, Frank Arthur"; http://www.anb.org/articles/10/10–01685.html; *American National Biography Online* Feb. 2000 (Dec. 1, 2010)

41. See, for example, John N. Ingham, *The Iron Barons: A Social Analysis of an American Urban Elite, 1874–1965* (Westport, CT: Greenwood Press, 1978): 30–31, 89–92.

42. This was the case for Junius Morgan, Pierpont Morgan's father. Juliet Pierpont, Junius Morgan's wife, was the daughter of a Unitarian minister from Boston. Joseph Morgan, Junius Morgan's father, was Congregationalist. Junius, however, moved toward the Episcopal Church in the 1840s. Chernow, *House of Morgan*, 51, 105.

Though most of the religious affiliations of the partners were determined through obituaries and other biographical sources, between 1900 and 1940, ten partners also stated their religious affiliation in *Who's Who in America*. www.marquiswhoswho.com (Oct. 8, 2007); Marquis, ed., *Who's Who in America*, vol. 21, 768; Marquis, ed., *Who's Who in America*, vol. 16, 909. Partners born after 1880 were more likely to list their religion. Seven were listed as Episcopalian (Francis D. Bartow, Henry Pomeroy Davison, William Ewing, Edward Hopkinson, Jack Morgan, Henry Sturgis Morgan, Thomas Newhall, George Whitney) and one as Presbyterian (William Arthur Mitchell). S. Parker Gilbert is listed as Baptist, but his funeral took place in an Episcopal church. "Funeral Tomorrow for Parker Gilbert," *NYT*, Feb. 25, 1938. Horatio Gates Lloyd is listed as Presbyterian, but his funeral also took place in an Episcopal church, and his obituary lists his church as Church of the Redeemer, Bryn Mawr. "Financial Leaders at Lloyd Funeral," *NYT*, Jan. 24, 1937.

43. Edward M. Lamont, *The Ambassador From Wall Street: The Story of Thomas*

W. Lamont, J. P. Morgan's Chief Executive (New York: Madison Books, 1994): 5; Albert Marquis, ed., *Who's Who in America*, vol. 21 (Chicago: A.N. Marquis Co., 1940): 1528–1529. When Lamont died, his funeral took place at Brick Presbyterian Church on Park Avenue and Ninety-First Street in New York City. "Lamont Funeral to be Saturday," *NYT*, Feb. 4, 1948.

44. Records of the Morgan Firms, Box 3, Folder: List of Partners, 1937, PML; Forbes, *Stettinius, Sr.;* Chernow, *House of Morgan*, 259.

45. Pierre Bourdieu, "Habitus," in Jean Hillier and Emma Rooksby, eds., *Habitus: A Sense of Place*, 2nd Edition (Burlington, VT: Ashgate Publishing Co., 2005): 42–45.

46. See "A. M. Anderson Expected to Be Morgan Partner," *New York Herald Tribune*, Dec. 29, 1926. Martin Egan (Hereafter Egan) papers, ARC 1222, Box 2, PML; "Thomas Cochran," *Quarter-Century Record Class of 1894 Yale College*, ed. Frank Dwight (New Haven: 1922): 115.

47. "Edward Farley Whitney," *NYT*, Feb. 10, 1928.

48. Nancy F. Cott, *Public Vows: A History of Marriage and the Nation* (Cambridge, MA: Harvard University Press, 2000): 1.

49. Letter to J. R. Carter from TWL, Apr. 13, 1927, TWL papers, Box 110–9, Baker Library Historical Collections, Harvard Business School. (Hereafter: HBS).

50. "Morgan Aides Form Investment House," *NYT*, Sept. 6, 1935. In 1941, Morgan Stanley & Co. changed its structure to a private partnership, which it remained until 1986 when it went public. Charles R. Geisst, *The Last Partnerships: Inside the Great Wall Street Money Dynasties* (New York: McGraw-Hill, 2001): 207; Jerry W. Markham, *A Financial History of the United States*, vol. 2 (Armonk, NY: M.E. Sharpe & Co., 2001): 169.

For Harold Stanley: "Stanley, Harold," *Who's Who in New York*, ed. Frank R. Holmes, 8th edition (New York: Who's Who Publications, 1924): 1174; "Miss Edith Thurston Engaged," *NYT*, Aug. 8, 1914; "Stanley and Joy Take Morgan Posts," *NYT*, Jan. 4, 1928; "Harold Stanley, 77, Is Dead; Led Investment-Banking Firm," *NYT*, May 15, 1963; "Bridal at Home for Mrs. Gilbert," *NYT*, Jan. 8, 1939.

For William Ewing: "William Ewing, 84, of Morgan Stanley," *NYT*, May 20, 1965; "Ewing, William," *Who Was Who in America*, vol. 4 (Chicago: Marquis Who's Who, 1968): 295; William Hyde and Howard L. Conrad, eds., *Encyclopedia of the History of St. Louis*, vol. 1 (New York: The Southern History Co., 1899): 290; Presley Kittredge Ewing and Mary Ellen (Williams) Ewing, *The Ewing Genealogy with Cognate Branches* (Houston: Hercules Printing & Book Co., 1919): 15; Paul Beckwith, *Creoles of St. Louis* (St. Louis: Nixon-Jones Printing Co., 1893): 65.

51. Interview with TWL and Frederick Lewis Allen, July 22, 1947, Bounded book titled "Morgan," Box 13, Frederick Lewis Allen (Hereafter: FLA) papers, Manuscripts and Archives, Library of Congress (Hereafter: LOC). See also "Col. Robert Bacon Dies in Hospital," *NYT*, May 30, 1919; "Loomis is Out, Robert Bacon In,"

NYT, Sept. 5, 1905; "Steel Trust's Report," *NYT,* Sept. 5, 1903. According to Carosso, another possible reason for Bacon's departure was greater national ambition (Carosso, *The Morgans,* 440). For George C. Thomas, see "G. C. Thomas to Retire From Drexel & Co.," *NYT,* Nov. 6, 1904; John W. Jordan, *Encyclopedia of Pennsylvania Biography,* vol. 10 (New York: Lewis Historical Publishing Co., 1918): 3–7.

52. "Morrow Won Fame in Only Four Years," *NYT,* Oct. 6, 1931; "Biographical Note," Elizabeth Cutter Morrow Papers, RG 32, Smith College Archives http://asteria.fivecolleges.edu/findaids/smitharchives/manosca12_bioghist.html (July 16, 2012).

53. Gates also took the position as university president without salary. See Lawrence Davies, "A Banker Rejoins His Old University," *NYT,* Aug. 3, 1930. See also letter to Bruce Bliven from TWL, Apr. 8, 1929, TWL papers, Box 110–1, HBS; "Dr. T. S. Gates Dies; Banker, Educator," *NYT,* Apr. 9, 1948; "Obituary Notes," *NYT,* Nov. 14, 1896; "Mrs. E. B. B. Waller Bride of T. S. Gates," *NYT,* July 20, 1929; *The Pennsylania Gazette,* vol. 20, issue 11 (Philadelphia: University of Pennsylvania, Jan. 6, 1922): 247; Daniel K. Cassel, *The Family Record of David Rittenhouse* (Norristown, PA: Herald Printing and Binding Rooms, 1897): 13; "Frederick Carroll Brewster," *NYT,* Dec. 27, 1929.

54. From *Tenth Report of the Secretary of the Class of 1871 of Harvard College* (Cambridge, MA: The University Press, 1911): 23. See also *Eleventh Report of the Class of 1871 of Harvard College June 1921: Fiftieth Anniversary* (Cambridge, MA: Riverside Press, 1921): 190; "Edward Farley Whitney," *NYT,* Feb. 10, 1928; "E. F. Whitney's Niece His Chief Beneficiary," *NYT,* Feb. 29, 1928; Frederick Clifton Pierce, *Whitney: The Descendants of John Whitney* (Chicago, IL: 1895): 160–161.

55. "Newhall, Thomas," *Who Was Who in America,* vol. 2 (Chicago: A.N. Marquis Co., 1963): 306; "Mrs. Thomas Newhall," *NYT,* Dec. 27, 1946; "Newhall, Financier, Is Found Shot Dead," *NYT,* May 13, 1947; "Thomas Newhall Shot Dead as He Cleans Gun," *Philadelphia Inquirer,* May 13, 1947; *Annual Proceedings Pennsylvania Society of the Sons of the Revolution, 1913–1914* (Philadelphia: Society of the Sons of the Revolution, 1914): 43.

56. As quoted in Chernow, *House of Morgan,* 143.

57. "Morgan Partner Retires," *NYT,* Jan. 1, 1922.

58. Letter to Mrs. JPM Sr. from JPM Jr., Sept. 12, 1923, JPM Jr. papers, ARC 1216, Box 233; Letter from JPM Jr. to Mrs. JPM Sr., Sept. 23, 1923, JPM Jr. papers, ARC 1216, Box 233, PML. See also "W. P. Hamilton, 81, Retired Financier," *NYT,* May 9, 1950.

59. *Money Trust Investigation,* Part 22, 1641.

60. Chernow, *House of Morgan* 92; Strouse, *Morgan: American Financier,* 620; John A. Garraty, *Right-Hand Man,* 238; "George W. Perkins Dies in 58th Year," *NYT,* June 19, 1920.

61. Interview with TWL and FLA, July 22, 1947, Bounded book titled "Morgan," Box 13, FLA papers, LOC.

62. As stated, though the formal connection between Morgan, Grenfell & Co. and the other Morgan houses was legally severed after 1934, they were included for consistency sake and also because the firms remained close. Records of Morgan Firms, ARC 1195, Box 4, Folder: Correspondence: J. P. Morgan & Co., 1934, June 16–Dec., PML.

Biographical sources for Morgan partners in England: "Lord St. Just, 71, British Financier," *NYT,* Nov. 29, 1941; "M. G. Herbert Dies; London Banker," *NYT,* Sept. 27, 1932; *Henry Adams and his Friends: A Collection of His Unpublished Letters* (New York: Houghton Mifflin Co., 1947): 469; "Regret in Newport," *NYT,* Oct. 1, 1903 (Michael G. Herbert's father); "Sir Clinton Dawkins Dead," *NYT,* Dec. 3, 1905; "New Morgan Partner," *NYT,* June 17, 1924; "Lord Bicester, 88, Financier, Dead," *NYT,* Feb. 18, 1956; "British Banker Dies in Hunting Accident," *NYT,* Feb. 14, 1938 (Charles F. Whigham); "Lord Catto, 80, British Banker," *NYT,* Aug. 24, 1959; "New Partner in Paris,". NYT, Jan. 1, 1933; Thomas Sivewright Catto, *Baron Catto of Cairncatto, Thomas Sivewright Catto, Baron Catto of Cairncatto, 1879–1959: A Personal Memoir and a Biographical Note* (London: T. and A. Constable, Ltd., 1962); D. E. Moggridge, *Maynard Keynes: An Economist's Biography* (London: Psychology Press, 1995): 904 (Francis Rennell Rodd); John Fforde, *The Bank of England and Public Policy, 1941–1958* (New York: Cambridge University Press, 1992): 525 f24 (Randal Hugh Vivian Smith); George Austin Morrison, *History of Saint Andrew's Society of the State of New York, 1756–1906* (New York: Order of the Society at Press of the Evening Post Job Printing Office, 1906): 111; *The Bulletin of the Metropolitan Museum of Art,* vol. 13, no. 1 (New York: Metropolitan Museum of Art, Jan. 1918): 160 (Robert Gordon); "Wilfred William M. Hill-wood," Ancestry.com *England & Wales, Death Index: 1916–2006* [database online]. Provo, UT, USA: Ancestry.com Operations Inc, 2007. General Register Office. *England and Wales Civil Registration Indexes,* London, England: General Register Office.

63. If we include Harry Ashton Watkins, who left in 1941 to join Bankers Trust in New York, the percentage increases to 88 percent. "Harry A. Watkins," *NYT,* May 29, 1976.

With Pierpont and Jack Morgan added, the numbers decrease to 75 percent and 78 percent, respectively, which was still much higher than the other branches. For example, Benjamin Joy, who was at Bankers Trust and Dillon, Read & Co. before becoming a Paris partner in 1928, was a Boston native and a Groton and Harvard graduate. He returned to Boston citing "poor health," but the New York partners doubted that this was the actual reason. See cable to J. P. Morgan New York from J. R. Carter, Dec. 29, 1930; Cable from J. P. Morgan to N. Dean Jay and Benjamin Joy, Dec. 3, 1930; Cable from Morgan to Benjamin Joy, Dec. 9, 1930; Cable from JPM Jr. to J. R. Carter, Dec. 30, 1930; Morgan Bank European Papers, Personal Name File, A–J, ARC 1221, Box 5, Folder: Joy, Benjamin, 1929–1930, PML.

Biographical sources for Morgan partners in France: "J. H. Harjes Dies in France," *NYT,* Feb. 16, 1914; "Harjes, Partner of Morgan, Dies of Polo Injury," *Chicago Daily*

Tribune, Aug. 22, 1926; "Mrs. Vanderbilt and H. H. Harjes Dead in France," *Hartford Courant*, Aug. 22, 1926; "H. H. Harjes Dies from Polo Injury," *NYT*, Aug. 22, 1926; "Oscar Siegel Dies in Paris," *NYT*, Dec. 21, 1917; "Benjamin Joy to Join Dillon, Read & Co.," *NYT*, Jan. 1, 1926; "Joy to Become a Partner of Morgan in Paris," *NYT*, Dec. 20, 1927; Henry L. Shattuck, "Benjamin Joy," *Proceedings of the Massachusetts Historical Society*, 3rd series, vol. 81 (1969): 211; "Benjamin Joy," NARA; Washington DC; Passport Applications, Jan. 2, 1906–Mar. 31, 1925; Collection Number; *ARC Identifier 583830/ MLR Number A1 534;* NARA Series: M1490; Roll #: 1949; "Benjamin Joy," Number: 014–22–9195; Issue State: Massachusetts; Issue Date: Before 1951. Social Security Administration. Social Security Death Index, Master File. Social Security Administration; Robert Sobel, *The Life and Times of Dillon Read* (New York: Truman Talley Books, 1991): 88; "John Ridgely Carter," *U.S. Department of State Office of the Historian http://history.state.gov/department history/people/carter-john-ridgely* (July 19, 2002); "Stanley and Joy Take Morgan Posts," *NYT*, Jan. 4, 1928; "Bernard Carter, Banker, 68, Dead," *NYT*, Nov. 9, 1961; "4 U.S. Business Men Pioneering in Paris," NYT, Jan. 4, 1945; "New Partner in Paris," *NYT*, Jan. 1, 1933; "Records of New Partners," *NYT*, Jan. 1, 1933 (Alan Vasey Arragon); "Alan Vasey Arragon," NARA; Washington DC; Passport Applications, Jan. 2, 1906–Mar. 31, 1925; Collection Number; *ARC Identifier 583830/ MLR Number A1 534;* NARA Series: *M1490;* Roll #: *1114;* "Alan Vasey Arragon," *Reports of the Deaths of American Citizens*, compiled 01/1835–12/1974. General Records of the Department of State, 1763–2002, RG 59–Entry 5166; Box Description: 1974 AA-BK, NARA; "Maurice Pesson-Didion," Year: *1935;* Arrival: *New York;* Microfilm Serial: *T715;* Microfilm Roll: *T715_5651;* Line: *6;* Page Number: *12*. Passenger Lists of Vessels Arriving at the Port of New York, New York, 1820–1897; Records of the U.S. Customs Service, RG 36; NARA.

Like Harry Watkins, Nelson Dean Jay, an Illinois native, was among those partners who stayed on after 1940 though unlike Watkins he returned to Morgan, Harjes in 1944. He went to Morgan, Harjes & Co. in 1919 from Guaranty Trust Co. of New York, and moved back to New York in 1955, where he died in 1972. "Nelson Dean Jay Going to Paris," *NYT*, July 19, 1919; "Nelson Dean Jay Is Dead at 89," *NYT*, June 7, 1972; "Nelsan Jay [sic], Ex-Banker, With Red Cross," *Washington Post*, Feb. 28, 1943; "Jay, Nelson Dean," *Who Was Who in America*, vol. 5 (Chicago: Marquis Who's Who, 1973): 370; "In Morgan Partnership," NYT, Jan. 11, 1934. Thanks to Martin Horn for the information on Jay.

64. Gertrude Himmelfarb, *Marriage and Morals Among the Victorians and Other Essays* (Chicago: Ivan R. Dee, 2001): 3–22.

65. Fanny was Pierpont Morgan's second wife. His first wife, Amelia Sturges Morgan (1835–1862), died very soon after their wedding from tuberculosis when Morgan was twenty-four years old. Strouse, *Morgan: American Financier*, 96–102, 207–212.

66. Strouse, *Morgan: American Financier*, 285–288, 294, 325–334, 632–33. Randolph eventually married William C. Whitney in 1896. She suffered a terrible

riding accident in 1898, was paralyzed, and died in 1899. "W. C. Whitney is to Wed," *NYT,* Sept. 29, 1896; "Mrs. Wm. C. Whitney Dead," *NYT,* May 7, 1899.

67. Strouse, *Morgan: American Financier,* 295–296, 570–71. See also Virginia Woolf, *Robert Fry: A Biography* (New York: Harcourt Brace & Co., 1940): 140–141; and cables from JPM Jr. to Lord Bicester, Sept. 11, 1940, Oct. 16, 1940 and cable from Vivian to J. P. Morgan, Oct. 21, 1940, Morgan Bank European papers, Boxes 2, 24, 33, PML.

68. Strouse, *Morgan: American Financier,* 295; Chernow, *House of Morgan,* 114.

69. Chernow, *House of Morgan,* 218; "H. Boocock Kills Wife and Himself," *NYT,* Mar. 23, 1915.

70. See K. Weigelt and C. Camerer, "Reputations and Corporate Strategy: A Review of Recent Theory and Applications," *Strategic Management Journal,* vol. 9 (September–October 1988): 443–454.

71. Strouse, *Morgan: American Financier,* 295–296, 330–331.

72. Strouse, *Morgan: American Financier,* 286–294, 325–326, 331.

73. Chernow, *House of Morgan,* 50, 62.

74. Chernow, *House of Morgan,* 113.

75. Letter to Mrs. JPM Sr. from JPM Jr., Mar. 18, 1889, JPM Jr. papers, ARC 1216, Box 121, Folder 12:1, PML.

76. Strouse, *Morgan: American Financier,* 468, 522–524, 528–531. Thanks also to Annelise Orleck for this point about A. Morgan.

77. Chernow, *House of Morgan,* 277, 403, 467.

78. See notations of payments for Miss Annie T. Morgan from Pierpont Morgan's account in the amount of $5,000 in January of multiple years, Pierpont Morgan's datebooks, ARC 1196, Box 28, PML. To give a sense of comparison, average annual earnings for industries and selected industries and occupations between 1902 and 1911 (including farm labor) was between $467 and $575. Average weekly hours worked and earnings in 1902 for manufacturing and "lower-skilled labor" was 58.3 hours @ .227 cents per hour for a total of $13.23 per week and for 1911 was 56.4 hours @ .263 cents per hour for a total of $14.83 per week. U.S. Bureau of the Census, *Historical Statistics of the United States: Colonial Times to 1957* (Washington, DC, 1960): 91. When Pierpont Morgan died, Anne Morgan was also left $3 million in his will. "$3,000,000 to Each Child and $1,000,000 to Mrs. Morgan," *NYT,* Apr. 20, 1913.

79. See letter to Mrs. JPM Sr. from JPM Jr., Mar. 24, 1889 and letter to Mrs. JPM Sr. from JPM Jr., Aug. 22, 1889, ARC 1216, Box 233, PML. This was consistent for elites across national boundaries at this time. For the German context, see Dolores L. Augustine, *Patricians and Parvenus: Wealth and High Society in Wilhelmine Germany* (Providence: Berg Publishers, 1994): 116, 189–242.

80. Letter to Mrs. JPM Sr. from JPM Jr., Mar. 16, 1898, JPM Jr. papers, ARC 1216, Box 121, Folder 14:2, PML.

81. Kenneth T. Jackson, *Crabgrass Frontier: The Suburbanization of the United States* (New York: Oxford University Press, 1985): 21; Sven Beckert, *The Monied*

Metropolis: New York City and the Consolidation of the American Bourgeoisie, 1850–1896 (New York: Cambridge University Press, 2003): 56.

82. Jackson, *Crabgrass Frontier*, 22; Paul Porzelt, *The Metropolitan Club of New York* (New York: Rizzoli, 1982): 7.

83. Jackson, *Crabgrass Frontier*, 22.

84. Beckert, *Monied Metropolis*, 55; Ingham, *Iron Barons*, 85–87.

85. Clifton Hood, *722 Miles: The Building of the Subways and How They Transformed New York* (Baltimore, MD: Johns Hopkins University Press, 1993): 39–40; Jackson, *Crabgrass Frontier*, 33–36; Notes by Frederick L. Allen of Pierpont Morgan's personal ledger, Box 13, FLA papers, LOC; Charles W. Cheape, *Moving the Masses: Urban Public Transit in New York, Boston, and Philadelphia, 1880–1912* (Cambridge, MA: Harvard University Press, 1980): 3. See Cheape for a comparative study of three different American cities.

86. Jackson, *Crabgrass Frontier*, 40–41.

87. Hood, *722 Miles*, 37–55.

88. Ida M. Tarbell, *The Life of Elbert H. Gary: The Story of Steel* (New York: D. Appleton and Company, 1925): 121–123.

89. Notes and interview with Leonhard Keynes by Frederick L. Allen, Nov. 3, 1947, Box 13, FLA papers, LOC; Letter to Mrs. JPM Sr. from JPM Jr., Dec. 2, 1889, JPM Jr. papers, ARC 1216, Box 121, Folder 12:2, PML. See Siegfried Blum, "The Elder Morgan," *Saturday Evening Post*, Apr. 22, 1933. Blum was Pierpont Morgan's private chauffeur from 1909 until 1913. Morgan had several automobiles and Blum lived with his family above the garage.

90. Pierpont Morgan and his partners headed the syndicate to finance the IRT though the primary financer, who had the contract with the city, was August Belmont. Hood, *722 Miles*, 74–91.

91. Hood, *722 Miles*, 91–93; *Money Trust Investigation*, Part 21, 1554. Letter to the Superintendent of the Broadway & Seventh Avenue RR, January 30, 1893 from JPM Jr., JPM Jr. papers, ARC 1216, Letterpress book #1, Page 60, PML.

92. Hood, *722 Miles*, 161, 183; Jackson, *Crabgrass Frontier*, 159. This did not mean that one in five Americans owned a car. Morgan partner Stettinius had, for example, six cars in 1923: two Cadillacs, three Fords, and one Buick. Forbes, *Stettinius, Sr.*, 189.

Jack Morgan also commuted to Wall Street by car or by boat, particularly during the summer when he lived in his Long Island home in Glen Cove. He bought his Glen Cove home in 1909 though he had been renting a home during the summer for several years. John Douglas Forbes, *J. P. Morgan, Jr. 1867–1943* (Charlottesville: University Press of Virginia, 1981): 66–68, 91.

93. Murray Hill Neighborhood Association, "A Bit of Murray Hill History," http://www.neighborhoodlink.com/manhattan/murrayhill-na/genpage/438521076.html (Jan. 24, 2010).

94. Paul S. Byard, *The Making of the Morgan from Charles McKim to Renzo Piano* (New York: The Morgan Library and Museum, 2008): 13. Morgan subsequently bought the other two brownstones in 1903 and 1904. The middle one was destroyed and a garden was created. The one on the northern corner became his son Jack Morgan's home.

95. In this period, 1900–1910, Charles Steele lived on Forty-Ninth Street, closer to his father-in-law, Seth Barton French, a prominent financier, who was a good friend of Pierpont Morgan. French lived on Fifty-Fourth Street about five blocks away from Steele and his wife, Nannie, whom he married in 1885. This may have been one of the reasons why he lived further uptown from the other Morgan partners because he already had long-standing ties to his neighborhood closer to his wife's family. "Seth Barton French Dead," *NYT,* Feb. 18, 1910; "The Real Estate Field," *NYT,* Sept. 15, 1912.

96. The geographic map was created in ArcGIS and is based on map data from Sanborn Fire Insurance Maps from the late nineteenth and early twentieth centuries. Sanborn maps copyright is held by Environmental Data Resources (EDR), an environmental risk management information company founded in 1990 and based in Milford, Connecticut. http://www.edrnet.com/index.php.

Between 2007 and 2008, EDR made a significant innovation to existing Sanborn maps by marrying them to a geographic coordinate system, Universal Transverse Mercator (UTM), which can be read by contemporary GIS programs such as ArcGIS. UTM is a grid system that is superimposed onto a map of the globe, which is divided into different zones. It is extremely accurate and can account for the curvature of the earth's surface. Steven Dutch, "The Universal Transverse Mercator System," University of Wisconsin-Green Bay (http://www.uwgb.edu/DutchS/FieldMethods/UTM System.htm). See also http://www.maptools.com/UsingUTM/UTMdetails.html. (January 23, 2010).

By physically locating addresses on EDR's digitized and UTM-coordinate Sanborn maps, hundreds of historic addresses (including those of the top syndicate participants from JPM & Co.'s syndicate books) were matched with UTM coordinates, which were then translated into LAT/LONG coordinates. This map, which visualizes these points in ArcGIS, gives a relatively accurate picture of where the historical addresses were *in relation to* one another in historic New York. The grid that is imposed upon it is that of the modern day New York City map and should only be used as reference. That said, New York City or Manhattan's grid pattern/street layout has remained remarkably consistent since the late nineteenth century.

All of the Morgan residential addresses were gathered from their *Social Register* listings. For the business addresses that are mapped in Figures 4 and 5, the sample of businesses was first gathered from looking at the circulars and letters of cooperation of the Morgan syndicates that were found in the syndicate books. (See Chapter Three.) All of those addresses were then located in the *Rand McNally International Bankers Directory: The Bankers Blue Book* (Chicago: Rand McNally & Co.) for every year between 1895 and 1925. In this project, the Montana State University and Yellowstone National Park online UTM converter was used. The Map Datum used was NAD83/WGS84. New York City is in zone 18. http://www.rcn.montana.edu/resources/tools/coordinates.aspx?nav=11 (January 23, 2010). http://www.esri.com/company/about/history.html and http://www.esri.com/software/arcgis/. See also Tim Ormsby, *Getting to Know ArcGIS Desktop: Basics of ArcView, ArcEditor, and ArcInfo* (Redlands, CA: ESRI Press, 2008). A very special thanks goes to Jon Walker and Hank Chin. Thanks also to Gerry Tsui, Paul Schiffer, and Amy Callahan, EDR.

97. Between 1906 and 1910, there were twenty partners in the House of Morgan: twelve in JPM & Co. and Drexel & Co., with eight New York City-based partners. All eight New York City partners are identified on the map.

98. Note on the datebooks: Pierpont Morgan's existing datebooks were translated into an Excel file. Every event was listed and coded by the time, date, place, event, address, and type of location, among other details. Though we cannot know if Morgan attended any or all of the listed engagements (preliminary total: 1955), we do know that they were important enough to be included in the datebooks. Not knowing if Morgan actually attended any of the meetings is, however, a serious limitation. Thus, other archival sources were consulted to gauge to what extent the datebooks could be used as evidence of his actual day-to-day world. Because a large percentage of Morgan's meetings involved the New York Central & Hudson River Railroad (NYC) and the New York, New Haven & Hartford Railroad (New Haven Road) and their subsidiary lines, these were used as the primary sample. They made up 734 out of 1955 events or 38 percent of the events listed in the datebooks.

The records for the NYC and the New Haven Road railroads reside at the New York Public Library (NYPL) Manuscript and Archives Division and the Thomas J. Dodd Research Center at the University of Connecticut, respectively. They were consulted to provide independent verification of how many NYC and New Haven Road meetings Morgan attended out of the ones listed in his datebooks, and in some cases, to fill in missing data as to where they were held. Morgan's datebooks list a total of fifty different railroads and related companies, such as steamship companies. Between the NYPL and the Dodd Center, twenty-nine of these railroads and companies, or 58 percent, had their boards of directors and/or executive committee minutes available. Out of 734 unique events for these 50 railroads, 665 were consulted or 91 percent. Out of these 665 unique events, Morgan was present at 414 meetings or 62 percent.

In addition, Jim Moske, Managing Archivist at the Metropolitan Museum of Art, very generously had the 105 Metropolitan Museum of Art meetings listed in Morgan's datebooks checked to see if Morgan actually attended and where they took place, if known. (Moske also found additional meetings and could not identify two for a final total of 107.) Out of these meetings, Morgan attended seventy meetings, did not attend twenty-five, and twelve could not be found. Of those meetings, Morgan attended 74 percent. Thus, out of the 1955 events listed in Morgan's datebooks between 1899, 1904–1912, the organizations related to the New York Central, the New Haven Road, and the Metropolitan Museum of Art constituted 839 or roughly 43 percent of all the events. Having checked 760 events out of 839, we know that Morgan attended 64 percent. The combined railroad and museum findings were used to confirm that the datebooks were a reliable source of Morgan's activities.

In the process of checking the events, a number of meetings were found that Morgan did attend but were not listed in his datebooks. These meetings were noted and added to another file. Morgan also spent several months a year abroad, and during those months, very few or no meetings are listed. Meetings were also sometimes listed during a time when Morgan was known to be out of the city. And finally, notes were made on meetings that stated Morgan declined an invitation or could not go. These were eliminated from the edited file. The edited file has 2,060 events, or 105 additional events compared to the original list based on the datebooks alone. Comparing the two files, there was little difference in the results of the two, so the edited file was used. The findings do not contradict other sources as to the organizations that he was known to have been committed.

99. James M. Mayo, *The American Country Club: The Origins and Development* (New Brunswick, NJ: Rutgers University Press, 1998): 11–12. See also Porzelt, *Metropolitan Club*, 1 and Jackson, *Crabgrass Frontier*, 97–99.

100. See G. William Domhoff, *Who Rules America? Power, Politics & Social Change*, 5th edition (New York: McGraw Hill, 2006): 49.

According to Clifton Hood, The *New York Times* reported that there were 350 private men's clubs in New York in 1890, twenty-five to thirty of which were "socially prestigious." The select clubs "had an aggregate membership of about 25,000" though the total number considering overlap between members "was probably no more than 15,000." Clifton Hood, "A Collision of Aspirations: Elite Men's Clubs and Social Competition in Gilded Age New York City," paper presented at 2011 Business History Conference, St. Louis. Special thanks to Clifton Hood for permission to cite this paper. See also Ingham, *Iron Barons*, 96–98.

101. Beckert, *Monied Metropolis*, 56, 58.

102. Mark Granovetter, "The Impact of Social Structure on Economic Outcomes," *Journal of Economic Perspectives*, vol. 19, no. 1 (Winter 2005): 34.

103. Susie J. Pak and Daniel S. Halgin, "The Significance of Social Clubs," March 2012.

104. Mayo, *American Country Club*, 16–17; Beckert, *Monied Metropolis*, 60. One exception was the Down Town Club, which was a businessmen's club in the business district.

105. Mayo, *American Country Club*, 27–29. The membership of the Century Club, which was founded in 1847, was limited to 100, though it was eventually expanded. Mayo, *American Country Club*, 14.

In 1895, the number of club members in the Union League Club was limited to 1600. *The Union League Club of New York* (New York: The Union League Club of New York, 1896): 47.

106. As quoted in Chernow, *House of Morgan*, 140. Thomas W. Lamont served on the advisory board of the Colony Club as early as 1915 and remained on the advisory board until at least 1940. For a full list of members and organizers in the first year as reported in the press, see "The Colony Club Has First Birthday," *NYT*, April 17, 1908. See also "Colony Club Formed By Woman A Very Exclusive Organization," *NYT*, May 7, 1905. For an official register, see *Officers, Members, Constitution & By-Laws of the Colony Club* (New York: The Club, 1908); *Officers, Members, Constitution & By-Laws of the Colony Club* (New York: Press of George Harjes Company, 1915, 1916, 1920); *Officers, Members, Constitution & By-Laws of the Colony Club* (New York: The Knickerbocker Press, 1926, 1930); *Officers, Members, Constitution & By-Laws of the Colony Club* (New York, 1933, 1938, 1940). Note that in general, women were listed by their husbands' names (not their own first names) unless they were not married. See also Anne F. Cox, *The History of the Colony Club, 1903–1984* (New York: The Colony Club, 1984): 85–96.

107. Morgan was, however, a member of a secret society called the Zodiac Club. (Chernow, *House of Morgan*, 254). His son, Jack, was also a member. See Datebooks, Pierpont Morgan papers, ARC 1196, Boxes 28–29, PML.

108. Porzelt, *Metropolitan Club*, 107; Guy St. Clair, *A Venerable and Cherished Institution: The University Club of New York, 1865–1990* (New York: The University Club, 1991): 254.

109. "The Social Register: Just a Circle of Friends," *NYT*, Dec. 21, 1997; Andy Logan, "That was New York, 'Town Topics,'" *New Yorker*, Aug. 14, 1965: 78.

110. *Who's Who* was more like an almanac of important national positions, such as members of the British royal family and parliament. http://www.acblack.com/whoswho/whoswho.asp?page=default.asp (Jan. 27, 2010).

111. E. Digby Baltzell, *Philadelphia Gentlemen: The Making of a National Upper Class* (Piscataway, NJ: Transaction Publishers, 1997): 8, 19–30; Cox, *The History of the Colony Club*, 53.

112. Letter from Herbert L. Satterlee (Hereafter: HLS) to his father, Aug. 15, 1900; letter from HLS to his mother, Aug. 17, 1900; letter from HLS to his mother, Aug. 23, 1900, Satterlee Family papers, ARC 1220, Part 3, Folder 6, PML. Thanks to Atiba Pertilla for this reference.

113. "An extract from the notes made by Benjamin Strong concerning his friendship and relations with Henry P. Davison. These notes loaned to H.L.S. by T.W.L., Feb. 1, 1929." HLS papers, ARC 1219, Box 12, Folder 2, PML.

114. Some accounts place this meeting at Delmonico's, a restaurant in downtown Manhattan, but according to U.S. Steel's centennial history and Schwab's biography, the dinner took place at the University Club. Robert Hessen, *Steel Titan: The Life of Charles Schwab* (Pittsburgh, PA: University of Pittsburgh Press, 1990): 114–118. Hessen writes that Schwab was also reluctant at first to meet Morgan in a pre-planned meeting because he did not want to give the impression to Carnegie that he was being

disloyal. Meeting Morgan in these social spaces helped to mitigate that impression. Carnegie was also at the dinner but left early to go to another engagement. See also W. Ross Yates, "Schwab, Charles Michael"; http://www.anb.org/articles/10/10 –01469.html; *American National Biography Online*, Feb. 2000.

115. Carosso, *The Morgans,* 303–304, 467–469.

116. See also for Willard Straight's diary description of his lunch meeting with Jacob Schiff at the Lawyer's Club as a key moment in the history of the American private banking alliance in China. Cyrus Adler, *Jacob H. Schiff: His Life and Letters,* vol. 1 (Garden City, NY: Doubleday, Doran and Co., 1928): 252.

117. For example, George Perkins reported that during the Panic of 1907, rumors of the insolvency of certain banks were circulating in "the Clubs" though the direct impact of those rumors is difficult, if not impossible, to pin down. "Copy of memorandum the Panic of 1907 written by George W. Perkins and sent to Henry P. Davison. Sent to H.L.S. and sent to G.W.P. Jr. Jan. 4, 1921," HLS papers, ARC 1219, Box 12, Folder 2, PML.

See also for meetings that took place for the Chinese Consortium at private clubs "that is to say no reporters present," letter from Sir Charles Addis to his wife, Eba McIsaac Addis, Oct. 13, 1920, Sir Charles Addis papers, PPMS14/267–277, Box 30, School of Oriental and African Studies Special Collections, University of London (Hereafter: SOAS).

118. *Money Trust Investigation,* Part 25, 1841–1842.

119. Thanks to Alan Dye and the Columbia Economic History Seminar and Robert E. Wright and other Business History Conference members for their questions, which helped me to clarify this point.

120. The Morgan partners' social club membership, and that of other banks, such as National City Bank, First National Bank, Lee, Higginson & Co., Kidder, Peabody & Co., Kuhn, Loeb & Co., J. & W. Seligman & Co., and Speyer & Co., were analyzed by using direct population data from their self-described affiliations, which included, for the most part, private men's clubs, political and social organizations, boards of companies, and universities. While not strictly a membership tie (as in the partners were members of the same organization at the same time), cases of self-identified educational affiliations (including honorary recognitions) were also included as organization affiliations. The partners' ties were analyzed for every five-year period of the firm's history, 1895–1940. Direct population data was found in the *Social Register, New York* published by the Social Register Association for the years 1897, 1900, 1905, 1910, 1915, 1920, 1925, 1930, 1935, and 1940 and for comparable years for the *Social Register, Philadelphia* and the *Social Register, Boston.* In addition, personal information was inputted for *Who's Who in America* published by Albert N. Marquis & Co. for the years 1899–1900, 1903–1905, 1910–1911, 1914–1915, 1920–1921, 1924–1925, 1928–1929, 1934–1935, and 1938–1939; and *Who's Who* (UK) published by AC Black for 1900, 1905, 1910, 1915, 1920, 1925, 1930, 1935, and 1940.

According to E. Digby Baltzell, *Who's Who in America* was more of a listing of "leading individuals in contemporary American life," who were an elite class, and the *Social Register* was "a listing of families of high social class position," who were the upper class. For this reason, the two registries have been analyzed separately, with a listing in *Who's Who* representing an identification as nationally elite but not necessarily socially elite. Here, I refer to what Baltzell called "upper class" as socially elite. Baltzell, *Philadelphia Gentlemen: The Making of a National Upper Class*, 8, 19–30.

With regard to the British social registry *Who's Who* (UK), though several of the European partners were listed in the American registries, the only American partner listed in *Who's Who* (UK) was the senior partner, Pierpont Morgan. In fact between 1895 and 1910, Pierpont Morgan was the only House of Morgan partner listed in *Who's Who* (UK), with the exception of Clinton E. Dawkins, who was in the civil service before he joined J. S. Morgan & Co. (Burk, *Morgan, Grenfell*, 57–59). Given the fact that the *Who's Who* (UK) data is negligible, the findings indicate that the British registry was either organized differently in terms of admission of members and/or that membership in British clubs was not as important for the House of Morgan overall. There is also the possibility that club membership was important for the cohesion and status of the British partners, specifically, but that this information cannot be found in the *Who's Who* (UK) directory until later. The presence of an established aristocracy and a constitutional monarchy in Britain as a dominant model suggests that we should not expect to find the non-British partners and instead we must rely on more qualitative data to analyze their social cohesion.

In general, the qualitative data suggest that the Morgan American partners and the Morgan London partners were deeply embedded in their own national contexts but not in the other, with the exception of the senior partner, Pierpont or Jack Morgan.

121. They were I. C. Raymond Atkin, Henry C. Alexander, and William A. Mitchell. Atkin and Mitchell both worked at the Royal Bank of Canada before joining the firm. Alexander was a member of the law firm of Davis, Polk, Wardwell & Gardiner, which was the Morgan bank's law firm.

Biographical sources on new partners: "William Mitchell Dead; Officer of Morgan & Co.," *NYT*, Mar. 5, 1980; "George Brown," Year: *1900;* Census Place: *Cleveland Ward 32, Cuyahoga, Ohio;* Roll: *1258;* Page: *7B;* Enumeration District: *158;* FHL microfilm: *1241258.* United States of America, Bureau of the Census. Twelfth Census of the United States, 1900. Washington, DC, NARA; "Raymond Atkin, Banker, 65, Dies," *NYT*, Jan. 26, 1957; "Atkin, Isaac Cubitt Raymond," *Who Was Who in America*, vol. 3 (Chicago: Marquis Who's Who, 1966): 35; "Alexander, Henry Clay," *The National Cyclopaedia of American Biography*, vol. 60 (New York: James T. White & Co., 1981): 149–150; "Henry C. Alexander, First Head of Morgan Guaranty, Dies at 67," *NYT*, Dec. 15, 1969; "Ely C. Hutchinson, Engineer, Is Dead," NYT, Nov. 15, 1955.

122. Between 1895 and 1940, the House of Morgan had sixty-seven partners.

Forty-one were partners in the American branches of JPM & Co. and Drexel & Co., or 61 percent of the total.

123. Thanks to Chris McKenna and members of the Oxford University Said School of Business seminar, particularly David Chambers, who made the suggestion to study the staff.

124. Of the aides, Willard D. Straight (1880–1918), who worked for the Morgan firm from 1909 to 1915, probably had the most in common with the newer partners in terms of social background. He was not from a wealthy family and his father passed away when he was still very young. He was unusual, however, in that his mother was a missionary and taught English in Japan. He spent his early years in Asia. His mother also died when he was still young and he was orphaned by the age of 10. He was able to graduate, however, from Cornell University (1901) and later entered the American diplomatic service. In 1911, Straight married Dorothy Payne Whitney, an heiress and the daughter of William C. Whitney, former secretary of the Navy, who married Morgan's former mistress. "Guide to the Willard Dickerman Straight papers, 1825–1925," Division of Rare and Manuscript Collections, Cornell University. http://rmc.library.cornell.edu/ead/htmldocs/RMM01260.html (November 14, 2012) Straight was not listed in the *Social Register* in 1910, the year before he married Whitney. He was clearly of a different social class than the Whitneys. But after 1911, his marriage to Whitney and their joint membership was listed in the *Social Register*.

125. Martin Egan was a journalist and a friend of Willard Straight. He was introduced to the Morgan firm through Straight, whom he met in East Asia at the turn of the century while working as a reporter for the Associated Press. Frank McKnight's first wife was Henrietta Davison. He was also close friends with Willard Straight and his wife, Dorothy. See letter to W. Cameron Forbes from Martin Egan, May 16, 1922, Egan papers, ARC 1222, Box 46, PML. Martin Egan left extensive papers to the PML. See also "Martin Egan Dies," *NYT,* Dec. 8, 1938.

126. Carosso, "The Morgan Houses: The Seniors, Their Partners, and Their Aides," 28. The sample of the aides was taken from Carosso's article, which contains brief biographical backgrounds of some of the aides, a list of J. P. Morgan employees in 1913, and a telephone list in the Morgan Firm papers in 1918. Only those aides after 1895 were included in the *Social Register* sample, and for 1913, only those who were at the top salary level in the employee lists ($10,000 in 1913). Note that in this period, Keyes was at the lower end of the salary scale ($2,000), the lowest being ($1,100). "Employees of J. P. Morgan & Co.," Mar. 1913, JPM Jr. papers, ARC 1216, Box 220, Folder 391. For 1918, only those persons listed as "Staff" were included. See Records of the Morgan Firms, Box 3, Folder: Telephone List: 1918 July, PML. The sample included: Christian T. Christensen, Henry G. Currier, Leonhard A. Keyes, Frank H. McKnight, Frederick W. Stevens, Willard D. Straight, Martin Egan, Thomas W. Joyce, Edwin S. Pegram, Charles H. Pond, Edward T. Sanders, Ernest Tuppen, J. A. M.

de Sanchez, Vernon Munroe, R. C. C. St. George, Walter H. Wilson. See also "Memories Persist at the House of Morgan," *NYT,* Feb. 16, 1964; "Robert C. C. St. George," *NYT,* Dec. 12, 1948; "Vernon Munroe, Banker, 82, Dead," *NYT,* July 16, 1957; "Frederick W. Stevens, Financier, Dies at 61," *NYT,* Nov. 3, 1926.

127. Again, this does not mean that the partners had to come from an elite background to have social capital, because they did not. Social club data are highly correlated, but do not prove causality. With the exception of some clear racial criteria, which are discussed below, the social club data do not answer the question of how some were able to become socially elite and others were not. It acts more like a prediction. To answer the question about how one becomes a member of socially elite clubs, we would need not only more data about the admissions policies of the clubs, which are difficult to come by because they remain "private," but also the social networks of individual partners beyond the scope discussed above. It would also require looking more closely at the unique international contexts. For example, British partners also had evidence of high social status but were slightly different from the American partners in the fact that they simultaneously maintained positions in the highest levels of British government. See, for example, the history of E. C. Grenfell, who had been the director of the Bank of England since 1905 and became a member of parliament in 1922. Kathleen Burk, "The House of Morgan in Financial Diplomacy, 1920–30," in *Anglo-American Relations in 1920s: The Struggle for Supremacy,* ed. B. J. C. McKercher (Edmonton: University of Alberta, 1990): 127–129.

128. The percentage capital of a partner in the firm is distinguished from individual partner accounts and balances with the firm or capital invested in the firm in excess of the partnership requirements. Only the former was included, as per the partnership agreement. For example, individual partners also took portions of syndicates for their own account. Between 1894 and 1934, the partner with the greatest amount of syndicate participations (in total) was TWL with approximately $44 million (four had amounts unknown). Dwight Morrow was second with $39 million (two had amounts unknown). The only person, who had more than both Lamont and Morrow as an individual was not a partner of the firm (John D. Rockefeller with $109 million [one was unknown]). George F. Baker Sr. came in fourth with $26 million (four were unknown).

129. The percentage capital allotted to an individual partner was determined entirely by Pierpont Morgan, and it could be different from the actual percentage of the capital of the bank. For example, Pierpont Morgan was allotted 35 percent between 1895 and 1899, but in 1895 when the firm was first organized, his "personal share" of the capital was 65 percent of the total ($4.6 million of $7.1 million). Carosso, *The Morgans,* 307.

130. A representative example of the relationship between club centrality and activity within the partnership is the history of Charles Steele. Steele was a railroad lawyer before he joined the firm and he quickly became an important adviser to Pierpont Morgan. Steele's club membership indicated a high level of centrality

between 1900 and 1925, meaning that he was in the same clubs at the same time with other partners who had the most number of connections to the most highly connected clubs. Starting in 1925 to 1930, however, Steele's centrality in the firm began to change. While still an important member of the firm, he no longer had the strongest ties to the other core members. Between 1930 and 1935, Steele's centrality in the firm decreased. In 1935 to 1940, Steele's connection to other core members of the firm dropped even further relative to the other core partners' strength of ties to each other. Steele, who was born in 1857, was less active in the firm from 1923 onward. (Steele was then sixty-six years old). When Steele's wife died in 1932, Leffingwell, wrote, "[Steele] took less interest in business, although he continued to be a partner in J. P. Morgan & Co." R. C. Leffingwell, "Memorial of Charles Steele" in the *Yearbook of the Association of the Bar of the City of New York* (New York: The Association of the Bar of the City of New York, 1940). Records of the Morgan Firm, Box 3, Folder: Correspondence: Charles Steele, 1920–1927, 1940, PML Archive.

Note: The specific measure of centrality used was eigenvector centrality, which looks not only at the number of connections that an individual or club has, it also weights that sum according to the ties they have to other well-connected nodes. See also Stephen P. Borgatti, "Centrality and Network Flow," *Social Networks,* vol. 27 (2005): 55–71; See also Robert A. Hanneman and Mark Riddle, *Introduction to Social Network Methods* (Riverside, CA: University of California, Riverside) (http://faculty.ucr.edu/~hanneman/).

The study of the partners' centrality using their club ties was created through a social network analysis of their club ties using UCINET. S.P. Borgatti, M.G. Everett, and L.C. Freeman, *Ucinet for Windows: Software for Social Network Analysis* (Harvard, MA: Analytic Technologies, 2002). The two-mode dataset of a person to club matrix was transformed into a one-mode dataset of persons to persons with their clubs in common. For more on two-mode networks, also called affiliation networks, see Stanley Wasserman and Katherine Faust, *Social Network Analysis: Methods and Applications* (New York: Cambridge University Press, 1994): 291–343. See also Stephen P. Borgatti and Martin G. Everett, "Network Analysis of 2–mode Data," *Social Networks* 19 (1997): 245; Allison Davis, Burleigh Bradford Gardner, and Mary R. Gardner, *Deep South: A Social Anthropological Study of Class and Caste* (Los Angeles: CAAS Publications, 1988).

131. Chernow, *House of Morgan,* 70; Carosso, *The Morgans,* 439.

132. Pak and Halgin used a longitudinal fixed effect time series analysis to investigate changes in percentage capital among Morgan partners in five-year periods between 1895 and 1940. Their findings indicate, "Morgan partners active in core social club circles with other partners obtained greater increases in capital ownership in the firm over time than others (Model 1, ß = 3.59)." They also found "a direct negative relationship between volume of clubs and change in ownership suggesting that not all clubs provided value. In other words, partners who were members of multiple social clubs did not reap the same benefits as those who were members in clubs with

other Morgan partners. In tandem this indicates that partners were rewarded for strategic social club memberships and certain core clubs were especially important." Susie J. Pak and Daniel S. Halgin, "The Significance of Social Clubs: Syndicates, Interlocking Directorates, and the Network of J. P. Morgan," March 2012.

133. Club ties also suggest that partners' individual differences and preferences were reflected in their function within the firm. Some partners were more inclined to be clubmen than others, and some were more involved in sports clubs, for example, or civic clubs. For notes on different partner functions, see Interview with TWL by FLA, July 22, 1947, Box 13, FLA papers, LOC.

134. "Morgan to Announce New Partners Soon," *The World*, Dec. 29, 1926; "A. M. Anderson Expected to Be Morgan Partner," *New York Herald Tribune*, Dec. 29, 1926, Egan papers, ARC 1222, Box 2, PML. See also "Sons of Three Partners Enter Morgan Firm," *NYT*, Jan. 1, 1929.

135. The *Social Register, Philadelphia* was also included as a source. In this period, Henry Davison and Pierpont Morgan were directors in First National, and Jack Morgan and George W. Perkins were directors in National City, so there is some overlap in the data.

To compare different five-year periods for the *Social Register, New York* only: Between 1895 and 1900, 56 percent of First National and 68 percent of National City directors were listed; between 1901 and 1905, 80 percent of First National and 75 percent of National City directors were listed; between 1906 and 1910, 69 percent of First National and 68 percent of National City directors were listed; between 1911 and 1915, 79 percent of First National and 72 percent of National City directors were listed. Director lists for First National and National City Bank were taken from Harold van B. Cleveland and Thomas F. Huertas, *Citibank, 1812–1970* (Cambridge, MA: Harvard University Press, 1985): 311–318 and Sheridan A. Logan, *George F. Baker and His Bank: 1840–1955: A Double Biography* (New York: The George F. Baker Trust, 1981): 402–405.

Social Register data for Boston was analyzed for Lee, Higginson & Co. and Kidder, Peabody & Co. to verify social elite (albeit regional) status. Partnership lists for those firms were determined by *New York Stock Exchange Co-Partnership Records*, v. 1 (1875–1903) and v. 2 (1904–1930), and *New York Stock Exchange Directory* (1931–1940), New York Stock Exchanges Archives. Sources were: *Social Register, Boston* (New York: Social Register Association, 1901, 1905, 1910, 1915, 1920, 1925, 1930, 1935, and 1940). In 1901, 100 percent of Lee, Higginson and 80 percent of Kidder, Peabody partners were listed. In 1905, 100 percent of Lee, Higginson and 83 percent of Kidder, Peabody partners were listed. In 1910, 55 percent of Lee, Higginson and 80 percent of Kidder, Peabody partners were listed. Starting around 1920, the percentage dips below 50 percent for both banks, but notably, the number of partners listed in the *Social Register, New York* also began to increase. (Lee, Higginson established an office in new York in 1906 and Kidder, Peabody had had a representative there since the late nineteenth century). Between 1920 and 1940, Kidder, Peabody partners had an average 65 percent of partners listed in the *Social Register, New York* or *Social Register, Boston*. Between 1920 and 1930, the average for Lee, Higginson was 57 percent of partners (the bank was dissolved after the Crash of 1929).

136. The eighteen firms were: J.P. Morgan & Co. with Drexel & Co., First National Bank of New York, Guaranty Trust Co., Bankers Trust Co., National City Bank, Chase National Bank, Astor Trust Co., Blair & Co., Speyer & Co., Continental & Commercial National Bank, Chicago, First National Bank, Chicago, Illinois Trust & Savings Bank, Chicago, Kidder Peabody & Co., and Lee, Higginson & Co. See *Money Trust Investigation*, Part 14, 980–1003. Club memberships were located in the *Social Register, New York* (New York: Social Register Association, 1912) and the *Social Register Locater* (New York: Social Register Association, 1912). Special thanks to Leslie Hannah for the suggestion to look at the Locater.

137. Twenty were private firms: August Belmont & Co., Baring Magoun & Co., Blair & Co., Brown Bros. & Co., Clark Dodge & Co., Hallgarten & Co., Harris Forbes & Co., Harvey Fisk & Sons, Hayden Stone & Co., Kidder Peabody & Co., Kissel Kinnicutt & Co., Kountze Brothers, Kuhn, Loeb & Co., Lazard Freres, N.W. Harris & Co., P.J. Goodhart & Co., Redmond Kerr & Co., Speyer & Co., W.S. Fanshawe & Co., and Winslow, Lanier & Co. Twelve were commercial banks: American Exchange National Bank, Chase National Bank, Corn Exchange Bank, First National Bank of New York, Grace National Bank, Hanover National Bank, Liberty National Bank, Mechanics & Metals National Bank, National Bank of Commerce, National City Bank, and National Park Bank. Nine were trust companies: Central Trust Co. of New York, Equitable Trust Co. of New York, Fifth Avenue Trust Co., Guaranty Trust Co., Mercantile Trust Co., New York Trust Co., Standard Trust Co. of New York, and United States Mortgage & Trust Co. Four were associated firms: The Federal Reserve Bank of New York and the New York Clearing House (which overlapped in terms of the leadership of the above banks), Standard Oil Co. of New York, and Cravath, Henderson, Leffingwell & De Gersdorff (and its predecessors), a key New York law firm. The leading members of these firms were identified from *Rand McNally International Bankers Director: The Bankers Blue Book* (Chicago: Rand McNally & Co.), the *Directory of Directors in the City of New York* (New York: Directory of Directors Company), or newspaper accounts. An effort was made to broaden the pool of banks in terms of time period and type, but all three datasets studied had some overlap because the leading national banks and J.P. Morgan & Co.'s syndicate participants overlapped.

138. Kuhn, Loeb & Co. partners, 1895–1940 (In order of entry into the firm): Solomon Loeb, Jacob H. Schiff, Abraham Wolff, Louis A. Heinsheimer, James Loeb, Felix M. Warburg, Otto H. Kahn, Mortimer L. Schiff, Paul M. Warburg, Jerome J. Hanauer, Gordon Leith, George W. Bovenizer, Lewis L. Strauss, William Wiseman, Frederick M. Warburg, Gilbert H. Kahn, John M. Schiff, Benjamin J. Buttenwieser,

Hugh Knowlton, Elisha Walker, Percy M. Stewart, Robert F. Brown. See "Kuhn, Loeb & Co. Partnership Agreements," Lehman Brothers Records, Boxes 517 and 518, HBS.

To compare different five-year periods for the *Social Register, New York* only for JPM & Co. and Kuhn, Loeb & Co.: Between 1895 and 1900, 88 percent of JPM & Co. and 0 percent of Kuhn, Loeb & Co. partners were listed; between 1901 and 1905, 100 percent of JPM & Co. and 17 percent of Kuhn, Loeb & Co. partners were listed; between 1906 and 1910, 100 percent of JPM & Co. and 33 percent of Kuhn, Loeb & Co. partners were listed; between 1911 and 1915, 89 percent of JPM & Co. partners (Pierpont Morgan was the only exception because he died in 1913) and 33 percent of Kuhn, Loeb & Co. partners were listed.

139. Partners in Kuhn, Loeb & Co., 1906–1910: Louis A. Heinsheimer, Otto H. Kahn, Jacob H. Schiff, Mortimer L. Schiff, Felix M. Warburg, and Paul M. Warburg; Partners in Speyer & Co.: Eduard Beit, Ferdinand Hermann, Gordon MacDonald, Henry Ruhlender, Richard Schuster, James Speyer, Charles H. Tweed, and Hans Winterfeldt; Partners in J. & W. Seligman & Co.: Emil Carlebach, Henry Seligman, Isaac Newton Seligman, James Seligman, Jefferson Seligman, Albert Strauss, and Frederick Strauss.

Partnership lists for Speyer & Co. and J. & W. Seligman & Co. were based on *New York Stock Exchange Co-Partnership Records,* v. 1 (1875–1903) and v. 2 (1904–1930), and *New York Stock Exchange Directory* (1931–1940), New York Stock Exchanges Archives. Other sources include: Linton Wells, *The House of Seligman,* unpublished, 1931, in Seligman family papers, New York Historical Society, James Speyer papers, 1896–1972, NYPL, and obituaries in the *New York Times.*

The club memberships of Jewish (as opposed to non-Jewish) partners in Speyer & Co. and J. & W. Seligman & Co. listed in the *Social Register* were similar to that of the two Kuhn, Loeb partners listed in the *Social Register* in that they did not include the top elite men's clubs in residential areas, such as the Metropolitan, Union, or Union League Clubs.

140. For the eight banks dataset, the club with the highest eigenvector centrality for 1900, 1905, 1915, and 1920 was the Metropolitan Club. It had the second highest centrality for 1910, 1925 and 1930. For the Pujo dataset of the eighteen top financial institutions in 1912, the Metropolitan club also had highest centrality. Similar findings apply to the population of the leading partners in forty-five firms, who were Morgan participants between 1900–1925. The Metropolitan Club was among the top five clubs for every five-year period (and the top club in 1910, 1915, 1920, and 1925).

It is also important to note that for all three datasets used to study overlapping social ties (eighteen leading national financial institutions in 1912, forty-five financial firms and associated firms in the Morgan syndicates between 1900–1925, eight key Anglo-American and German Jewish banks between 1900–1940), the individual with the highest centrality was (with few exceptions) the senior Morgan partner of that time. For the eight key banks between 1900–1910, it was Pierpont Morgan. Immediately after he died, it was Charles Steele. Then by 1920, it was Jack Morgan. By 1935 until 1940, it was Thomas Lamont. The one exception was 1930 when George Baker's son, George Baker, Jr., had the highest score. Jack Morgan was, however, a close second. For the dataset of forty-five firms, the most central person was James Stillman in 1900 and 1915 (closely followed by Pierpont Morgan in 1900 and Jack Morgan in 1915), Pierpont Morgan in 1905 and 1910, and Jack Morgan in 1920 and 1925. For the eighteen financial institutions in 1912, the most central and connected person with regard to social ties was also Pierpont Morgan.

Note that partnerships of private banks were usually much smaller in size than the directorships of national commercial banks like National City, i.e, the Morgans did not have the highest eigenvector centrality simply because it was the largest component in the network. The fact that the Morgan partners were socially elite and had many club ties in common would play a role in their centrality, but one that would not contradict their social position in the network. The size of a bank might affect a bank's centrality measure if a bank were as small as Kuhn, Loeb & Co., for example, which was about a third of the size of the Morgan partnership. But Kuhn, Loeb & Co. also had very limited representation in the *Social Register,* so the results are in part confirmation of their general social position in the network. Again, the centrality measure indicates how connected an actor or club was to another actor or club through these social ties. A tie, at whatever the strength, shows the potential for communication and identification but it does not actually tell us what flowed through that link. In order to know what was actually transferred, we would have to turn to the qualitative data.

141. James L. Grant, *Bernard M. Baruch: Adventures of a Wall Street Legend* (New York: John Wiley & Sons, 1997): 93–96. See also "New Club for Financiers," *NYT,* May 4, 1911. Grant writes that no Schiffs or Seligmans were listed in the *Social Register* before 1920, and though that was not the case, Bernard Baruch's experiences in the club world did resonate with that of Kuhn, Loeb partners.

142. Like their male counterparts, the Colony Club had an informal bar against Jewish women. However, a Gentile wife of an elite German Jewish banker could be a member. For example, Eleanor Robson, who was the wife of August Belmont Jr., was a member, as was Ellen Prince Lowery, the wife of James Speyer. Both were not Jewish. (Speyer and his wife were married by Bishop Potter in an Episcopalian ceremony in 1897). Mrs. Speyer had been one of the original members and Mrs. Belmont joined in 1913. "The Colony Club Has First Birthday," *NYT,* April 17, 1908; "Speyer-Lowery Nuptials," *NYT,* Nov. 12, 1897; *Officers, Members, Constitution & By-Laws of the Colony Club* (New York: The Knickerbocker Press, 1930): 9.

Anne Morgan did not support the bar against women on the basis of their religion, but even she could not guarantee a candidate's admission. In 1914 she proposed a candidate, who was Jewish, and was told that it was not desirable. She wrote a stern rebuttal that stated in part, "It is impossible for me to endorse your attitude about

Jews. . . ." Letter to Eunice (Mrs. Walter Maynard) from Anne T. Morgan, Dec. 29, 1914, ARC 1215, Box 27:1, PML. Eventually Morgan was forced to drop the issue because she was told there were no vacancies on the non-resident membership list. She withdrew the name of her candidate and asked the club to destroy the letters of endorsement and not to file them, presumably to protect the reputation of her candidate from having on record that she was "rejected." Morgan remained a member of the club. Letter to Mrs. J. S. Cushman from Anne T. Morgan, Jan. 14, 1915; Letter to Miss Ruth Twombly from Anne T. Morgan, Feb. 6 and Feb. 25, 1915, Anne Tracy Morgan papers, ARC 1215, Box 27:1, PML.

The Colony Club had the highest centrality status by 1940 among clubs that connected the leading members of a dataset made up of partners of the eight Anglo American and German Jewish houses. Over time, it became more important as an indicator of a partner's status and influence within that network with regard to his social ties.

3. ANTI-SEMITISM IN ECONOMIC NETWORKS

1. Vincent P. Carosso, "A Financial Elite: New York's German-Jewish Investment Bankers," *American Jewish Historical Quarterly (1961–1978)*, vol. 66, no. 1–4 (Sept. 1976–1977): 80.

2. Carosso, "A Financial Elite," 20; See also Stephen Birmingham, *'Our Crowd': The Great Jewish Families of New York* (Syracuse: Syracuse University Press, 1967).

3. Niall Ferguson, *The House of Rothschild: The World's Banker, 1849–1999, vol. 2* (New York: Penguin Books, 2000): xxviii.

4. Ralph W. Hidy, *The House of Baring in American Trade and Finance: English Merchant Bankers at Work, 1763–1861* (Cambridge, MA: Harvard University Press, 1949); Peter E. Austin, *Baring Brothers and the Birth of Modern Finance* (London: Pickering and Chatto Publishers, 2007).

5. Vincent Carosso, *Investment Banking in America: A History* (Cambridge, MA: Harvard University Press, 1970): 29.

6. According to their partnership agreements, Pierpont Morgan and Jacob Schiff had absolute authority to make the final decisions for their firms, held the majority stake in the firms' capital, and were responsible for the majority of its profits and losses. They also decided how the capital of the firm was allocated after a partner died or left. Morgan also "had the right to dissolve the partnership" without the consent of the other partners. The partnership agreement also stipulated that a partner's capital could not be withdrawn unless all the parties consented to it.

7. Cable to Mortimer L. Schiff (Hereafter: MLS) from Otto H. Kahn, Apr. 17, 1931, Otto H. Kahn (Hereafter: OHK) papers, Box 238–15, Department of Rare Books and Special Collections, Princeton University Library (Hereafter PUL).

8. That partner was Jerome Hanauer, who worked as an office boy in Kuhn,

Loeb from the age of sixteen starting in 1891. It took him about twenty years to become a partner. "Bankers Take in Partners," *NYT,* Dec. 31, 1911. Hanauer's daughter, Alice, married Lewis Strauss, who also became a Kuhn, Loeb & Co. partner. "Jerome Hanauer, Financier, is Dead," *NYT,* Sept. 4, 1938; Naomi W. Cohen, *Jacob H. Schiff: A Study in American Jewish Leadership* (Hanover: Brandeis University Press, 1999): 7.

9. For example, Mortimer Schiff married Adele Neustadt, the daughter of Sigmund Neustadt, a partner in Hallgarten & Co., another private bank. "Mrs. Schiff Willed $95,000 to Charity," *NYT,* July 19, 1932.

10. "Mrs. Isaac Seligman, 91," *NYT,* June 15, 1956. See letter to Isaac N. Seligman from JHS, June 12, 1917, JHS, MS 456, 450/5, American Jewish Archives (Hereafter: AJA).

11. "F. M. Warburg Dies at 66 in Home Here," *NYT,* Oct. 21, 1937. The Loeb sisters did not all share the same mother. Therese's mother was Loeb's first wife, who died later giving birth to another child, who also died during the birth. Betty was Loeb's second wife and the mother to his other children. John Kobler, *Otto the Magnificent: The Life of Otto Kahn* (New York: Charles Scribners & Sons, 1988): 13, 19.

12. Barry E. Supple, "A Business Elite: German-Jewish Financiers in Nineteenth-Century New York," *Business History Review,* vol. 31 (Summer 1957): 164.

13. "Percy A. Rockefeller Weds Miss Stillman," *NYT,* Apr. 24, 1901; "P. A. Rockefeller's Widow Dies at 50," *NYT,* Aug. 23, 1935.

In 1924, Anne Stillman, James Stillman's granddaughter (James A. Stillman's daughter), was married to Henry P. Davison Jr., who was the son of the late Henry P. Davison, a Morgan partner. Davison Jr. was then working at the Morgan bank, but he did not become a partner until 1929. They divorced in 1946. "Anne Stillman to Wed Henry P. Davison; Childhood Romance to Culminate in the Fall," *NYT,* June 4, 1924; "Henry P. Davison, Banker, 63, Dead," *NYT,* July 3, 1961.

In 1925, the Stillman Rockefeller and Carnegie clans were connected by marriage when James Stillman Rockefeller, Stillman's grandson (William G. and Elsie's son), married Nancy Carnegie, Andrew Carnegie's grandniece (Andrew Carnegie II's daughter). "Miss Rockefeller Wed in Baltimore," *NYT,* Sept. 2, 1937; "Miss Nancy Carnegie to Wed on Apr. 15," *NYT,* Mar. 30, 1925; "Andrew Carnegie Dies in Greenwich," *NYT,* June 10, 1947. Andrew Carnegie II was the son of Carnegie's younger brother, Thomas.

14. Pierpont Morgan was also a director during this time. Francis D. Bartow was also a director of First National Bank before becoming partner, though he started in the 1920s. Sheridan A. Logan, *George F. Baker and His Bank: 1840–1955: A Double Biography* (New York: The George F. Baker Trust, 1981): 402–405. "Francis Bartow, Banker 41 Years," *NYT,* Sept. 25, 1945; "Obituary Notes: Jacob Field Bartow," *NYT,* Oct. 26, 1901; "Bartow-Martin," NYT, May 9, 1906; "H. S. Bartow Dies, Retired Banker," *NYT,* Jan. 2, 1934; "Bartow, Francis Dwight," *Who Was Who in America,*

vol. 2 (Chicago: A.N. Marquis Co., 1963): 48; "Bartow, Francis Dwight," *Who's Who in New York,* ed. Frank R. Holmes, 8th edition (New York: Who's Who Publications, 1924): 81; Henry Whittemore, *The Founders and Builders of the Oranges, 1666–1896* (Newark, NJ: L.J. Hardham, 1896): 333; "Frank E. Martin," Year: *1900;* Census Place: *West Orange, Essex, New Jersey;* Roll: *968;* Page: *18A;* Enumeration District: *184;* FHL microfilm: *1240968.* United States of America, Bureau of the Census. Twelfth Census of the United States, 1900. Washington, DC, National Archives Records Administration (Hereafter: NARA).

15. Mary Jane Matz, *The Many Lives of Otto Kahn: A Biography* (New York: The Macmillan Company, 1963): 18–19; Kobler, *Otto the Magnificent,* 14. In 1928, Gordon Leith became a London-based partner. He also started with the Speyers, the London branch of Speyer Brothers (1900, partner 1911–1919). "Gordon Leith, 62, Banker of London," *NYT,* Apr. 3, 1941.

Kuhn, Loeb also, however, had a conflicted relationship with Speyer. In the early 1900s, Schiff spoke favorably about working together with Speyer & Co. In 1904, he referred to the banks as "joining hands" [his words were "to join hands"] in working together. He also wrote Robert Fleming, his friend and a prominent British banker, that the combined "prestige" of Kuhn, Loeb & Co. and Speyer & Co. could "assure the necessary deposits of all classes of securities." Letter to Robert Fleming from JHS, Mar. 29, 1904, JHS papers, MS 456, 437/11, AJA. This feeling of joining hands with the Speyers appears to have faded somewhat by the First World War. Schiff wrote to Mortimer in 1915 about some business with the consolidation of two railroads, saying that if they absolutely had to, maybe they should "in this one instance undertake the business officially with Speyers." Letter to MLS from JHS, Apr. 8, 1915, JHS papers, MS 456, 444/4a, AJA. He also wrote that he did not want to appear publicly with Speyers. See letter by JHS, Mar. 17, 1915, JHS papers, MS 456, 444/16, AJA. See also Theresa M. Collins, *Otto Kahn: Art, Money, & Modern Time* (Chapel Hill: University of North Carolina Press, 2002): 48–51.

16. For example, Russell Leffingwell, who became a partner in 1923, was a partner in the law firm of Cravath, Henderson, Leffingwell & de Gersdorff. S. Parker Gilbert, who became a partner in 1931, came from the same firm. For a history of the firm, see Robert T. Swaine, *The Cravath Firm and Its Predecessors, 1819–1948,* vols. I & II (New York: Ad Press, Ltd., 1946 and 1948).

The Cravath firm was actually Kuhn, Loeb & Co.'s counsel. At the time it became counsel to Kuhn, Loeb (1880), the firm was called Blatchford, Seward, Griswold & Da Costa. In 1900, it became Guthrie, Cravath & Henderson, and in 1910, it was Cravath, Henderson & De Gersdorff, and in 1944, it became Cravath, Swaine & Moore. For a full list of all the different titles of the firms and partners, see http://www.cravath.com/Cravath.html. (January 5, 2010)

Though the Morgans recruited from the Cravath firm, their primary counsel was Francis Stetson of Bangs, Stetson, Tracey & MacVeagh, later called Stetson, Jennings & Russell, and still later known as Davis, Polk & Wardwell. Stetson's former partner was Charles E. Tracy, Pierpont Morgan's brother-in-law. Vincent P. Carosso, *The Morgans: Private International Bankers, 1854–1913* (Cambridge, MA: Harvard University Press, 1987): 366. Davis, Polk's John W. Davis was attorney general from 1913 to 1918 and American ambassador to Great Britain until 1921, when he joined the law firm. Jean Strouse, *Morgan: American Financier* (New York: Perennial, 2000): 535. Davis, Polk served as Morgan counsel throughout the twentieth century representing the firm on deals with the Japanese government in the 1920s, during the Pecora Hearings, and through the separation of Morgan, Stanley from J.P. Morgan & Co. See also http://www.davispolk.com/firm/history (January 16, 2010)

Harold Stanley was at Guaranty Trust Company before becoming a partner in 1928. JPM & Co. merged with Guaranty Trust Company in 1959; Henry Clay Alexander was a partner in the law firm of Davis, Wardwell, Gardiner & Reed before becoming a partner in 1939. Marquis, ed., *Who's Who in America*, vol. 18 (Chicago: Albert Marquis & Co., 1935): 1435, 2239; Marquis, ed., *Who's Who in America*, vol. 21 (Chicago: Albert Marquis & Co., 1940): 159; "Morgan, Guaranty Deal Cleared," *NYT,* Apr. 3, 1959.

17. Schiff's grandson, John Schiff, married Edith Baker, the granddaughter of George F. Baker of First National Bank, in a civil ceremony at her parents' home in 1934. They were married for over forty years. "Edith Baker to Wed John M. Schiff," *NYT,* May 4, 1934; "Mrs. David T. Schiff Has a Son, David Baker," *NYT,* Aug. 20, 1969; "Edith Baker Schiff, Dead at 61, A Leader in Community Affairs," *NYT,* June 9, 1975; "John M. Schiff to Wed Mrs. Fell This Winter," *NYT,* Jan. 16, 1976; "John M. Schiff Marries Josephine L. Fell on L.I.," *NYT,* Mar. 1, 1976.

18. Kuhn, Loeb & Co. admitted Hugh Knowlton as a partner in 1933. He was Morgan & Co. partner Harold Stanley's brother-in-law. Harold Stanley was president of Guaranty Trust Co. of New York before he became a Morgan partner in 1927. His sister, Christine Stanley, married Knowlton in 1917 in Grace Church. Stanley's first wife died in 1934, and he married the widow of S. Parker Gilbert, another Morgan partner, in 1939. Thus, his sister, Christine, and his second wife were sisters-in-law, making Knowlton related distantly by marriage to another Morgan partner after the fact (Gilbert died in 1938). Both H. Stanley and Knowlton were from Massachusetts and both attended Yale though Knowlton was about six years younger. "Harold Stanley, 77, is Dead; Led Investment Banking Firm," *NYT,* May 15, 1963; "Hugh Knowlton, 87, Specialist for Financing Aviation Industry," *NYT,* May 5, 1981; "Miss Stanley Weds Lieut. Knowlton," *NYT,* Dec. 7, 1917; "Kuhn, Loeb Make Changes in Firm," *NYT,* Dec. 30, 1932.

19. Carosso, *The Morgans,* 362, 386–88, 394. See also Carosso, *Investment Banking,* 100–101; Naomi W. Cohen, *Jacob H. Schiff,* 24.

20. For most Kuhn, Loeb partners, it was not possible to get their addresses from the *Social Register* because they were not listed. In those cases, an attempt was made to find their addresses through the U.S. Census, *Who's Who,* obituaries, passport applications, or personal papers.

21. Precedents in the European context are not discussed here due to considerations of space. However, the lack of integration of the German banking community
elite into the dominating social elite, which distinguished it from the London context in particular, involved very clearly a consideration of their Jewish background.
For bankers like Schiff, who came to the United States as an adult and came from a
German banking family, this structure of social separation would not have been
extraordinary. Because the Morgans' French branch was mostly made of American
partners, the most important comparative international contexts would be that of the
English and German banks.

For the study of Jews in a German economic context and definitions of how "economic elites" and "Jews" are defined, see Dolores L. Augustine, *Patricians and Parvenus: Wealth and High Society in Wilhelmine Germany* (Providence: Berg Publishers,
1994) and Werner E. Mosse, *Jews in the German Economy: The German-Jewish Economic Elite, 1820–1935* (Oxford: Clarendon Press, 1987). For a comparative study
that looks at the social integration of elites in London, Paris, and Berlin during the
same period of study, see Youssef Cassis, "Financial Elites in Three European Centres:
London, Paris, Berlin, 1880–1930s" in Geoffrey Jones, ed., *Banks and Money: International and Comparative Finance in History* (London: Frank Cass, 1991): 53–71.

22. Strouse, *Morgan: American Financier,* 20.

23. For brief histories of these and other banks before the Civil War, see Carosso,
Investment Banking, 6–13, 20–26. For more extensive histories, see Barrett Wendell,
History of Lee, Higginson & Company, 1848–1918 (Boston: privately printed, 1921)
(Located in Houghton Library, Harvard University); Vincent P. Carosso, *More Than
a Century of Investment Banking: The Kidder, Peabody & Co. Story* (New York:
McGraw Hill, 1979); Charles Rappleye, *Sons of Providence: The Brown Brothers, The
Slave Trade, and the American Revolution* (New York: Simon & Schuster, 2006);
Edwin J. Perkins, *Financing Anglo-American Trade: The House of Brown, 1800–1880*
(Cambridge, MA: Harvard University Press, 1975). See also for the earlier history of
the Brown Brothers patriarch, *The Story of Alex Brown & Sons, 1800–1975* (Baltimore: Barton Gillet & Co., 1975). For the history of the connection between Alex
Brown & Sons and Brown Bros., which is now known as Brown Brothers Harriman,
a private partnership reorganized in 1931, see http://www.bbh.com/company/history
.shtml (Nov. 28, 2010).

24. Harold van B. Cleveland and Thomas F. Huertas, *Citibank, 1812–1970*
(Cambridge, MA: Harvard University Press, 1985): 315.

25. For example, Kahn was not observant at all while Schiff was. Kobler, *Otto the
Magnificent,* 10, 19; Supple, "A Business Elite," 162–163.

26. David Farrar, *The Warburgs: The Story of a Family* (New York: Stein and Day,
1974): 117–119, 247. See also for an extensive biography of the family, Ron Chernow,
The Warburgs: The Twentieth-Century Odyssey of a Remarkable Jewish Family (New
York: Random House, 1993).

27. See also Naomi W. Cohen, *Jacob H. Schiff* and Birmingham, *'Our Crowd'*; Carosso, *Investment Banking*, 17–23, 26.

28. Mark Granovetter, "The Strength of Weak Ties," *American Journal of Sociology*, vol. 78 (May 1973): 1360–1380; Mark Granovetter, "The Strength of Weak Ties: A Network Theory Revisited," *Sociological Theory*, vol. 1 (1983): 201–223.

29. Eyatar Friesel, "Jacob H. Schiff and the Leadership of the American Jewish Community," *Jewish Social Studies*, vol. 8, no. 2/3 (2002): 63.

30. Naomi W. Cohen, *Jacob H. Schiff*, 75; Friesel, "Jacob H. Schiff," 63.

31. Naomi W. Cohen, *Jacob H. Schiff*, 54; Sven Beckert, *The Monied Metropolis: New York City and the Consolidation of the American Bourgeoisie, 1850–1896* (New York: Cambridge University Press, 2003): 266; Birmingham, *'Our Crowd'*, 142–148; Leonard Dinnerstein, *Antisemitism in America* (New York: Oxford University Press, 1995): 41; Friesel, "Jacob H. Schiff," 63.

32. August Belmont was born August Schonberg in Prussia in 1816. In 1848, he married the daughter of Commodore Matthew Perry in an Episcopal ceremony at Grace Church in New York. Birmingham, *'Our Crowd'*, 57–62.

33. Supple, "A Business Elite," 164–166. See Supple for an extensive map of marriage ties within the German Jewish community.

34. Seligman, Speyer, and Belmont all immigrated to the United States in 1837. See Supple for greater detail on German Jewish immigration in the 1830s to the 1850s, including place of origin, marital status and push factors. Supple, "A Business Elite," 146–152.

35. The London branch of Seligman Bros. was opened in 1864, Seligman & Stettheimer in Frankfurt in 1864, Seligman, Hellman & Co. was established in 1865, the San Francisco firm of J. Seligman & Co. (founded 1852) became a banking house in 1867, and the French branch of Seligman Freres et. Cie. was founded in 1868. Linton Wells, *The House of Seligman*, carbon typescript (1931): 54–69. Seligman Family papers, The New York Historical Society (Hereafter: NYHS).

36. See letter from S. Schechter (?) to Louis Marshall, July 26, 1908, Louis Marshall papers, Series A, Correspondence Sub-Series 1, General, Di-H, Box 4, AJA. The writer sent Marshall, who was Samuel Untermyer's law partner, a pamphlet for a hotel establishment, which he pointed out to Marshall stated "No Jews. No Dogs." The pamphlet was titled, "In the Catskills," vol. 3, no. 3, July 18, 1908.

37. Birmingham, *'Our Crowd'*, 142–148; Dinnerstein, *Antisemitism in America*, 41.

38. James M. Mayo, *The American Country Club: The Origins and Development* (New Brunswick, NJ: Rutgers University Press, 1998): 27; Beckert, *Monied Metropolis*, 56, 58.

39. Paul Porzelt, *The Metropolitan Club of New York* (New York: Rizzoli, 1982): 3, 6, 9–10; *The Union League Club of New York* (New York: The Union League Club, 1896): 111.

40. See "Death of Judah P. Benjamin," *NYT*, May 8, 1884.

41. Will Irwin, Earl Chapin May, and Joseph Hotchkiss, *A History of the Union League Club of New York City* (New York: Dodd, Mead & Company): 23; Mayo, *The American Country Club,* 27.

42. Mayo, *The American Country Club,* 30; Linton Wells, *The House of Seligman,* carbon typescript (1931): 359. Seligman Family papers, NYHS.

43. "Eugene Seligman, Attorney, Is Dead," *NYT,* Nov. 29, 1936; "Theodore Seligman Dies," *NYT,* Sept. 11, 1907.

44. Mayo, *The American Country Club,* 14.

45. Porzelt, *Metropolitan Club,* 107; Guy St. Clair, *A Venerable and Cherished Institution: The University Club of New York, 1865–1990* (New York: The University Club, 1991): 107, 179; "James H. R. Cromwell Dies at 93, Married 'Richest Girl in the World,'" *NYT,* Mar. 23, 1990.

46. Linton Wells, *The House of Seligman,* carbon typescript (1931): 359. Seligman Family papers, NYHS; Mayo, 30.

NOTE: Race, religion, ethnicity, and culture were often used interchangeably. For examples within correspondence, see: Letter to Philip Cowen from JHS, May 16, 1900, Philip Cowen papers, P-19, Box 1, Folder 29, and letter to Philip Cowen from Isaac N. Seligman, Dec. 10, 1902, Philip Cowen papers, P-19, Box 1, Folder 32, American Jewish Historical Society, Boston, MA and New York, NY.

See also Eric L. Goldstein, "'Different Blood Flows in Our Veins': Race and Jewish Self-Definition in Late Nineteenth Century America," *American Jewish History,* vol. 85, no. 1 (1997): 29–55. Goldstein looks at the ways in which Jews self-identified as a race and the conditions under which they did so.

47. "Editorial," *Christian Advocate,* Apr. 20, 1893. See also "Union League Silent on Loeb Rejection," *NYT,* Dec. 29, 1910; "Hebrews are Angry," *Chicago Daily,* Apr. 23, 1893; "Mr. Seligman's Rejection," *NYT,* Apr. 17, 1893; "The Vice President of the Union League Club," *Washington Post,* Jan. 17, 1886; "Mr. Seligman's Blackballing," *NYT,* Apr. 23, 1893; "Has Many Troubles On Hand," *NYT,* Apr. 16, 1893; "Censure for Union League," *NYT,* Apr. 21, 1893; "Censure for the Union League," *NYT,* Apr. 20, 1893; "The Union League Policy," *NYT,* Apr. 24, 1893; "Mr. Seligman Blackballed," *NYT,* Apr. 15, 1893. See also Richard L. Zweigenhaft and G. William Domhoff, *Jews in the Protestant Establishment* (New York: Praeger, 1982): 9–13.

48. Linton Wells, *The House of Seligman,* carbon typescript (1931): 359. Seligman Family papers, NYHS.

49. "Edwin Einstein Resigns," *NYT,* Jan. 7, 1895.

50. "William Loeb, 70, Executive, Is Dead," *NYT,* Sept. 20, 1937.

51. Both clubs counted Morgan partners as members at that time: Pierpont Morgan (Metropolitan, Washington and Union League) and Henry Davison, Thomas W. Lamont, George Perkins, William Henry Porter, and Edward Stotesbury (Union League). See "Union League Silent on Loeb Rejection," *NYT,* Dec. 29, 1910. See also "Club Snobbery Scored by Taft," *Boston Daily Globe,* May 18, 1911; "Dr. Wise Talks of Jews," *New York Tribune,* Dec. 12, 1910; "Victim of Club's Ban,"

Washington Post, May 22, 1911; "Club Bars Jew Congressman," *Chicago Daily Tribune,* May 22, 1911. Other incidents include the Republican Club of New York (Edward Robinson and William H. Porter were members during these general periods). See "No Race Prejudice, Republicans Say," *NYT,* Mar. 21, 1913; "The Republican Club," *NYT,* Dec. 19, 1888.

52. Ron Chernow, *The House of Morgan: An American Banking Dynasty and the Rise of Modern Finance* (New York: Touchstone, 1990): 48; Porzelt, *Metropolitan Club,* 3, 6, 9–10; *The Union League Club of New York* (New York: The Union League Club, 1896): 111.

53. Beckert, *Monied Metropolis,* 59, 266–267. Porzelt writes that there was one Jewish charter member in the Metropolitan Club and several Catholic members, but that almost all the members of the club in the early twentieth century were "Episcopalian of English and Dutch descent." Porzelt, *Metropolitan Club,* 108.

54. Benjamin's wife was from "a prominent Creole Catholic family" in New Orleans and they married in the Catholic Church. Terry L. Jones, "The Jewish Rebel," *NYT,* Apr. 18, 2012; Michael B. Chesson, "Benjamin, Judah Philip"; http://www.anb.org/articles/04/04–00093.html; *American National Biography Online* Feb. 2000 (May 17, 2012).

55. "Mr. E. P. Fabbri's Retirement," *NYT,* Jan. 1, 1886; "Egisto P. Fabbri," *NYT,* June 27, 1894; "Will of Ernesto P. Fabbri," *NYT,* Dec. 27, 1894; "Ernesto G. Fabbri," *NYT,* July 4, 1883. Ernesto, Egisto's brother, had a son also named Ernesto, whom Egisto adopted after his brother died in 1883. Ernesto, the younger, married the granddaughter of William K. Vanderbilt, Edith Shepard, in 1897. They divorced in 1923. "Lakewood Club Opened," *NYT,* Feb. 12, 1903; "Mrs. Fabbri Gets Divorce," *NYT,* Feb. 16, 1923; "Mrs. E. G. Fabbri and Sister Dead," NYT, Jan. 27, 1934.

56. The one aspect of Fabbri's social background that was similar to that of the other partners was that he was Episcopalian. In the area of religion, as far as can be known, the Morgan partners were majority Protestant Christian, including Pierpont's senior partner in Drexel, Morgan & Co., Anthony Drexel. Drexel's father, Francis, who was from a Catholic family in Austria, immigrated to the United States from Germany in 1817. Anthony Drexel converted to Episcopalianism though his brother, Frank, did not. See "Anthony J. Drexel is Dead," *NYT,* July 1, 1893. "John R. Drexel, 72, Dies in Paris Home," *NYT,* May 19, 1935. Dan Rottenberg, *The Man Who Made Wall Street: Anthony J. Drexel and the Rise of Modern Finance* (Philadephia: University of Pennsylvania Press, 2001): 43–44, 46, 52, 103, 104, 114. "J. P. Morgan & Co. Will Incorporate as a State Bank," *NYT,* Feb. 16, 1940.

57. See Reginald Horsman, *Race and Manifest Destiny: The Origins of American Racial Anglo-Saxonism* (Cambridge, MA: Harvard University Press, 1981).

58. See John Higham, *Strangers in the Land: Patterns of American Nativism, 1860–1925* (New Brunswick, NJ: Rutgers University Press, 2002); Nell Painter, *Standing at Armageddon: A Grassroots History of the Progressive Era* (New York: W.W. Norton, 2008); Mae Ngai, *Impossible Subjects: Illegal Aliens and the Making of*

Modern America (Princeton, NJ: Princeton University Press, 2005); Gary Y. Okihiro, *Margins and Mainstreams: Asians in American History and Culture* (Seattle, WA: University of Washington Press, 1994); David C. Hammack, *Power and Society: Greater New York at the Turn of the Century* (New York: Russell Sage Foundation, 1982): 27.

59. Ellis W. Hawley, *The Great War and the Search for a Modern Order: A History of the American People and Their Institutions, 1917–1933* (New York: St. Martin's Press, 1979): 11.

60. Ronald Steel, *Walter Lippmann and the American Century* (New York: Vintage, 1980): 7. See also Angelo N. Ancheta, *Race, Rights, and the Asian American Experience* (New Brunswick, NJ: Rutgers University Press, 1998): 1–18.

61. See Slavoj Zizek as quoted in Naoki Sakai, *Translation and Subjectivity: On 'Japan' and Cultural Nationalism* (Minneapolis: University of Minnesota Press, 1997): 143; Michael N. Dobkowski, "American Anti-Semitism: A Reinterpretation," *American Quarterly*, vol. 29, issue 2 (Summer 1977): 176; Albert S. Lindemann, *Anti-Semitism before the Holocaust* (New York: Longeman, 2000): 47.

62. For a discussion on the ambiguity of race and the issue of naturalization law in particular, see Ian Haney Lopez, *White By Law: The Legal Construction of Race* (New York: NYU Press, 1997).

63. Noel Ignatiev, *How the Irish Became White* (New York: Routledge, 1995): 112.

64. Strouse, *Morgan: American Financier,* 218, 537–538. See Mayo, *The American Country Club,* 7–34, esp. 28–30. See also Irwin, May, and Hotchkiss, *A History of the Union League Club of New York City;* St. Clair, *Venerable and Cherished Institution,* 134–135, 174–177.

65. Carosso, *The Morgans,* 10. Supple suggests that if German Jewish houses had not existed, Jewish American men would not have been able to enter into the field of American banking otherwise because of "their race and background." Supple, "A Business Elite," 170.

66. That was Boris S. Berkovitch, who became vice-chairman, in 1984. Chernow, *House of Morgan,* 581, 605, 656.

67. Albert Marquis, ed., *Who's Who in America,* vol. 21 (Chicago: A.N. Marquis Co., 1940): 379; "George W. Bovenizer Dies at 81; Bank and Civic Leader Here," *NYT,* May 11, 1961.

68. As quoted in Naomi W. Cohen, *Jacob H. Schiff,* 53.

69. Naomi W. Cohen, *Jacob H. Schiff,* 52, 54, 75.

70. Naomi W. Cohen, *Jacob H. Schiff,* 34–35, 124–152. See also cable from Henry P. Davison to JPM Jr., Mar. 23, 1912, JPM Jr. papers, ARC 1216, Box 32, PML. See also letter to Sir Edward Grey from Mr. Bryce, Apr. 9, 1910, FO 405/202, Public Records Office (PRO).

71. Naomi W. Cohen, *Jacob H. Schiff,* 45–47.

72. According to Chernow, "Our Crowd," "came from the German phrase '*Unser Kreis*' (literally, 'Our Circle')." Chernow, *The Warburgs,* 46. See also Birmingham, *'Our Crowd'.*

73. Supple, "A Business Elite," 145, 164. The members of this elite community had their own exclusionary leanings. Most had immigrated largely before the Civil War, and tried to distance themselves from the new immigrants by excluding Russian Jews from their own socially elite clubs, such as the Harmonie Club (f. 1852), even while also working to uplift their less fortunate brethren. Beckert, *Monied Metropolis,* 266. See also Mayo, *The American Country Club,* 30; Birmingham, *'Our Crowd',* 131, 345; Dinnerstein, *Antisemitism in America,* 35–57. The Harmonie Club was originally called *Harmonie Gesellschaft.* It changed its name in 1894. Until 1893, German was the official language of the club.

74. Chernow, *House of Morgan,* 197.

75. Interview with TWL by Frederick L. Allen, July 22, 1947, Box 13, FLA papers, LOC. Repeated interactions were par for the course in private banking and did not just apply to the seniors. For the extensive interaction over periods of decades, see for example, correspondence between TWL and OHK, OHK papers, Boxes 15–1, 145–16, PUL.

76. Letter to Gaston Meyer from JHS, June 19, 1914, JHS papers, MS 456, Box 438, Folder 4, AJA. See also Naomi W. Cohen, *Jacob H. Schiff,* 55; Friesel, "Jacob H. Schiff and the Leadership of the American Jewish Community," 64.

77. According to Strouse, "Morgan privately supplemented Potter's salary with $12,500 a year, and raised $50,000 to insure he had an income for life." Strouse, *Morgan: American Financier,* 74–75, 270–271.

78. Letter to JHS from Bishop Potter, Jan. 11, 1898, JHS papers, MS 456, 2541/2, AJA.

79. Letter from JHS to Bishop Potter, Jan. 18, 1898, JHS papers, MS 456, 2541/2, AJA. Schiff wrote about Potter's views two years later in a letter to Philip Cowen, the editor of *American Hebrew.* In that letter he also wrote about "the prejudice and insults under which we have so frequently to suffer." Letter to Philip Cowen from JHS, May 16, 1900, Philip Cowen papers, P-19, Box 1, Folder 29, American Jewish Historical Society, Boston, MA and New York, NY.

80. Marilyn Nissenson, *The Lady Upstairs: Dorothy Schiff and the New York Post* (New York: Macmillan, 2008): 6.

81. Naomi W. Cohen writes, "[Schiff] kept his Jewish life distinctly separate from his business." Naomi W. Cohen, *Jacob H. Schiff,* 40.

82. Naomi W. Cohen, *Jacob H. Schiff,* 5; Birmingham, *'Our Crowd',* 187.

83. Chernow, *House of Morgan* 113, 170, 171, 602. See also John A. Garraty, *Right-Hand Man: The Life of George W. Perkins* (New York: Harper & Brothers, 1957): 90.

84. Supple, "A Business Elite," 170.

85. Carosso, *The Morgans,* 452. Carosso's primary text on the Morgan bank only goes up until World War I, which may be one reason for this conclusion.

86. Supple, "A Business Elite," 171.

87. Carosso, "A Financial Elite," 78.

88. Supple, "A Business Elite," 167–168, 171.

89. Both men had three participations for which the amount was unknown.

90. During Schiff's lifetime, Kuhn, Loeb & Co. and National City Bank had a strong alliance and their different roles in originating issues or placing them were extremely complementary. After Schiff died, however, Kuhn, Loeb's representation on the board was not replaced. Cleveland and Huertas, *Citibank, 1812–1970,* 37–47, 58.

91. Carosso, *More Than a Century of Investment Banking,* 3.

92. Carosso, *More Than a Century of Investment Banking,* 16, 17, 19, 27, 30–33.

93. Thanks to David Weiman for the suggestion of noting private banks separately from commercial banks.

94. This evidence is particularly striking because Kidder, Peabody did not always have friendly relations with the Morgans. Their competition over AT&T, for example, was intense, and Kidder, Peabody felt under pressure to maintain their position having been AT&T's original bankers. When they did work together even with negative feelings, they did so because of their position and ties within a community of international bankers, which included the Morgans' British branch, Baring Bros., other American brokerage houses like Harvey, Fisk & Sons, competitors like Kuhn, Loeb and Speyer & Co., and clients like AT&T and New York Telephone Co. The aggregate syndicate evidence thus suggests that the ethno-religious structure also played a role even when affective ties between Yankee banks were not present or strong. Kidder, Peabody & Co. Records, letter to Messrs. Baring Brothers & Co., Ltd., London from Kidder, Peabody & Co., Mar. 15, 1910, Letter books, v. 7, pgs. 295–296; Letter to Messrs. Baring Brothers & Co., Ltd., London from Kidder, Peabody & Co., Feb. 20, 1912, Letter books, v. 8, pg. 56, Baker Library Historical Collections, Harvard Business School (HBS); Carosso, *The Morgans,* 493–494.

95. Cleveland and Huertas cited the "Kuhn, Loeb Syndicate Book(s)," but they did not indicate where the books were located. See Cleveland and Huertas, *Citibank, 1812–1970,* 347–348. The main repository for Kuhn, Loeb & Co. papers is the Lehman Brothers collection at Baker Library Historical Collections, Harvard Business School, but it does not house the syndicate books. The syndicate books are also not housed in the American Jewish Archives, which is the repository for Jacob Schiff and Felix Warburg's papers.

96. Thanks to Chris Weiss and the MA students of Columbia University Institute for Social and Economic Research and Policy Quantitative Methods in the Social Sciences Seminar, particularly May Ling Lai, for the suggestion to look at the profits of the syndicates.

97. The Argentine loan was part of a bank syndicate that called itself the South

American Group in which JPM & Co. was a member. Kuhn, Loeb & Co. gave the South American Group 96 percent of its $1.5 million interest in that deal.

98. This point was something that Schiff himself emphasized. See letter to JHS from Charles Eliot, Mar. 13, 1917; Response to Charles Eliot from JHS, Mar. 14, 1917; Response to JHS from Charles Eliot, Mar. 15, 1917; Response to JHS from Charles Eliot, Mar. 22, 1917, JHS papers, MS 456, 452/9, AJA.

99. See Louise Michele Newman, *White Women's Rights: The Racial Origins of Feminism in the United States* (New York: Oxford University Press, 1999): 1–5.

4. DISRUPTING THE BALANCE: THE GREAT WAR

1. Jack Morgan also died at the age of seventy-five like his father. "J. P. Morgan Dies, Victim of Stroke at Florida Resort," *NYT*, Mar. 13, 1943.

2. Interview with Leonhard Keynes by Frederick L. Allen, Nov. 3, 1947, and Thomas W. Lamont (Hereafter: TWL), July 22, 1947, Box 13, Frederick Lewis Allen (Hereafter: FLA) papers, Manuscripts and Archives, Library of Congress (Hereafter: LOC). See letter to Clinton Dawkins from JPM Jr., Dec. 10, 1901, J. P. Morgan Jr. letter book, Dec. 1901, Morgan, Grenfell & Co. papers, MS 21797, Guildhall Library.

3. Letter to Mrs. JPM Sr. from JPM Jr., July 12, 1887, JPM Jr. papers, ARC 1216, Box 233, Pierpont Morgan Library (Hereafter: PML).

4. Ron Chernow, *The House of Morgan: An American Banking Dynasty and the Rise of Modern Finance* (New York: Touchstone, 1990): 95–97, 266–267; John Douglas Forbes, *J. P. Morgan, Jr. 1867–1943* (Charlottesville: University Press of Virginia, 1981): 25.

5. Juliet, Louisa's younger sister, married William Pierson Hamilton in 1894 when she was twenty-four years old. "Marriage of Miss Juliet Morgan," *NYT*, Apr. 13, 1894. After Louisa married, her place as Pierpont's companion was taken by up her sister, Anne. "Mrs. Satterlee, Wife of Lawyer, Dies," *NYT*, Oct. 8, 1946.

6. Before he got married, most of Jack Morgan's letters to his mother were addressed to "Mama" or "Mamma." Almost immediately after he was married to Jessie Morgan, his letters were addressed to "Mother." See letter to Mrs. JPM Sr. from JPM Jr., Dec. 18, 1890, ARC 1216, Box 233, PML.

7. Jessie died in 1925 from lethargic encephalitis, also known as "sleeping sickness." Jack never remarried. "Mrs. J. P. Morgan Dies at Glen Cove Home," *NYT*, Aug. 15, 1925; "J. P. Morgan Dies, Victim of Stroke at Florida Resort," *NYT*, Mar. 13, 1943; Chernow, *House of Morgan*, 267–269.

8. Naomi W. Cohen, *Jacob H. Schiff: A Study in American Jewish Leadership* (Hanover: Brandeis University Press, 1999): 195; Paul Windolf, "The German-Jewish Economic Elite (1900 to 1930)," *Zeitschrift für Unternehmensgeschichte. Journal of Business History*, no. 2 (2011): 140. Thanks to Roy Barnes for this reference.

9. Alan Brinkley, *American History: A Survey*, vol. 2, 12th edition (New York: McGraw Hill Higher Education, 2007): 615.

10. Chernow, *House of Morgan,* 170, 191. Morgan also had a hunting lodge in Gannochy, Scotland.

11. Priscilla Roberts, "J. P. Morgan and Company" in Spencer C. Tucker and Priscilla M. Roberts, eds., *Encyclopedia of World War I,* vol. 2 (Santa Barbara, CA: ABC Clio, 2005): 603. For a study of the Morgan bank's relationship with France, which cannot be conflated with its ties to Great Britain, see Martin Horn, "A Private Bank at War: J. P. Morgan & Co. and France, 1914–1918," *The Business History Review,* vol. 74, no.1 (Spring 2000): 85–112. See also Martin Horn, *Britain, France, and the Financing of the First World War* (Montreal: McGill-Queen's University Press, 2002)

12. See, for example, letter from JPM Jr. to Jessie N. Morgan, Nov. 24, 1918, Morgan Family papers, ARC 1194, Box 1, PML.

13. "As British Envoy Saw Morgan Shot," *NYT,* July 6, 1915; "Holt an American of German Descent," *NYT,* July 4, 1915; "Intruder Has Dynamite," *NYT,* July 4, 1915; "Muenter, Once German Teacher Here, Killed Wife, Shot Morgan, Sabotaged in World War 1," *Crimson,* Feb. 14, 1942; "Holt is Muenter, Says Associates," *NYT,* July 5, 1915. See also Chernow, *House of Morgan,* 192–195.

14. Holt as quoted in "Holt Tells Why He Shot Morgan," *NYT,* July 4, 1915.

15. "Climbs Bar for Plunge," *NYT,* July 7, 1915.

16. "J. P. Morgan Dies, Victim of Stroke at Florida Resort," *NYT,* Mar. 13, 1943; "Intended Bomb for J. P. Morgan & Co.," *NYT,* May 2, 1917.

17. Rev. Henry Anstice, *History of St. George's Church in the City of New York, 1752–1811–1911* (New York: Harper & Brothers, 1911): 473–475.

18. "Lunatic Kills Dr. James W. Markoe at Service in St. George's Church," *NYT,* Apr. 19, 1920.

19. "To Hurry Markoe's Slayer to Asylum," *NYT,* Apr. 20, 1920.

20. *Money Trust Investigation,* Part 25, 1803; "Havoc Wrought in Morgan Offices," *NYT,* Sept. 17, 1920; "Detectives Guard Wall St. Against New Bomb Outrage," *NYT,* Dec. 19, 1921; James Barron, "After 1920 Blast, The Opposite of 'Never Forget'," *NYT,* Sept. 17, 2003. A longer treatment of the 1920 bombing can be found in Beverly Gage, *The Day Wall Street Exploded: A Story of America in its First Age of Terror* (New York: Oxford University Press, 2009).

21. Chernow, *House of Morgan,* 194–195.

22. Edward Marshall, "Jacob H. Schiff Points a Way to European Peace," NYT, Nov. 22, 1914;

23. Letter to Louis Wiley, *NYT,* from Jacob H. Schiff (Hereafter: JHS), Oct. 1, 1914, JHS papers, MS 456, Box 438, Folder 4, American Jewish Archives. (Hereafter: AJA).

24. Letter to Dr. J. E. Noeggerath from JHS, Sept. 1, 1914, JHS papers, MS 456, Box 438, Folder 4, AJA.

25. Cable to Minister of Finance from JHS, Aug. 23, 1914, JHS papers, MS 456,

Box 438, Folder 6, AJA. See Richard J. Smethurst, *From Foot Soldier to Finance Minister: Takahashi Korekiyo, Japan's Keynes* (Cambridge, MA: Harvard University Asia Center, 2009): 156. Thanks to Robert Dannin for this reference.

NOTE: In this book, Japanese names are written with the given name first and family name last.

26. "Jacob H. Schiff Has Quit Japan Society," *NYT,* Dec. 2, 1914.

27. Letter to Baron K.T. from JHS, Oct. 7, 1914, JHS papers, MS 456, Box 438, Folder 6, AJA.

28. Letter to Lucien Wolf from JHS, June 14, 1915, JHS papers, MS 456, Box 438, Folder 4, AJA.

29. Naomi W. Cohen, *Jacob H. Schiff,* 196–197; Stephen Birmingham, *'Our Crowd': The Great Jewish Families of New York* (Syracuse: Syracuse University Press, 1967): 316–319.

30. Naomi W. Cohen, *Jacob H. Schiff,* 38.

31. Chernow, *House of Morgan,* 196. According to Cohen, Schiff "threatened to resign from the board of the National City Bank if it floated a Russian loan." Naomi W. Cohen, *Jacob H. Schiff,* 135.

32. Priscilla M. Roberts, "A Conflict of Loyalties: Kuhn, Loeb and Company and the First World War, 1914–1917," in *Studies in the American Jewish Experience,* vol. 2, ed., Jacob R. Marcus and Abraham J. Peck (Lanham, Md.: University Press of America and the American Jewish Archives, 1985): 17.

33. Schiff (1847–1920) was twenty years older than Jack Morgan though ten years younger than Pierpont. Otto Kahn was Jack Morgan's age (1867–1934) and also around the same age as Lamont (1870–1948) and Felix Warburg (1871–1937). Mortimer (1877–1931) was ten years younger than Jack.

34. Chernow, *House of Morgan,* 197. See interview with TWL by F. L. Allen, July 22, 1947, Box 13, FLA papers, LOC.

35. See, for example, letter from Mortimer Schiff to JHS, March 23, 1916, JHS papers, MS 456, 445/6 which also gives a description of an incident involving Lee, Higginson. See also letter to Mortimer from JHS, April 11, 1917, JHS papers, MS 456, 450/5, AJA, which talks about an incident involving the Federal Reserve Board of New York.

36. Letter to partners from JHS, Mar. 20, 1916, JHS papers, MS 456, Box 449/4b, AJA.

37. See letter to JHS from Mortimer L. Schiff (Hereafter: MLS), Mar. 23, 1916, JHS papers, MS 456, Box 445/5, AJA.

38. Henry Fairfield Osborn (1857–1935) was the son of Virginia Reed Sturges Osborn (1831–1902), who was the sister of Amelia Sturges, Pierpont Morgan's first wife who died in 1862. "Dr. Henry F. Osborn Dies in His Study," *NYT,* Nov. 17, 1935.

39. As quoted in Jean Strouse, *Morgan: American Financier* (New York: Perennial, 2000): 560.

40. Birmingham, *'Our Crowd'*, 333–334.

41. Naomi W. Cohen, *Jacob H. Schiff*, 7.

42. "Life as a Boy Made Kahn Arts Patron," *NYT*, Mar. 30, 1934. For biographies on Kahn, which detail his interest in art and music, see Theresa M. Collins, *Otto Kahn: Art, Money, & Modern Time* (Chapel Hill: University of North Carolina Press, 2002); Mary Jane Matz, *The Many Lives of Otto Kahn: A Biography* (New York: The Macmillan Company, 1963).

43. Chernow, *House of Morgan*, 114. See also Strouse, *Morgan: American Financier*, 560–561.

44. Letter to Adele Schiff from MLS, Jan. 8, 1919, JHS papers, MS 456/461/166, AJA.

45. David Farrar, *The Warburgs: The Story of a Family* (New York: Stein and Day, 1974): 117–119, 247.

46. "Paul M. Warburg Dies of Pneumonia," *NYT*, Jan. 25, 1932; "F. M. Warburg Dies at 66 in Home," *NYT*, Oct. 21, 1937. Regarding Max Warburg's role in Versailles after the war, see letter to Gerald Warburg from Felix Warburg, Mar. 17, 1919, Felix M. Warburg papers (Hereafter: FMW papers), MS 457, 184/54, AJA.

47. Paul Warburg felt compelled to leave the Federal Reserve Board as a result of the anti-German agitation. See letter to the president from Paul Warburg, May 27, 1918, Paul Moritz Warburg (Hereafter: PMW) papers, Box 4–53, Manuscripts and Archives, Yale University Library. (Hereafter: YUL). For Wilson's response, see letter to Paul M. Warburg, Aug. 9, 1918 and for Benjamin Strong's reaction, see letter to Paul Warburg, Aug. 9, 1918, among others, PMW papers, Box 4–56, YUL.

48. Undated letter from Otto H. Kahn (Hereafter: OHK) to JHS and letter from Schiff to Kahn, July 21, 1916, JHS papers, MS 456/449/46; Letter to OHK from JHS, Sept. 27, 1916, JHS papers, MS 456, 449/4b; Letter to JHS from OHK, Sept. 21, 1916, JHS papers, MS 456, 449/4b, AJA. See also Priscilla M. Roberts, "A Conflict of Loyalties," 1–32. Roberts also gives more extensive details on the views of the other partners and other bankers.

49. Mortimer felt the same way. See letter to OHK from MLS, May 28, 1910, OHK papers, Box 238–13, Princeton University Library (Hereafter: PUL).

50. Undated, untitled, and unsigned letter to partners though most certainly from OHK, JHS papers, MS 456, 449/4b, AJA.

51. Letter to JHS from OHK, Sept. 21, 1916, JHS papers, MS 456, 449/4b, AJA. Kahn did not send the letter. He instead handed it directly to Schiff, and Schiff later wrote him on September 27, which Kahn also forwarded to Mortimer. Letter to MLS from OHK, Oct. 2, 1916, JHS papers, MS 456, 449/4b, AJA.

52. Translation: Anna P. Kim.

53. Letter to OHK from JHS, Sept. 27, 1916, JHS papers, MS 456, 449/4b, AJA. Translation: Ellen Roh.

54. In December 1916, Jacob Schiff wrote James Loeb, his brother-in-law, that he

and Felix wanted to make the loans to German municipalities, "and we were practically on the point of coming to something in this respect through Max Warburg, when the Federal Reserve Board issued a mandate in the form of a warning against war finance, which, while both right and timely, cut us off, for the time being, from the possibility of further issuing European Municipal Bonds." Letter to James Loeb from JHS, Dec. 22, 1916, JHS papers, MS 456, 447/17, AJA. See also Carosso, *Investment Banking in America,* 211.

55. Letter to OHK from MLS, July 21, 1916, JHS papers, MS 456, 449/4b, AJA.

56. Letter to MLS from OHK, July 23, 1916, JHS papers, MS 456, 449/4b, AJA.

57. Letter to MLS from OHK, Oct. 2, 1916, JHS papers, MS 456, 449/4b, AJA.

58. Naomi W. Cohen, *Jacob H. Schiff,* 208.

59. Letter to Philip Schiff from JHS, Apr. 6, 1917, JHS papers, MS 456, 450/4, AJA.

60. Letter to Charles Eliot from JHS, Mar. 14, 1917, JHS papers, MS 456, 452/9, AJA. Schiff also wrote his friend, Alfred Heinsheimer, in Nov. 1918 that the kaiser was a "coward," for whom he had lost what little respect he had. Cable from MLS to JHS in White Sulphur Springs, West Virginia, Mar. 22, 1917, JHS papers, MS 456, 452/12, AJA. Letter to Alfred Heinsheimer from JHS, Nov. 12, 1918, JHS papers, MS 456, 457/19, AJA.

61. Priscilla Roberts, "A Conflict of Loyalties," 28. For more on Schiff's activities on behalf of Jews during the First World War, see Naomi W. Cohen, *Jacob H. Schiff,* 210–214.

62. "Davison's Life Story Reads Like Fiction," *NYT,* May 7, 1922; Naomi W. Cohen, *Jacob H. Schiff,* 203.

63. "Red Cross Fund to be $110,000,000," *NYT,* June 24, 1917. Lamont declined, however, to be associated with Untermyer even in the context of a war effort if it were a "small committee." See letter to Florence Lamont from TWL, May 15, 1917, TWL papers, Box 81–1, Baker Library Historical Collections, Harvard Business School. (Hereafter: HBS).

64. "20,000 Marchers in Loan Pageant," *NYT,* Oct. 26, 1917; "Rain Fails to Halt Liberty Day Fervor," *NYT,* Oct. 25, 1917; "Loan Sales Here Nearly a Billion," *NYT,* Oct. 25, 1917.

65. "Morgan's Team Leads in New York Campaign," *NYT,* June 20, 1917; "Red Cross Total $4,500,000," *NYT,* May 21, 1918. For more on Schiff's involvement with the Red Cross during the war, see JHS papers, MS 456, 462/1, AJA.

66. Lamont's son Thomas S. joined the army; Morgan's son Junius, Davison's son Henry P., and Paul Warburg's son James joined the navy. "Sons of 3 Partners Enter Morgan Firm," *NYT,* Jan. 1, 1929; "Junius Spencer Morgan is Dead," *NYT,* Oct. 20, 1960; "Ensign Warburg Weds Miss Swift," *NYT,* June 2, 1918.

67. Henry P. Davison's son F. Trubee Davison was also seriously wounded. "Death Notices: Porter," *NYT,* Oct. 21, 1918; "F. Trubee Davison Dies at 78; Led Natural History Museum," *NYT,* Nov. 16, 1974; "Howard Avenel Bligh St. George," Baker Family papers, Box 12, HBS; Sheridan A. Logan, *George F. Baker and His Bank: 1840–1955: A Double Biography* (New York: The George F. Baker Trust, 1981): 192; Cyrus Adler, *Jacob H. Schiff,* 204; "Capt. M. H. Schiff Missing," *NYT,* Oct. 25, 1917.

68. Edward Weeks, *Men, Money and Responsibility: A History of Lee, Higginson Corporation* (Boston: Lee, Higginson Corporation, 1962): 16; "Blair Fortune to Sons," *NYT,* June 17 1915; "Lord Rothschild, Financier, Dead," *NYT,* Apr. 1, 1915; "J. J. Hill Dead in St. Paul Home at Age of 77," *NYT,* May 30, 1916; "James Seligman, Aged Banker, Dies," *NYT,* Aug. 21, 1916; "Fall From Horse Kills I. N. Seligman," *NYT,* Oct. 1, 1917; "J. A. Stillman Takes His Father's Place," *NYT,* Apr. 3, 1918; "Luther Kountze, Banker, Dies at 76," *NYT,* Apr. 18, 1918; "Major H. L. Higginson, Boston Banker Dies," *NYT,* Nov. 16, 1919; "George C. Clark Dead," *NYT,* Feb. 26, 1919; "Col. Robert Bacon Dies in Hospital," *NYT,* May 30, 1919; "Henry C. Frick Dies," *NYT,* Dec. 3, 1919; "Levi P. Morton Dies at Rhinebeck Home on 96th Birthday," *NYT,* May 17, 1920; "E. C. Converse Dies of Heart Disease," *NYT,* Apr. 5, 1921.

69. Richard Sylla, Richard Tilly, and Gabriel Tortella, *The State, the Financial System, and Economic Modernization* (New York: Cambridge University Press, 1999): 3.

70. Marilyn Nissenson, *The Lady Upstairs: Dorothy Schiff and the New York Post* (New York: Macmillan, 2008): 7–8, 15, 27–28; Ron Chernow, *The Warburgs: The Twentieth-Century Odyssey of a Remarkable Jewish Family* (New York: Random House, 1993): 50.

71. Nissenson, *The Lady Upstairs,* 7, 10–13, 20. "Mrs. Schiff Willed $95,000 to Charity," *NYT,* July 19, 1932.

72. "Schiff, Mortimer L.: Last Will and Testament, 1930," Box 212, f. 3; "The Story of Schiff," Lehman Brothers papers: Kuhn, Loeb, Box 165, f. 10, HBS.

73. Chernow, *The Warburgs,* 45.

74. Chernow, *The Warburgs,* 50–51, 163.

75. "Mortimer L. Schiff Has Simple Burial," *NYT,* June 9, 1931. See FMW papers, MS 457, 176/8, 179/33, 183/16, 184/5, 184/54, 229/11, 232/1, 251/5, 338/10, AJA.

76. Chernow, *The Warburgs,* 163. Supple also writes that over time, the next generation of German Jews did not feel the compulsion to directly participate in the family business and branched off into other fields. Barry E. Supple, "A Business Elite: German-Jewish Financiers in Nineteenth-Century New York," *Business History Review,* vol. 31 (Summer 1957): 166–167.

77. Vincent P. Carosso, "A Financial Elite: New York's German-Jewish Invest-

ment Bankers," *American Jewish Historical Quarterly (1961–1978)*, vol. 66, no. 1–4 (Sept. 1976–1977): 87.

78. Only first marriages are listed. "Ensign Warburg to Marry Miss Swift," *NYT,* June 2, 1918; "George Backer Weds Mrs. Dorothy Hall," *NYT,* Oct. 25, 1932; "Miss Maud Kahn's Bridal on June 15," *NYT,* June 8, 1920; "Roger Kahn Weds Miss Edith Nelson," *NYT,* Apr. 8, 1933; "Gilbert Kahn To Study Bank Methods Abroad," *NYT,* May 23, 1926; "Mrs. Anne W. Kahn Dies of Pneumonia," *NYT,* Nov. 20, 1933; James Barron, "Margaret Kahn Ryan, 93, Financier's Daughter, Dies," *NYT,* Jan. 27, 1995. NOTE: Thomas F. Ryan was of Irish Protestant background. When he married Ira Barry (who was Roman Catholic), he converted to Catholicism. Stephen Birmingham, *Real Lace* (Syracuse: Syracuse University Press, 1973): 149–156.

79. Dorothy Schiff was a graduate of Brearley School in New York City and Bryn Mawr College. She married three times. Her first husband, Richard B. W. Hall, was an Englishman. She became the owner of the *New York Post* in 1939, which she sold to Rupert Murdoch in 1976. See Nissenson, *The Lady Upstairs.*

80. Quoted in Nissenson, *The Lady Upstairs,* 24. At the same time, Nissenson writes, "Several biographers report that Schiff included in his will the threat that any grandchild marrying a non-Jew would forfeit all claims against Schiff's estate, but this is not true." Nissenson, *The Lady Upstairs,* 17. Jacob Schiff's will confirms Nissenson's statement. There is no such stipulation in his will. See "Last Will and Testament of Jacob H. Schiff," Dorothy Schiff papers. Manuscripts and Archives Division. The New York Public Library. Astor, Lenox, and Tilden Foundations. (Hereafter: NYPL)

81. Judy Michaelson, "What Generation Gap?" *New York Post,* Dec. 13, 1968.

82. James Warburg and his wife, a pianist, "met in connection with the conservatory" that was established by James Loeb (Solomon Loeb's son). Letter to John Warburg from Felix Warburg, Mar. 27, 1918, FMW papers, MS 457, 179/33, AJA.

83. Warburg was talking about his feelings with regard to the relations between Jews and Arabs in the Middle East through the reference to intermarriage. Letter to Dr. Stephen Wise from Felix Warburg, July 7, 1937, FMW papers, MS 457, 338/10, AJA.

84. See Eric L. Goldstein, *The Price of Whiteness: Jews, Race, and American Identity* (Princeton, NJ: Princeton University Press, 2006).

85. For a discussion on Jewish women's social interaction with non-Jews in the late nineteenth century and the reactions of Jewish leaders to intermarriage, see Eric L. Goldstein, "'Different Blood Flows in Our Veins': Race and Jewish Self-Determination in Late Nineteenth Century America," *American Jewish History,* vol. 85, no. 1 (1997): 34.

86. While these views were present in the 1920s before the rise of Hitler, it was firmly established by the Second World War. For example, Dorothy Schiff considered the use of the term race to be the use of "the malicious Hitler terminology"

instead of using the term "creed or nationality." She wrote her brother in 1960, "As you know, there are three races of mankind: white, yellow and black or Caucasian, Mongolian and Negro. There are Jews among all three races, but most Jews are white." Memorandum from Dorothy Schiff to John M. Schiff, Feb. 17, 1960. See also letter from Mr. Donovan Rowse to Mrs. Dorothy Schiff, Sept. 1, 1949 and letter to Mr. Donovan Rowse, Editor, Historical Committee, Town Hall, from Dorothy Schiff, Sept. 14, 1949 and letter from John M. Schiff to Dorothy Schiff, Sept. 13, 1949, Dorothy Schiff papers, NYPL.

87. See, for example, "Banker Purchases East 69th Street," *NYT,* Apr. 30, 1927.

88. In the 1920s, "a group of neighbors of the lawyer Paul D. Cravath formed a syndicate to buy for $1,200,000 his estate at Locust Valley just east of Glen Cove on the north shore of Long Island." Syndicate members included Henry P. Davison, Edward R. Stettinius, and George F. Baker Jr. Davison already had an estate on Peacock Point. Jack Morgan had a home on East Island, near Davison. Stettinius also built a house in that area. John Douglas Forbes, *Stettinius, Sr.: Portrait of a Morgan Partner* (Charlottesville: University Press of Virginia, 1974): 185–187.

89. Notes on "HSM to author, Nov. 14, 1979," Vincent P. Carosso papers, ARC 1214, Box 8, Folder 2, PML.

90. See J. P. Morgan & Co. Syndicate Books, ARC 108–ARC 119, PML.

91. Chernow, *House of Morgan,* 215–216. See also letters to MLS from OHK, April 7, 1923, May 1, 1923, June 4, 1923 regarding Jack Morgan's interaction with him on issues during 1923, OHK papers, Box 238–15, PUL.

92. The Dawes Plan was replaced by the Young Plan in 1929. Germany under Hitler repudiated the reparations agreement in 1933. See Melvyn P. Leffler, *The Elusive Quest: America's Pursuit of European Stability and French Security, 1919–1933* (Chapel Hill: University of North Carolina, 1979). See also Horn, *Britain, France, and the Financing of the First World War,* 183–186.

93. Edward M. Lamont, *The Ambassador From Wall Street: The Story of Thomas W. Lamont, J. P. Morgan's Chief Executive* (New York: Madison Books, 1994): 210.

94. Morgan drew the line at Speyer & Co., who had been excluded from the Morgan syndicates since 1905 after allegedly violating the boundaries of the gentlemen's code. Given Speyer & Co.'s international connections and status, the partners in New York (Steele, Porter, Morrow, Cochran, Leffingwell, and Whitney) felt the firm should be included in the German loan because Speyers was an influential German American house. The Morgan partners were careful to note though they did not "mean that we desire or intend to re-establish personal relations with [Speyers] which would be obnoxious to all of us." Jack Morgan did not want to include Speyers and said, ". . . Our name appearing with Speyers degrades us . . ." But he agreed to go along with the decision or "allow himself to be overruled." The partners eventually decided not to include Speyer & Co. because "the complete contentment of J. P. Morgan is more valuable contribution to the success of the loan than the inclusion of Jimmie [Speyer]." They cabled Morgan, "Jimmie is out." Morgan replied,

"Quite impossible express happiness your cable has given me." See cables between JPM & Co. and Morgan, Grenfell & Co., Oct. 2, 1934, Oct. 3, 1924, Oct. 4, 1924, Oct. 6, 1924, TWL papers, Box 177–22, 23 & 24, HBS.

95. For international loans, Kuhn, Loeb attributed this to the fact that Great Britain or the Bank of England was the leading institution. In those cases, Kahn wrote, ". . . the leadership will again fall to Morgan's with ourselves in second place . . . I have made no attempt to secure the lead for us." Letter to MLS from OHK, Oct. 12, 1923, OHK papers, Box 238–15, PUL.

96. Memorandum dated June 14, 1927 written by TSL (Thomas S. Lamont), J. P. Morgan & Co. Syndicate Book #11, ARC 108–119, between pages 117 and 118, PML.

97. See Forbes, *J. P. Morgan, Jr.,* 116.

98. For just one example, see Schiff's correspondence with Henry Lee Higginson, the senior partner of Lee, Higginson & Co., throughout the years. Letter to JHS from H. L. Higginson, Mar. 19, 1891, JHS papers, MS 456, Box 2541, Miscellaneous letters, telegrams, etc., AJA. See also letter to JHS from Henry Lee Higginson, May 11, 1915, JHS papers, MS 456, Box 438, Folder 4, AJA. See also Werner E. Mosse, *Jews in the German Economy: The German-Jewish Economic Elite, 1820–1935* (Oxford: Clarendon Press, 1987): 201–202.

99. See letter from OHK to MLS, Aug. 5, 1924, OHK papers, Box 238–15, PUL.

100. Leonard Dinnerstein, *Antisemitism in America* (New York: Oxford University Press, 1995): 78–104.

101. Letter to TWL from Herman Harjes, May 15, 1922, TWL papers, Box 112–18, HBS; Forbes, *J. P. Morgan, Jr.,* 124.

102. Letter to TWL from Herman Harjes, May 16, 1922, TWL papers, Box 112–18, HBS.

103. Letter from TWL to Herman Harjes, May 17, 1922, TWL papers, Box 112–18, HBS.

Lamont also referred to Speyers as being part of a "tribe" in 1915. He also accused KL& Co. "our friends" for leaking details of a deal to the newspapers about a gold deal. Letter to E. C. Grenfell from TWL, June 2, 1915, TWL papers, Box 111–11, HBS.

104. Letter to George Whitney from TWL, May 23, 1922, TWL papers, Box 137–11, HBS. Rosen is possibly Walter T. Rosen of Ladenburg, Thalman & Company, a German Jewish private bank founded in 1879.

105. Jack Morgan also wrote in the same letter that he would not want to have "his name publicly associated with that of Mr. Speyer for any purpose whatsoever." Letter to TWL from JPM Jr., Aug. 16, 1922, TWL papers, Box 108–13, HBS.

106. Letter to Mrs. JPM Sr. from JPM Jr., Sept. 19, 1922, JPM Jr. papers, ARC 1216, Box 233, PML.

107. See letter from Clinton Dawkins to Jack Morgan, Feb. 16, 1904, Morgan Grenfell & Co. papers, MS 21, 800, 2, Guildhall Library.

108. Cable to Vivian H. Smith from TWL, Jan. 10, 1927, TWL papers, Box 111–19, HBS.

109. Chernow, *House of Morgan*, 198–99. For a history of Jews in the British context, see Todd M. Endelman, *The Jews of Britain, 1656 to 2000* (Los Angeles: University of California Press, 2002).

110. In a letter to his children, Thomas Lamont wrote of Lippmann, who was a friend for many years, "We never think of him as a Jew because he is the least like the traditional type that you can suppose." Letter to Tommy, Ellie, young Tommy, Teddy, Lansing, Corliss, Margaret, little Margaret, and my darling Ellie from TWL, April 17, 1931, TWL papers, Box 284-1, HBS. For more on Lippmann, see Ronald Steel, *Walter Lippmann and the American Century* (New Brunswick, NJ: Transaction Publishers, 1999); Barry D. Riccio, *Walter Lippmann: Odyssey of a Liberal* (New Brunswick, NJ: Transaction Publishers, 1994). For Lord Reading, see "Lord Reading Began as Cabin Boy," *NYT,* Dec. 31, 1935; "Lady Reading, the First Woman in the House of Lords is Dead at 77," *NYT,* May 23, 1971.

111. See also Strouse, *Morgan: American Financier,* 218, 349, 353, 359, 480, 537–538, 560, 601.

112. Letter to Mrs. JPM Sr. from JPM Jr., May 18, 1922, JPM Jr. papers, ARC 1216, Box 233, PML. See for similar sentiments by Henry P. Davison before the War, letter to E. C. Grenfell from Henry Davison, Sept. 5, 1914, E. C. Grenfell papers, Box 9C, Folder: Dec. 1906–Sept. 1914, Deutsche Bank AG Archives. (Hereafter: DBAG).

113. Letter to Mrs. JPM Sr. from JPM Jr., Aug. 1, 1924, JPM Jr. papers, ARC 1216, Box 233, PML.

114. Letter to TWL from Charles F. Whigham, undated but 1925, TWL papers, Box 111–15, HBS. Lamont did not make any remark about Whigham's comment about the other passengers. Letter to Charles F. Whigham from TWL, July 9, 1925, TWL papers, Box 111–15, HBS.

These sentiments were not new or unique to the Morgans. Earlier references can also be found, such as when Henry Davison wrote Teddy Grenfell in 1914, ". . . [I] fully appreciate the many annoying incidents for which our 'Jewish-American' travelers are responsible." Letter from Henry Davison to E. C. Grenfell, Sept. 15, 1914, Morgan Grenfell papers, Box 9C, Folder: Dec. 1906–Sept. 1914, DBAG. Sir Charles Addis of the Hong Kong Shanghai Banking Corporation (London) made similar comments about being forced into smaller quarters on his journey to Brazil. He wrote to his wife, "Oh! Those Jews!" See letter from Sir Charles Addis to his wife, Dec. 14, 1923, Sir Charles Addis papers, PPMS14/267–277, Box 30, School of Oriental and African Studies Special Collections, University of London.

115. See Dinnerstein, *Antisemitism in America,* 78–104.

116. Letter to Edward Grenfell from JPM Jr., May 17, 1929, Records of Morgan Firms, ARC 1195, Box 5, Folder: Correspondence: Sports ground, 1938–1931, PML.

117. Notes on "HSM to author, Nov. 14, 1979," Vincent P. Carosso papers, ARC 1214, Box 8, Folder 2, PML.

118. Ellis W. Hawley, *The Great War and the Search for a Modern Order: A History of the American People and Their Institutions, 1917–1933* (New York: St. Martin's Press, 1979): 12.

5. THE SIGNIFICANCE OF SOCIAL TIES: HARVARD

1. Between 1900 and 1909, JPM & Co. and Drexel & Co. admitted five partners. Between 1910 and 1919, the firms admitted six partners. Between 1920 and 1929, the firms admitted fourteen partners. Between 1930 and 1939, the firms admitted five partners.

London branch: Between 1900 and 1909, J. S. Morgan & Co. admitted two partners. Between 1910 and 1919, Morgan, Grenfell & Co. admitted one partner. Between 1920 and 1929, Morgan, Grenfell & Co. admitted two partners. Between 1930 and 1939, the firm admitted two new partners and two new managing directors.

Paris branch: Between 1900 and 1909, Morgan, Harjes & Co. admitted no new partners. Between 1910 and 1919, Morgan, Harjes & Co. admitted one new partner. Between 1920 and 1929, Morgan, Harjes & Co./Morgan et. Cie. admitted three new partners. Between 1930 and 1939, Morgan et. Cie. admitted three new partners.

2. American partners in 1920: Elliot C. Bacon (Robert Bacon's son), Junius Spencer Morgan Jr. (Jack Morgan's son), George Whitney (Robert Bacon's son-in-law and Edward F. Whitney's nephew); Partners between 1921 and 1925: Thomas S. Gates and Russell C. Leffingwell; Partners between 1926 and 1930: Arthur M. Anderson, Francis Bartow, William Ewing, Harold Stanley, Henry P. Davison Jr. (Henry P. Davison's son), Edward Hopkinson Jr., Thomas Stillwell Lamont (Thomas W. Lamont's son), Henry Sturgis Morgan (Jack Morgan's son), Thomas Newhall.

Sources: "Elliot C. Bacon Marries," *NYT,* June 6, 1915; "E. C. Bacon's Will Filed," *NYT,* Oct. 9, 1924; "Bacon, Elliot Cowdin," *Who's Who in New York,* ed. Frank R. Holmes, 8th edition (New York: Who's Who Publications, 1924): 50; "Lieut. Guy Norman Dead," *NYT,* June 4, 1918; "F. S. Converse Dies; A Leader in Music," NYT, June 9, 1940 (Junius S. Morgan's father-in-law); "Henry S. Morgan Is Dead at 81, Member of the Banking Family," *NYT,* Feb. 8, 1982; "George Whitney, Banker, 77, Dies," *NYT,* July 23, 1963; "Mrs. George Whitney Dies; Widow of J. P. Morgan Head," *NYT,* Oct. 16, 1967; "Whitney, George," *The National Cyclopaedia of American Biography,* vol. 50 (New York: James T. White & Co., 1968): 167–168.

3. Martin J. Sklar, *The Corporate Reconstruction of American Capitalism, 1890–1916: The Market, The Law, and Politics* (New York: Cambridge University Press, 1988): 28.

4. There were exceptions, of course. Edward Hopkinson Jr., who became the leading partner in Drexel & Co. after Edward Stotesbury, was the "great-great-

grandson of Francis Hopkinson, one of the signers of the Declaration of Independence." "E. Hopkinson, Jr., Dies at 85, Financier and Former City Official," *Philadelphia Inquirer,* Apr. 7, 1966. See also "Edward Hopkinson Jr., 80, Dies; Philadelphia Investment Banker," *NYT,* Apr. 8, 1966; "Edward Hopkinson, Attorney, 85, Dies," *NYT,* Dec. 25, 1935; "William F. Hopkinson Dead of Heart Disease," *NYT,* Jan. 28, 1932; Hopkinson Family papers, 1736–1941, Collection 1978, The Historical Society of Pennsylvania; "E. Hopkinson Jr. to Wed," *NYT,* Mar. 4, 1928; "James Sullivan," Year: *1920;* Census Place: *Philadelphia Ward 8, Philadelphia, Pennsylvania;* Roll: *T625_1629;* Page: *8B;* Enumeration District: *183;* Image: *205.* Fourteenth Census of the United States, 1920. Records of the Bureau of the Census, RG 29, NARA.

5. Four of the seven, Jack Morgan, Robert Bacon, Edward Whitney, and Thomas W. Lamont, went to Harvard. One, William P. Hamilton, Pierpont Morgan's son-in-law, went to Yale. Two others, both lawyers, Charles Steele and Temple Bowdoin, went to Columbia. In the post-war period, those who did not go to college include Arthur M. Anderson, Francis D. Bartow, and Thomas Newhall.

For Arthur Anderson: "A. M. Anderson Expected to be Morgan Partner," *New York Herald Tribune,* Dec. 29, 1926; "Morgan to Announce New Partners Soon," *World,* Dec. 29, 1926; "A. M. Anderson, 85, Morgan Partner," *NYT,* Aug. 11, 1966; "Anderson, Arthur Marvin," *The National Cyclopaedia of American Biography,* vol. 54 (New York: James T. White & Co., 1973): 111; "Anderson, Arthur Marvin," *Who Was Who in America,* vol. 4 (Chicago: A.N. Marquis Co., 1968): 28; "Frederick Anderson," Year: *1880;* Census Place: *East Orange, Essex, New Jersey;* Roll: *780;* Family History Film: *1254780;* Page: *496A;* Enumeration District: *098;* Image: *0253.* Tenth Census of the United States, 1880. (NARA microfilm publication T9, 1,454 rolls). Records of the Bureau of the Census, RG 29, NARA; "Frederick W. Anderson," Year: *1900;* Census Place: *East Orange Ward 3, Essex, New Jersey;* Roll: *968;* Page: *9B;* Enumeration District: *175;* FHL microfilm: *1240968.* United States of America, Bureau of the Census. Twelfth Census of the United States, 1900. Washington, DC, NARA.

In the 1930s, two of the three partners who did not go to college were Canadian, William Mitchell and Raymond Atkin.

6. Elliot C. Bacon, Junius S. Morgan Jr., Thomas S. Lamont, and Henry S. Morgan all went to Harvard. Russell C. Leffingwell, Harold Stanley, William Ewing, and Henry P. Davison Jr. went to Yale. With the exception of Davison, all the members who went to Yale were not related to other Morgan partners. All of those who graduated from Harvard were related to senior partners. Two others went to the University of Pennsylvania, with which Drexel partners had been traditionally affiliated (Thomas S. Gates and Edward Hopkinson Jr.) and one went to Amherst (Dwight Morrow).

7. See Wyndham Robertson, "Inside Morgan, Stanley," *Fortune,* Feb. 27, 1978, Vincent P. Carosso papers, ARC 1214, Box 29, PML.

8. This trend was reflective of a change in the national leadership of the country. See findings of Mabel Newcomer, *The Big Business Executive: The Factors that Made Him, 1900–1950* (New York: Columbia University Press, 1955); Walter A. Friedman and Richard S. Tedlow, "Statistical Portraits of American Business Elites: A Review Essay," *Business History,* vol. 45, no. 4 (Oct. 2003): 100.

9. Sklar, *Corporate Reconstruction,* 26.

10. With regard to the J. S. Morgan & Co./Morgan, Grenfell & Co. partners, the educational background of the partners differs somewhat in the chronology. Partners with kinship ties on both sides of the Atlantic made partner much earlier than those without those ties and the appropriate pedigree or university background. But by the time Jack Morgan and his cousin, both family members, entered the London partnership, the London partners were mostly British and not American (which was not the case during the early JSM period or the George Peabody period) and they were also educated at the elite British public schools like Eton, Harrow, and Cheltenham, and then Cambridge or Oxford. In particular, for the London firm, the 1900s were a time of introducing British partners with elite backgrounds and education while the 1930s were a time of introducing the next generation of kinship members, who were also educated at the most elite schools. The 1900–1929 period in contrast saw the entry of three partners who did not have either of those kinds of ties as far as we know. For more on British public schools and British leaders, see Rupert Wilkinson, *Gentlemanly Power: British Leadership and the Public School Tradition: A Comparative Study in the Making of Rulers* (New York: Oxford University Press, 1964).

The Paris house was a much smaller operation and it was different from the London house in that most of the partners were American. Like the American branches, it does not appear that the partners, who were with the firm at the beginning of the reorganization in 1895, had a university background, but this is not definitive. In general, information on the older partners is harder to come by, but the educational pattern of the younger partners followed the pattern of the American branches. Seven partners entered the firm between the start of the First World War and the start of the Second World War. Six of those partners were college graduates, or 86 percent. Of those six, two were Harvard graduates, one was a Williams College graduate, one was a Northwestern University graduate, one was a Knox College graduate, and one was a Trinity College (CT) graduate.

11. Over the course of the early twentieth century, Harvard's importance as a social connection between financiers steadily increased. For the dataset that included the partners/directors of the House of Morgan, First National Bank of New York, National City Bank, Kuhn, Loeb & Co., Speyer & Co., J. & W. Seligman & Co., Lee, Higginson & co., and Kidder, Peabody & Co., it was the third most central "club" by 1940.

Ties to Harvard were also a major point of commonality between New York banks and Boston Brahmin banks though elite Boston banks had much stronger (and older) ties starting earlier in the century. In this regard, the Boston Brahmin bank of Lee,

NOTES TO PAGES 142–143

Higginson & Co. was more similar to the Morgans' English partners. For example, by 1900, 67 percent of Lee, Higginson partners had gone to Harvard. By 1905, 100 percent had gone to Harvard. By 1910, 78 percent had gone to Harvard. Between 1915 and 1940, the percentage remained at about the 48 percent range.

12. *Harvard University Catalogue of Names, 1922–23* (Cambridge, MA: Harvard University, 1922): 4–5; *Quinquennial Catalogue of the Officers and Graduates, 1636–1920* (Cambridge, MA: Harvard University, 1920): 20–21.

13. This does not include James Pierpont, Morgan's ancestor, who attended Harvard in the late seventeenth century. (See Pierpont Family Papers Finding Aid, ARC 1289, Pierpont Morgan Library [Hereafter: PML], 2006). It also does not include Jack Morgan's uncle, Walter Hayes Burns (1838–1897), who married his father's sister, Mary Lyman Morgan, in 1867. Burns, who was a partner in J. S. Morgan & Co., was born in New York and graduated from Harvard in 1856, but was based mostly in London. See Frank Farnsworth Starr, *The Miles Morgan Family of Springfield, Massachusetts In the Line of Joseph Morgan of Hartford, Connecticut, 1780–1847* (Hartford, CT: Tuttle, Morehouse & Taylor, Co., 1904): 57.

14. Edward M. Lamont, *The Ambassador From Wall Street: The Story of Thomas W. Lamont, J. P. Morgan's Chief Executive* (New York: Madison Books, 1994): 6.

15. "Hammond Lamont Dies," *NYT,* May 7, 1909. Thomas W. Lamont's father, Thomas Lamont (1832–1916), graduated from Union College in 1856 (AB) and received an AM degree in 1859. Andrew Van Vranken Raymond, *Union University: Its History, Influence, Characteristics and Equipment,* vol. 3 (New York: Lewis Publishing Company, 1907): 107–108; "The Rev. Mr. Lamont's Will," *NYT,* Apr. 18, 1916.

16. Lamont, *Ambassador From Wall Street,* 17.

17. Jack Morgan went to St. Paul's preparatory school in New Hampshire (1880–1884), where he did not have the best of experiences. Both of his sons went to Groton School, which opened in 1884, in Massachusetts. John Douglas Forbes, *J. P. Morgan, Jr. 1867–1943* (Charlottesville: University Press of Virginia, 1981): 8–12. "J. P. Morgan Dies, Victim of Stroke at Florida Resort," *NYT,* Mar. 13, 1943; "Junius Spencer Morgan is Dead," *NYT,* Oct. 20, 1960; "Henry S. Morgan is Dead at 81," *NYT,* Feb. 8, 1982. For a discussion of private schools among elites, see John N. Ingham, *The Iron Barons: A Social Analysis of an American Urban Elite, 1874–1965* (Westport, CT: Greenwood Press, 1978): 92–95.

18. Ron Chernow, *The House of Morgan: An American Banking Dynasty and the Rise of Modern Finance* (New York: Touchstone, 1990): 479–480.

19. Thomas S. Lamont became a Morgan partner. According to the *New York Times,* "Thomas S. Lamont was elected an Overseer of Harvard in 1945 and became one of seven life members of the Harvard Corporation in 1952." Corliss Lamont became a socialist and a philosopher. Austin Lamont became a medical doctor. Lamont also had a daughter named Eleanor. "Thomas Lamont, Banker, 68, Dead," *NYT,* Apr. 11, 1967; "Lamont, Thomas Stilwell," *The National Cyclopaedia of American Biography,*

vol. 53 (New York: James T. White & Co., 1972): 426; "Lamont, Thomas Stilwell," *Who Was Who in America,* vol. 4 (Chicago: A.N. Marquis Co., 1968): 551; "Dr. Austin Lamont Dead at 64; Banker's Son, Medical Teacher," *NYT,* June 22, 1969; "Corliss Lamont Dies at 93; Socialist Battled McCarthy," *NYT,* Apr. 28, 1995; "Edward G. Miner," Year: *1920;* Census Place: *Rochester War 12, Monroe, New York;* Roll: *T625_1123;* Page: *18A;* Enumeration District: *147;* Image: *365.* Fourteenth Census of the United States, 1920. Records of the Bureau of the Census, RG 29, NARA (T. S. Lamont's wife's father).

20. "Harvard Boards Changes," *NYT,* Nov. 5, 1922: 32; "Alumni Committees Named for Harvard," *NYT,* Jan. 7, 1923: E3; *Harvard University Catalogue,* Call no. HU20.41 mfP, 1920/21–1922/23, Reel 16, Courtesy of Harvard University Archives (Hereafter: HUA); "J. P. Morgan Selected to Head Alumni Association for Year as Successor to Allston Burr," *Harvard Crimson,* Oct. 17, 1929; "Boston Major," *Time,* Apr. 6, 1931 (http://www.time.com/time/magazine/article/0,9171,741391,00.html ?promoid=googlep) (Sept. 19, 2008).

21. "Dr. C. W. Eliot Dies at Summer Home in Maine, Aged 92," *NYT,* Aug. 23, 1926.

22. Charles W. Eliot, "What is a Liberal Education?" in *Educational Reform: Essays and Addresses* (New York: The Century Co., 1898): 89–122.

23. Henry Wilder Foote, "Charles W. Eliot," *Christian Register,* 1953. Reprinted in Herbert F. Vetter, ed., *Harvard's Unitarian Presidents* http://www.harvardsquare library.org/HVDpresidents/eliot.php (June 20, 2010).

24. James Loeb was a member of Kuhn, Loeb & Co., though he retired early in 1901 and lived in Europe from 1905 until his death in 1933. Harvard University received the largest public legacy from his will. It was given $800,000, of which $300,000 was used to create the Loeb Classical Library Foundation. "James Loeb Left $2,258,996 Estate," *NYT,* July 8, 1936; "James Loeb Dies on German Estate," *NYT,* May 29, 1933; Naomi W. Cohen, *Jacob H. Schiff: A Study in American Jewish Leadership* (Hanover: Brandeis University Press, 1999): 76.

25. Mortimer went to Amherst but never graduated. He did, however, receive an honorary degree (A.M.) in 1906. Naomi W. Cohen, *Jacob H. Schiff,* 4; Stephen Birmingham, *'Our Crowd': The Great Jewish Families of New York* (Syracuse: Syracuse University Press, 1967): 186–187; "Mortimer L. Schiff," *Scenic and Historic America,* vol. 3, no. 2 (June 1931): 35.

26. "John Schiff, Philanthropist and Investment Banker, Dies," *NYT,* May 10, 1987.

27. The exception was their son, Paul F. Warburg (1904–1965). Felix and Frieda's daughter Carola Warburg (1897–1987) married into the Rothschilds family, and she did not go to university. See Lehman Brothers Records: Kuhn, Loeb & Co., Subseries I.4 Warburg family records, 1913–1968, Baker Library Historical Collections, Harvard Business School. (Hereafter: HBS.)

28. Endicott Peabody's father, Samuel Endicott Peabody, was a relative of George Peabody, the original founder of what became the House of Morgan. The Peabodys were also a pre-Revolutionary War, old Boston family (though George Peabody eventually settled in Baltimore). "Endicott Peabody of Groton School," *NYT,* Nov. 18, 1944; Edwin P. Hoyt, *The Peabody Influence: How a Great New England Family Helped to Build America* (New York: Dodd, Mead & Company, 1968). "F. Trubee Davison Dies at 78," *NYT,* Nov. 16, 1974; "F. T. Davison Wed to Miss Peabody," *NYT,* Apr. 17, 1920.

29. Naomi W. Cohen, *Jacob H. Schiff,* 49; Birmingham, *'Our Crowd',* 185–187.

30. "Groton Celebrates Its Fiftieth Year," *NYT,* June 3, 1934.

31. As quoted in Marcia Synnott, *The Half-Opened Door: Discrimination and Admissions at Harvard, Yale, and Princeton, 1900–1970* (Westport, CT: Greenwood Press, 1979): 30. Schiff also remembered Harvard and the Semitic Museum in his will.

32. Lamont served on the Board of Overseers from 1912 to 1925. Lowell was president from 1909 until 1933. Katia Svachuk, "Abbot Lawrence Lowell," *Harvard's Unitarian Presidents* http://www.harvardsquarelibrary.org/HVDpresidents/lowell .php (Apr. 5, 2010).

33. Nell Painter, "Jim Crow at Harvard: 1923," *The New England Quarterly,* vol. 44, no. 4, (Dec. 1971): 627.

34. Marcia G. Synnott, "The Admission and Assimilation of Minority Students at Harvard, Yale, and Princeton, 1900–1970," *History of Education Quarterly,* vol. 19, issue 3 (Autumn 1979): 294.

35. "Harvard Boards Changes," *NYT,* Nov. 5, 1922: 32; "Alumni Committees Named for Harvard," *NYT,* Jan. 7, 1923: E3; *Harvard University Catalogue,* Call no. HU20.41 mfP, 1920/21–1922/23, Reel 16, HUA.

36. Raymond Wolters, "The Harvard Dormitory Crisis (1921–23)" in Werner Sollers et al., eds., *Blacks at Harvard: A Documentary History of African American Experience at Harvard and Radcliffe* (New York: New York University Press, 1993): 208; "United States: Annual Report, 1922," June 21, 1923, pg. 59, FO 371/8525, Public Records Office (UK).

37. Randall Kennedy, "Introduction: Blacks and the Race Question at Harvard" in Sollers et al., *Blacks at Harvard,* xxi.

38. "Letter to the Editor," *Boston Herald,* Jan. 17, 1923: 16; Painter, "Jim Crow at Harvard: 1923," 632; Synnott, *Half-Opened Door,* 25.

39. "Why Independents Support Wilson," *NYT,* June 19, 1916. One of the supporters cited in the article is Jacob Schiff.

40. "United States: Annual Report, 1922," June 21, 1923, pg. 59, FO 371/8525, Public Records Office.

41. Synnott, "The Admission and Assimilation of Minority Students at Harvard, Yale, and Princeton, 1900–1970," 290. As a reference for the size of the class, Oliver B. Pollak writes, "In Sept. 1921 Harvard University enrolled its largest freshman class: 856 out of a total student body of 2,620." Oliver B. Pollak, "Antisemitism, the

Harvard Plan, and the Roots of Reverse Discrimination," *Jewish Social Studies*, vol. 45, no. 2 (Spring 1983): 113.

42. Synnott, *The Half-Opened Door*, 21, 23–24, 58; Synnott, "The Admission and Assimilation of Minority Students at Harvard, Yale, and Princeton, 1900–1970," 293; Wolters, "Harvard Dormitory Crisis," 198. See "Harvard Alumni Fight Negro Ban: Prepare Memorial for College Corporation Calling for Perpetuation of Traditions," *New York Sun*, June 16, 1922: front page.

43. Synnott, *The Half-Opened Door*, 46.

44. David Levering Lewis, *W. E. B. Du Bois: The Fight for Equality and the American Century, 1919–1963* (New York: Henry Holt & Co., 2000): 91.

45. Letter to Dr. E. F. Du Bois from Lewis S. Gannett, Mar. 3, 1922, W. E. B. Du Bois (Hereafter: Du Bois) papers, Reel 10, Manuscripts and Archives, Library of Congress (Hereafter: LOC). See also Wolters, "Harvard Dormitory Crisis," 198; "Harvard Alumni Fight Negro Ban: Prepare Memorial for College Corporation Calling for Perpetuation of Traditions," *New York Sun*, June 16, 1922: front page. On Yale and Princeton's discrimination of blacks and Jews, and their conversations with other colleges like Dartmouth, see Synnott, *The Half-Opened Door*, 139–142, 151, 155, 188–197.

46. Synnott, *The Half-Opened Door*, 44.

47. As quoted in Chernow, *House of Morgan*, 214–215; John T. Bethell, *Harvard Observed: An Illustrated History of the University in the Twentieth Century* (Cambridge, MA: Harvard University Press, 1998): 95; David H. Gellis, "Five New Members Elected to Harvard Board of Overseers," *Harvard Crimson*, July 12, 2002. See also Peter J. How, "The Corporation: Who's on It, What It Does," *Harvard Crimson*, Feb. 27, 1985.

48. The elections were made in June 1919. "Five Elected to Board of Overseers," *Harvard Crimson*, Sept. 19, 1919.

49. James Byrne served as member of Harvard Corporation from 1920 until 1926. "Harvard's New Fellow," *Harvard Crimson*, April 14, 1920; "Byrne Resigns as a Member of Harvard Corporation," *Lewiston Evening Journal*, October 12, 1926.

Born in Springfield, Massachussetts, Byrne was of Irish-Catholic background. After Harvard, he became a partner in the law firm of Hornblower & Byrne (f. 1888), which was the predecessor firm to Willkie Farr & Gallagher. In the early twentieth century, Charles Evans Hughes and Felix Frankfurter were both associates of the firm. http://www.willkie.com/firm/firm.aspx?type=history (November 20, 2012); "James Byrne, 85, Lawyer 60 Years," *NYT*, November 5, 1942. NOTE: In 1938, Bryne's daughter, Helen, married Walter Lippmann with whom she had had an affair while she was married to Hamilton Fish Armstrong, the founder of *Foreign Affairs*. Lippmann also divorced his wife, Faye, in order to be with Helen, which led to a rift with Lamont, who had been close friends with both Walter and Faye. "Mrs. Armstrong Bride of Writer," NYT, Mar. 27, 1938; Lamont, *Ambassador From Wall Street*, 404–405.

The first Catholic member of the Harvard Board of Overseers was Charles Joseph Bonaparte (Class of 1871), who was also a lawyer and served as secretary of the navy and attorney general under President Theodore Roosevelt. Bonaparte was an overseer from 1891 until 1903. Synnott, *The Half-Opened Door,* 10. See also John T. Bethell, *Harvard Observed: An Illustrated History of the University in the Twentieth Century* (Cambridge, MA: Harvard University Press, 1998): 94–98.

50. Painter, "Jim Crow at Harvard: 1923," 628. According to Bethell, the first case involved a student named William Knox Jr., who was given a space at the dormitory because he was mistakenly thought to be white. Knox was asked to give back his room confirmation. Bethell, *Harvard Observed,* 95.

51. Samuel Eliot Morison, "A Memoir and Estimate of Albert Bushnell Hart," *Proceedings of the Massachusetts Historical Society,* vol. 77 (1965): 28–52.

52. "Death of Senator Sumner; Last Hours of the Great Statesman," *NYT,* Mar. 12, 1874. See also David Herbert Donald, *Charles Sumner* (1960) (New York: Da Capo Press, 1996).

53. "Moorfield Storey, Leader of Bar, Dies," *NYT,* Oct. 25, 1929; William B. Hixson Jr., "Moorfield Storey and the Defense of the Dyer Anti-Lynching Bill," *The New England Quarterly* 42:1 (Mar. 1969): 65–81; William B. Hixson Jr., "Moorfield Storey and the Struggle for Equality," *The Journal of American History* 55:3 (Dec. 1968): 533–554. See also William B. Hixson Jr., *Moorfield Story & The Abolitionist Tradition* (New York: Oxford University Press, 1972).

54. "Death of E. L. Godkin," *NYT,* May 22, 1902.

55. Villard inherited the *New York Evening Post* and the *Nation* from his father, Henry Villard, a German immigrant and railroad financier, who was also a journalist. Villard was president of the *Post* from 1897 until 1918, when he sold the paper to Thomas Lamont. Villard and Lamont, in general, did not get along. Villard had been good friends with Lamont's older brother, Hammond, who was the managing editor for the *Evening Post* from 1901 to 1906 and the editor of the *Nation* until his death in 1909. In the 1930s, there was some debate over whether Villard intentionally sold the *Post* to Lamont or whether he thought he was selling it to someone else. See letter to Oswald Garrison Villard from TWL, June 13, 1939, TWL papers, Box 135–2, HBS. See also letter to TWL from A. W. Noyes, Aug. 7, 1939 and letter to TWL from John Palmer Gavit, Aug. 21, 1939, TWL papers, Box 135–2, HBS. Letter to Oswald Garrison Villard from TWL, June 9, 1915, Box 117–10, HBS; See also Warren I. Cohen, *The Chinese Connection: Roger S. Greene, Thomas W. Lamont, George E. Sokolsky and American-East Asian Relations* (New York: Columbia University Press, 1978): 127–128.

56. Letter to Harvard alumni from William Channing Gannett et al., undated, in letter to Moorfield Storey from Lewis S. Gannett, June 2, 1922, Moorfield Storey papers, Box 4, Subject File: Harvard dormitories (Exclusion of Negroes) Correspondence, 1922–23, LOC.

57. "Lewis Gannett, Book Critic, Dies," *NYT,* Feb. 4, 1966. Gannett later became well known for writing a book critic column for the *New York Herald Tribune.*

58. Ernest Gruening was the editor of the *Nation,* 1920–1923, and the editor of the *New York Evening Post,* 1932–1933. He was later governor of Alaska and senator for Alaska, 1959–1969. http://bioguide.congress.gov/scripts/biodisplay.pl?index= g000508 (June 16, 2010).

59. Letter to Moorfield Storey from Lewis S. Gannett, June 2, 1922, Moorfield Storey papers, Box 4, Subject File: Harvard dormitories (Exclusion of Negroes) Correspondence, 1922–23, LOC.

60. Letter to Moorfield Storey from Lewis S. Gannett, July 26, 1922, Moorfield Storey papers, Box 4, Subject File: Harvard dormitories (Exclusion of Negroes) Correspondence, 1922–23, LOC; Painter, "Jim Crow at Harvard: 1923," 628.

61. Letter to Harvard alumni from William Channing Gannett et al., undated, in Letter to Moorfield Storey from Lewis S. Gannett, June 2, 1922, Moorfield Storey papers, Box 4, Subject File: Harvard dormitories (Exclusion of Negroes) Correspondence, 1922–23, LOC.

62. "In re Memorial to the Corporation at Harvard," in letter to Moorfield Storey from Lewis S. Gannett, July 26, 1922, Moorfield Storey papers, Box 4, Subject File: Harvard dormitories (Exclusion of Negroes) Correspondence, 1922–23, LOC.

63. Synnott, "The Admission and Assimilation of Minority Students at Harvard, Yale, and Princeton, 1900–1970," 295.

64. Kennedy, "Introduction: Blacks and the Race Question at Harvard" in Sollers et al., *Blacks at Harvard,* xxi.

65. Wolters, "Harvard Dormitory Crisis," 203.

66. As quoted in Painter, "Jim Crow at Harvard: 1923," 628.

67. As quoted in Wolters, "Harvard Dormitory Crisis," 204.

68. As quoted in Wolters, "Harvard Dormitory Crisis," 219.

69. "Lowell Denied Attacking Jews in Private Talk," *New York Evening Post,* Jan. 15, 1923: front page; "Lowell's Interviewer is Bronx Laundryman; Fish Raps Bruce Action: Former Harvard Captain, Now in Congress, Sends Lowell Sharp Letter: Calls Negro Policy 'Jim Crow Method': Victor Kramer, Harvard '18, Stands by Statement at Jewish Forum: Talked with Crimson Head," *Boston Herald,* Jan. 16, 1923: 5.

70. "Eliot Opposes Line on Color: Says Racial Discrimination would Violate Harvard Traditions: Hallowell Scores Bruce Case Action," *Boston Herald,* Jan. 15, 1923: 16.

71. "Letter to the Editor," *Boston Herald,* Jan. 17, 1923: 16; Painter, "Jim Crow at Harvard: 1923," 632; Synnott, *Half-Opened Door,* 25.

72. As quoted in Wolters, "Harvard Dormitory Crisis," 201. The letter was written on February 7, 1923. R. S. Wallace was most likely Roy Smith Wallace of the National Recreation Association. "R. S. Wallace Rites Today," *NYT,* Sept. 7, 1935.

73. Synnott, *The Half-Opened Door,* 59–60; "Julian Mack Dies; 40 Years on Bench," *NYT,* Sept. 6, 1943. See also Harry Barnard, *The Forging of an American Jew: The Life and Times of Judge Julian W. Mack* (New York: Herzl Press, 1974): 292.

74. Letter to President Charles W. Eliot from Jerome D. Greene, June 10, 1922, Jerome D. Greene (Hereafter: JDG) papers, HUG 4436.14, Specialized Subject file Harvard, Box 1, unnamed folder, HUA; Lewis, *W. E. B. Du Bois: 1919–1963,* 91.

75. Edward Weeks, *Men, Money and Responsibility: A History of Lee, Higginson Corporation* (Boston: Lee, Higginson Corporation, 1962): 27.

76. "Jerome Greene of Harvard Dies," *NYT,* Mar. 30, 1959.

77. Lee, Higginson & Co.'s London office was established in 1907. It also opened a Chicago office in 1905. Weeks, *Men, Money, and Responsibility,* 9, 20.

78. "Jerome Greene of Harvard Dies," *NYT,* Mar. 30, 1959.

79. JDG papers, Call no. HUG 300, Folder: 1896 Greene, Jerome D., Folder: Greene, Evarts Boutell, HUA; "R. S. Greene, Aided Chinese Medicine," *NYT,* Mar. 29, 1947; "Dr. Daniel C. Greene Dies," *NYT,* Sept. 16, 1913; "E. B. Greene Dead; History Professor," *NYT,* June 25, 1947. See also Warren I. Cohen, *The Chinese Connection.*

80. "Jerome C. Greene to Wed," *NYT,* May 13, 1929: 25.

81. One organization in particular was the Institute for Pacific Relations, to which Lamont had been introduced in 1925 by Greene. See letter to TWL from J. Merle Davis with "supplementary facts about IPR," Dec. 19, 1925; Memorandum to Martin Egan from TWL, Dec. 31, 1925, TWL papers, Box 35–13, HBS; Letter to Jerome D. Greene from Martin Egan, Jan. 27, 1926, Institute of Pacific Relations papers, Box 112, Folder: Greene, Jerome D., Columbia University, Rare Book and Manuscript Library (Hereafter: RBML)

82. Letter to TWL from Jerome D. Greene, Jan. 12, 1923, TWL papers, Box 267–8, HBS.

83. Letter to Jerome D. Greene from Abby A. Rockefeller, Feb. 5, 1923, JDG papers, HUG4436.7, Subject File, Box K–R, Folder: Lawrence Lowell, HUA.

84. Letter to President Charles W. Eliot from Jerome D. Greene, Jan. 18, 1923, JDG papers, HUG 4436.14, Specialized subject file Harvard, Box 1, unnamed folder, HUA.

85. Letter to TWL from A. Lawrence Lowell, Sept. 16, 1922, TWL papers, Box 267–8, HBS.

86. See letter to Julian Street from Martin Egan, April 27, 1926, Egan papers, Box 70, PML; Letter to Mrs. Harry L. Roosevelt [Eleanor] from Martin Egan, June 29, 1927, Egan papers, Box 63, PML; "Because you were having a novel" section of Martin Egan's biography, Egan papers, Box 4, Addenda 1, PML; Letter to Arthur M. Anderson from Martin Egan, July 28, 1927, Egan papers, Box 2, PML; Letter to Martin Egan from Conrad Hathaway, Feb. 11, 1933, Egan papers, Box 31, PML.

87. February 11 and February 16, 1927, "Diaries and Papers, 1927," Box 172–31, HBS. See also letter to Thomas S. Lamont from TWL, Feb. 13, 1927, TWL papers, Box 283–4, HBS, which stated regarding Cape Haytien, Haiti: "It is a grubby little place—nothing but darkies, with a couple of American consuls (white)." See also letter to Austin Lamont from TWL, February 1927, TWL papers, Box 281–9, HBS.

88. Lamont was asked to look at the issue by Eleanor Robson Belmont, the wife of financier August Belmont Jr., the son of the founder of August Belmont & Co., who was not happy about it. Vernon Munroe was a Harvard graduate (1875–1957, Class of 1896) with whom he worked closely at the bank and who had been a JPM & Co. staff member since 1920. Memorandum to Vernon Munroe [V.M.] from TWL, Nov. 25, 1942, TWL papers, Box 84–6, HBS; "Vernon Munroe Jr., Retired Lawyer, 84," *NYT*, Sept. 20, 1993. See also letter to Florence Lamont from TWL, Oct. 6, 1943, TWL papers, Box 81–2, HBS.

Survey Graphic was a progressive publication on philanthropy and social work originally called *Charities,* the magazine of the Charity Organization Society of New York, which had been founded by Josephine Shaw Lowell, the sister of Robert G. Shaw, the leader of the 54th Massachusetts Infantry. Founded in 1897, *Charities* changed its named in 1909 and eventually turned into a magazine called *Survey Midmonthly* and a journal called *Survey Graphic* in 1923. They merged again to form the monthly *Survey* in 1949. Clarke A. Chambers, *Paul U. Kellogg and the Survey: Voices for Social Welfare and Social Justice* (Minneapolis: University of Minnesota Press, 1971): 7, 84.

89. Given that the issue was published during the war, it was a direct comment on the meaning of democracy and the fight for freedom as having to include the recognition of "the equal rights of peoples of all colors." Chambers, *Paul U. Kellogg and the Survey,* 182.

The issue featured a number of articles on the status of African Americans in the United States, including an article by Alain Locke, "The Unfinished Business of Democracy," Walter White's article "The right to fight for democracy" on African Americans and the war, an article by A. Philip Randolph on the need to march on Washington, and articles on India, Africa, and China by Pearl Buck and Edward C. Carter of the YMCA and Institute of Pacific Relations. The issue also included a series of graphs on "The Negro in the U.S.A." illustrating statistics on the black population, their geographic location, their life expectancy, education, and income compared to white people.

In 1939, the *Survey*'s circulation was about 25,000 regular subscriptions and 5,000 sold on newsstands. The November 1942 issue sold more than a regular issue but less than other special issues. Chambers, *Paul U. Kellogg and the Survey,* 162–163, 172–75, 182, 193.

90. Letter to Jerome D. Greene from TWL, Jan. 19, 1923, TWL papers, Box 267–8, HBS.

91. Painter, "Jim Crow at Harvard: 1923," 634; Lewis, *W. E. B. Du Bois: 1919–1963*, 90.

92. Letter to President Charles W. Eliot from Jerome D. Greene, January 18, 1923, JDG Papers, HUG 4436.14, Specialized subject file Harvard, Box 1, unnamed folder, HUA.

93. "W. E. B. DuBois Dies in Ghana; Negro Leader and Author, 95," *NYT*, Aug. 28, 1963.

94. Letter to Lewis S. Gannett from W. E. B. Du Bois, Mar. 13, 1922, Du Bois papers, Reel 10, LOC.

95. Letter to Dr. E. F. Du Bois from Lewis S. Gannett, Mar. 3, 1922, Du Bois papers, Reel 10, LOC; Letter to Dr. W. E. B. Du Bois from Lewis S. Gannett, Mar. 10, 1922, Du Bois papers, Reel 10, LOC. See "N.P. Hallowell, Financier, Was 85," *NYT*, Feb. 14, 1961.

96. For a discussion of where Du Bois lived during his time at Harvard as well as his social sphere, see W. E. B. Du Bois, *The Autobiography of W. E. B. Du Bois: A Soliloquy on Viewing My Life on the Last Decade of Its First Century* (New York: International Publisher Co., 1968): 132–136.

97. Lewis, *W. E. B. Du Bois: Biography of a Race, 1868–1919*, 80.

98. "W. E. B. Du Bois: Courses taken at Harvard University, Apr. 4, 1973, Call no. HUG 300, Folder: 1890 Du Bois, William Edward Burghardt, HUA.

The class met on Mondays, Wednesdays, and Fridays at 11. There were 122 students. Du Bois got a B, Lamont got a C. *Yearly (Annual) returns, 1890–91*, Call no. UAIII15.28, HUA; *Harvard University Catalogue 1889–90*, Call No. HU20.41 mfP, 1889/90–1893/94, Reel 7, HUA.

See record of T. W. Lamont '92, "Student Records," Call no. UAIII15.75.10, HUA; Harvard University, *Quinquennial Catalogue of the Officers and Graduates, 1636–1930* (Cambridge: Harvard University, 1930). For a verification of the men, who are listed only by last name and first initial in the quinquennial, see "Class reports of the Harvard College Class of 1890," Twenty-fifth anniversary report, HUD.290.25, HUA; "Class reports of the Harvard College Class of 1892," Twenty-fifth anniversary report, HUD.292.25, HUA.

99. For example, in 1889–1890, Du Bois took "History 13—American history" with Jeremiah Smith Jr., a close friend of Lamont. There were 138 men in the class, which met on Tuesdays, Thursdays, and Saturdays at 9. Du Bois received an A+, Smith a B+. *Yearly (Annual) returns, 1889–90*, Call no. UAIII15.28; *Harvard University Catalogue 1889–90*, Call No. HU20.41 mfP, 1889/90–1893/94, Reel 7, HUA; "Jeremiah Smith, Financier, Dead," *NYT*, Mar. 13, 1935.

100. "Norman Hapgood, Editor, Dies at 69," *NYT*, Apr. 30, 1937. Hapgood was editor of *Hearst's International*, 1923–5. He went on to edit *The Christian Register*, a magazine of the Unitarian Church.

101. Smith and Hapgood were not the only overlaps. Looking at class schedules

for Jerome Greene's brother Evarts (A.B. 1890, A.M. 1891, Ph.D. 1893), Oswald Villard's brother Harold (A.B. 1890), and two of Lamont's good friends, Jeremiah Smith Jr. (A.B. 1892), and Norman Hapgood (AB 1890), we would find that Du Bois took three classes with Hapgood, four classes with Evarts Greene, two classes with H. Villard, two classes with Smith.

For example, in 1888–89, Du Bois took "Philosophy 4-Ethics." Norman Hapgood. There were only forty people in the class. Du Bois got an A, Hapgood also got an A. The class met on Tuesdays, Thursdays, and Saturdays at 11. There do not seem to be any sections for this or any other class that Du Bois took. Du Bois also took "English C-Forensics" with Hapgood, Villard, and Evarts Greene. Du Bois got a C, Hapgood an A, Greene a C and Villard (listed by last name only) a B. There were 270 men in the class. No time is listed for class meetings, which consisted of ten lectures. Faculty of Arts & Sciences, Yearly *(Annual)* returns, *1888–89,* Call no. UAIII15.28; Harvard University Catalogue, Call no. HU20.41 mfP, 1884/85-1888/89, Reel 6, HUA.

The following year Du Bois took "English D-Forensics." His classmates included Evarts B. Greene, Norman Hapgood, and Harold G. Villard. The class met on Thursdays at 12 until Christmas and included 289 students. Du Bois got a "B (A)- "Comm. Part for 2," Greene got a B, Hapgood an A, Villard a B. According to the catalogue, the students of course D could also attend the lectures in course C which met on Thursdays at 3. Faculty of Arts & Sciences, Yearly *(Annual)* returns, 1889–90, Call no. UAIII15.28; *Harvard University Catalogue 1889–90,* Call No. HU20.41 mfP, 1889/90-1893/94, Reel 7, HUA.

102. Caldwell Titcomb, "The Black Presence at Harvard: An Overview," *Blacks at Harvard,* 2.

103. The only group Du Bois tried to join was the Glee Club and he was rejected. W. E. B. Du Bois, *The Autobiography of W. E. B. Du Bois,* 134.

104. Lewis, *W. E. B. Du Bois: 1919–1963,* 90; Lewis, *W. E. B. Du Bois: Biography of a Race, 1868–1919,* 81.

105. For Du Bois' views on Storey's leadership, see letter to Louis Gannett, Feb. 14, 1923, Du Bois papers, Reel 11, LOC.

106. Letter to Moorfield Storey from Lewis Gannett, Feb. 8, 1923, Moorfield Storey papers, Box 4, Subject File: Harvard dormitories (Exclusion of Negroes) Correspondence, 1922–23, LOC.

107. Copy of letter to Lewis S. Gannett, Feb. 9, 1923, Du Bois papers, Reel 12; Letter to W. E. B. Du Bois from Lewis S. Gannett, Feb. 10, 1923, Du Bois papers, Reel 11, LOC.

108. Letter to Louis Gannett, Feb. 14, 1923, Du Bois papers, Reel 11; Letter to W. E. B. Du Bois from W. R. Valentine, May 11, 1922, Du Bois papers, Reel 11, LOC.

109. Re: Board of Overseers: That person was Ralph J. Bunche (1904–1971, MA 1928, PhD 1934). Bunche won the Nobel Peace Prize in 1950, was a former professor

of government at Harvard and the undersecretary for the United Nations at the time of his election. He served on the board from 1959 to 1965. "Dr. Bunche of U.N., Nobel Winner, Dies," *NYT,* Dec. 10, 1971; "Graduates State Candidates for Overseers' Board," *The Harvard Crimson,* Jan. 28, 1959. To give a sense of comparison, Yale had its first black Board of Trustee in 1970. He was Judge A. Leon Higginbotham Jr., who was a U.S. District Court Judge in Philadelphia. "Negro is Elected Trustee of Yale," *NYT,* June 15, 1970.

Re: Harvard Corporation: He was Conrad K. Harper, a law partner at Simpson, Bartlett & Thatcher, who graduated from Harvard Law in 1965. Harper stepped down in 2005 and he was replaced by Patricia A. King, who became the first African American woman to serve on the board. Vasugi V. Ganeshananthan and Erica B. Levy, "Corporation Announces Two New Members," *The Harvard Crimson,* Feb. 7, 2000. Zachary M. Steward, "First Black Female Named to Corporation," *The Harvard Crimson,* Dec. 4, 2005; "Harvard Corporation Member Resigns," *The Boston Globe,* July 29, 2005.

110. Synnott, *The Half-Opened Door,* 105.

111. Lewis, *W. E. B. Du Bois: 1919–1963,* 108.

112. Report to Board of Overseers from executive committee of Board for 1922–23, undated, TWL papers, Box 267–10, HBS.

113. "Votes to Maintain Traditional Policy of Non-Discrimination: Men of White and Colored Races Will Not Be Forced to Live and Eat Together," *Harvard Crimson,* Apr. 10, 1923.

114. Synnott, *The Half-Opened Door,* 109.

115. Synnott, "The Admission and Assimilation of Minority Students at Harvard, Yale, and Princeton, 1900–1970," 291.

116. Letter to Jerome D. Greene from Charles W. Eliot, Feb. 12, 1924, JDG papers, Specialized subject File Harvard, HUG 4436.14, Box 4, Folder: 1924, HUA.

117. Synnott, *The Half-Opened Door,* 112–120.

118. Synnott, *The Half-Opened Door,* 47.

119. Synnott, "The Admission and Assimilation of Minority Students at Harvard, Yale, and Princeton, 1900–1970," 295; Painter, "Jim Crow at Harvard: 1923," 634.

120. On Yale and Princeton's discrimination of African Americans and Jews, and their conversations with other colleges like Dartmouth, see Synnott, *The Half-Opened Door,* 139–142, 151, 155, 188–197.

121. Letter to Mrs. John D. Rockefeller Jr. from Jerome D. Greene, Feb. 21, 1923, JDG papers, HUG4436.7, Subject File, Box K–R, Folder: Lawrence Lowell, HUA.

6. COMPLEX INTERNATIONAL ALLIANCES: JAPAN

1. "Thomas W. Lamont, Banker, Dies at 77 in Florida Home," *NYT,* Feb. 3, 1948.

2. See for example, letter to Mrs. JPM Sr. from JPM Jr., Sept. 21, 1924; Letter to Mrs. JPM Sr. from JPM Jr., Sept. 28, 1924, JPM Jr. papers, ARC 1216, Box 233, Pierpont Morgan Library (Hereafter: PML).

3. In 1930, Jack Morgan owned 24.4 percent of the firm's capital and Lamont 9.8 percent. In 1934, Jack Morgan owned 12.5 percent of the firm's capital and Lamont 10 percent. By 1939, Jack Morgan owned 12.5 percent of the firm's capital and Lamont 11.5 percent. See "Articles of copartnership, J. P. Morgan & Co., 1916–1939," ARC 1195, Morgan Firm papers, Boxes 1 and 5, PML.

4. Lamont started both books in 1943 after he became very ill. He was not able to finish the second volume, which was edited by his children, wife, and former secretary. The title of *Across World Frontiers* was chosen by them as "descriptive of the contents." Thomas W. Lamont, *Across World Frontiers* (New York: Harcourt, Brace & Co., 1951): vi–vii.

5. Letter to Colonel Harry Roosevelt from Martin Egan, Oct. 11, 1922, Martin Egan (Hereafter: Egan) papers, Box 63, PML; Harold Nicolson, *Dwight Morrow* (New York: Arno Press, 1975).

6. Letter to Breckenridge Long from H. D. Marshall, May 24, 1919 and June 16, 1919, Breckenridge Long papers, Box 180, Folders: Chinese Loan Jan–May 1919 & Chinese Loan June 1919, Manuscripts and Archives, Library of Congress (Hereafter: LOC); Thomas W. Lamont, "America and the Far East," *The Far Eastern Fortnightly: Bulletin of the Far Eastern Bureau,* vol. 7, no. 21, Oct. 11, 1920, Box 84, Folder: Lamont, T.W.: 1920 "America and the Far East," Stanley K. Hornbeck (Hereafter: SKH) papers, Hoover Institution Archives (Hereafter: HIA).

7. Warren I. Cohen, *The Chinese Connection: Roger S. Greene, Thomas W. Lamont, George E. Sokolsky and American-East Asian Relations* (New York: Columbia University Press, 1978): 279. See also Lamont's diary entry for July 5, 1919 regarding Versailles, Box 164–19, for month of January 1924, Box 172–21, and for July 25, 1927 regarding Junnosuke Inouye, his main contact at the Bank of Japan, Thomas W. Lamont (Hereafter: TWL) papers, Box 273–4, Baker Library Historical Collections, Harvard Business School. (Hereafter: HBS). See also letter to Austin Lamont from TWL, TWL papers, Box 81–8, February 6, 1924 and letter to Austin Lamont, Nov. 13, 1924, Box 281–8, HBS. See also letter to TWL from RCL, Dec. 14, 1932, Russell Cornell Leffingwell (Hereafter: RCL) papers, MS 1030, Box 4, Folder 95, Manuscript and Archives, Yale University Library (Hereafter: YUL); Letter to TWL from Kakutaro Suzuki, Mar. 10, 1933; Memorandum for Thomas S. Lamont from TWL, Mar. 13, 1933 and letter to Kakutaro Suzuki from TWL, Mar. 13, 1933, TWL papers, Box 187–20, HBS. See also for examples of use by family members,

such as Florence Lamont (Lamont's wife) in excerpts from her letters sent from TSL to his children, July 16, 1964, TWL papers, Box 81–4, HBS.

8. In keeping with their practice of sharing a respectable portion of the other's issues, JPM & Co. took two participations totaling £200,000. See J. P. Morgan & Co. Syndicate Book #3, pages 223–224, PML.

9. Naomi W. Cohen, *Jacob H. Schiff: A Study in American Jewish Leadership* (Hanover: Brandeis University Press, 1999): 33–34.

10. Takahashi was Japanese Finance Minister, 1913–1914, 1918–1922, 1927, 1931–1936, Japanese Premier, 1921–1922. "Takahashi, Korekiyo," in Paul Lagasse, ed., *The Columbia Encyclopedia,* Sixth Edition (New York: Columbia University Press, 2004): 2781.

11. Takahashi was married twice. His first wife died in 1884. Wakiko was his daughter from his second wife, whom he married in 1887. Richard J. Smethurst, *From Foot Soldier to Finance Minister: Takahashi Korekiyo, Japan's Keynes,* (Cambridge, MA: Harvard University Asia Center, 2009): 9, 10, 19, 23, 29, 41, 59, 141, 148, 149, 196. See also Richard Smethurst, "Takahashi Korekiyo, the Rothschilds and the Russo-Japanese War, 1904–1907," http://www.rothschildarchive.org/ib /articles/AR2006Japan.pdf (June 27, 2010).

12. Smethurst, *Takahashi Korekiyo, Japan's Keynes,* 142, 149–165; Naomi W. Cohen, *Jacob H. Schiff,* 34–39.

13. Ron Chernow, *The House of Morgan: An American Banking Dynasty and the Rise of Modern Finance* (New York: Touchstone, 1990): 235.

14. This was a note that Takahashi wrote in his diary. Quoted in Smethurst, *Takahashi Korekiyo, Japan's Keynes,* 167. Kaneko Kentaro was a graduate of Harvard (BA 1878) and one of the writers of the Japanese constitution in 1889. "Kaneko, Kentaro," in Janet Hunter, ed., *Concise Dictionary of Modern Japanese History* (Los Angeles: University of California Press, 1984): 85–86.

15. Smethurst, *Takahashi Korekiyo, Japan's Keynes,* 192–196. Schiff wrote an account of his trip, which was printed in 1906. Jacob H. Schiff, *Our Trip to Japan* (New York: The New York Co-operative Society, 1906).

16. See also letter to Mrs. Schiff from Baron Takahashi, July 17, 1920, Jacob H. Schiff (Hereafter: JHS) papers, MS 456, 463/11. American Jewish Archives (Hereafter: AJA); Letter to Baron Takahashi from JHS, June 18, 1920, JHS, MS 456, 463/11, AJA; Letter to Wakiko (Mrs. T. Okubo) from JHS, Jan. 15, 1918, 456/3, AJA; Letter to Mr. Okubo from JHS, Mar. 7, 1916, JHS, MS 456 445/5, AJA; Letter to Wakiko Okubo from JHS, Jan. 19, 1916, JHS, MS 456, 445/5, AJA. See also note from Dorothy Schiff to Lester Mallets, May 19, 1972, Dorothy Schiff papers, Manuscripts and Archives, New York Public Library (Hereafter: NYPL).

Masakazu Iwata, *Ōkubo Toshimichi: The Bismarck of Japan* (Los Angeles: University of California Press, 1964): 252; Takahashi Korekiyo, *Takahashi Korekiyo Jiden,* ed. Uetsuka Tsukasa (Tokyo: Chuo Koronshinsha 1976): 116; Yomiuri Shimbun

Shuzai Han, *Kensho Nichirosenso* (Tokyo: Chuo Koronshinsha, 2005): 150–151; Umetani Noboru, *Oyatoi Gaikokujin: Kinyu, Zaisei,* vol. 8 (Tokyo: Kajima Kenkyūjo Shuppankai, 1969): 143; "Ōkubo Toshikata," Kanagawa Prefectural Museum of Cultural History (http://ch.kanagawa-museum.jp/dm/syoukin/ysb_ayumi/nenpyo/d _toudori13.html) (July 15, 2012). Special thanks to Ken Okamura for the references to Toshikata Ōkubo.

17. Naomi W. Cohen, *Jacob H. Schiff,* 189, 195–198.

18. Jacob Schiff wrote Lamont a letter of introduction to Takahashi in Feb. 1920. See letter to Baron K. Takahashi from JHS, Feb. 10, 1920, JHS, MS 456, 463/11, AJA.

Baker Library, *Guide to the papers of Thomas William Lamont in Baker Library, Harvard University. Compiled by John V. Miller* (Cambridge: Baker Library, Graduate School of Business Administration, 1966): 237. Lamont was appointed as a delegate to the U.S. Treasury by President Woodrow Wilson. Letter to TWL from Woodrow Wilson, Feb. 13, 1919, TWL papers, Box 171–28, HBS.

When Lamont left Paris, he was represented by Martin Egan. Letter to Breckenridge Long from H. D. Marshall, June 4, 1919, Breckenridge Long papers, Box 180, Folder: Chinese Loan Jan.–May 1919, LOC.

19. JPM & Co.'s syndicate books date this loan as 1924: "$150,000,000 Imperial Japanese Government External Loan of 1924 30 Year Sinking Fund 6 ½% Gold Bond Syndicate." Edward Lamont dates it at 1923. Edward M. Lamont, *The Ambassador From Wall Street: The Story of Thomas W. Lamont, J. P. Morgan's Chief Executive* (New York: Madison Books, 1994): 195–196. See also letter to Corliss and Austin Lamont from TWL, Feb. 17, 1924, TWL papers, Box 81–8, HBS.

20. Chernow, *House of Morgan,* 235–236.

21. Lamont, *Ambassador From Wall Street,* 309.

22. Peter Duus, *Modern Japan* (New York: Houghton Mifflin & Co., 1997): 99.

23. Duus, *Modern Japan,* 136–142.

24. Korea did not gain its independence until after the Second World War. Duus, *Modern Japan,* 138–146.

25. "Again Admits Japanese," *NYT,* Mar. 14, 1907. See also for the Japanese government's reactions to San Francisco and naturalization (Uchida Sadatsuchi, Consul based in New York, Aoki Shuzo, the Japanese Ambassador, Hayashi Tadasu, the Foreign Minister: all last names listed first) in Yuji Ichioka, "The Early Japanese Immigrant Quest for Citizenship: The Background of the 1922 Ozawa Case," *Amerasia Journal* 4:2 (1977): 3–4

26. Bill Ong Hing, *Making and Remaking Asian America Through Immigration Policy 1850–1990* (Stanford, CA: Stanford University Press, 1993): 29; Alexander Saxon, *The Indispensable Enemy: Labor and the Anti-Chinese Movement in California* (Los Angeles: University of California Press, 1971): 257; Ichioka, "Japanese Immigrant Quest," 3.

27. Angelo N. Ancheta, *Race, Rights, and the Asian American Experience* (New Brunswick: Rutgers University Press, 1998): 177. See also Ichioka, "Japanese Immigrant Quest," 8.

28. During the First World War, the U.S. Congress passed the 1917 Immigration Act, which attempted to reduce immigration from Southern and Eastern Europe and Japan. Instead of specifying directly that it was discriminating on the basis of race and national origin, the law established a literacy test. It also created an "Asiatic barred zone," which extended the scope of the Chinese Exclusion Act to a wider geographic area. Filipinos were not affected because of their status as U.S. nationals. That loophole would be closed when the Philippines was granted nominal independence in 1934.

29. Alan Sharp, *The Versailles Settlement: Peacemaking in Paris, 1919* (London: Macmillan, 1991): 23.

30. Makino Nobuaki (1861–1949) was the second son of Toshimichi Ōkubo, one of the founders of modern Japan, "but he was adopted immediately after birth into the heirless Makino family." Thomas W. Burkman, *Japan and the League of Nations: Empire and World Order, 1914–1938* (Honolulu: University of Hawai'i Press, 2008): 46. See also Naoku Shimazu, *Japan, Race and Equality: The Racial Equality Proposal of 1919* (New York: Routledge, 1998): 13; Paul Gordon Lauren, *Power and Prejudice: The Politics and Diplomacy of Racial Discrimination* (Boulder: Westview Press, 1988): 82–107.

31. "Says Japan Must Join as Equal," *NYT,* Apr. 3, 1919. Like the American government, the British kept tabs on Japan's propaganda of racial discrimination in the United States and India, fearing that it would stir up trouble in its own colonies. See "Press service of issue circular announcing Japanese condemnation of American lynchings," Call no. P1610/1610/145, *Index to the Correspondence of the Foreign Office for the Year 1921,* Part II, M to Q, Klaus-Thomson Organization Ltd., Neudeln/ Liechtenstein, 1969, pg. 176); F. Ashton-Gwatkin, "Racial Discrimination and Immigration," Oct. 10, 1921, pg. 14, Japan, F4212/223/23, FO 371/6684, Public Records Office (UK).

32. Shimazu, *Japan, Race and Equality,* 29.

33. Shimazu, *Japan, Race and Equality,* 29–31, 81; Lauren, *Power and Prejudice,* 99–100; Brenda Gayle Plummer, *Black Americans and U.S. Foreign Affairs, 1935–1960* (Chapel Hill: The University of North Carolina Press, 1996): 20; Marc Gallicchio, *The African American Encounter with Japan and China: Black Internationalism in Asia, 1895–1945* (Chapel Hill: University of North Carolina Press, 2000): 24.

34. Gallicchio, *African American Encounter,* 17, 24. See also Roberta Allbert Dayer, *Bankers and Diplomats in China, 1971–1925: The Anglo-American Relationship* (New York: Frank Cass and Company Limited, 1981): 4–8; Reginald Kearny, *African American Views of the Japanese: Solidarity of Sedition?* (Albany: State University of New York, 1998): xvii, 27, 60; Lauren, *Power and Prejudice,* 102.

35. Gallicchio, *African American Encounter*, 74–76, 54–57. For negative views of China, see also Kearny, *Views of Japanese*, 8–9.

Though the British foreign office and the American state department were aware of Japan's brutality in Korea and other colonies, they did nothing to champion their goal of independence. Letter to Roland S. Morris from J. V. A. MacMurray, Feb. 5, 1919, J. V. A. MacMurray papers, Box 22, Folder: Jan.–Mar. 1919, 20th Century Public Policy papers, Princeton University Library (Hereafter: PUL).

For the most part, the Korean position was virtually ignored by the power players. During the Paris Peace Conference, a provisional Korean government attempted to push forward its claims for liberation based on its reading of Wilson's self-determination ideals, but it was unsuccessful. Henry Chung, *The Case of Korea: A Collection of Evidence on the Japanese Domination of Korea, and on the Development of the Korean Independence Movement* (New York: Fleming H. Revell, 1921). For more on Japan and the British vis-à-vis Korea, Dae-yeol Ku, *Korea under Colonialism: the March First Movement and Anglo-Japanese Relations* (Seoul, Korea: Seoul Computer Press, 1985). For a personal look at the March First movement, see Peter Hyun, *Man Sei! The Making of a Korean American* (Honolulu, HI: University of Hawaii Press, 1986).

36. Gallicchio, *African American Encounter*, 50–51, 61. See also Kearny, *Views of Japanese*, xvi.

37. Tomoko Akami, *Internationalizing the Pacific: The United States, Japan and the Institute of Pacific Relations in War and Peace, 1919–45* (New York: Routledge, 2002): 24–25.

38. This fact was not lost on African Americans. Gallicchio, *African American Encounter*, 52. For both anti- and pro-Japanese African American sentiment on the Immigration Act, see also David J. Hellwig, "Afro-American Reactions to the Japanese and the Anti-Japanese Movement, 1906–1924," *Phylon (1960–)*, vol. 38, issue 1 (First Quarter 1977): 93–104.

39. Dayer, *Bankers and Diplomats in China*, 180; See also Chernow, *House of Morgan*, 236.

40. Letter Adolph S. Ochs from TWL, Apr. 23, 1924, TWL papers, Box 186–18, HBS. For discussion of Japan's adherence to the Gentleman's Agreement, see letter to J. V. A. MacMurray from George H. Blakeslee, June 6, 1924, J. V. A. MacMurray papers, Box 24, Folder: May–June 1924, PUL.

41. Letter to TWL from Viscount Shibusawa, Oct. 28, 1922, TWL, Box 188–34, HBS.

42. Letter to Malcolm W. Davis from J. V. A. MacMurray, Feb. 9, 1924, J. V. A. MacMurray papers, Box 24, Folder: Feb.–Mar. 15, 1924, PUL.

43. Letter to Congressman Rogers from Otto T. Mallery, May 21, 1924, Box 24, Folder: May–June 1924, J. V. A. MacMurray papers, PUL. Albert N. Marquis, ed., *Who's Who in America*, vol. 20 (Chicago, IL: A.N. Marquis Company, 1939): 1613; Memorandum to Martin Egan from TWL, Oct. 30, 1919, TWL papers, Box 186–6, HBS.

44. Letter to Joseph K. Hutchinson from J. V. A. MacMurray, Apr. 8, 1924, J. V. A. MacMurray papers, Box 24, Folder: Mar. 16–Apr. 1924, PUL. See also Ellis W. Hawley, *The Great War and the Search for a Modern Order: A History of the American People and Their Institutions, 1917–1933* (New York: St. Martin's Press, 1979): 65.

45. Letter from Theodore Roosevelt to President Taft, Dec. 22, 1910, SKH papers, Box 249, Folder: Japan: Roosevelt-Taft Diplomacy, 1910, HIA.

46. Letter to Hon. Charles E. Hughes from H. C. Lodge, Apr. 15, 1924, Charles Evans Hughes (Hereafter: CEH) papers, Reel 4, Folder: General Correspondence: 1924, Jan.–Apr.; Letter to Hon. Charles E. Hughes from H. C. Lodge, Apr. 17, 1924, CEH papers, Reel 4, Folder: General Correspondence: 1924, Jan.–Apr.; "For immediate release: Representative Albert Johnson, chairman of the House Committee on Immigration and Naturalization," Apr. 21, 1924, CEH papers, Reel 121, Subject file, Secretary of State, Immigration Act of 1924, LOC.

47. Letter to Hon. Charles E. Hughes from H. C. Lodge, Apr. 15, 1924, CEH papers, Reel 4, Folder: General Correspondence: 1924, Jan.–Apr., LOC; Letter to Dr. Payson J. Treat from Roland S. Morris, June 2, 1924, Payson J. Treat papers, Box 48, Folder: Japanese in the United States, HIA; Letter to Dr. Robert E. Speer from Cyrus E. Woods, Nov. 24, 1924 in letter to TWL from Reverend Sidney Gulick, Dec. 18, 1924, TWL papers, Box 186–19, HBS; Letter to Jane Addams from Mary Windsor, May 8, 1926, Women's International League for Peace and Freedom (Hereafter: WILPF) papers, University of Colorado at Boulder, Western Historical Collections, Jane Addams papers, Series 1, Reel 18, LOC; Letter to SKH from Jerome D. Greene, Oct. 10, 1930, SKH papers, Box 182, Folder: Jerome Greene, HIA.

48. Hing, *Remaking Asian America*, 33.

49. Akami, *Internationalizing the Pacific*, 40.

50. Letter to Dr. Takuma Dan from TWL, June 2, 1924, TWL papers, Box 188–4, HBS; Letter to TWL from Takuma Dan, June 25, 1924, TWL papers, Box 188–4, HBS.

51. Letter to TWL from Takuma Dan, June 25, 1924, TWL papers, Box 188–4, HBS.

52. "American Declare Amity for Japan," *NYT*, July 2, 1924: 21. For comments on Japan's reactions, see letter to Edgar A. Bancroft from Martin Egan, Oct. 18, 1924, Egan papers, Box 4, PML; Letter to Martin Egan from Edgar A. Bancroft, Nov. 6, 1924, Egan papers, Box 4, PML.

53. Letter to SKH from Jerome D. Greene, Oct. 10, 1930, SKH papers, Box 182, Folder: Jerome Greene, HIA. See also letter to Jerome D. Greene from Inazo Nitobe, Mar. 22, 1932, HUG4436.12, Specialized subject file Far Eastern Crisis 1930s, Box. No. 1, Folder: The League Indispensable, Courtesy of Harvard University Archives (Hereafter: HUA). "Questionnaire of Heizer Wright for the News (New York's Picture Newspaper) Submitted with his letter of May 24th 1934" in letter to Frederick V. Field from Jerome D. Greene stating that they were Greene's answers, Institute of

Pacific Relations papers, June 1, 1934, Box 111, Folder: Greene, Jerome D., Columbia University, Rare Book and Manuscript Library (Hereafter: RBML).

54. Letter to Raymond B. Fosdick, Charles H. Strong, and George Wickersham from TWL, Nov. 9, 1931, TWL papers, Box 29–17, HBS; Letter to "Dear Sir" from the American Boycott Association signed Mrs. Corliss Lamont (Margaret) and William Loeb Jr., Executive Secretaries, Jerome D. Greene (Hereafter: JDG) papers, HUG 4436.14, Specialized subject file, Box 1, Folder: Harvard Boycotts Japan 1932, HUA; In letter to K. Wakasugi, Consul General of Japan, from TWL, Sept. 17, 1937, TWL papers, Box 188–4, HBS; Letter to Eigo Fukai from TWL, Sept. 13, 1935, TWL papers, Box 188–1, HBS; "Morgan & Company and the Japanese 'Hands-off' Doctrine," *China Weekly Review*, June 30, 1934 in letter to Ambassador Hiroshi Saito from Martin Egan, Dec. 8, 1934, Egan papers, Box 39, PML; Letter to James Shotwell from TWL, Oct. 10, 1935, TWL papers, Box 216–27, HBS; Memorandum to RCL from TWL, Feb. 24, 1941, TWL papers, Box 103–24, HBS.

55. Letter to TWL from W. Cameron Forbes, Dec. 2, 1930, TWL papers, Box 187–5, HBS.

56. Letter to W. Cameron Forbes from TWL, Dec. 20, 1930, TWL papers, Box 187–5, HBS.

57. Letter to SKH from Jerome D. Greene, Oct. 10, 1940, SKH papers, Box 182, Folder: Jerome Greene, HIA; Memorandum to TWL from RCL, Feb. 2, 1942, RCL papers, MS 1030, Box 4, Folder 99, YUL.

58. William Appleman Williams, *The Tragedy of American Diplomacy* (New York: Dell Publishing Co., Inc., 1972): 78; William H. Becker, *The Dynamics of Business-Government Relations: Industry and Exports 1893–1921* (Chicago: The University of Chicago Press, 1982) 120–121; Carl Parrini, *Heir to Empire: United States Economic Diplomacy, 1916–1923* (Pittsburgh: University of Pittsburgh Press, 1969): 143; Michael J. Hogan, *Informal Entente: The Private Structure of Cooperation in Anglo-American Economic Development, 1918–1928* (Chicago: Imprint Publications, 1991): 80.

59. Becker, *Business-Government Relations,* 136–143. See also Williams, *Tragedy of American Diplomacy,* 85; Parrini, *Heir to Empire,* 27–30, 80–83.

60. Refusal to accept arbitration would nullify the provision "which forbade the use of force to collect international debts," also known as the Calvo or Drago doctrine, which was adopted by the Hague Convention of 1907. The rhetoric of the contract, law, and finance gave the impression that the powers were acting in good faith, or under equal terms for all parties. Emily Rosenberg, *Financial Missionaries to the World: The Politics and Culture of Dollar Diplomacy, 1900–1930* (Cambridge: Harvard University Press, 1999): 73–75.

61. Rosenberg, *Financial Missionaries,* 2.

62. For a history of American expansion in Central America, see Walter LaFeber, *Inevitable Revolutions: The United States in Central America,* Second Edition (New

York: W.W. Norton & Co., 1993): 19–85; Edward Rhodes, "Charles Evans Hughes Reconsidered, or: Liberal Isolationism in the New Millennium" in Anthony Lake and David Ochmanek, eds., *The Real and the Ideal: Essays on International Relations in Honor of Richard H. Ullman* (Lanham, Maryland: Rowman & Littlefield, 2001): 160. See also Emily Rosenberg, *Spreading the American Dream*, 121, 138, 139, 152.

   63. As quoted in Cleveland and Huertas, Citibank, 1812–1970, 147. Original is in Charles Evans Hughes, *Observations on the Monroe Doctrine: An Address* (Washington, DC: Government Printing Office, 1923): 17.

   64. In order to study the overlapping ties between the Morgans, other elite New York bankers, and the state, a sample of state representatives between 1900 and 1940 was created and their social ties, if listed in the *Social Register, New York,* were compiled for every five year period. Most of the positions were consistent for the entire period but some were not formed until after 1910, e.g., the Federal Reserve Board of New York or the Securities Exchanges Commission, and so they were only added in those years when they were in existence.

   Included in the sample were the leading members of the following departments: Senate, House, Executive, Department of State (including members of the diplomatic service for Great Britain, France, Germany, China, Japan), Department of Treasury, Treasurer of the United States, Department of War, Department of Justice, Department of Navy, Department of Labor, Supreme Court of the United States; Department of Commerce, Territories and Insular Possessions: Philippines Commission, Federal Reserve Board, Federal Trade Commission, Securities and Exchange Commission, Mayor of the City of New York, Comptroller of the City of New York, Governor of the Federal Reserve Bank of New York. An average of 14 departments and 88 positions was studied for every five year period.

   Sources: *Official Register of the United States: Officers and Employees in the Civil, Military, and Naval Service on July 1, 1901,* vol. 1 (Washington: Government Printing Office, 1901 and 1911); *Official Register of the United States: Person in the Civil, Military, and Naval Service Exclusive of the Postal Service* (Washington: Government Printing Office, 1919, 1921, 1931, and 1940); *Foreign Service of the United States: Diplomatic and Consular Service* (Washington: Government Printing Office, 1925): 1–6; *Foreign Service List* (Washington: Government Printing Office, 1931): 1–29; *Foreign Service List* (Washington: Government Printing Office, 1940): 1–35; "Elected Mayors of New York City, 1898–1998," http://www.nyc.gov/html/nyc100 /html/classroom/hist_info/mayors.html (July 10, 2009); http://www.newyorkfed .org/aboutthefed/historical_speeches.html (July 10, 2009); Kenneth T. Jackson, ed., *The Encyclopedia of New York City* (New Haven, CT: Yale University Press, 1995): 270.

   The social overlaps of these state representatives were then compared to the social club ties of eight Anglo-American and German Jewish commercial banks and private banks in general and J.P. Morgan & Co. partners in particular for every five year period between 1900 and 1940. During this time, out of list above, only members from the following departments were listed in the *Social Register, New York*: Executive, Department of State, especially the diplomatic service, the Departments of War, Navy, Justice, Labor, and Treasury, the Supreme Court, the Federal Trade Commission (FTC), the Federal Reserve Board (FRB). The specific overlap of club ties between this group and the Morgans was then analyzed, starting with the Washington D.C. clubs in which many of the government officials were members.

If we were to look at the Morgan bank's overlaps with the state actors through elite Washington, D.C. men's clubs between 1900 and 1925, only the senior partner, either Pierpont or Jack Morgan, maintained membership in the Metropolitan Club, Washington (f. 1863). (Pierpont Morgan became a non-resident member in 1891). Carl Charlick, *The Metropolitan Club of Washington: The Story of Its Men and of Its Place in City and Country* (Washington, D.C.: Metropolitan Club of Washington, D.C., 1965): 92, 229, 242.

In many ways, Pierpont and Jack Morgan's membership in D.C.'s most elite club is similar to that of their membership in the elite gentlemen's clubs in London, such as White's, in which no other Morgan partners were members. The relatively smaller number of overlapping ties between the firm and D.C. clubs indicate that they were more important for the relationships they created outside the firm as opposed to within the firm.

By the 1930s, Morgan partners, who had been recruited with government experience (S. Parker Gilbert and Russell C. Leffingwell), assumed the role of having D.C. elite clubs ties within the firm though Jack Morgan remained a member of the Metropolitan Club, Washington. (Gilbert and Leffingwell were also members of Chevy Chase (f. 1892), an offshoot of the Metropolitan Club that was founded as a country club with an emphasis on hunting.) The first iteration of the Chevy Chase Club was founded in 1885 and called the Dumblane Club, which was a club for fox hunting. John M. Lynham, *The Chevy Chase Club: A History, 1885–1957* (Chevy Chase, Maryland: The Chevy Chase Club, 1958): 3.

The fact that the partners with former government experience had social club ties in D.C. suggests that an individual partner's particular background and personal inclination had an impact on his club membership. But because specific ties could come and go, the aggregate and qualitative nature of the ties between business and state were much stronger indicators of how they integrated the firm into a larger network of state/capital relations through club ties, if they did. In general, the majority of the Morgan partners in the 1920s and 1930s did not have former government experience or ties, but the ties they did have were part of a long tradition of men in certain government positions with similar social and cultural priorities as private bankers, such as those in the diplomatic service and in the departments stated above. Of those state officials, who did have common club ties with the Morgans after 1930, they also had club memberships outside of DC as well. Many went to Harvard or Yale and were also members of the Metropolitan Club, Washington, the University Club of New York, Century Association, or Piping Rock Club (both New York clubs).

65. "Memorandum on the China Consortium," September 1, 1924, in letter to Mr. Waterlow from C.S. Addis, September 3, 1924, FO 405/246, Public Records Office (UK).

66. As quoted in Naomi W. Cohen, *Jacob H. Schiff*, 38. See also letter to Baron Korekiyo Takahashi, Feb. 11, 1915, JHS papers, MS 456, 444/13, AJA.

67. See, for example, Schiff's letter to Baron Korekiyo Takahashi, June 18, 1915, letter to Takahashi, July 28, 1915, JHS papers, MS 456, 444/13, and letter to Frank Polk, Counselor to the Dept. of State, Oct. 10, 1916, JHS papers, MS 456, 445/12, AJA.

68. After the First World War when the United States rejoined the IBC, Lamont also personally negotiated Japan's admission to the IBC. Japan was not a member of the original IBC. See "A Review of the Interests of the United States Government and its Nationals in Financial Questions in China," undated without an author, most likely 1919, SKH Papers, Box 51, Folder: China: American Interests In, HIA; Letter to TWL from George Sokolsky, May 24, 1920, letter to George Sokolsky from TWL, July 1, 1920, letter to George Sokolsky from TWL, July 21, 1920, George Sokolsky papers, Box 76, Folder: Thomas W. Lamont, 1919–20, HIA; Letter to Breckenridge Long from TWL, August 30, 1919, Breckenridge Long papers, Box 180, Folder: Chinese Loan July-Sept. 1919, letter to TWL from Breckenridge Long, December 20, 1919, Breckenridge Long papers, Box 180, Folder: Chinese Loan Oct.-Dec. 1919, LOC. See also Michael Hogan, *Informal Entente*, 88–89; Dayer, *Bankers and Diplomats*, 82; Rosenberg, *Spreading the American Dream*, 149; Warren I. Cohen, *The Chinese Connection*, 52–55; and Parrini, *Heir to Empire*, 201–202.

69. The leading banker in the Continental and Commercial Trust and Savings Bank was John Jay Abbott. "John Jay Abbott, A Chicago Banker," *NYT*, Oct. 19, 1942.

70. E. T. Williams, "Report of conversation with John Jay Abbott," Jan. 31, 1917, Breckenridge Long papers, Box 179, Folder: China Jan. 31–Sept. 23, 1917, LOC; Dayer, *Bankers and Diplomats in China*, 49; Joan Hoff Wilson, *American Business & Foreign Policy, 1920–33* (Boston: Beacon Press, 1973): 201; Parrini, *Heir to Empire*, 55; Naomi W. Cohen, *Jacob H. Schiff*, 34.

71. "A Review of the Interests of the United States Government and its Nationals in Financial Questions in China," undated without an author, most likely 1919, SKH papers, Box 51, Folder: China: American Interests In, HIA; Arthur N. Young, *China's Nation-Building Effort, 1927–1937: The Financial and Economic Record* (Palo Alto: Hoover Institution Press, Stanford University, 1971): 129; "Extract from Moody's Government and Municipal Manual, last edition, issued as of Jan. 1, 1936," July 3, 1936, Arthur N. Young papers, Box 22, Folder: Hukuang, From May 1 to July 31, 1936, HIA. See also Arthur N. Young, *China's Nation-Building Effort*, 24.

72. As quoted in Wilson, *American Business & Foreign Policy*, 106.

73. Duus, *Modern Japan*, 143; "Russo-Japanese War," Encyclopedia Britannica's

Guide to the Nobel Prizes, http://www.britannica.com/nobelprize/article-9064492 (July 8, 2010).

74. Louise Young, *Japan's Total Empire* (Los Angeles: University of California Press, 1998): 31–33; Gavan McCormack, *Chang Tso-lin in Northeast China, 1911–1928: China, Japan, and the Manchurian Idea* (Stanford: Stanford University Press, 1977) 5–8; Rana Mitter, *The Manchurian Myth: Nationalism, Resistance, and Collaboration in Modern China* (Los Angeles, CA: University of California Press, 2000): 41; "Manchuria: Japanese Railway Policy and Results. Effect of Concession Railways (Excerpts from report on CONSOLIDATION AND NEUTRALIZATION OF TRANSPORTATION IN CHINA by Trade Commissioner Paul Page Whitham, dated Peking, Dec. 1918)," SKH papers, Box 291, Folder: Manchuria: Railways, HIA.

75. Yoshihisa Tak Matsusaka, *The Making of Japanese Manchuria, 1904–1932* (Cambridge, MA: Harvard University Press, 2003): 4–5; Mitter, *The Manchurian Myth,* 41; Barbara Brooks, *Japan's Imperial Diplomacy: Consuls, Treaty Ports, and War in China: 1895–1938* (Honolulu, HI: University of Hawai'i Press, 2000): 124; James B. Crowley, *Japan's Quest for Autonomy: National Security and Foreign Policy: 1930–1938* (Princeton: Princeton University Press, 1966): 3–10; Herbert P. Bix, *Japanese Imperialism and Manchuria, 1890–1931* (Harvard University PhD dissertation): 109–110; Julean Arnold, "Special Report re: The Open Door in Manchuria," July 9, 1932, Julean Arnold papers, Box 6, Bonded book, no title, HIA. See also Chi-ming Hou, *Foreign Investment and Economic Development in China, 1840–1937* (New York: Routledge, 2000): 18.

76. Letter from Theodore Roosevelt to President Taft, Dec. 22, 1910, SKH papers, Box 249, Folder: Japan: Roosevelt-Taft Diplomacy, 1910, HIA.

77. Julean Arnold, "Proposed Thirty Million Dollar American Loan to the South Manchuria Railway," Nov. 26, 1927, Julean Arnold papers, Box 4, Folder: U.S. Commercial Attaché, China/Despatches, 1926–27, HIA; Letter to Inouye from TWL, Mar. 22, 1922, TWL papers, Box 186–14, HBS; Lamont, *Ambassador From Wall Street,* 195.

78. Letter to His Excellency Tsuneo Matsudaira from TWL, Dec. 9, 1927, TWL papers, Box 189–32, HBS.

79. Julean Arnold, "Proposed Thirty Million Dollar American Loan to the South Manchuria Railway," Nov. 26, 1927, Julean Arnold papers, Box 4, Folder: U.S. Commercial Attaché, China/Despatches, 1926–27, HIA.

80. Akami, *Internationalizing the Pacific,* 65, 287, 145; Chernow, *House of Morgan,* 232–234; Rosenberg, *Financial Missionaries,* 189; "Inoue, Junnosuke, 1869–1932," in Hunter, *Concise Dictionary,* 69; Letter to Governor Junnosuke Inouye from TWL, Oct. 26, 1927, TWL papers, Box 189–17, HBS; "Inouye Long Guided Japanese Finances," *NYT,* Feb. 10, 1932.

81. Norio Tamaki, *Japanese Banking: A History, 1859–1959* (New York: Cambridge University Press, 1995): 120.

82. "Inouye, Junnosuke," Portraits of Modern Japanese Historical Figures, National Diet Library, Japan, http://www.ndl.go.jp/portrait/e/datas/235.html (July 11, 2010); "Inouye Long Guided Japanese Finances," *NYT,* Feb. 10, 1932.

83. Cable to Morgan New York from TWL, Dec. 5, 1927, TWL papers, Box 189–30, HBS. Inouye, for example, was a strong supporter of the gold standard. William Miles Fletcher III, *The Japanese Business Community and National Trade Policy, 1920–42* (Chapel Hill: The University of North Carolina Press, 1989): 40, 50–64.

84. Letter to Governor Junnosuke Inouye from TWL, Oct. 26, 1927, TWL papers, Box 189–17, HBS; Untitled report from SMR to TWL, undated but most probably 1927 after Oct., TWL papers, Box 189–27, HBS.

85. Letter to Inouye from TWL, Jan. 9, 1928, TWL papers, Box 189–32, HBS.

86. Letter to Frederick W. Stevens from TWL, Mar. 16, 1921, TWL papers, Box 186–3, HBS.

87. Draft letter to Frederick W. Stevens from TWL, undated, TWL papers, Box 186–3: China, Apr.–May 1921, HBS.

88. Letter to R. E. Olds from TWL, Nov. 11, 1927, TWL papers, Box 189–29, HBS; "South Manchurian Railway" memo by TWL, Oct. 19, 1927, TWL papers, Box 189–30, HBS; "Cable retransmitted from Imperial Hotel Tokio to SS. President Pierce" to TWL from Morgan New York, Oct. 20, 1927, TWL papers, Box 189–30, HBS.

89. Cable to TWL from Morgan New York, Oct. 18, 1927, TWL papers, Box 189–30, HBS.

90. "Lamont in Tokio, Denies Banking Aim," *NYT,* Oct. 4, 1927. See also Lamont's speech to the Japan Society, Jan. 5, 1928, which was published and distributed. In TWL papers, Box 150–7, HBS.

91. "Cable correspondence between Governor Inouye and T. W. Lamont, Esq. re South Manchurian Railway Loan," in letter to Ambassador Tsuneo Matsudaira, Dec. 9, 1927, TWL papers, Box 189–32, HBS.

92. Rosenberg, *Financial Missionaries,* 168; "Manchurian Railway Loan," *NYT,* Oct. 29, 1927.

93. Letter to Jeremiah Smith Jr. from TWL, Aug. 15, 1927, TWL papers, Box 189–5, HBS. Kengo Mori had been Financial Attaché for the Japanese embassy in the United States (based in the Equitable Building in New York City), 1923–1927. He was also a member of the House of Peers. *Diplomatic List* (Washington, DC: Department of State) for years 1923–1927, Jan. edition.

94. Letter to Oswald Garrison Villard from TWL, Dec. 10, 1928 draft letter, TWL papers, Box 186–30, HBS. See also Warren I. Cohen, *The Chinese Connection,* 160 on the questionable accuracy of Lamont's statements to Villard. For information on the role of the *Nation* as a voice of anti-imperialism, starting with their reporting of Haiti in 1916 and the difference between the *Nation* and the *New York Times,* see Rosenberg, *Financial Missionaries,* 84, 128–129.

95. Letter to Martin Egan from James A. Thomas, Jan. 6, 1928, Egan papers, Box 72, PML; Letter to TWL from Ambassador Charles MacVeagh, Jan. 24, 1928, TWL papers, Box 186–23, HBS; Letter to Martin Egan from John Earl Baker, Dec. 20, 1921, Egan papers, Box 3, PML; Letter to Martin Egan from J. A. Thomas of Chinese American Bank of Commerce, Apr. 29, 1922, Egan papers, Box 72, PML; Letter to SKH from George Sokolsky, Aug. 26, 1931, SKH papers, Box 391, Folder: George Sokolsky, HIA.

96. Wilson, *American Business & Foreign Policy,* 158–159.

97. Letter to TWL from George Sokolsky, Sept. 29, 1927, TWL papers, Box 189–9, HBS.

Lamont's diaries state that Lamont, Smith, Egan, and three other men left New York on September 17, 1927 and arrived in Japan on October 3, 1937. Lamont diary entries, TWL papers, Box 273–4, HBS.

98. Warren I. Cohen, *The Chinese Connection,* 151–153.

99. "Loan of $40,000,000 for Japanese in View: Financing for South Manchurian Railway Expected to Lead Many Flotations," *NYT,* Nov. 4, 1927: 4.

100. Henry F. Misselwitz, "Chinese Request Us to Bar Morgan Loan to Manchurian Line," *NYT,* Nov. 24, 1927: front page.

101. Julean Arnold, "Weekly Report: Dec. 3 to Dec. 19, inclusive," Dec. 19, 1927, Julean Arnold papers, Box 4, Folder: U.S. Commercial Attaché, China/Despatches, 1926–27, HIA.

102. See Henry F. Misselwitz, "Nanking Abrogates Treaties of Peking," *NYT,* Nov. 25, 1927: 5; "Chinese Request US to Bar Morgan Loan to Manchurian Line," *NYT,* Nov. 24, 1927; "U.S. Not to Act On Japanese Loan," *New York Evening Post,* Nov. 15, 1927: front page; "Manchurian Loan Called Blow at China," *NYT,* Nov. 28, 1927: 2; "Japan Threatens Manchurian Action," *NYT,* Dec. 1, 1927: 8; "Chinese Protest at Railway Loan," *New York Evening Post,* Dec. 5, 1927: 8; Henry F. Misselwitz, "China Asks Kellogg to Ban Morgan Loan," *NYT,* Dec. 5, 1927: 7.

103. See "American Capital and Manchuria," *NYT,* Nov. 25, 1927: 20; "Lamont Consults Kellogg on Orient," *NYT,* Nov. 18, 1927.

104. Warren I. Cohen, *The Chinese Connection,* 155.

105. "Simeon Ford Dies; Noted Raconteur," *NYT,* Aug. 31, 1933. See also TWL papers, Box 234–4 Folder: Ford, Simeon and Julia, 1904–1916, HBS.

106. "Guide to the Julia Ellsworth Ford papers," Yale Collection of American Literature, Beinecke Rare Book and Manuscript Library. (Hereafter: BRBML) (http://hdl.handle.net/10079/fa/beinecke.fordje) For more on the Lamonts' social ambitions, see Lamont, *The Ambassador From Wall Street,* 275–277, 315–317 and Ron Chernow, *The House of Morgan,* 260–262. Albert Marquis, ed., *Who's Who in America,* vol. 8 (Chicago, IL: A.N. Marquis and Company, 1915): 817.

107. "Chinese Students' Alliance of Eastern States, U.S.A.," *The Chinese Students' Monthly,* vol. 15, no. 1 (Dec. 1919): 3. In 1926, W. Cameron Forbes was honorary president of the China Society of America, while Martin Egan was also on the board

of directors. "Annual Report of China Society of America," Jan. 1926, Egan papers, Box 9, PML. Egan also served as president of the American Asiatic Association from 1928 to 1930 and was followed by Jerome D. Greene (1930–1932). Their predecessors included Willard Straight (1908–1913). *American Asiatic Association,* 1937, Box 1, Egan papers, PML.

108. Robert Dallek, *Franklin D. Roosevelt and American Foreign Policy, 1932–1945* (New York: Oxford University Press, 1979): 85.

109. For a history of this movement, see Robert David Johnson, *The Peace Progressives & American Foreign Relations* (Cambridge, MA: Harvard University Press, 1995).

110. "Opposes Forces in China," *NYT,* Dec. 4, 1926.

111. "American Committee for Justice in China Newsletter," Dec. 20, 1927, Egan papers, Box 39, PML.

112. Letter to Florence Lamont from Julia Ellsworth Ford, Nov. 28, 1927, TWL papers, Box 189–29, HBS.

113. Letter to Florence Lamont from Julia Ellsworth Ford, Dec. 31, 1927, TWL papers, Box 189–32, HBS.

114. Letters to Roblo Ogden, James G. McDonald, Walter Lippmann, Herbert Croly, and Robert E. Olds from TWL, Dec. 1, 1927, TWL papers, Box 189–31, HBS; Letter to Ernest Hamlin Abbott from TWL, Dec. 7, 1927, TWL papers, Box 189–32, HBS.

115. See internal J. P. Morgan document, "Memorandum for Mr. A. M. Anderson from B.A." discussing SMR Co. and Morgan & Co. history regarding the railway, dated Sept. 15, 1927, "Memorandum for Mr. A. M. Anderson: South Manchuria Ry. Co.," Sept. 15, 1927, TWL papers, Box 189–29, HBS; Letter to Oswald Garrison Villard from TWL, Dec. 10, 1928 draft letter, TWL papers, Box 186–30, HBS; Letter to Ogden L. Mills, under secretary of the treasury, from TWL; also for the reference to Secretary of Treasury Andrew Mellon, Sept. 24, 1927, TWL papers, Box 189–9, HBS.

116. Letter to Julia Ellsworth Ford from TWL, Jan. 4, 1928, TWL papers, Box 189–32, HBS.

117. Letter to Julia Ellsworth Ford from TWL, Jan. 4, 1928, TWL papers, Box 189–32, HBS.

118. Letter to R. E. Olds from TWL, Nov. 11, 1927, TWL papers, Box 189–29, HBS.

119. Letter to TWL from Julia Ellsworth Ford, Jan. 10, 1928, TWL papers, Box 189–32, HBS.

120. Letter to Martin Egan from James A. Thomas, Jan. 6, 1928, Egan papers, Box 72, PML.

121. Letter to TWL from Dorothy Detzer, Jan. 24, 1928, TWL papers, Box 189–32, HBS.

122. Emily Rosenberg, *Financial Missionaries,* 129–131. For more on the Women's International League, see Catherine Foster, *Women for all Seasons: The Story of the Women's International League for Peace and Freedom* (Athens: The University of Georgia Press, 1989); Linda K. Schott, *Reconstructing Women's Thoughts: The Women's International League for Peace and Freedom Before World War II* (Stanford: Stanford University Press, 1997).

123. Allen F. Davis, *American Heroine: The Life and Legend of Jane Addams* (New York: Ivan R. Dee, 2000).

124. Rosenberg, *Financial Missionaries,* 138–147.

125. Letter to Mrs. Hannah Hull from Jane Addams, Mar. 15, 1927, Jane Addams papers, Series 1, Swarthmore College Peace Collection, Reel 18, LOC.

126. The Women's International League decided to send a delegation to China to meet with a women's group led by Chinese Nationalist leader Sun Yat-sen's wife. Letter to Mrs. Hannah Hull from Jane Addams, Mar. 15, 1927, Jane Addams papers, Series 1, Swarthmore College Peace Collection, Reel 18, LOC. Eventually, two Chinese women were brought to the United States instead. Letter to Emily S. Balch from Rufus M. Jones, Apr. 19, 1927; Letter to Jane Addams from Madeleine Doty, Apr. 7, 1927; Letter to Mrs. Grover Clark from Jane Addams, May 10, 1927; Letter to Jane Addams from Madeleine Doty, May 10, 1927; Jane Addams papers, Series 1, Swarthmore College Peace Collection, Reel 18; Letter to Jane Addams from Madeleine Doty, June 22, 1927, Jane Addams papers, Series 1, Swarthmore College Peace Collection, Reel 19; Letter to Madeline Doty from Jane Addams, May 10, 1927, WILPF papers, University of Colorado at Boulder, Western Historical Collections, Reel 18, LOC.

127. Letter to Jane Addams from Madeleine Doty, June 27, 1927, Jane Addams papers, Series 1, Swarthmore College Peace Collection, Reel 19, LOC.

128. Letter to TWL from Dorothy Detzer, Jan. 24, 1928, TWL papers, Box 189–32, HBS.

129. Letter to Jane Addams from Julia Ellsworth Ford, Dec. 24, 1927, TWL papers, Box 189–32, HBS. See letter to Mrs. Ford from Jane Addams, Dec. 28, 1927, Box 1, Folder 1, Julia Ellsworth Ford Papers, BRBML. A very special thanks to Moira Fitzgerald for her assistance in accessing this collection. Thanks also to Jennifer Meehan.

See also "Manchuria Viewed as World Problem," NYT, Dec. 18, 1927; Letter to Mrs. J.V.A. MacMurray from C.E. Howe, April 2, 1921, J.V.A. MacMurray Papers, Box 23, Folder: Mar.–April 1921, PUL; Lillian M. Li, *Fighting Famine in North China: State, Market, and Environmental Decline, 1690s–1990s* (Palo Alto, CA: Stanford University Press, 2007): 297; *Twenty Years of the Foreign Policy Association* (New York, 1939): 4; George W. Wickersham, America's Next Step Abroad (New York: Foreign Policy Association, May 1922).

130. John Palmer Gavit and Lucy Lamont married in 1890. Gavit was also the managing editor of the *New York Evening Post* (1913–1918), Washington bureau

chief for the Associated Press (1909–1911), and vice-president and director of the *Post* (1920–1922) during the time Lamont was the *Post*'s owner. "Dr. John Gavit, 86, Newsman, Author," *NYT,* Oct. 28, 1954; "Mrs. John P. Gavit," *NYT,* Jan. 9, 1941.

131. Letter to TWL from Lucy Lamont Gavit, Jan. 5, 1928; Letter to Lucy Lamont Gavit from Jane Addams, Jan. 2, 1928; Letter to Jane Addams from Balch with note from Gavit to TWL, undated, TWL papers, Box 189–32, HBS.

132. Memorandum for TSL from TWL, Jan. 14, 1928, TWL papers, Box 189–32, HBS.

133. Letter to TWL from Lucy Lamont Gavit, Jan. 5, 1928; Letter to Lucy Lamont Gavit from Jane Addams, Jan. 2, 1928; and Letter to Jane Addams from Balch with note from Gavit to TWL, undated, TWL papers, Box 189–32, HBS.

134. Letter to Florence Lamont from Julia Ellsworth Ford, Dec. 31, 1927, TWL papers, Box 189–32, HBS.

135. Cable to Inouye from TWL, Dec. 1, 1927 in letter to His Excellency Tsuneo Matusudaira, Dec. 9, 1927, TWL papers, Box 189–32, HBS.

136. Letter to Inouye from TWL, Jan. 9, 1928, TWL papers, Box 189–32, HBS.

137. Lamont, *Ambassador From Wall Street,* 243–244; Wilson, *American Business & Foreign Policy,* 211–212.

138. See J. P. Morgan & Co. Syndicate Book #11, pgs. 95–96 and Syndicate Book #12, pgs. 65–66, PML. The American portion of the 1930 loan was $50,000,000.

139. Letter to His Excellency Tsuneo Matsudaira from TWL, Dec. 9, 1927, TWL papers, Box 189–32, HBS; "Cable correspondence between Governor Inouye and T. W. Lamont, Esq. re South Manchurian Railway Loan," in letter to Ambassador Tsuneo Matsudaira, Dec. 9, 1927, TWL papers, Box 189–32, HBS; Letter to Bank of Japan from TWL, Nov. 23, 1927, TWL papers, Box 189–30, HBS.

140. Though the networks of Chinese nationalists themselves have to be considered elsewhere, this point would apply to them as well, particularly for the western-educated Chinese leaders that dominated the foreign ministry of the Peking government during the interwar period and included men such as: V.K. Wellington Koo (Ku Wei-chün) (1888–1986), Dr. Cheng-t'ing Wang or C.T. Wang (1882–1961), Sao-ke Alfred Sze (Shih Chao-chi) (1877–1958), who were China's delegates at Versailles. Others like H.H. Kung (1881–1967) and T.V. Soong (1894–1971) were prominent in the Ministry of Finance.

Despite their Western education, these Chinese diplomats were not powerful enough or close enough to the financiers of the IBC to change their pre-existing ideas with regards China. Their university background gave them a certain social capital in China, but their minority status in the United States put limits on their creation of strong personal ties even to peace reformers, who were sympathetic to their cause. China also did not have the political or economic leverage of a country like Japan. What they did have, however, was an advantage when it came to presenting a moral imperative.

141. See for an example of Florence Lamont's letter to Lamont, undated, TWL papers, Box 81, f. 3, HBS. Though the letter is undated and the cause of Florence's worry is not directly stated, it is a very good example of how deeply she could feel both segregated from his work and left in the dark (She writes, "Won't you please, dear Tom, take me into your confidence?") and how tied she felt to him and his interests. (She writes, "You hint that some great disaster is about to befall us, meaning not only financial ruin, but the ruin of your reputation as well.")

142. Letter to Jane Addams from Julia Ellsworth Ford, Jan. 13, 1928, Jane Addams papers, Series 1, Swarthmore College Peace Collection, Reel 9, LOC.

143. "Statement made by the Japanese Government regarding the dispatch of contingent to Shantung," Apr. 20, 1928, Egan papers, Box 39, PML.

144. "China's protest to Japanese Government," cable received from Waichiaopu, Frank W. Lee, Representative of Nationalist Government, May 5, 1928, Egan papers, Box 39, PML.

145. "Japanese Government's statement on Mukden Incident issued Sept. 24," Egan papers, Box 39, PML.

146. "Puyi." *Encyclopædia Britannica. Encyclopædia Britannica Online.* Encyclopædia Britannica, 2010. Web. 16 July 2010 <http://www.search.eb.com/eb/article-9061784>. (July 15, 2010)

147. Lamont, *Ambassador From Wall Street,* 309.

148. The ¥127 million advance was made on Jan. 10, 1932 but confirmed by Lamont on Mar. 18, 1932. Wilson, *American Business & Foreign Policy,* 233–234.

149. Letter to TWL from Kakutaro Suzuki, Oct. 16, 1931, TWL papers, Box 187–10, HBS. In letter to K. Wakasugi, Consul General of Japan, from TWL, Sept. 17, 1937, TWL papers, Box 188–4, HBS; Letter to S. Sonoda from TWL, Mar. 7, 1932, TWL papers, Box 188–22, HBS.

150. "Memo of the visit of Consul General Sawada" written by Martin Egan, Nov. 26, 1929, Egan papers, Box 39, PML.

151. Memorandum to Kakutaro Suzuki from TWL, Oct. 17, 1931, TWL papers, Box 187–10, HBS.

152. Chernow, *House of Morgan,* 236.

153. Members of Lamont's own family were critical of Japan. See letter to "Dear Sir" from the American Boycott Association signed Mrs. Corliss Lamont (Margaret, Lamont's daughter-in-law) and William Loeb Jr., Executive Secretaries, JDG papers, HUG 4436.14, Specialized subject file, Box 1, Folder: Harvard Boycotts Japan 1932, HUA; George Abell, "Senior Lamont Japan's Friend, Young Lamont is Pro-Chinese," *New York City World,* Mar. 8, 1932. Article was apparently sent to Lamont from McDonald in letter from E. T. Sanders, secretary, Mar. 11, 1932, TWL papers, Box 29–8, HBS; Memorandum to J. G. McDonald from T.W.D. [sic], Mar. 11, 1932, TWL papers, Box 29, Folder 8, HBS; Letter to James G. McDonald from TWL, Nov. 16, 1931, TWL papers, Box 29–8, HBS; Letter to TWL from Raymond Leslie Buell, Nov. 19, 1931, TWL papers, Box 29–8, HBS; Letter to James G. McDonald

from TWL, Nov. 28, 1931, TWL papers, Box 29–8, HBS; Letter to Joseph C. Grew from TWL, Sept. 28, 1934, TWL papers, Box 187–27, HBS.

154. "Morgan & Company and the Japanese 'Hands-off' Doctrine," *China Weekly Review*, June 30, 1934 in letter to Ambassador Hiroshi Saito from Martin Egan, Dec. 8, 1934, Egan papers, Box 39, PML. See also letter to Walter Lippmann from TWL, Oct. 1, 1931, TWL papers, Box 104–29, HBS, which is a representative example of TWL blaming China for the problems with Japan. See also letter to E. C. Grenfell from RCL, Feb. 18, 1932, RCL papers, MS 1030, Box 3–69, YUL.

155. The term is taken from Warren I. Cohen, *The Chinese Connection*, 209. While Cohen and Tomoko Akami argue that Lamont's "love affair" ended in 1937, Dayer argues, "Morgans continued to be sympathetic to Tokyo even after the Japanese invasion of China proper in 1937, in fact until 1941, the year of Pearl Harbor." Dayer, *Bankers and Diplomats in China*, 238; Akami, *Internationalizing the Pacific*, 221. See for support of both views, memorandum to TWL from RCL, Oct. 19, 1937, RCL papers, MS 1030, Box 4, Folder 97, YUL; Memorandum to TWL from RCL, Nov. 7, 1940, RCL papers, MS 1030, Box 4, Folder 98, YUL; Letter to Masao Shibusawa from TWL, Dec. 1, 1937, TWL papers, Box 188–5, HBS; Letter to Nelson Johnson from TWL, Feb. 26, 1938, TWL papers, Box 184–14, HBS.

Others, like Jerome Greene, had reached this conclusion much sooner. Letter to Horinouchi from Jerome D. Greene, Apr. 20, 1934, JDG papers, HUG 4436.7, Subject file, Box I-Jap., Folder: Japan, HUA. It is unclear, however, if this letter was sent. See also memorandum to RCL from TWL, Feb. 24, 1941, TWL papers, Box 103–24, HBS.

156. "Tokyo Leader Slain by Young Assassin," *NYT*, Feb. 10, 1932.

157. See state department knowledge of Japanese brutality in Nanjing/Nanking in letter to SKH from Nelson T. Johnson, Feb. 10, 1938, Nelson T. Johnson papers, Box 66, Folder: Stanley Hornbeck correspondence, 1937, LOC.

158. Dallek, *Roosevelt and Foreign Policy*, 148–151.

159. Letter to Dr. Dickson from Junius Spencer Morgan, Sept. 30, 1937, TWL papers, Box 188–5, HBS.

160. Letter to E. Araki from TWL, Sept. 27, 1937, TWL papers, Box 188–5, HBS.

161. Memorandum for Martin Egan from TWL, Sept. 29, 1937, TWL papers, Box 188–5, HBS.

162. Memorandum for TWL from Martin Egan, Oct. 4, 1937, TWL papers, Box 188–5, HBS.

163. Letter to Mrs. John D. Rockefeller Jr. from TWL, Dec. 30, 1937, TWL papers, Box 188–6, HBS.

164. Akira Iriye, *After Imperialism: The Search for a New Order in the Far East, 1921–1931* (Chicago: Imprint Publications, 1990): 125, 191. See also Akami, *Internationalizing the Pacific*, 61; Brooks, *Japan's Imperial Diplomacy*, 24. See also letter to

E. Guy Talbott from Frederick Field, Nov. 14, 1935, Institute of Pacific Relations papers, Box 136, Folder: National Council for Prevention of War, RBML.

165. Memorandum to TWL from RCL, Nov. 7, 1940, RCL papers, MS 1030, Box 4, Folder 98, YUL.

By 1932, the United States invested $466 million in Japan, almost twice the amount invested in China (Wilson, *American Business & Foreign Policy*, 210–213). And with some exceptions like the SMR loan, "Most Japanese loans were readily floated in [the United States], especially those for public utility companies and municipalities" in the 1920s. Letter to Thomas Millard from Martin Egan, Dec. 4, 1923, Egan papers, Box 49, PML; William Miles Fletcher III, *The Japanese Business Community and National Trade Policy*, 107.

166. Memorandum for Walter Lippmann on America-Japan from TWL, Nov. 13, 1941, TWL papers, Box 188–13, HBS.

167. Memorandum to RCL from TWL, Dec. 24, 1941, TWL papers, Box 103–24, HBS.

7. THE END OF PRIVATE BANKING AT THE MORGANS

1. Letter to H. S. Morgan from JPM Jr., Aug. 29, 1938, P. Morgan Miscellaneous Files, Pierpont Morgan Library (Hereafter: PML).

2. Jerry W. Markham, *A Financial History of the United States*, vol. 2 (Armonk, NY: M.E. Sharpe & Co., 2001): 169.

3. John E. Wiltz, *In Search of Peace: The Senate Munitions Inquiry, 1934–36* (Baton Rouge, Louisiana: Louisiana State University Press, 1963): 3.

4. Nathan Miller, *New York Coming: The 1920s and the Making of Modern America* (Cambridge, MA: Da Capo Press, 2003): 270; Robert McElvaine, *The Great Depression, America, 1929–1941* (New York: Three Rivers Press, 2009): 16–24.

5. Ellis W. Hawley, *The New Deal and the Problem of Monopoly: A Study in Economic Ambivalence* (New York: Fordham University Press, 1995): 12.

6. Anthony J. Badger, *The New Deal: The Depression Years, 1933–40* (Chicago: Ivan R. Dee, 1989): 29.

7. Charles P. Kindleberger, *The World in Depression, 1929–1939* (Los Angeles: University of California Press, 1986): 104–105, 130–136, 142–167; Badger, *The New Deal*, 18.

8. Badger, *The New Deal*, 18.

9. Badger, *The New Deal*, 22; William E. Leuchtenberg, *Franklin D. Roosevelt and the New Deal* (New York: Harper Torchbacks, 1965): 7–8.

10. See *Rand McNally International Bankers' Directory: The Bankers' Bluebook* (Chicago: Rand, McNally and Company). Pliny Fisk, the leading partner of Harvey Fisk & Sons, who was a good friend of Pierpont Morgan, had a breakdown in 1919. He died in poverty in 1939. "Pliny Fisk is Dead, Retired Banker, 78," *NYT*, Mar. 31, 1939.

11. "Kountze Brothers, Old Firm, Suspend," *NYT,* Oct. 14, 1931.

12. "Philip J. Goodhart, Retired Broker, 88," *NYT,* Apr. 27, 1944.

13. Frank Partnoy, *The Match King: Ivar Kreuger, The Financial Genius Behind a Century of Wall Street Scandals* (New York: Public Affairs, 2009): 6–7.

14. "Ivar Kreuger." *Encyclopaedia Britannica.* 2010. Encyclopaedia Britannica Online. 16 Dec. 2010 http://www.britannica.com/EBchecked/topic/323451/Ivar-Kreuger.

15. Frank Partnoy, *The Match King,* 6–7; "Kreuger Financed on Unproved Assets," *NYT,* May 4, 1932; "Lee, Higginson Men Quit Kreuger Group," *NYT,* May 20, 1932; "How Kreuger Myth Swayed Banks Told," *NYT,* May 12, 1932; "F. W. Allen, Banker, Dies at Home Here," *NYT,* Nov. 25, 1933.

16. Frank Partnoy, *The Match King,* 199.

17. For more on Lee, Higginson & Co. and the Ivan Kreuger scandal that bankrupted them, see Charles R. Geisst, *Wall Street: A History* (New York: Oxford University Press, 1997) 166–169. See also "Lee, Higginson, 84 Years Old, To Liquidate: Banking House Hart [sic] Hit by Kreuger Failure; New Securities Firm is Planned," probably *New York Tribune,* June 15, 1932, Jerome D. Greene (Hereafter: JDG) papers, HUG.4436.1, General Correspondence 1922–42, Unnamed folder, Courtesy of Harvard University Archives (Hereafter: HUA). See also letter to Walter B. Cannon from Jerome D. Greene, Mar. 2, 1936; letter to Jerome D. Greene from Cannon, Mar. 6, 1936; letter to Cannon from Greene, Mar. 16, 1936; letter to Greene from Cannon, Mar. 18, 1936; and letter to Cannon from Greene, Mar. 22, 1936; JDG papers, HUG.4436.1, General Correspondence 1922–42, Folder: 1936, HUA; Letter to Professor Joseph P. Chamberlain from Jerome D. Greene, July 2, 1932, JDG papers, HUG4436.18, Specialized subject file Lee, Higginson & Co, Box 1, unmarked folder, HUA.

18. Carosso writes that Hovey was Webster's son-in-law, but Hovey was actually Webster's brother-in-law. Vincent P. Carosso, *More Than a Century of Investment Banking: The Kidder, Peabody & Co. Story* (New York: McGraw Hill, 1979): 65–74; Charles R. Geisst, *The Last Partnerships: Inside the Great Wall Street Money Dynasties* (New York: McGraw-Hill, 2001): 128–129; "Kidder, Peabody: New Style," *Time,* vol. 17, issue 13, March 30, 1931; "Edwin S. Webster, Engineer, is Dead," *NYT,* May 11, 1950; "Webster, Banker, Found Shot Dead," *NYT,* November 22, 1957; "Kidder, Peabody is Reorganized," *NYT,* March 17, 1931.

19. As quoted in Ron Chernow, *The House of Morgan: An American Banking Dynasty and the Rise of Modern Finance* (New York: Touchstone, 1990): 325. Chernow compares the Morgans' treatment of Kidder, Peabody with the partners' refusal to come to the aid of the Bank of the United States, which failed in 1930. The Bank of United States's owners were Jewish and its clientele was largely Jewish and foreign. Chernow, *The House of Morgan,* 326–327.

20. Of 670 private firms, Kissel, Kinnicutt was ranked number nine for the

period between 1895 and 1934. Of 2,466 total syndicate participants, it was ranked number twenty-two.

21. Carosso, *More Than a Century of Investment Banking*, 68–79; "G. H. Kinnicutt, 66, Investment Banker," *NYT*, Dec. 7, 1943. Kinnicutt was married to May Tuckerman, who was the descendant of Rev. Cotton Smith. "Personal and Otherwise," *NYT*, Aug. 25, 1907.

After a scandal involving one of their top bond traders, Kidder, Peabody & Co. met its end in 1994 after it was sold to Paine Webber & Co. by General Electric, which bought a majority stake in the firm in 1986. See Kurt Eichenwald, "Paine Webber Reported Near Deal for Kidder," *NYT*, Oct. 17, 1994; Kenneth N. Gilpin, "Paine Webber's Plan for Kidder," *NYT*, Oct. 18. 1994; "Paine Webber Will Cut Its Staff by 5% as Part of a Revamping," *NYT*, Mar. 22, 1995; Saul Hansell, "Former Bond Trader Wins a Round Against Kidder," *NYT*, Dec. 20, 1996.

22. "$2,000,000,000 Bank, Largest in Country, Formed By Merger," *NYT*, Feb. 22, 1929; "Guaranty Trust Marks Centenary," *NYT*, Jan. 2, 1939.

23. "Bank Stocks Rise on Chase Merger," *NYT*, Mar. 20, 1930.

24. John Atlee Kouwenhoven, *Partners in Banking: An Historical Portrait of a Great Private Bank, Brown Brothers Harriman & Co., 1818–1968* (New York: Doubleday, 1968): 13–14.

25. "Mortimer Schiff Dies Unexpectedly," *NYT*, June 5, 1931.

26. Letter to Max Warburg from Felix Warburg, June 5, 1931, Felix M. Warburg (Hereafter: FMW) papers, Letterpress Book No. 83, MS 457, Box 5, American Jewish Archives (Hereafter: AJA).

27. Paul Warburg had been seriously ill since 1931. See letter to Baron Theodore de Guinsburg from Felix Warburg, Dec. 28, 1931, FMW papers, MS 457, 267/, AJA. Letter to Max Warburg from Felix Warburg, Jan. 5, 1932, Jan. 13, 1932, Jan. 22, 1932, Jan. 29, 1932, FMW papers, Letterpress Book No. 81, MS 457, Box 5, AJA.

28. Letter to Jim Loeb from Felix Warburg, Nov. 21, 1932, FMW papers, MS 457, 283/9, AJA.

29. "Otto Kahn, 67, Dies of Heart Attack in Bank's Offices," *NYT*, Mar. 20, 1934.

30. See also letter to Russell Leffingwell from Felix Warburg, June 9, 1931, FMW papers, Letterpress Book No. 81, MS 457, Box 5, AJA. Leffingwell wrote to express the Morgan firm's sympathies with regard to Mortimer's death.

31. Cable from TWL to JPM Jr., Nov. 11, 1932, Morgan Bank European papers, J. P. Morgan Jr. Personal Cables 1928–1935, ARC 1221, Box 23, Folder 3, PML; "Shifts at Year-End in Kuhn, Loeb & Co.," *NYT*, Nov. 18, 1932.

32. The other partners were George W. Bovenizer, Gordon Leith, Lewis L. Strauss, William Wiseman, Benjamin J. Buttenwieser, Hugh Knowlton, and Elisha Walker.

33. Cable from TWL to JPM Jr., Nov. 11, 1932, Morgan Bank European papers, J. P. Morgan Jr. Personal Cables 1928–1935, ARC 1221, Box 23, Folder 3, PML.

34. Ron Chernow, *The Warburgs: The Twentieth-Century Odyssey of a Remarkable Jewish Family* (New York: Random House, 1993): 163. By the mid-1930s, Warburg was the chairman of the Federation for the Support of Jewish Philanthropic Society of New York City, the American Jewish Joint Distribution Committee, president of the New York Foundation, vice-president of the Charity Organization Society, and the Jewish Welfare Board, to name just a few. Proof for *Who's Who in Commerce and Industry,* stamped received from Kuhn, Loeb & Co. Nov. 14, 1935, FMW papers, MS 457, 333/11, AJA.

Felix Warburg started much of this work in the early twentieth century, and when Jacob Schiff was still alive, they had this commitment in common. See untitled memo, Kuhn, Loeb & Co. date stamped Mar. 27, 1934, FMW papers, MS 457, 252/10, AJA. Also see FMW papers, MS 457, 179/20, AJA.

35. See FMW papers, MS 457, 288/8, 288/10, 285/14, 296/3, 308/8, AJA. For letter regarding his health see letter to Hans Meyer from Felix Warburg, Mar. 10, 1933, FMW papers, MS 457, 285/14, AJA.

36. Stephen Birmingham, *'Our Crowd': The Great Jewish Families of New York* (Syracuse: Syracuse University Press, 1967): 369.

37. Robert Dallek, *Franklin D. Roosevelt and American Foreign Policy, 1932–1945* (New York: Oxford University Press, 1979): 166–168.

38. The name was changed to Warburg, Brinckmann, Wirtz & Co. in 1970. It retook its original name in 1991. David Farrar, *The Warburgs: The Story of a Family* (New York: Stein and Day, 1974): 117–119, 247. See also "Hans J. Meyer, 77, of E. M. Warburg," *NYT,* June 28, 1968. http://www.mmwarburg.de/en/bankhaus/historie/kurzueberblick.html (June 9, 2010).

39. Martin Gilbert, *The Second World War: A Complete History* (New York: Henry Holt and Company, 1989): 373. See, for example, letter to Mrs. August Belmont from Thomas W. Lamont (Hereafter: TWL), Jan. 15, 1934, TWL papers, Box 84–6, Baker Library Historical Collections, Harvard Business School. (Hereafter: HBS).

40. In November 1938, Vernon Munroe devised a series of memoranda for Lamont on the issue of anti-Semitism and Jewish immigration from Europe. Lamont used the materials developed by Munroe and other J.P. Morgan & Co. staff for his correspondence. See, for example, of this research, Vernon Munroe, "Memorandum," (I, II, III) Nov. 17, 1938 and letter to F.J.R. Rodd from Thomas W. Lamont, November 18, 1938, TWL papers, Box 45–6, HBS.

41. Memorandum to Thomas S. Lamont from TWL, Dec. 20, 1938, TWL papers, Box 45–7, HBS.

42. Letter to Eleanor [Belmont] from TWL, Nov. 27, 1942, TWL papers, Box 84–6, HBS.

43. Memorandum to TWL from Russell C. Leffingwell (Hereafter: RCL), May 4, 1939, RCL papers, MS 1030, Box 4, Folder 97, Manuscripts and Archives, Yale University Library (Hereafter: YUL).

44. Letter to JPM Jr. from RCL, May 20, 1937, RCL papers, MS 1030, Box 6, Folder 127, YUL.

45. Memorandum to TWL from RCL, Jan. 12, 1942, TWL papers, Box 103–24, HBS.

46. Letter to President Franklin D. Roosevelt from RCL, Dec. 24, 1940, RCL papers, MS 1030, Box 7, Folder 147, YUL.

47. Cables to JPM Jr. from Vivian H. Smith, Jan. 6, 7, 8, 1937; Cables to Vivian H. Smith from JPM Jr., Jan. 6, 7, 8, 1937; Cable to Lord Wigram from JPM Jr., Jan. 15, 1937; Cable to Archbishop of Canterbury from JPM Jr., Jan. 15, 1937; Cable to Morgan Grenfell & Co. from JPM Jr., Mar. 31, 1937; Cable to Junius S. Morgan from JPM Jr., May 8, 1937; Handwritten note from Junius Morgan and JPM & Co. to J. P. Morgan, undated, Morgan Bank European papers, ARC 1221, Box 24, J. P. Morgan, Jr. personal cables, 1936–1941, PML.

48. "British Banker Dies in Hunting Accident," *NYT,* Feb. 14, 1938; Vincent P. Carosso, *The Morgans: Private International Bankers, 1854–1913* (Cambridge, MA: Harvard University Press, 1987): 445.

49. Partnership agreement for Mar. 1916, "Articles of copartnership: J. P. Morgan & Co., 1916–1939," Morgan Firms' papers, Box 1, PML, *NYT,* Oct. 30, 1936; Records of the Morgan Firms, Box 3, Folder: List of Partners, 1937, PML. "Horatio Lloyd, 70, Financier, is Dead," *NYT,* Jan. 22, 1937; "Thomas Cochran, Financier, Is Dead," *NYT,* Oct. 30, 1936.

50. "S. Parker Gilbert Is Dead Here at 45," *NYT,* Feb. 24, 1938.

51. "Articles of copartnership, 1932–33," Morgan Firms papers, ARC 11215, Box 5, PML.

52. Kathleen Burk, *Morgan, Grenfell 1838–1988: The Biography of a Merchant Bank* (New York: Oxford University Press, 1989): 158.

53. See interview with Leonhard Keynes by Frederick L. Allen, Nov. 3, 1947, and interview with TWL by F. L. Allen, July 22, 1947, Box 13, Frederick Lewis Allen (Hereafter: FLA) papers, Manuscripts and Archives, Library of Congress (Hereafter: LOC); Russell Leffingwell, "Memorial of Charles Steele," The Association of the Bar of the City of New York Yearbook, 1940, Records of the Morgan Firm, Box 3, Folder: Correspondence: Charles Steele, 1920–1927, 1940, PML; "$5,000,000 in Gifts Left by Steele," *NYT,* Aug. 11, 1939.

54. The new American partners were S. Parker Gilbert (joined in 1931), who had been with the law firm of Cravath, Henderson & De Gersdorff, though he died in 1938; Charles D. Dickey (joined in 1932), who had been with Brown Brothers; Henry Clay Alexander, who had been with Davis, Polk, Wardwell, Gardiner & Reed (joined in 1939); and I. Raymond Atkin and William A. Mitchell (both joined in 1939), who had both been with the Royal Bank of Canada. "3 Partners Added By

Morgan & Co.," *NYT,* Feb. 2, 1939; "Charles D. Dickey, Banker, 82, Dead," *NYT,* Apr. 29, 1976; "Charles D. Dickey Buried," *NYT,* Aug. 17, 1897 (Dickey's father); "Richard C. Colt, 74, A Retired Exporter," *NYT,* Nov. 12, 1938; "Bride of C. D. Dickey, Jr.," *NYT,* Apr. 16, 1917; "William Mitchell Dead; Office of Morgan & Co.," *NYT,* Mar. 5, 1980; "Henry C. Alexander, First Head of Morgan Guaranty Dies at 67," *NYT,* Dec. 16, 1969; "Raymond Atkin, Banker, 65, Dies," *NYT,* Jan. 26, 1957.

The new London partners/directors were Randal Hugh Vivian Smith (joined in 1930), who was the son of Vivian Smith; Francis James Rennell Rodd (made partner in 1933), who was Vivian H. Smith's son-in-law; Wilfred William Hill Hill-Wood, who was appointed managing director in 1939; and William Edward, 2nd Viscount Harcourt, who was also appointed managing director in 1939, and was the grandson of Walter Burns and the great-grandson of J. S. Morgan—"the last member of the founding families to work in the bank." Burk, *Morgan, Grenfell,* 98–100, 159.

The new Paris partners were Maurice Charles Alphonse Paul Pesson-Didion, who made partner in 1931; Alan Vasey Arragon, who made partner in 1933; and Harry Ashton Watkins, who made partner in 1934. Copartnership Article, Dec. 1934. Records of the Morgan Firms, Box 6, Folder: Articles of copartnership, 1934, PML; "Articles of copartnership, 1932–33," Morgan Firms papers, ARC 11215, Box 5, PML; "New Partner in Paris," *NYT,* Jan. 1, 1933; "In Morgan Partnership," *NYT,* Jan. 11, 1934; "Harry A. Watkins," *NYT,* May 29, 1976.

55. Letter to Norman Hapgood from TWL, Apr. 5, 1932, TWL papers, Box 97–8, HBS.

56. Memorandum to TWL from RCL, Jan. 2, 1934, RCL papers, MS 1030, Box 4, Folder 96, YUL.

57. Letter to Norman Hapgood from TWL, Apr. 5, 1932, TWL papers, Box 97–8, HBS. Lamont's letter to Hapgood was probably based in part on a March 26, 1932, memo written to him by Vernon Munroe, a Morgan staff member. Memorandum to TWL from Vernon Munroe, Mar. 26, 1932, TWL papers, Box 97–8, HBS.

58. Michael Perino, *The Hellhound of Wall Street: How Ferdinand Pecora's Investigation of the Great Crash Forever Changed American Finance* (New York: Penguin Press, 2010): 53.

59. "Ex-Justice Ferdinand Pecora, 89, Dead," *NYT,* Dec. 8, 1971; Chernow, *The House of Morgan,* 360.

60. The first prosecutor, Irving Ben Cooper, resigned. Vincent Carosso, *Investment Banking in America: A History* (Cambridge, MA: Harvard University Press, 1970): 322–327.

61. Carosso, *Investment Banking in America,* 328–329.

62. Ferdinand Pecora, *Wall Street Under Oath: The Story of Our Modern Money Changers* (New York: Simon & Schuster, 1939).

63. Chernow, *The House of Morgan,* 360–361. For original, see cable from JPM

Jr. to Junius Morgan, Oct. 9, 1933, Morgan Bank European papers, ARC 1221, J. P. Morgan Jr. personal cables, 1928–1935, Box 23, PML.

64. Stephen Salsbury, "Insull, Samuel"; http://www.anb.org/articles/10/10 –00858.html; *American National Biography Online* Feb. 2000 (Aug. 17, 2010).

65. Carosso, *Investment Banking in America,* 330–332.

66. Like National City Co. and National City Bank, First National Bank and First Security Co., its securities affiliate, had the same officers and directors. First Security Co. also used the same office and the same clerks. During the Pujo Hearings, Francis Hine, the president, tried to argue that the companies were separate and distinct, a claim that Untermyer did not buy for a second. *Money Trust Investigation,* Part 26, 2048.

67. This was the case for two multi-million dollar bond issues for a state in the Brazilian Republic in 1928 and 1929, three loans to Peru in 1927 and 1928 for a total of $90 million, "a $15 million loan for the Cuban Dominican Sugar Company and a $32 million bond issue for the Lautrato Nitrate Company of Chile." Carosso, *Investment Banking in America,* 330–332.

68. Carosso, *Investment Banking in America,* 333–337.

69. Franklin Delano Roosevelt, "Inaugural Address of the President," Mar. 4, 1933. http://www.archives.gov/education/lessons/fdr-inaugural/ (Sept. 30, 2011).

70. Carosso, *Investment Banking in America,* 333–337.

71. Ferdinand Pecora, *Wall Street Under Oath,* 3–4.

72. See, for example, Pecora Hearings, Part 1, 63.

73. Carter Glass's statement predated the Graf incident. It originally gave the Ringling Bros. agent the idea to bring Graf into the courtroom. Chernow, *House of Morgan,* 367.

74. Chernow, *House of Morgan,* 367–369; Carosso, *Investment Banking in America,* 337–339; "Midget Placed in Lap of Morgan in Hearing," *NYT,* June 2, 1933; "Notes regarding Mr. J. P. Morgan: typescript of interviews with TWL and Dwight W. Morrow," Morgan Firm papers, ARC 131798, Box 1, PML.

75. Quoted in Carosso, *Investment Banking in America,* 337–338.

76. Pecora Hearings, Part I, 4.

77. Letter to the Editor, *Arizona Silver Belt,* labeled "not for publication" from TWL, Oct. 20, 1933, TWL papers, Box 110–2, HBS.

78. Concerns about the firm's reputation and image extended to the international branches as the hearings were reported in the European presses. Cable to J. P. Morgan from London partners, July 14 (most likely 1933) including a *Times* article on trusts, Morgan Bank European papers, Box 23, Morgan, Grenfell & Co., PML; Telegram to JPM Jr. from J. S. Morgan Jr., Sept. 29, 1932, Morgan Bank European papers, Boxes 23, 24, 33, PML.

See also memorandum to TWL from Vernon Munroe, Mar. 26, 1932, TWL papers, Box 97–8, HBS.

79. "Richard Whitney, 86, Dies; Headed Stock Exchange," *NYT,* Dec. 6, 1974; "George Whitney, Banker, 77, Dies," *NYT,* July 23, 1963.

80. Chernow, *House of Morgan,* 421–429.

81. Helmuth C. Engelbrecht and Frank C. Hanighen, *Merchants of Death: A Study of the International Armaments Industry* (New York: Dodd, Mead & Co., 1934).

82. "H. C. Engelbrecht Stricken on Train," *NYT,* Oct. 10, 1939.

83. "Frank Hanighen, Editor, Dies at 64," *NYT,* Jan. 11, 1964.

84. Engelbrecht and Hanighen, *Merchants of Death,* 60–61, 140, 173–176.

85. Wayne S. Cole. "Nye, Gerald Prentice"; http://www.anb.org/articles/07/07 –00459.html; *American National Biography Online* Feb. 2000 (Aug. 13, 2010).

86. Dallek, *Roosevelt and American Foreign Policy,* 85–86.

87. Wiltz, *In Search of Peace,* 3. See also Matthew Ware Culter, *The Senate Munitions Inquiry of the 1930s: Beyond the Merchants of Death* (Westport: Greenwood Press, 1997).

88. Wiltz, *In Search of Peace,* 55, 134.

89. Chernow, *House of Morgan,* 399–401; Wiltz, *In Search of Peace,* 15.

90. Wiltz, *In Search of Peace,* 55.

91. As quoted in Edward M. Lamont, *The Ambassador From Wall Street: The Story of Thomas W. Lamont, J. P. Morgan's Chief Executive* (New York: Madison Books, 1994): 380–382; Carosso, *Investment Banking in America,* 350.

92. Cable to TWL from J. P. Morgan, Oct. 28, 1935; Lamont's cable response, Oct. 29, 1935; Cable to J. P. Morgan from TWL, Nov. 1, 1935; Cable to Lamont from Morgan, Nov. 1, 1935; Lamont's response, Nov. 2, 1935, Morgan Bank European papers, Boxes 23, 24, 33, PML.

93. Cable to J. P. Morgan from TWL, Nov. 1, 1935, Morgan Bank European papers, Boxes 23, 24, 33, PML.

94. Letter to Robert Nichols from Florence Lamont, Oct. 8, 1936, TWL papers, Box 121–18, Folder: Nicols, Robert, 1924–1936, HBS. In 1941, Lamont also wrote a draft of a letter for Florence to send to a publication called the *Arbitrator,* defending him for his role in the Crash of 1929 and foreign affairs. See letter to the Editor from Florence Lamont, Oct. 16, 1941 and TWL handwritten notes, TWL papers, Box 81–2, HBS.

95. Wayne S. Cole. "Nye, Gerald Prentice"; http://www.anb.org/articles/07/07– 00459.html; *American National Biography Online* Feb. 2000 (Aug. 13, 2010); Dallek, *Roosevelt and American Foreign Policy,* 103–110.

96. As quoted in Carosso, *Investment Banking in America,* 410. See also 408–409, 411.

97. Franklin D. Roosevelt, Oct. 12, 1937 in Russell D. Buhite and David W. Levy, eds., *FDR's Fireside Chats* (Norman: University of Oklahoma Press, 1992): 127.

98. Michael Janeway, *The Fall of the House of Roosevelt: Brokers of Ideas and Power From FDR to LBJ* (New York: Columbia University Press, 2004): 222.

99. James Stuart Olson, *Historical Dictionary of the Great Depression, 1929–1940* (Westport, CT: Greenwood Press, 2001): 279.

100. Carosso, *Investment Banking in America*, 423.

101. Carosso, *Investment Banking in America*, 424, 429.

102. Olson, *Historical Dictionary of the Great Depression*, 279; Dallek, *Roosevelt and American Foreign Policy*, 18, 97.

103. Temporary National Economic Committee, *Investigation of Concentration of Economic Power* (Washington, DC: United States Printing Office, 1941); Charles Geisst, *Deals of the Century: Wall Street, Mergers, and the Making of Modern America* (Hoboken, NJ: John Wiley & Sons, 2004): 128; David L. Porter, *The Seventy-sixth Congress and World War II, 1939–1940* (Columbia, MO: University of Missouri Press, 1979).

104. Dallek, *Roosevelt and American Foreign Policy*, 94.

105. Badger, *The New Deal*, 6–7.

106. Dallek, *Roosevelt and American Foreign Policy*, 18.

107. Franklin D. Roosevelt, Oct. 12, 1937 in Russell D. Buhite and David W. Levy, eds., *FDR's Fireside Chats* (Norman: University of Oklahoma Press, 1992): 127.

108. Letter to H. S. Morgan from JPM Jr., Aug. 29, 1938, P. Morgan Miscellaneous Files, PML.

109. TWL, "J. P. Morgan & Co. and Their Relations to the Public," TWL papers, Box 110–2, HBS. See also J. P. Morgan (Jr.), Statement of condition, June 16, 1934, TWL papers, Box 110–2, HBS.

110. Chernow, *House of Morgan*, 354–355; "Youth," *Time*, July 23, 1923; "Leffingwell, Russell Cornell," *Who's Who in New York*, ed. Frank R. Holmes, 8th edition (New York: Who's Who Publications, 1924): 775; "A New Partner," *Time*, July 9, 1923; "Leffingwell's Rites," *NYT*, Oct. 5, 1960; "Russell C. Leffingwell Is Dead; Ex-Chairman of Morgan Bank," *NYT*, Oct. 3, 1960.

111. Letter to E. C. Grenfell from RCL, Oct. 27, 1932, Box 3–69; Letter to FDR from RCL, Aug. 23, 1932; Letter from FDR to RCL, Sept. 14, 1932; Letter to FDR from RCL, Oct. 6, 1932, Box 7–146; letter to Vivian Smith from RCL, Nov. 11, 1932, Box 7–155; Letter to TWL from RCL, Aug. 27, 1936, RCL papers, MS 1030, Box 4–96, YUL.

112. Of course, individual relations were vulnerable and did not always act as a direct benefit to the banks. Leffingwell and Gilbert's former boss at the Treasury, Senator Carter Glass (after whom the Glass-Steagall Act was named), for example, went to great pains during the Pecora Investigation to undermine any impression that he was cozy with the Morgans because of his history with the partners. Glass's efforts during the hearings, however, contrast with his correspondence with Leffingwell over the years. They certainly did not have an easy relationship, but they had

an open line of communication. See letter to Carter Glass from RCL, Jan. 29, 1920, and letter from Carter Glass to RCL, Feb. 2, 1920, RCL papers, MS 1030, Box 3–64, YUL. For later correspondence, see letter to Carter Glass from RCL, Dec. 27, 1938, Apr. 25, 1939, and letter to RCL from Carter Glass, Dec. 31, 1938, Apr. 26, 1939, RCL papers, MS 1030, Box 3–67, YUL.

113. "Newest Morgan Partner Won Fame in War Loans," *NYT,* July 8, 1923.

114. "S. Parker Gilbert is Dead Here at 45," *NYT,* Feb. 24, 1938; "Funeral Tomorrow for Parker Gilbert," *NYT,* Feb. 25, 1938; "Notables Attend Gilbert Funeral," *NYT,* Feb. 27, 1938; "Mrs. Seymour Parker Gilbert," *NYT,* Nov. 16, 1937.

115. "Sir William Wiseman Dies at 77," *NYT,* June 18, 1962; W. B. Fowler, *British-American Relations, 1917–1918: The Role of Sir William Wiseman* (Princeton, NJ: Princeton University Press, 1969).

116. "Kuhn, Loeb & Co. Add Three Partners," *NYT,* Dec. 29, 1928. Strauss was first introduced to Mortimer Schiff by Herbert Hoover. His involvement with government work extended well into the twentieth century. He and Alice Hanauer married in 1923, after he entered the firm. "Lewis Strauss Dies; Ex-Head of A.E.C.," *NYT,* Jan. 22, 1974; "Reception for Miss Alice Hanauer," *NYT,* Jan. 1, 1923.

117. Rixey Smith and Norman Beasley, *Carter Glass: A Biography,* first published 1939 (Freeport, NY: Books for Libraries Press, 1970): 156.

118. Most of the younger generation of Morgan partners never knew Pierpont Morgan personally. Leffingwell only met Pierpont Morgan once. See memorandum from RCL to TWL, October 3, 1944, RCL papers, MS 1030, Box 5–10, YUL.

119. Memorandum to TWL from RCL, Oct. 6, 1934, RCL papers, MS 1030, Box 4, Folder 96, YUL.

120. Copy of letter to Morris L. Ernst from RCL, Feb. 9, 1940, TWL papers, Box 103–22, HBS.

121. Memorandum from RCL to TWL and RGW, Dec. 22, 1941, RCL papers, MS 1030, Box 4–98, YUL.

122. Professor Gras most likely refers to N.S.B. (Norman Scott Brian) Gras (1884–1956, Harvard Business School, 1927–1956). Memorandum from RCL to TWL, October 3, 1944, RCL papers, MS 1030, Box 5–10, YUL; "Norman Scott Brian Gras, 1884–1956," *Business History Review,* vol. 30, no. 4 (December 1956): 357–360.

123. See memorandum from RCL to TWL and RGW, Dec. 22, 1941, RCL papers, MS 1030, Box 4–98, YUL.

124. Memorandum by R. G. Wasson and possibly RCL and T. S. Lamont, pg. 11, June 27, 1939, TWL papers, Box 20–5, HBS. See also "Decorations, Degrees and Fraternities," "Miscellaneous Activities—Past and Present," and "Active Memberships," TWL papers, Box 286, Folder 255–3, 285–3, HBS.

125. Phrase taken from George M. Reynolds, president, Continental & Commercial National Bank, Chicago, *Money Trust Investigation,* Part 23, 1654.

WRITING THE HISTORY OF NETWORKS

1. Two years later, JPM & Co. went "public" and sold shares of the company to outsiders. Edward M. Lamont, *The Ambassador From Wall Street: The Story of Thomas W. Lamont, J. P. Morgan's Chief Executive* (New York: Madison Books, 1994): 449.

2. Pecora Hearings, Part I, 3–6.

3. Ron Chernow, *The House of Morgan: An American Banking Dynasty and the Rise of Modern Finance* (New York: Touchstone, 1990): 366.

4. See Rowena Olegario, *A Culture of Credit: Embedding Trust and Transparency in American Business* (Cambridge, MA: Harvard University Press, 2006).

5. See Douglass C. North, *Structure and Change in Economic History* (New York: W.W. Norton & Co., 1982).

6. See Martin J. Sklar, *The Corporate Reconstruction of American Capitalism, 1890–1916: The Market, The Law, and Politics* (New York: Cambridge University Press, 1988): 13–14.

Acknowledgments

A project such as this book inevitably incurs many debts. I must begin by thanking my editors, Geoff Jones and Walter Friedman, whose advice and critique have been invaluable and are deeply appreciated. Special thanks also go to Mike Aronson and Kathi Drummy, Harvard University Press. I am also indebted to Gary Y. Okihiro, Columbia University, and Naoki Sakai, Cornell University, who were extremely influential in the formation of this project and at its earliest stages. Special acknowledgment must go to Daniel S. Halgin, LINKS Center for Social Network Analysis, University of Kentucky, whose collaboration made it possible for me to pursue a network-based analysis of the archival and historical data. I would also like to thank my students and colleagues at St. John's University, especially the Department of History, the College of Liberal Arts and Sciences, the Center for Teaching and Learning, and the Institute for Writing Studies.

   While all of the archives referenced are noted throughout the text, special thanks must be made to certain libraries starting with the Pierpont Morgan Library. I spent several years going to the Morgan on a weekly basis, and I would like to express my appreciation to Inge Dupont, Maria Isabel Molestina, Sylvie L. Merian, Sandra Kopperman, Christine Nelson, Marilyn Palmeri, and the staff of the Morgan Library and Museum. I was also very fortunate to receive funding from the Harvard Business School in the form of the Alfred D. Chandler Jr. Traveling Fellowship in Business History and Institutional Economic History, which allowed me to conduct research at Baker Library Historical Collections (HC). Special thanks go to the Harvard Business School Business History Initiative and the staff at Baker HC, especially Laura Linard and Tim Mahoney. I am also indebted to the Jacob Rader Marcus Center of the American Jewish Archives (AJA). The Einstein Fellowship and the AJA Fellows program made it possible for me to conduct research at the AJA, and I would like to give a special thanks to Kevin Proffitt, Dr. Gary P. Zola, and the AJA staff for their assistance and support.

Given the nature of the archival data referenced in the manuscript, I spent many hours hunting down volumes of directories and sources or gathering obscure records and papers, which often required the active involvement of individual archivists. At the New York Public Library, I would like to thank Thomas Lannon, Laura Ruttum, and John Cordovez, Manuscript & Archives Division; Tony Mui, General Research Division; Sachiko Clayton and Philip Sutton, Milstein Local History and Genealogy Division; and Beth Wladis and Will Brister, Science, Industry, Business Library Division. Thanks also go to Laura Katz Smith, Thomas J. Dodd Research Center, University of Connecticut; Helyn Parr, Sue Ball, and Joanne Phillips, Deutsche Bank AG, London; Susannah Rayner, Library of the School of Oriental and African Studies Archives, University of London; James Moske, Metropolitan Museum of Art; Mark Bartlett, New York Society Library; Janet Linde and Steven Wheeler, New York Stock Exchange Archives; and Moira A. Fitzgerald, Jennifer Meehan, and Nancy Kuhl, Beinecke Rare Book & Manuscript Library, Yale University.

Particular acknowledgment must be made to Jon Walker, Environmental Data Resources, Inc. (EDR), whose generosity in allowing me access to Sanborn Fire Insurance map data made it possible for me to create the nineteenth-century and early-twentieth-century New York City maps included in the book. Thanks must also go the EDR team, particularly Hank Chin for his assistance in collecting and translating the geographic data. Funding to study the ArcGIS and social network analysis technologies used to create the maps was provided by a St. John's University Faculty Growth Grant and a grant from the Technology Fellows Program from St. John's Center for Teaching and Learning. I would also like to thank Isabelle Lewis, who helped me to render my drafts of the maps into a more accessible format.

Presentations at seminars and conferences allowed me to receive feedback to refine the arguments presented in the book. Thank you to the members of the Columbia University Economic History Seminar, Business History Conference, International Network for Social Network Analysis, Association of Business Historians, Eastern Economic History Association, Social Science History Association, St. John's University Junior Faculty Research Colloquium, Columbia University Center for the Study of Race and Ethnicity, and the Ford Foundation. Special thanks must go to Chris McKenna, Camilla Stack, and the Novak Druce Centre for Professional Service Firms Seminar Series, Said School of Business, University of Oxford. Thanks also to Chris Weiss and the Columbia University Quantitative Methods Seminar; Eric Wakin, Michael Ryan, and the Columbia University Business History Forum, the Rare Book and Manuscript Library, and the Herbert H. Lehman Center for American History; and Pamela Crossley, the Dartmouth College History Department and the Critical Seminar in Manuscript Development. I would also to express my appreciation to the Schoff Fund at the University Seminars at Columbia University for their help in publication. In addition to their support, the ideas presented in this book have greatly benefited from discussions in the University Seminar on Economic History. Special thanks also go to Robert Pollack, Alice Newton, Alan Dye, and David Weiman.

I deeply appreciate the generosity of colleagues who read all or portions of the manuscript. I am indebted to Martin Horn, who gave detailed comments on an early draft, three anonymous reviewers of the manuscript, and two anonymous reviewers of a draft article for *Business History Review,* which explored an early version of the book's argument on networks. I am also very thankful for the comments of Orlando Bagwell, Rebecca Kobrin, Eric Hilt, Ken Okamura, Teemu Ruskola, Rowena Olegario, and Pamela Laird. I would also like to thank Melinda Durham and Catherine Watterson for their assistance in guiding the book through the production process, Megan Smith-Creed for her assistance in copyediting, and Bernice Eisen for her assistance in creating the index.

To the many individuals, who answered my inquiries for references and information, and to my friends and colleagues, who were so generous with their time and support, thank you: Barbara Abrash, Randy Akee, Ayano Murofushi-Arno, Gavin Arno, Dolores Augustine, Leslie Alexander Austin, Fran Balla, Roy Barnes, Jason Barr, Peter Bearman, Sven Beckert, Harnet Berhe, Elizabeth Mendez Berry, Steve Borgatti, Mauricio Borrero, Ronald Breiger, Gregory Brennan, Matt Briones, Ray Bulman, Leslie Butler, Leon Bynum, Elaine Carey, Desma Casimir, David Chambers, Roberta Chase, Dimitri Christopoulos, Elizabeth Chung, John Clarke, Polly Cleveland, Phyllis Conn, Tracey-Anne Cooper, Frank Coppa, Bruce Cronin, Neil Cummins, Robert Dannin, Harry Denny, John Devereux, Jana Diesner, Kathy Donovan, Rich DeJordy, Emmanuel Deonna, Michael Edelstein, Ann Marie Ellis, David Eng, Martin Everett, Robert Fanuzzi, Maura Flannery, Gene Garthwaite, Anne Geller, Chris Genovese, Lisa Getman, Manuel A. Bautista Gonzalez, Nicole Guidotti-Hernandez, Lulie Haddad, Leslie Hannah, Robert A. Hanneman, Jason Hecht, Lisa Heller, Marina Henriquez, Betsy Herbin-Triant, Theresa Hernandez, Caroline Hong, Clifton Hood, Peter Hudson, Kim Ima,

Matthew Jacobson, Richard John, Victoria Johnson, Daniel Kaplan, Martin Kenner, Anna P. Kim, Jean J. Kim, Jeff Kinkley, John Kleeberg, Riam Sarah Knapp, Chris Kobrak, Michael Krenn, Sharon La Cruise, May Ling Lai, Judy Lam, Ed Lee, Jen Lee, Richard Lee, Kathy Lopez, Pretha Mani, Anna Marie Mannuzza, Laurence Martinaud, Dave Mazzoli, Lisa McGirr, Ramsey McGlazer, Stephen Mihm, Timothy Milford, Richard Miller, Aaron Moore, Deborah Dash Moore, Dean Morris, Alan Morrison, Petra Moser, Angel David Nieves, Frank Ninkovich, Annelise Orleck, Mary O'Sullivan, Julia Ott, Derek Owens, Alia Pan, Ed Perkins, Atiba Pertilla, Tom Philipose, Alejandro Quintana, Malika Ra, Adrian Randolph, Amy Rasmussen, Mary Tone Rodgers, Dylan Rodriguez, Ellen Roh, William Roy, Ariel Rubin, Nerina Rustomji, Gaby Sandoval, Abraham Samuel Schiff, Susan Schmidt-Horning, Mike Schneider, Stefan Schwarzkopf, Michelle Scott, Setsu Shigematsu, David Sicilia, Audrey Simon, Jenny Skoglund, Diane Spielmann, Jean Strouse, Richard Sylla, Kristin Szylvian, Elda Tsou, Konrad Tuchscherer, Lara Vapnek, Trac Vu, Xiao-chun Wang, KJ Ward, Peter Wardley, Simone Wegge, Bill Wilhelm Jr., Jen Wilks, and Michael Wolfe. I am especially grateful to my parents, Hee Sang and Chai Hee Lee, my sister, Grace, my brothers, David and Daniel, my extended family in New York, California, Korea, and Canada, and my husband's family, particularly my parents-in-law, Charles and Jane Pak.

My husband, Greg, occupies the traditional place at the end of the acknowledgments usually reserved for those who have the dubious privilege of being the closest in proximity to the writing of a book. Years ago I wrote an article that compared the writing process to Frodo Baggins's journey in *The Lord of the Rings*, J.R.R. Tolkien's epic novel. It is no accident that Greg's favorite character then and now is Sam, Frodo's long-suffering companion. If Sam had hiked to Mordor while also carrying a small baby, then one might approximate the work that Greg has done so I could bring this book to fruition. For this and many reasons, this book is dedicated to him and to our son.

Index

Whitney, George, 207
Whitney, Richard, 207
Whitney, William C., 21
Williams College, 21
Who's Who in America, 71, 74
Wilson, Woodrow, 36; at Princeton University, 145; racial issues and, 166–167
Wiseman, William, 216
Women: peace and reform efforts of, 176, 182–187; political protest and, 176; position in society, 103; social life in financial community and, 64–65, 95–96
Women's International League, 184–185
Woods, Cyrus E., 168
Woodward, James T., 22
World War I. *See* First World War
Wright, J. Hood, 49

Yale University, 13, 78, 139, 144, 146, 159, 215